Developing Academics

Academics work in a highly complex world where they must build integrative capabilities and outcomes as teachers, researchers and leaders. As they progress from novice to expert their evolving identities, methodologies and strategies need to be well-attuned to their own strengths and the sectoral expectations: a process that is greatly facilitated by the guidance of leaders and specialist developers. *Developing Academics* offers guidance to developers, senior leaders and academics on the principles and practices that support high-performing and adaptive academic communities. As the first work to explore the complex nature of academic capacity building, it offers comprehensive development principles, learning theories and specific strategies to encourage academic growth and development.

Developing Academics explores academic capacity from a range of perspectives, including:

- What makes a high-performing, well-rounded academic?
- How can our academics be equipped to meet the demands of their current and future roles?
- What are the essential characteristics of an outstanding developer and development service?
- How can leaders support and guide high-performing academics who wish to excel?

This book is divided into five parts. The first explores academic capacity building and the role developers, leaders and academics play. The second part offers comprehensive guidance to higher education developers, providing the theoretical grounding, methodologies and advanced professional techniques that support their service delivery. The third explores the academic development context, mapping the key capabilities that academics need to acquire as they progress from early career to senior roles across their various portfolios. The fourth explores strategies to evaluate and research the impact of higher education development on learners and their performance. In the final part, the design of higher education services and their interaction with university leaders is explored, illustrating the critical importance of building influence and impact across the university community. The positioning of higher education development as a discipline is also mapped.

Developers, leaders and academics will find this handbook to be an essential resource for regular reference: full of useful insights, tips and strategies to help them increase their outcomes and impact. Readers are challenged to reflect on their own leadership and effectiveness throughout this work, as individuals and contributors to academic capacity building.

Shelda Debowski holds a PhD in organizational learning and a Masters in education. She has an extensive background in higher education development and leadership.

Developing Academics

The essential higher education handbook

Shelda Debowski

LONDON AND NEW YORK

First published 2017
by Routledge
2 Park Square, Milton Park, Abingdon, Oxon OX14 4RN

and by Routledge
711 Third Avenue, New York, NY 10017

Routledge is an imprint of the Taylor & Francis Group, an informa business

© 2017 S. Debowski

The right of S. Debowski to be identified as author of this work has been asserted by her in accordance with sections 77 and 78 of the Copyright, Designs and Patents Act 1988.

All rights reserved. No part of this book may be reprinted or reproduced or utilised in any form or by any electronic, mechanical, or other means, now known or hereafter invented, including photocopying and recording, or in any information storage or retrieval system, without permission in writing from the publishers.

Trademark notice: Product or corporate names may be trademarks or registered trademarks, and are used only for identification and explanation without intent to infringe.

British Library Cataloguing in Publication Data
A catalogue record for this book is available from the British Library

Library of Congress Cataloging in Publication Data
Names: Debowski, Shelda, author.
Title: Developing academics : the essential higher education handbook / Shelda Debowski.
Description: New York, NY : Routledge, 2016. | Includes bibliographical references.
Identifiers: LCCN 2016007307 (print) | LCCN 2016019167 (ebook) | ISBN 9781138910102 (hbk : alk. paper) | ISBN 9781138910119 (pbk : alk. paper) | ISBN 9781315693583 (ebk)
Subjects: LCSH : Education, Higher–Handbooks, manuals, etc.
Classification: LCC LB2322.2 .D44 2016 (print) | LCC LB2322.2 (ebook) | DDC 378–dc23
LC record available at https://lccn.loc.gov/2016007307

ISBN: 978-1-138-91010-2 (hbk)
ISBN: 978-1-138-91011-9 (pbk)
ISBN: 978-1-315-69358-3 (ebk)

Typeset in Galliard
by Deanta Global Publishing Services, Chennai, India

Dedication

This book is dedicated to:

Emeritus Professor Alan Robson, a long-term sponsor of higher education development and model of good executive leadership.

My dear Organisational and Staff Development Services (OSDS) team at The University of Western Australia who came with me on my higher education journey and taught me so much about leadership, development and service delivery.

The many colleagues and participants who have shared their wisdom, experiences, insights, journeys and dilemmas as leaders, academics and developers with me. May this book offer a rich stimulus for your ongoing academic journey.

Vivienne, Ree and Ross for generously sharing your knowledge and professional insights.

Sandra and Sue: my first higher education development (HED) mentors who taught me to dance in time to the music.

John, ever patient as I continue to be distracted by new projects.

And to Alysia for your unending support and willingness to be a critical litmus tester.

Contents

List of figures — xvii
List of tables — xviii
List of boxes — xix
Preface — xx

PART I
Understanding higher education development — 1

1 Why develop academics? — 3

   Navigating an academic career 5
   Learning to be academic 6
   Prioritising academic learning 7
   Key principles for academic success 8
   Supporting the development of academics 9
   Defining development and capacity building 10
   About this book 11
   References 14

2 The emergence of higher education development — 17

   Identifying and addressing academic capability enhancement 17
      Supporting higher education teaching and learning 18
      The changing research context 19
      Supporting higher education leadership 20
   Introducing higher education development (HED) 21
   Mapping higher education development 22
   Progressing toward disciplinary status 23
   Conclusion 24
   Note 25
   References 25

PART II
Designing and delivering quality higher education development 27

3   How higher education development operates in
    university and college settings 29

   The location of HED service groups 30
   Higher education development units 31
   Core portfolios supported by HED services 32
      Types of services offered by HED providers 32
   HED sponsors 33
   The role of the HED leader 34
   HED challenges 34
   Conclusion 36
   References 36

4   The higher education development service framework 38

   The focus of higher education development services 38
   Framing the HED focus 39
   Service and client: the HED identity 41
   Potential HED services 43
   Core and customised services 43
   Targeted support 47
   The dilemma of individualised support 48
   Modes of delivery 49
   Features of high-quality service delivery 50
   Conclusion 50
   References 50

5   The role of the higher education developer 52

   The higher education development role 52
   The multi-faceted developer 53
   Core capabilities of HE developers 53
   Critical development competencies 58
      Relationship management 59
      Diagnostic, evaluative and analytic skills 59
      Communication skills 60
      Group management skills 60
      Learning design 61
      Self-management 61

Establishing a professional identity as a developer 62
Conclusion 63
References 63

6 Foundational principles of higher education development 66

The academic learning context 66
Designing meaningful academic learning experiences 69
Learning formats 71
  Information sessions 72
  Seminars and conferences 72
  Workshops 72
  Online learning 73
  Blended learning 73
  Group facilitation 74
  Programs 75
  Communities of practice 76
Conclusion 76
References 76

7 Delivering high-quality experiences: the HED toolkit 79

The role of facilitator 80
  Facilitation tips and techniques 81
Clarifying the intentions of the development activity 81
Designing high-quality learning experiences 82
  Step 1: Develop a preliminary plan 83
  Step 2: Designing the learning activities 84
  Step 3: Plan the learning space and related accompaniments 88
Providing online support 89
Attracting and supporting the participants 90
Dilemmas and potential issues 92
  Make it short! 92
  Consistency or creativity? 92
University capability frameworks 92
Conclusion 93
Notes 93
References 93

8 Program development and management 95

Development programs 95
Types of programs 97

Possible program features 98
Program management 98
   Getting started 98
   The planning cycle 99
   Consultation and research 100
   Program sponsorship 100
   Costing the program 100
   Program scheduling 101
   Program recruitment 102
   Program design 102
   Interviews with participants 104
   Multi-source reviews 104
   Reflective activities 105
   Program evaluation 105
Conclusion 106
References 106

9 **Facilitating organisational change and transitions**   109

Understanding transitions 110
Culture as part of change 111
Planning and leading reforms 112
The communication strategy 112
Rollout of institutional initiatives 116
   Plan the rollout strategy 116
   Manage the rollout 117
   Evaluate the rollout implementation and impact 117
Determining the consultation strategy 118
The HE developer as provocateur, agent of change, partner in arms or anarchist 118
Conclusion 118
References 120

10 **A delicate alliance: establishing effective relationships with university executives and senior leaders**   122

The consultancy process 122
   Clarify the real issue/s 123
   Confirm the agreed process, costs and scope 123
   Map the options 123
   Document the preferred option with respect to timelines, roles, costs and outcomes 123

Maintain regular communications and catch-up meetings during the implementation phase 123
Work together to solve any issues 124
Review and monitor outcomes 124
Supporting senior leaders 124
Senior leader expectations and interactions 125
Some inherent tensions in the role of HED development 126
Indicators of a healthy client-focused executive service 128
Conclusion 129
References 129

PART III
Academic capacity building 131

11 The evolution of academic identity 133

Why be an academic? 133
Measuring academic success 135
The academic career cycle 135
   The early career academic 136
   The mid-career academic 138
   The senior academic 140
Identity challenges and dilemmas 141
Supporting identity and career development 142
Building a coherent narrative 143
Conclusion 144
Note 144
References 144

12 Entering academe 148

The aspirant academic/researcher 149
Future proofing the doctorate 149
Transitioning to academe from doctoral studies 151
Tenure track 152
Research-focused roles 152
Teaching-focused roles 153
Entering academe from the professions 154
Facilitating the growth of the new academic 154
Conclusion 155
References 155

13 Academic collegiality and service 158

Unpacking collegiality 160
The non-collegial academic 161
Service: an undervalued component of university activity 162
The non-contributory academic 164
Strategies to encourage collegiality and service 165
  University strategies 165
  Local group strategies 166
  Supervisor strategies 167
  Individual strategies 168
  Developer strategies 168
Conclusion 169
References 169

14 The engaged academic 172

Choosing engagement foci 173
Engagement skills and capabilities 176
Developing engaged academics 178
Conclusion 179
References 179

15 From novice researcher to research leader 182

Researcher capabilities 183
  Publishing 183
  Funding their research 185
  Research project management 186
  Collaboration 187
  Research supervision 188
  Research leadership and management 189
Conclusion 190
Notes 190
References 191

16 Developing research capacity 194

Research capacity building success indicators 195
Development options and strategies 195
Developing the research identity, narrative and portfolio 197
Building research capacity 198
Whole of institutional reforms 198
Research capability frameworks 199

Supporting doctoral candidates 200
Orientation and induction 201
Early career researchers 202
Mid-career researchers 203
Research leaders 204
Conclusion 206
Notes 206
References 206

17 From aspirant to excellent teacher — 209

Academics as teachers 209
Building a teaching identity 210
Understanding the educational context 211
Evaluating educational effectiveness 213
Extending reach and influence: scholarship and research on teaching 214
Leading learning and teaching initiatives and groups 215
Assessing teaching excellence 215
Conclusion 216
References 216

18 Developing learning and teaching capacity — 220

Evaluating the impact of learning and teaching capacity building 220
Setting the context for excellent teaching 221
Evidencing quality teaching 222
Starting right: the learning and teaching orientation program 224
Building good foundations in learning and teaching 225
Foundational programs for learning and teaching 226
Setting tutors and graduate assistants up for success 227
Supporting course coordinators 227
Encouraging scholarship of learning and teaching 228
Guiding teaching leaders 229
Institutional reforms 230
The faculty–central partnership 231
Conclusion 231
Notes 231
References 231

19 Leading academic communities — 235

Defining good academic leadership 235
Academic transitions to leadership 236

The adaptive academic head 237
Evaluating effective leadership 239
Institutional support for good academic leadership 240
Conclusion 241
Note 242
References 242

20 Developing academic leadership capacity   244

The university executive as leadership models and sponsors 245
The leadership community 246
The higher education development service 246
Developing reflexive leaders 247
Building leadership capacity 249
   Leadership attributes/framework 250
   Leadership orientations 250
   Workshops and forums 250
   Programs 251
   Multi-source feedback 251
   Coaching 252
   Leadership network 252
   Program scheduling 253
   Supporting heads and deans 254
   Women and under-represented minorities 254
   Leadership in context 255
Conclusion 255
Note 255
References 256

PART IV
Evaluating and researching HED practice and impact   259

21 Evaluating the impact and effectiveness of HED strategies   261

Why evaluate HED? 261
   The evaluation context 264
Determining the evaluation purpose 264
Evaluating the HED activity 268
   Was the design and delivery of the learning activity engaging and effective? 268
   What did the learners gain from participating? 269
   Did the experience influence their attitudes, beliefs or values? 270

Have learners changed their behaviours or practices? 271
*Did learners have the right disposition when they participated in
the learning opportunity? 273*
*Are learners able to transfer their learning back to their own
organisational context? 273*
Managing the evaluative process 274
Conclusion 275
References 276

22 Undertaking HED scholarship and research 278

Potential research foci 280
Research strategies 281
Research approaches and methods 281
Collaboration 283
Ethics and development 284
Disseminating the research 285
Conclusion 285
Note 286
References 286

PART V
Positioning the HED service for success 289

23 Leading high-performing HED services 291

Envisioning the HED service 292
Leading HED teams 293
  The nature of the HED team 293
  Recruiting developers 295
Building a high-performing HED team 295
Establishing role and performance expectations 296
Integrating a strong service ethic 296
Ensuring quality outcomes 297
  Performance reviews and targets 298
  Designing HED policies and systems 298
  Developing the HED capability 299
Resetting the goal posts 300
The integrated HED service 300
The adaptive HED service 301
Conclusion 301
References 302

24 Positioning the HED service in a political world 304

Being politically competent 305
Map the terrain 306
Build allies and coalitions 307
Achieve the desired results 309
Promote the outcomes and impact 310
Engaging the university community as partners 311
When things go wrong 312
Conclusion 313
References 313

25 The Age of Influence 316

The new age HED developer 316
Transitioning to the Age of Influence 317
Positioning the new HED service 319
The discipline of higher education development 320
Implications for university leaders 322
Conclusion 323
References 323

Index 325

Figures

4.1	Framing the HEDU mission and focus	40
11.1	Academic identity influences and enablers	142
14.1	A model of academic engagement	175
19.1	The adaptive academic head	238
20.1	Developing leadership capacity	248
21.1	Assessing HED impact on learner processes and outcomes	265
21.2	Sample capability assessment relating to research strategy	272

Tables

1.1	Developing academics: a roadmap	12
4.1	Potential HED services offered to university clients	44
5.1	Higher education development approaches and applications	54
7.1	Learning design plan template	84
7.2	Framing the learning experience	85
8.1	A comparison of workshops and programs	96
8.2	Program costing	101
9.1	Leading and facilitating university transition processes	113
9.2	Consultation strategy considerations	119
21.1	Assessing HED impact on learner processes and outcomes	263

Boxes

14.1	Evaluating an engagement option	176
15.1	Indicators of a successful publication track record	184
15.2	Indicators of a successful funding track record	186
15.3	Indicators of successful research project management	187
15.4	Indicators of successful collaboration	188
15.5	Indicators of successful research supervision	189
15.6	Indicators of successful research leadership	190
16.1	Evidence of high-impact research development	196
18.1	Indicators of successful teaching capacity building	221

Preface

This work has been long in the making. I first entered the field of higher education development (HED) in 2002 when I was recruited to head a central development service at the University of Western Australia. This service supported all facets of academic learning, including learning and teaching, research, leadership and career strategy. While this was the start of my formal career as a developer, I have since come to realise that my prior roles had reflected similar work in different guises.

My first discipline, for example, was teacher librarianship, a field that guides student learning through the delivery of high-quality educational services through individualised support, mediated instruction, and whole of school reforms. My early years managing school libraries supported the acquisition of teaching strategies, including the design of programs and engaging learning experiences, as well as marketing strategies and designing innovations. I learnt to lead staff, guide high-quality service delivery, and I received a grant to design online learning strategies. This role required the development of partnerships with teachers, who often acted as co-contributors to educational activities. The use of my service was highly contingent on my capacity to influence, engage and add value to my colleagues' programs. When I moved into lecturing in the same field, I also observed a field in transition, as it grappled with the challenge of building a separate identity from both teaching and librarianship.

Later, I completed my PhD, which explored the impact of learning and feedback on self-efficacy, motivation and performance. This wasn't an easy transition: I had two young children and was working in a field where there was little support to combine research with my substantive teaching responsibilities. The challenges, though, started me thinking about why research should be so hard to integrate and execute in some academic contexts.

My move to a business faculty where I lectured in organisational development and human resource management offered new insights into learning cultures and service delivery. I continued to observe academics struggling to manage their composite roles, and I ultimately moved toward leadership roles within my school, faculty and the university to learn more about how research was structured and encouraged. I also became more engaged with the various development groups that offered somewhat disjointed support. I observed the restructuring of two service areas and noted the disruption and distress that these decisions caused.

These diverse experiences encouraged my interest in being a Professor of Higher Education Development. I hadn't intended to move outside a faculty role, but the opportunity was enticing. Here was the chance to model best practice organisational development, to support teaching, research and leadership from the inside. Located in a Human Resources Department, we aimed to build the best service possible, based on educational and learning theory, human resource, research and knowledge management principles. The journey was smooth initially, with a fabulous senior sponsor who understood higher education development and was happy to trial new approaches. Later experiences of adversarial, ineffectual or indifferent sponsors illustrated the real difficulties that can occur when lines of authority change. For two years, for example, we did not receive an annual budget, innovative ideas were rejected and, for some time, it was better to be invisible. My integrated HED centre was split apart, with the resources re-allocated and all collaborative systems sundered. The seamless delivery of HED support became fractured and in some areas, contentious, as learning and teaching support shifted to a new sponsor and home. It was a tough time for my team as we grappled with the need to reshape our own identity and purpose.

But tough times can also be fertile, creative periods of innovation. Over those years we refined our functions, emphasising research, leadership and organisational development. The team increased its service orientation, built enhanced diagnostic skills and tools and moved toward more systemic influence as we shaped a number of institutional systems. We increased our focus on building partnerships and alliances with faculty leaders and commenced the brokering of networks. The key to our successful rebuilding related to these associations: we were integral to the leadership community and became their first contact when they experienced difficulties. In turn, this translated into a suite of new services and models that were grounded, relevant and valued. Our productivity escalated as more academics came to us for support and development. I continued to learn and reflect on the turbulent nature of higher education development and its positioning in universities.

Our innovative practices in research development led to a collaborative partnership with seven other Australian universities, where we developed one of the earliest blended learning programs for researchers. At one stage, my leadership of this project encompassed 161 stakeholders, including many executive leaders. Later, I led a range of other initiatives to support academic capacity building, particularly through collaborative blended learning programs. As a leader, author and collaborator in these projects, I learnt a vast amount about what works for academics and the challenges associated with encouraging them to engage with online learning for their own professional development.

At the same time, I moved toward external leadership roles in this field. As President of HERDSA (the Higher Education Development Society of Australasia) for six years and the International Consortium for Educational

Development (ICED) for two years, I built connections with colleagues across the world. In these roles, I interacted with many of the key thinkers in this field. I was able to visit a range of nations and see how they each configured higher education development. We shared different perspectives and lexicons. The efforts of different nations to move toward academic capacity building were tracked, and I contributed to the development of some national higher education networks. Invitations to present to development colleagues in China, Japan, the UK and the US affirmed the complexities of creating an inclusive space for higher education development.

Thus, my time as a Professor of Higher Education Development was educative, rich and enlightening. It taught me about politics, leadership, HE development, strategy and resilience in more ways than I could ever have imagined. I enjoyed the chance to shape new programs and products and to build evaluative frameworks for testing the impact of these support strategies. The boundary-spanning nature of the role opened up many fascinating insights into how university fiefdoms and leadership operated. I made mistakes and misjudgements: fruitful causes of reflection and learning. I continued to think about the holistic nature of academic capacity building and how we could better support both academics and leaders.

I found a paucity of good resources to assist those moving into development, and indeed, for those moving into academe. And so, I wrote *The New Academic* (2012) to fill one perceived gap: guiding those in the early career academic phase. This work drew on the existing research and literature about being academic, but also integrated much of the practical and evidence-based material that I had developed over that ten years. It explored all elements of academic work providing a comprehensive toolkit for academics, and a resource for HE developers.

Later, I moved to a deputy vice-chancellor role. As a member of the executive, I strove to build alignment across the university activities and to increase leadership capacity. The deans were key partners in this quest, demonstrating a strong desire to make a difference, but benefiting from guidance on ways to increase academic engagement with identified priorities. I explored a range of reforms with academics and witnessed their passion to do things better. The right guidance, incentives to participate and coherent messages made a very real difference to their efforts.

In the last few years, I have moved to my new role as a higher education consultant. My visits to multiple universities have continued to illustrate the challenges that leaders and academics face in acquiring the capabilities they need to succeed in an increasingly complex and challenging setting. My interactions with developers from all specialist fields also confirms the challenges of achieving effective positioning and outcomes of HED work. This is understandable, given that so little practice wisdom is shared and so few core principles are mapped. The field primarily operates from assumptions and peer learning. While this has its place, it keeps higher education development firmly located as a cottage industry, with each group shaping unique products according to their own particular interpretation of the field. As this book illustrates, the establishment of a theoretically-informed and methodologically-sound suite of tools and practices requires more rigorous research-informed frameworks that reflect educational, adult learning and human resource development principles, as well as higher education research and scholarship.

So this book has been developed as a response to these observations and reflections. However, the plan has morphed to some extent since its first inception. I had initially envisaged writing something that just explored HED. However, without recognising the context in which these services are situated and the need to be politically savvy and keyed into the university and its transitions, even excellent developers can find themselves marginalised. So this work now maps the field from four primary perspectives:

- providing executive leaders with a blueprint for thinking about the types of HED support they need or anticipate, and encouraging them to think about their own leadership journey and impact;
- offering senior leaders guidance on the ways they can build academic capacity, high-functioning academic communities and enhanced leadership capabilities;
- assisting academics with exploring their academic capabilities and practices to encourage more strategic positioning of their careers and roles;
- providing any developer facilitating academic capacity building with a foundational handbook to support their role and the positioning of their service.

The book therefore seeks to provide a full overview of the HED landscape. It maps core theories and research and integrates many of the resources and models that I have developed and tested across the last fifteen years. This practice wisdom fills many of the evident gaps I have identified. I have integrated some new frameworks and models that articulate the partnerships that underpin successful HED work.

However, the work also includes some messages that I hope will be considered. HED is at risk of remaining in the margins if it continues to assert its differences rather than commonalities, if its evidence base continues to be anecdotal and hard to source or if it remains peripheral to the real work being done in universities. This is a call to arms: it is time to think about this field as a professional discipline that can make a substantive difference. First though, it is necessary to start building a name and identity that is inclusive and can translate across all nations; thus, the framing of this field in this work as *higher education development*. A second key message is the importance of building alignment and collaborations between leadership and HED services. This is a partnership that can build significant impact once both groups are in sync. Finally, the necessity of being aligned with institutional strategy is emphasised: the reality of higher education has changed and so too, must HED. Thus, this book threads realism, pragmatism and idealism throughout its many chapters.

I hope you find this work stimulating, challenging and, at times, confronting! While it integrates considerable reflection from my own professional journey, it also draws on the experiences of hundreds of others. I hope it adds new perspectives and enrichment.

Shelda Debowski
February 2016

Part I

Understanding higher education development

Higher education development (HED) has emerged as a response to the challenges that academics now encounter in building and maintaining a highly competitive professional base. Part I explores the emergence of the field of HED, explaining why academics need support and how universities and the sector have approached the development of academics. This section also establishes the rationale for using the term *higher education development* and introduces the three professional areas that contribute to the field.

Chapter 1 explores the academic employment context, outlining the factors that influence academic outcomes and capacity. The need for support and development is also outlined. Chapter 2 introduces the field of higher education development, mapping the progressive growth of learning and teaching, research and leadership development in supporting academic capacity building.

Chapter 1

Why develop academics?

Across the world, millions of academics are employed to deliver high-quality, engaging education and research. They come in all shapes and sizes: full-time, part-time, casual, tenured, on probation, baby-boomers, Generation X, different nationalities, ex-professionals, current clinicians or practitioners. They come with wide-ranging backgrounds, motivations and experiences. They work in diverse contexts, including research-intensive, high-prestige universities, public and private institutions, colleges or specialist educational communities. Despite these differences, they all face a common challenge: maintaining their currency and edge as valued, credible and reputable members of the academic community.

Academics are university or college employees who are directly engaged in the core university functions of research and/or teaching. Their roles and responsibilities are highly diverse, ranging across full-time research, a mix of teaching and research, full-time teaching or, in some institutions, supporting academics across the university. Despite the different titles they may carry, they are expected to demonstrate a scholarly and research-informed approach to their roles and their contribution to the university's mission and priorities.

The world of higher education has grown more precarious and unpredictable as the impact of societal expectations, national and regional policy, globalisation, funding and consumer demand has influenced the positioning and practices of institutions (Altbach 2013a; Altmann and Ebersberger 2013; McGettigan 2013; Williams 2014; Zajda 2015). Universities and colleges face escalating global competition in their efforts to capture a viable share of the student market. Students have access to an astonishing array of information and can select from a vast range of choices and educational experiences. At the heart of these offerings is the drawcard of expert academics who support students in finding their desired future paths.

The calibre of each university's academics is recognised as a key factor in ensuring institutional distinctiveness, with many institutions placing great importance on recruiting the best and brightest academics (Teichler *et al.* 2013). However, there is considerable evidence of increasing expectations of academics as they are asked to absorb new roles and responsibilities, particularly in the changing fiscal context. To illustrate, teaching academics must deliver high-quality experiences to their students, acting as educators, curriculum designers, team leaders, administrators, communicators and counsellors. They may support diverse student groups across multiple locations via a range of modes of delivery. Enhanced educational technologies have further devolved administrative loads to the academic and increased expectations with respect to their support of students. They may oversee work-integrated learning programs (Ferns 2014), research-informed educational experiences, team learning, service-learning (Cipolle 2010) or problem-based learning programmes (Barrett and Moore 2010; France 2004) as part of their duties. In addition, teachers are expected to demonstrate a scholarly approach to their educational practice, researching and publishing on their educational innovations and insights (Jones 2013). They will also assume leadership roles to support educational innovations and initiatives (Debowski 2012a).

In tandem, they must maintain or build their research track record (Debowski 2012b; Delamonte and Atkinson 2004). Academics are expected to be successful scholars, evidencing a stream of research, high-quality publications and a national or international profile. The capacity to disseminate and achieve high impact through their research is an important translational capability. Obtaining external funding has become another significant marker of research success. At the same time, academics are expected to supervise the next generation of researchers, providing them with support and guidance as they undertake their research apprenticeship and embark on their postdoctoral careers (Denholm and Evans 2007).

Over time, each academic should also demonstrate a progressive shift toward leadership roles (Jones *et al.* 2012; Knight and Trowler 2000; Macfarlane 2012; Middlehurst 1993). They will assume responsibility for events, institutional initiatives, committees, working groups, programs, teams, projects, schools, institutes and collaborations. Institutional formalisation of leadership roles, responsibilities, accountabilities and performance expectations has escalated pressure to perform credibly as a leader who reflects high integrity, impact and effectiveness (Scott *et al.* 2008; Buller 2011; Middlehurst 2013). The capacity to establish constructive, productive, goal-oriented communities and agendas, while maintaining research and/or teaching roles, creates considerable tension for many leaders.

A fourth facet of academic performance relates to the ability to build relationships and collaborations. The capacity to engage with others, communicate in a meaningful way and build communal ideas about innovative practice is another feature of a successful, modern academic (Cipriano 2011). The modern academic is wired, connected to a myriad of other colleagues, university stakeholders and groups that intersect with the university and its activities. They are encouraged to engage with diverse groups as a collaborator, consultant or expert source (Jones 2013). Thus, academics need to be good communicators, able to empathise with groups and individuals. They need to be culturally competent, adaptive and flexible.

Navigating an academic career

A complicating factor in building academic careers is the fragile employment environment in which many individuals now find themselves (Bexley et al. 2011; Kimber 2003). Entry into academic careers has become increasingly difficult with lower numbers of doctoral graduates successfully moving toward university employment (Cyranoski et al. 2011). An established track record of scholarly publishing is becoming necessary to secure entry-level roles as tutors or postdoctoral researchers. Thus, the threshold for entering academe has been raised. As a result, there is growing concern for ensuring doctoral candidates are able to demonstrate their capabilities and career potential by the time they graduate (Akerlind 2009; Denholm and Evans 2009; Lee et al. 2009).

Unfortunately, there is increased precariousness with respect to securing ongoing employment in the sector, even with a doctorate. The financial upheavals across the world have created a more risk-averse sector, with many universities aiming to build a flexible workforce that can be sculpted according to demand. Recent statistics for the United States, United Kingdom and Australia all indicate that around 50% of the academic workforce is now employed in part-time or casual capacities (HESA 2014; Knapp et al. 2012; Norton 2014). New generations of academics face a challenging time as they seek to gain a more secure foothold in a turbulent industry. The transition from short-term appointments to more assured employment will be predicated on evidence of high competitiveness and a track record of successful performance (Bazeley 2010). Those who gain a foothold will be offered limited time to demonstrate their capabilities in readiness for a longer-term appointment in the university. There is increased pressure to act as hyper-professionals who exemplify high performance and high productivity (Gornall and Salisbury 2012). At the same time, academics who are tenured also face reduced certainty as to their security.

Universities have markedly increased their concern for measuring and evaluating academic performance (Fitzgerald et al. 2012). Academics must regularly monitor and document their outputs to demonstrate their effectiveness. Processes to measure the impact, effectiveness, efficiency and overall performance of academics have taken hold in a number of nations. Institutions are closely defining academic performance expectations to assist regular performance reviews, better recruitment and selection processes, and more rigorous advancement practices. While these processes can offer recognition, guidance and support to academics, they can also be an invidious way of micromanaging the academic workforce, particularly if workloads and performance expectations are highly prescriptive.

The notion of what is valued and what is recognised continues to be vigorously contested and discussed across the sector (Altbach 2013b; Rust and Kim 2015). Many universities have introduced performance metrics, with research acting as a proxy for academic performance, thereby increasing the pressure to be research active. There is evidence of diverging paths within and away from academe with the introduction of role specialisation and academic-related roles outside faculties. The latter now fill specialist research project management, research support services or teaching and learning support roles, either as academics or professionals.

Unlike other professional fields where initial identification with the discipline creates a solid platform to launch and maintain a career, academe is increasingly reflective of a dynamic and shifting context. Career management has escalated in importance as academics navigate progressive reincarnations of their academic personas. Opportunities, collaborations, changes in institutional priorities or the ongoing evolution of an academic may result in progressive shifts across disciplines, institutions, roles and/or identities. The capacity to build a robust and resilient identity that draws on one's strengths and passions ensures individuals can weather these unpredictable climes. Each individual needs to ensure they remain "future-proofed," capable of moving into new roles or other institutions, while also reflecting their current university's requirements. Given the time-lag between commencing new initiatives and demonstrating outcomes, impact and/or high performance, academics are well advised to commence preparing for their next career shift as early as possible.

This changing higher education environment has created a notable tension for many individuals. Every career choice has consequences for the future and for the way the individual is perceived by their institution. At the same time, their particular approaches and priorities are influenced by their talents, expertise and passion. There are many paths through academe, offering the opportunity to straddle teaching, research and leadership, or to specialise in some of those areas. The challenge, however, is that the relative effort and contribution of each may be valued differently, depending on what the university administration emphasises. Thus, choices as to the direction and prioritisation of academic work have potential consequences for future career progression.

In summary, then, the world of universities and colleges has changed. Modern, successful academics must demonstrate high performance across a diverse range of activities. They face stiff competition in establishing a profile that ensures they are competitive and worthy of continuing employment. Universities have created an environment where ongoing assessment and evaluation of academic performance informs many employment decisions, including retention. Each choice an academic makes can have wide-reaching consequences, opening new doors or closing others. The capacity to balance and execute myriad roles and responsibilities can determine whether an academic is perceived to be a high performer or moderate contributor by supervisors and administrators. No matter the level or past track record, no academic is secure as universities grapple with large-scale reform and change (Vukasović 2012).

Learning to be academic

So how do academics develop the critical skills and capabilities to ensure they are valued as high performers? The capabilities necessary to undertake academic roles are largely missing from the professional grounding that people acquire prior to embarking on university work. Doctoral training has been criticised for its minimal focus on building advanced academic and professional capabilities (Denholm and Evans 2009; Kubler and Western 2007). Doctoral programs primarily offer an introductory grounding in critical thinking, academic writing and, possibly, communication, signalling that people have the capacity to develop academic capabilities and skills. They are generally poor in providing a comprehensive grounding to allow an individual to move into the complex realm of teaching, research, engagement and leadership. A particular challenge for those entering academe as early career academics is that they may have only 3–5 years to prove their worth. In that time, they will need to produce a range of worthy publications, demonstrate teaching competence and build effective relationships across the academic fraternity. Even experienced academics face increasing pressure to progress from their entry-level capabilities toward more responsible and influential roles that support their ongoing career escalation and their university's own ambitions. While there is now much greater understanding as to the core capabilities that underpin academic success (e.g. Debowski 2012b), the provision of support to build these foundations remains limited and erratic.

Prioritising academic learning

Academics can find it difficult to develop these complex and critical skills, with a number of influences affecting their prioritisation of ongoing learning and development. These can be grouped into three factors: the individual, the academic community and institutional sponsorship.

At the *individual* level the academic plays a key role in deciding if and when they will engage with possible learning opportunities. Some of the factors that may influence their choices include:

- the ability to self-review their performance and success;
- their knowledge of available learning opportunities;
- the perceived match between learning opportunities and their own developmental needs;
- the value they place on professional development;
- a willingness to invest in their learning;
- the perceived importance of particular capabilities;
- their capacity to manage workloads or commitments to make time for development;
- the prioritisation of career management and planning;
- the nature of past learning experiences.

The *academic community* also plays a key role in setting up expectations as to ongoing learning and development. In their research on learning transfer, for example, Holton and his colleagues found that the transfer climate had a very large impact on an individual's capacity to integrate newly acquired abilities or skills (Bates *et al.* 2012; Holten *et al.* 1997). Factors such as the opportunity to test and use the new skills in a non-judgemental setting, support from supervisors and peers and the perception of benefits attached to demonstrating learning gains all impact on an individual's confidence in learning and applying that capability. Thus, the environment in which an individual works will have a very important influence over whether they choose to engage with learning opportunities.

At the broader level, the degree to which an *institution* sponsors the development of its academics also plays a key role in setting the right context for ongoing learning. The allocation of resources to support learning and development, as well as positive and proactive sponsorship by university executives, deans and heads of school, all play a part in setting up a positive and dynamic learning context where learning and development is acknowledged as important.

The key points to highlight here are that academics do not learn in isolation. They are dependent on being supported and guided as to what matters. The provision of mentors and sponsors to assist their ongoing learning and reflection creates a positive and supportive setting. They will need focused time and the capacity to attend to their learning. The ability to practice and take risks as they test new ideas and methods also sets up a positive learning environment. While on-the-job learning and mentorship continue to play a critical role in setting academics up for success, strong reliance on this approach for the majority of academics creates an *ad hoc* and unpredictable outcome for many. If they do not have the support of key people, or are not the highly talented protégés that generally get more attention, it is likely that they will not receive the necessary support and guidance. This can generate concerning career consequences. Thus, the academic workforce relies on the provision of high-quality development experiences, the opportunity to participate, and the capacity to apply the skills and capabilities in ongoing roles.

Key principles for academic success

From this short introduction, it can be seen that there are some key principles that will ensure an academic is well poised for success. Academics benefit from:

- a realistic and knowledgeable understanding of the academic and higher education context, including performance expectations;
- a realistic assessment of their skills, capabilities and development needs;
- an ability to articulate their career goals, identify any ambitions and to map the learning goals they will need to achieve to accomplish these aspirations;
- access to appropriate support and learning experiences to progressively build the array of skills needed to be successful, modern academics;
- a learning environment that is conducive to accessing learning and development and applying this learning to their ongoing professional practice;

- institutional expectations that provide clarity and useful guidance on what is valued and what is deemed to be high performance;
- the provision of appropriate and well-designed learning experiences that are high quality, relevant and accessible.

Supporting the development of academics

There has never been a more pressing need for academics to be offered support as they develop and extend their core professional skills to match shifting sectoral expectations. Their personal will and commitment to participate in, learn from and apply their learning is a critical factor in this developmental process. However, they also benefit from the support of their academic colleagues and leaders as well as higher education developers.

The provision of guidance, mentorship and sponsorship from colleagues and the academic community provides the necessary context to take risks, test new ideas and gain expert feedback (Evans *et al.* 2013). A faculty, school or centre that encourages high performance and collective capacity building offers the ideal setting for promoting learning as a key institutional advantage (Debowski 2014; Di Napoli 2014; Peseta 2014; Szkudlarek and Stankiewicz 2014). Deans, heads of school, senior colleagues and all members of the academic community are important sources of influence and guidance. They fill important functions in:

- creating a supportive culture to explore, test and learn new capabilities and strategies;
- modelling good practices;
- sharing knowledge and discipline-related expertise;
- sponsoring new academics into established networks and academic communities;
- mapping the core capabilities that underpin success for that discipline and providing performance feedback;
- mentoring.

Thus, they are uniquely placed to ensure each individual is able to achieve their learning and development goals. They offer the contextual knowledge and emotional support to guide the transferral of new capabilities into academic practices and strategy.

In addition, the increasing sophistication of academic work requires specialist support and guidance. There have been great advancements in our understanding of higher education theory and practice. It is no longer necessary to rely on trial and error or osmosis to become an academic and advance one's capabilities. There is a burgeoning field of knowledge relating to academic capacity building throughout various career stages. Higher education (HE) developers are learning and development professionals who meld learning and development expertise with an in-depth, professional knowledge of teaching, research, leadership and/or career management. They offer an important interface between the professional skills and capabilities that underpin academic work, the learner and their academic community. Their role is to offer:

- expert guidance on the professional and academic practices to be acquired;
- powerful and engaging learning experiences;
- specialist guidance and advice at point of need;
- support for university leaders focused on capacity building;
- guidance on problems or issues that need to be addressed.

These professionals may be located within faculties or central service areas of universities.

HE developers have the potential to build strong partnerships with faculty and university leaders to ensure academics are strongly poised for success. However, as this book will outline, the success of these roles depends on many things: the developer's capacity to partner with faculty leaders; their credibility as experts in their particular speciality; their willingness to collaborate with other HE development groups; and their effectiveness in designing and delivering desirable, relevant, accessible, valued and effective learning experiences to the academic community. Their roles are complex, drawing on various professional disciplines. Unfortunately, in many cases, these professionals have been expected to develop these skills on the run, thereby reducing their capacity to provide the quality support that is needed.

Defining development and capacity building

This work explores the ways in which academics explore and acquire new intellectual, mental, emotional and social schema to support the acquisition and enhancement of their professional knowledge, capabilities and strategies. These processes require the progressive and iterative acquisition of skills, capabilities, confidence and, in some cases, courage, with a view to building new levels of expertise and insight that support their advancement.

Development can be described as the process of identifying a learning need, identifying and developing new capabilities and approaches and consolidating their application into one's ongoing practice. This learning process benefits from clearly mapping the key capabilities that need to be acquired and providing a conducive learning context. The progression from novice to academic leader will be an iterative and ongoing journey that requires evidence of increasingly sophisticated capabilities, skills and knowledge. This is likely to span complex areas, including research, teaching, leadership, engagement, career strategy and generic capabilities.

In this work, *capacity building* describes the process of building collective capabilities, processes and strengths that facilitate high-functioning institutions and communities. It encourages academic performance, adaptive behaviours, supportive academic cultures and productive outcomes. This book will prompt considerable reflection by leaders about the role they play in building the right environment and context for learning and capacity building. It will be seen that the attitudes, infrastructure, systems, policies and practices all influence an academic's capacity to learn, as well as influencing their resultant skills, knowledge and confidence to be academic. This holistic overview of academe and the progression of an academic from novice to leader will challenge many leaders at faculty and institutional level to explore the role they play in building capacity.

However, the cultivation of academic capabilities benefits from support beyond that offered by excellent leaders and supportive communities. The HE developer fills an important partnership role with other university leaders, acting as a confirmatory, transformational and sometimes destabilising source of guidance (Di Napoli 2014; Debowski 2014; Peseta 2014; Szkudlarek and Stankiewicz 2014). As a boundary-spanning function, higher education developers act as a bridge between different academic groups and leaders, providing specialist knowledge of capacity building and capability enhancement. The successful enactment of their roles is contingent on building strong relationships across the organisation; aligning with institutional goals; facilitating organisational renewal; and encouraging academics to engage with their learning.

A key theme throughout this book is the intertwined roles that developers, leaders and the individual all play in building capacity. This partnership benefits from commitment at all levels to build the right context for learning.

About this book

This book has therefore been designed as the essential higher education development handbook to guide academics, academic and university leaders, and higher education developers in the various facets of academic capacity building. Structured in five parts, it is intended as a practical and detailed professional toolkit to assist those who support academic learning, whether as individual mentors, deans, heads or dedicated developers. Designed as a handbook, it integrates theoretical guidance, research and scholarship, and *practice wisdom* (Bamber and Stefani 2015) to fill in the gaps. The latter draws on an extensive history as a higher education development professor, scholar, director and practitioner, deputy vice-chancellor, a leader of international academic development networks and development consultant to many universities, where these different contexts have offered considerable scope to apply, test and validate the documented principles and ideas.

The last 15 years have offered many opportunities to review the level of accessible professional guidance for developers, illustrating the challenges many experience in interpreting their role and building additional, more specialised capabilities. The limited understanding of academic learning and development across universities is a further concern, with evidence of many institutions undervaluing academic capacity building. This work has therefore been designed to fill these two gaps and offer holistic coverage to support the different roles that are played in setting academics up for success.

Academics will find considerable guidance relating to the strategic positioning of their careers and the different ways they can build their capabilities and impact. Those who mentor will also build greater insights into strategies to assist their protégés. Part II of this book, which explores HED methodologies, offers extensive insight into engagement strategies that can be applied to external groups just as readily as internal stakeholders.

University leaders will be encouraged to consider their own development as well as the ways they can build capacity within their teams, schools or faculties.

Senior and executive leaders are offered additional guidance on systemic capacity building. Those who have the capacity to sponsor, establish, influence or disestablish higher education development centres will build a more nuanced understanding of the features of successful HED services and how they might be structured – at either faculty or central university levels.

The entire work supports *higher education developers* in building and maintaining a comprehensive professional base that integrates good practice from a range of related fields. It also provides valuable scaffolds to increase systemic influence, impact and better positioning of HED activities.

The following table provides a quick roadmap to guide prospective readers based on their roles and likely areas of interest.

Universities rely on high-performing communities that are staffed by reflective, adaptive and talented academics. The development of academics is a critical factor in achieving this ambition.

Table 1.1 Developing academics: a roadmap

Part I: Understanding higher education development

This first section explores the context in which higher education development has emerged. It maps the convergence of various areas of academic capacity building, illustrating the common concerns that have become apparent and some of the challenges that have been encountered in creating appropriate support within universities.

Chapter	Title	Academics	Leaders	Developers
1	Why develop academics?	√	√	√
2	The emergence of higher education development		√	√

Part II: Designing and delivering quality higher education development

Higher education development principles, models, roles and types of activities are overviewed. This part offers a professional grounding for developers, encouraging the provision of meaningful, productive and high-impact learning for academics, schools and the institution. It explores a number of core services, including learning design, programs, change leadership and consultancy services. An exploration of the partnership role of the HE developer highlights the importance of relationship building in these roles.

Chapter	Title	Academics	Leaders	Developers
3	How higher education development operates in university and college settings		√	√
4	The higher education development service framework		√	√
5	The role of the higher education developer		√	√
6	Foundational principles of higher education development			√
7	Delivering high-quality experiences: the HED toolkit			√
8	Program development and management		√	√
9	Facilitating organisational change and transitions		√	√
10	A delicate alliance: establishing effective relationships with university executives and senior leaders		√	√

Part III: Academic capacity building

In this section, the ways in which academics learn as they evolve from novice to expert are explored. The transition from early career academic to influential leader requires many shifts in identity and professional practice. The specific challenges inherent in progressing in research, teaching, engagement and leadership are explored. Central to these transitions is the progressive evolution of academic identity. A range of development approaches are mapped, illustrating how different aspects of academic learning needs may be assisted by HE developers, academic leaders and their colleagues.

Chapter	Title	Academics	Leaders	Developers
11	The evolution of academic identity	√	√	√
12	Entering academe	√	√	√
13	Academic collegiality and service	√	√	√
14	The engaged academic	√	√	√
15	From novice researcher to research leader	√	√	√
16	Developing research capacity		√	√
17	From aspirant to excellent teacher	√	√	√
18	Developing learning and teaching capacity		√	√
19	Leading academic communities	√	√	√
20	Developing academic leadership capacity		√	√

Part IV: Evaluating and researching HED practice and impact

An important element of HED is the assessment of impact and outcomes. In this short section, some key principles to support effective evaluation and ongoing research into the discipline are offered.

Chapter	Title	Academics	Leaders	Developers
21	Evaluating the impact and effectiveness of HED strategies		√	√
22	Undertaking HED scholarship and research			√

(*continued*)

Table 1.1 Continued

Part V: Positioning the HED service for success

In this final part, the positioning of HED services is reviewed. While largely focusing on the establishment of a highly functional and politically attuned HED service, this analysis also highlights the criticality of building robust partnerships across the university with executives, senior leaders and other contributors. The final chapter maps the future for HED and leaders in building increased academic capacity.

Chapter	Title	Academics	Leaders	Developers
23	Leading high-performing HED services			√
24	Positioning the HED service in a political world		√	√
25	The Age of Influence		√	√

References

Akerlind, G., 2009. Making your doctorate work in an academic career. In C. Denholm and T. Evans, eds, *Beyond doctorates downunder*, Camberwell, Vic.: ACER Press, pp. 138–145.

Altbach, P.G., 2013a. Advancing the national and global knowledge economy: the role of research universities in developing countries. *Studies in Higher Education*, 38(3), pp. 316–330.

Altbach, P.G., 2013b. *International imperative in higher education*, Rotterdam: Sense Publishers.

Altmann, A. and Ebersberger, B. (eds), 2013. *Universities in change: managing higher education institutions in the age of globalization*, New York: Springer.

Bamber, V. and Stefani, L., 2015. Taking up the challenge of evidencing value in educational development: from theory to practice. *International Journal for Academic Development*, pp. 1–13.

Barrett, T. and Moore, S., 2010. *New approaches to problem-based learning: revitalising your practice in higher education*, Hoboken, NJ: Taylor & Francis.

Bates, R., Holton, E.F. and Hatala, J.P., 2012. A revised learning transfer system inventory: factorial replication and validation. *Human Resource Development International*, 15(5), pp. 549–569.

Bazeley, P., 2010. Conceptualising research performance. *Studies in Higher Education*, 45(3), pp. 257–279.

Bexley, E., James, R. and Arkoudis, S., 2011. *The Australian academic profession in transition: addressing the challenge of reconceptualising academic work and regenerating the academic workforce*, Melbourne, Vic.: Centre for Studies in Higher Education.

Buller, J.L., 2011. *Academic leadership day by day: small steps that lead to great success*, 1st edition, San Francisco, CA: Jossey-Bass.

Cipolle, S.B., 2010. *Service-learning and social justice: engaging students in social change*, Lanham, MD: Rowman & Littlefield.

Cipriano, R.E., 2011. *Facilitating a collegial department in higher education: strategies for success*, 1st edition., San Francisco, CA: Jossey-Bass.

Cyranoski, D., Gilbert, N., Ledford, H., Nayar, A. and Yahia, M., 2011. Education: the PhD factory. *Nature*, 472(7343), pp. 276–279.

Debowski, S., 2012a. Leading higher education learning, teaching and innovation. In J.E. Groccia, M.A.T. Alsudairi and W.H. Bergquist, eds, *Handbook of university and college teaching: a global perspective*, San Francisco, CA: SAGE Publications, chpt. 17.

Debowski, S., 2012b. *The new academic: a strategic handbook*. London: Open University Press.

Debowski, S., 2014. From agents of change to partners in arms: the emerging academic developer role. *International Journal for Academic Development*, 19(1), pp. 50–56.

Delamonte, S. and Atkinson, P., 2004. *Successful research careers: a practical guide*, Maidenhead, Berkshire: Society for Research in Higher Education and Open University Press.

Denholm, C.J. and Evans, T.D., 2007. *Supervising doctorates downunder: keys to effective supervision in Australia and New Zealand*, Camberwell, Vic.: ACER Press.

Denholm, C.J. and Evans, T.D., 2009a. *Beyond doctorates downunder: maximising the impact of your doctorate from Australia and New Zealand*, Camberwell, Vic.: ACER Press.

Di Napoli, R., 2014. Value gaming and political ontology: between resistance and compliance in academic development. *International Journal for Academic Development*, 19(1), pp. 4–11.

Evans, L., Homer, M. and Rayner, S., 2013. Professors as academic leaders: the perspectives of 'the Led'. *Educational Management Administration and Leadership*, 41(5), pp. 674–689.

Ferns, S. (ed.), 2014. *Work integrated learning in the curriculum*, Milperra, NSW: Higher Education Research and Development Society of Australasia.

Fitzgerald, T., Gunter, H. and White, J., 2012. *Hard labour? Academic work and the changing landscape of higher education*, Bingley, UK: Emerald Group.

France, K., 2004. Problem-based service-learning: rewards and challenges with undergraduates. In C.M. Wehlberg and S. Chadwick-Blossey, eds, *To improve the academy: resources for faculty, instructional, and organizational development*, San Francisco, CA: Jossey-Bass, pp. 239–250.

Gornall, L. and Salisbury, J., 2012. Compulsive working, 'Hyperprofessionality' and the unseen pleasures of academic work. *Higher Education Quarterly*, 66(2), pp. 135–154.

HESA (Higher Education Statistics Agency), 2014. *Free Online Statistics*. Available online at www.hesa.ac.uk/index.php?option=com_content&view=article&id=1898&Itemid=634

Holten, E.F., Seyler, D.L. and Carvalho, M.B., 1997. Toward a construct validation of a transfer climate instrument. *Human Resource Development Quarterly*, 8(2), pp. 95–113.

Jones, S., 2013. Beyond the teaching-research nexus: the Scholarship-Teaching-Action-Research (STAR) conceptual framework. *Higher Education Research & Development*, 32(3), pp. 381–391.

Jones, S., Lefoeb, G., Harvey, M. and Ryland, K., 2012. Distributed leadership: a collaborative framework for academics, executives and professionals in higher education. *Journal of Higher Education Policy and Management*, 34(1), pp. 67–78.

Kimber, M., 2003. The tenured 'Core' and the tenuous 'Periphery': the casualisation of academic work in Australian universities. *Journal of Higher Education Policy and Management*, 25(1), pp. 41–50.

Knapp, L.G., Kelly-Reid, J.E. and Ginder, S.A., 2012. *Employees in postsecondary institutions, Fall 2011 and student financial aid, Academic Year 2010–11: first look*, (provisional data), Washington, DC: National Center for Education Statistics.

Knight, P. and Trowler, P., 2000. *Departmental leadership in higher education*, Philadelphia, PA: Society for Research into Higher Education.

Kubler, M. and Western, M., 2007. *PhD graduates 5 to 7 years out: employment outcomes, job attributes and the quality of research training: summary results for The Australian National University*, Brisbane, Qld: University of Queensland.

Lee, A., Brennan, M. and Green, B., 2009. Re-imagining doctoral education: professional doctorates and beyond. *Higher Education Research & Development*, 28(3), pp. 275–287.

Macfarlane, B., 2012. *Intellectual leadership in higher education: renewing the role of the university professor*, NY: Routledge.

Mcgettigan, A., 2013. *The great university gamble: money, markets and the future of higher education*, London: Pluto Press.

Middlehurst, R., 1993. *Leading academics*, Buckingham, UK: Society for Research into Higher Education.

Middlehurst, R., 2013. Changing internal governance: are leadership roles and management structures in United Kingdom universities fit for the future? *Higher Education Quarterly*, 67(3), pp. 275–294.

Norton, A., 2014. *Mapping Australian higher education*, Melbourne, Vic.: Grattan Institute. Available online at grattan.edu.au/wp-content/uploads/2014/10/816-mapping-higher-education-2014.pdf

Peseta, T.L., 2014. Agency and stewardship in academic development: the problem of speaking truth to power. *International Journal for Academic Development*, 19(1), pp. 65–69.

Rust, V.D. and Kim, S., 2015. Globalization and global university rankings. In J. Zajda, ed., *Second international handbook on globalisation, education and policy research*, Dordrecht: Springer, pp. 167–180.

Scott, G., Coates, H. and Anderson, M., 2008. *Learning leaders in times of change: academic leadership capabilities for Australian higher education*, Melbourne, Vic.: ACER Press.

Szkudlarek, T. and Stankiewicz, Ł., 2014. Future perfect? Conflict and agency in higher education reform in Poland. *International Journal for Academic Development*, 19(1), pp. 37–49.

Teichler, U., Arimoto, A. and Cummings, W.K., 2013. *The changing academic profession: major findings of a comparative survey*, Dordrecht: Springer.

Vukasović, M., 2012. *Effects of higher education reforms change dynamics*, Rotterdam: Sense Publishers.

Williams, J., 2014. A critical exploration of changing definitions of public good in relation to higher education. *Studies in Higher Education*, 41(4), pp. 1–12.

Zajda, J. (ed.), 2015. *Second international handbook on globalisation, education and policy research*, Dordrecht: Springer. Available online at http://link.springer.com/10.1007/978-94-017-9493-0

Chapter 2

The emergence of higher education development

Messer-Davidow *et al.* (1993) suggest that disciplines act as instruments to establish a professional identity; identify problems; develop tools to address challenges; reward intellectual achievements; distribute status and recognition; encourage the enhancement of relevant expertise and capabilities; demarcate novices and experts; and encourage intellectual engagement, knowledge production and communication. New disciplines take time to evolve and to build a clear identity. They often emerge in response to identified needs that must be addressed, attracting passionate advocates who seek to make a better context for their colleagues and stakeholders.

The discipline of higher education development has emerged in response to the sector's concern for supporting the academic enterprise of teaching and research (Gibbs 2013; Lee *et al.* 2008). It comprises three fields that all play an integral part in preparing academics for their complex roles in university learning and teaching, research and leadership. Each has been informed and guided by different historical, organisational and political influences. This book encourages an integrated view of the field, arguing that the academic target audience, methodologies and common challenges support an enriched, holistic approach. However, it is helpful to understand how these different strands have come into being, and for what purposes.

In this chapter, some of the influences that have contributed to the evolution of this discipline are outlined. This potted history illustrates the emergent nature of the field and its influences. This chapter also identifies key challenges that need to be addressed as the field matures and establishes a more cohesive identity.

Identifying and addressing academic capability enhancement

Universities first moved to develop their academics through the provision of sabbaticals, recognising the need to provide periods of time away from teaching to facilitate a focus on research and renewal of one's academic knowledge base (Lewis 1996). This has continued as an important form of renewal, remaining a significant and highly valued form of development into the present day. Certainly, the competitiveness and currency of academics is essential to faculties seeking to develop reputable scholarly communities that are known to be at the forefront of their practice and knowledge. However, there are many questions regarding the equity of access to such opportunities (Smith 2010).

Furthermore, the reliance on self-education and renewal has proven to be insufficient for the complex roles that academics now assume. Chapter 1 outlined the many different activities that underpin academic work. The capabilities that ensure success in performing these roles are largely missing from a novice academic's repertoire and are difficult to acquire without substantial support and guidance. This has stimulated considerable focus on enhancing academic capabilities via institutional support.

Supporting higher education teaching and learning

Support for teaching and learning has spearheaded the emergence of higher education development. The 1960s and 1970s saw a pronounced expansion of higher education access and participation. This massification of the learning community challenged traditional teaching practices as class sizes grew and students became much more diverse. Initial attempts to address the burgeoning demand for quality teaching were led by a handful of champions across the world (Biggs 2013; Gibbs 2013; Lee *et al*. 2008). As Gibbs notes, these initial efforts focused on working with individual teachers and sharing effective, tested practices. In effect, early development efforts operated from an apprenticeship model, enabling the development of effective practices, scholarly thinking and self-reflection.

The establishment of learning and teaching development coincided with the expansion in size and complexity of universities over the 1960s and 1970s. Various university sponsors of teaching and learning emerged, with the goal of promoting a higher standard of educational experience (Austin and Sorcinelli 2013; Lee *et al*. 2008). Universities moved toward establishing centres for teaching and learning to guide more consistent educational practices (Sorcinelli *et al*. 2006). They recognised the value in building hubs that could act as centres of expertise, excellence and innovation. The positioning and roles of these centres were, and still are, influenced by institutional priorities, the presence or absence of champions, and the established organisational structures.

Developers progressed from their initial focus on helping individuals to building more impact and influence by working with groups and academic communities (Gibbs 2013). There was increased recognition of the need for building foundational teaching skills so that students could be assured of a consistent, well-designed educational experience. This sparked the establishment of development programs, workshops and other mechanisms to encourage wider adoption of good practice. This focus on building new entry faculty skills has continued to the present day as a core element of these services. A range of development approaches were introduced, including intensive programs to educate new teachers; various workshops and colloquia to share good practice; the establishment of expert centres that provided concentrated support; and the provision of funding to stimulate studies relating to learning and teaching. The staffing of the expert centres generally comprised people perceived to be excellent, passionate or experienced teachers.

We have seen considerable growth in learning communities, knowledge exchange, the sharing of models and scholarly work relating to learning and teaching. The mapping of university teaching approaches and methodologies encouraged a more detailed exploration of the ways in which students might best learn. Universities moved toward mapping the criteria and indicators of teaching quality and building assessment tools to evaluate teaching practises. This concern for quality enhancement continues as innovative educational design, diverging modes of delivery and our understanding of higher education learning theory gathers momentum. Scholarship has progressed through many iterations. Initial concern for the pragmatic management of classrooms (Svinicki *et al.* 2011) has progressed to the establishment of a body of literature that guides our understanding of higher education learning theory (e.g. Peseta and Kandlbinder 2011). Grants to promote in-depth research relating to learning and teaching and awards for teaching excellence encourage academic engagement.

Teaching and learning has been well supported by a strong disciplinary community. The *Higher Education Research and Development Society of Australasia* (HERDSA) was established in 1972 to facilitate the exchange of ideas and support the growth of teaching and learning (Lee *et al.* 2008). The *Professional and Organizational Development Network* (POD) was similarly established in 1974 to guide US academic practice and methodologies. These and similar societies ensured that there was a critical mass and collective voice across the nations, including the development of conferences, journals and professional development opportunities. The United Kingdom has also provided considerable national support through its Higher Education Academy (www.heacademy.ac.uk).

A notable achievement was the establishment of the *International Consortium for Educational Development* (ICED), which hosts an international network comprising the leading educational networks from a number of nations. ICED has provided an important forum for many new networks as they consolidated their identity and presence. Ethiopia, India, China, Japan and Thailand, for example, are recent additions to the consortium, gaining valuable support while building their national strategies to promote professional academic practices.

The changing research context

Research has undergone a similar metamorphosis. Faculties continue to sponsor research capability development through sabbaticals, mentorship and in-house learning activities. However, universities and governments have become more instrumental in guiding research development as they continue to invest vast sums of money into the research enterprise through direct funding of research training and grants; support for research centres and institutes; the provision of research infrastructure and services; and the allocation of time for academics to research (Roberts 2002). With this investment comes an increasing expectation that funded research activities will be conducted in an efficient, well managed and viable manner. This has led to a stronger focus on how research is undertaken and the capabilities that underpin successful research outcomes.

The United Kingdom has offered an interesting case study for the growth of research development. Roberts funding stimulated the appointment of UK research developers and the promotion of research development activities within universities (Roberts 2002). It increased scrutiny on practices and strategies that could generate improved research outcomes (Haynes 2010). Many universities established a team of research developers to facilitate the promotion of higher-order research capabilities, often through existing research offices or human resource departments. In other universities, research development has been located in faculties or research centres.

Concern for justifying public expenditure on research has encouraged many different initiatives, including mapping critical research capabilities (see, for example, the VITAE framework[1]) and the development of networks, guides and resources to support identified needs.

Research metrics and public cross-institutional comparisons have prompted institutional concern for supporting and developing high-performing researchers. The UK, Australia, Hong Kong and New Zealand, for example, all rely on competitive assessment schemes to evaluate the calibre of academic research. These reviews contribute to funding allocations and carry significant influence in guiding institutional practices and priorities. Notably, the performance expectations keep rising and expanding, in line with the monitored performance of competitors.

As a consequence, many universities and faculties have initiated a stronger focus on research development. There is increasing recognition of the need to build collective research capacity, mentorship and leadership of research communities that promote the best use of academics' research talent and potential. Thus, the field of research development has been stimulated by a concern for increasing institutional research capacity across the full community. This is allied with an ongoing concern for research to be compliant with ethical and legislative expectations.

Supporting higher education leadership

The latter half of the twentieth century saw a significant shift toward recognising that academics needed to acquire ongoing capabilities to support their roles and careers (Ouellett 2010). There was increasing focus on the context in which academics operate and their capacity to act, lead and engage as well-balanced and informed academics.

University leadership operates in diverse forms encompassing informal, influencing or formal roles. Universities are reliant on academic leaders to achieve their mission and outcomes. This has stimulated a stronger recognition of the need to build robust and strategic leaders who can embrace change and ensure their academic communities are functional and effective (Blackmore and Sachs 2007; Fullan and Scott 2009). Universities have increased their expectations as to the role academic leaders play and the priorities they must pursue. This concern has resulted in increased framing of academic leadership in terms of capabilities and impact. In turn, institutional concern for mapping the behaviours and evidence of good leadership has encouraged increased formalisation of discussions of leadership and measurement of outcomes.

This recognition has led to the establishment of human resource development staff in universities. Commonly, these staff sit within the human resource departments, offering services that may include support for academic leaders and their development, guidance of academic career management, mentorship programs, organisational reviews, change initiatives and other culturally driven agendas. These developers may find that they are key agents in progressing institutional changes in systems (e.g. performance management), standards (including academic standards and role statements) and in promoting major institutional changes to academic practice. While this field is informed by the discipline of human resource development (Werner 2014), there is limited literature exploring the HE sector and its particular complexities (Debowski 2012). Few networks have been established to support these professionals, although the UK Leadership Foundation for Higher Education has had considerable influence relating to higher education leadership (www.lfhe.ac.uk).

Introducing higher education development (HED)

While the three fields supporting academic, research and leadership development have travelled different paths and emerged to address particular concerns, all three have focused on creating a better, more supportive context to ensure academics can be effective, successful and resilient. The early work of those in teaching and learning has supported the rapid escalation of their allied colleagues in the more recent specialisms. At this stage, it is possible to see the emergence of a discipline that can build strength from the collective interests of those working in this dynamic field.

This book will therefore employ the term *higher education development* (HED) to describe the scope of activities and functions that support the development of academics, their work communities and institutional academic priorities. Each country has developed particular ways of describing their developers, variously labelling them as faculty, educational, research, human resource, organisational or academic developers. The title of higher education developer offers an inclusive mechanism to integrate the different lexicons that have emerged over the last 40 years. It also encourages a broader framing of the roles that are filled and deeper thinking around the possible functions that might be fulfilled. The melding of different professional orientations to support complex academic learning needs is a particular benefit of perceiving higher education development as a multi-faceted and adaptive learning space. This reframing encourages the positioning of these groups as an integrated alliance that can better support academic capacity building.

Thus, this term will be used to describe any professional or academic who is involved in:

- facilitating improved academic practice;
- guiding academics or academic communities toward enhanced skills or capabilities that will support their roles;
- encouraging improved cultural and performance outcomes across academic communities;
- ensuring there is strong support for academics across all facets of their role and across their career life-cycle.

Mapping higher education development

When mapping the current state of higher education development there are some clear trends evident:

1 The HE development sphere has been informed by our growing understanding of academics and their learning context. The increasing recognition of the need to support learning across a full continuum of academic practice has become a key driver.
2 There is high diversity in the interpretation and enactment of each institution's services. This necessitates careful identification of the particular activities that a HED unit will support from the larger set of possibilities (Gibbs 2013).
3 Within each institution, developers are experiencing dynamic shifts in expectation, methodologies and the framing of their services. Their work may be influenced by multiple stakeholders with variant interpretations of their functions, thus creating a complex and somewhat unpredictable context.
4 Many HED units (HEDUs) will have established a range of core services that remain important in building institutional capacity. They also seek ways to contribute innovative approaches to multi-faceted problems (Sorcinelli *et al.* 2006).
5 There is an increasing expectation that they will work in partnership with faculty leaders and other higher education development specialists to ensure academics are supported in the most effective manner (Sorcinelli *et al.* 2006).
6 The complexity of academic capacity building encourages interaction across the different HED sub-disciplines. Human resource/leadership developers, for example, often work in partnership with other HED colleagues to host various programs or activities.

Despite these advancements, the volatility and fragility of universities has created a less stable and predictable environment for those who work in higher education development. As this book will illustrate, it is increasingly critical to be politically attuned, influential and credible in order to guide desirable outcomes. Tightened fiscal contexts and the competition for sponsorship has necessitated a stronger evidence-based professional focus to build impact, capacity and institutional benefit. This is a time where the desire to make a difference needs to be matched with opportunity, sponsorship, credibility, professionalism, adaptive practices and a rich repertoire. There are many challenges, including the potential marginalisation of these services within the university. Thus, the higher education developer needs to build influence and partnerships to ensure their work is relevant and valued. This is a central premise throughout this book.

Progressing toward disciplinary status

Is HED a discipline (Messer-Davidow *et al.* 1993)? Not quite yet, but it has the potential to be so. This book explores a number of issues that are evident in the field as HED grapples with building identity, impact and influence. Ten key themes are threaded throughout this work, illustrating the various ways in which this field can consolidate its influence and visibility.

1 *The consolidation of a professional identity*: There is evidence of considerable angst as to what a HE developer is or does (Kensington-Miller *et al.* 2015; Kinash and Wood 2013; van Schalkwyk *et al.* 2013; Timmermans 2014). The functions and capabilities that underpin HE development roles are articulated in this work, offering a foundation for these discussions.
2 *The identification of scope and focus*: There has been some exploration of HED methodologies or services in the literature, particularly relating to learning and teaching (Gibbs 2013; Gillespie 2010; Loads and Campbell 2015; Sorcinelli *et al.* 2006). *Developing Academics* offers detailed guidance on the different activities and foci that effective HED services may integrate, promoting a focus on the academic learner as the framing device.
3 *The identification of problems and tools to address those challenges*: Again, the absence of a clear HED methodology, scholarship or toolkit means that HE developers from any of the sub-specialisms must generally build their capabilities from the ground up. This is both wasteful and risky. This book provides practical guidance on core methodologies that will assist in diagnosing and addressing institutional and systemic problems that can be facilitated through the deployment of consistent methodologies.
4 *The recognition and rewarding of intellectual and professional achievements*: How do we judge developers? This is a pressing question as the field is outside the normal academic context (Gravett and Bernhagen 2015; Green and Little 2015; Little and Green 2012). This work offers guidance on the standards and capabilities that support excellent performance as a HE developer. It will assist those seeking recognition or simply wishing to discuss how they undertake their role.

24 Understanding higher education development

5 *The capacity to distribute status and recognition*: The first step in building reputation and recognition is to encourage an understanding of the field across the wider community. University leaders currently evidence a limited understanding of the HED sphere. This work promotes better delineation of possible services and functions to support improved inclusion in important discussions. Evaluation and research of the field to build a stronger evidence base is also explored.
6 *The enhancement of relevant expertise and capabilities*: The provision of practical guidance and tools that can be applied to one's professional practice is a critical part of building professional capabilities (DiPietro 2014). Central to this work is the goal of providing a valuable, practical guide to those moving into the development space and encouraging mastery of more advanced strategies. The methodologies promoted in this work are drawn from all three sub-fields, encouraging a strengthening of HED capabilities.
7 *Demarcate novices and experts*: This work explores HED roles, mapping the capabilities that need to be developed by entry-level HE developers, specialist providers and HED leaders. It has been designed to support the professional growth of developers so that there is increased clarity as to the professional toolkit that underpins successful role enactment.
8 *Encourage intellectual engagement, knowledge production and communication*: There are many different societies and journals that explore the representative fields, but they largely miss each other in sharing their collective knowledge. This work is hopefully the start of a collective effort to find and learn from each other. The development of a HED scholarly space may emerge as a result.
9 *Attract passionate advocates who seek to make a better context for their colleagues and stakeholders*: The HED discipline is filled with passionate people. But it is also notable for its protective silos between the sub-groups that contribute to this field. This work encourages more collaboration, integration and communication, including through communal evaluative and research-driven outcomes and adoption of core principles.
10 *Advocate and influence*: The development of various societies within the different sub-fields has created a strong presence. However, they are not particularly influential. There is a notable absence of advocacy or voice in national and international discussions of HED and academic capacity building. The development of an integrated field that is recognised as a discipline is the first step toward being advocates, standards-setters and a voice for those working in the field.

Conclusion

As outlined in Chapter 1, academics need access to specialist support services to develop their capabilities and, more broadly, to build institutional capacity. This review of the emerging field of higher education development illustrates the recognition across the sector of the need to provide specialist support to achieve these goals. However, HED has been challenged by its many identities, names and structures within universities. The mapping of HED methodologies and principles can support the building of a professional identity and collective strength, and assist those who are seeking support from these services.

Note

1 See: www.vitae.ac.uk/researchers-professional-development/about-the-vitae-researcher-development-framework/researchers-how-you-can-use-the-vitae-researcher-development-framework.

References

Austin, A.E. and Sorcinelli, M.D., 2013. The future of faculty development: where are we going? *New Directions for Teaching and Learning*, 133, pp. 85–97.

Biggs, J.B., 2013. *Changing universities: a memoir about academe in different places and times*, Hawthorn: Strictly Literary.

Blackmore, J. and Sachs, J., 2007. *Performing and reforming leaders: gender, educational restructuring, and organizational change*, Albany, NY: State University of New York Press.

Debowski, S., 2012. Applying learning and organization development principles to specific organizational contexts: the higher education development experience. In W.J. Rothwell, R.K. Prescott, J. Lindholm, K.K. Yarrish, A.G. Zaballero and G.M. Benscoter, eds, *The encyclopedia of human resource management*, San Francisco, CA: Pfeiffer, pp. 23–33.

DiPietro, M., 2014. Tracing the evolution of educational development through the POD Network's Institute for New Faculty Developers. *To Improve the Academy*, 33(2), pp. 113–130.

Fullan, M. and Scott, G., 2009. *Turnaround leadership for higher education*, San Francisco, CA: Jossey-Bass.

Gibbs, G., 2013. Reflections on the changing nature of educational development. *International Journal for Academic Development*, 18(1), pp. 4–14.

Gillespie, K.H., 2010. *A guide to faculty development*, 2nd edition, San Francisco, CA: Jossey-Bass.

Gravett, E.O. and Bernhagen, L., 2015. A view from the margins: situating CTL staff in organizational development. *To Improve the Academy*, 34(1–2), pp. 63–90.

Green, D.A. and Little, D., 2015. Family portrait: a profile of educational developers around the world. *International Journal for Academic Development*, pp. 1–17.

Haynes, K., 2010. *Analysis of university reports on career development and transferable skills training (Roberts) payments*, Newmarket Suffolk, UK: The Professional and Higher Partnership Ltd.

Kensington-Miller, B., Renc-Roe, J. and Morón-García, S., 2015. The chameleon on a tartan rug: adaptations of three academic developers' professional identities. *International Journal for Academic Development*, 20(3), pp. 279–290.

Kinash, S. and Wood, K., 2013. Academic developer identity: how we know who we are. *International Journal for Academic Development*, 18(2), pp. 178–189.

Lee, A., Manathunga, C. and Kandlbinder, P., 2008. *Making a place: an oral history of academic development in Australia*, Milperra, NSW: Higher Education Research and Development Society of Australasia.

Lewis, K.G., 1996. Faculty development in the United States: a brief history. *International Journal for Academic Development*, 1(2), pp. 26–33.

Little, D. and Green, D.A., 2012. Betwixt and between: academic developers in the margins. *International Journal for Academic Development*, 17(3), pp. 203–215.

Loads, D. and Campbell, F., 2015. Fresh thinking about academic development: authentic, transformative, disruptive? *International Journal for Academic Development*, 20(4), pp. 355–369.

Messer-Davidow, E., Shumway, D.R. and Sylvan, D. (eds), 1993. *Knowledges: historical and critical studies in disciplinarity*, Charlottesville, VA: University Press of Virginia.

Ouellett, M.L., 2010. Overview of faculty development: history and choices. *A guide to faculty development*, Jossey-Bass, pp. 3–20.

Peseta, T. and Kandlbinder, P. (eds), 2011. *Higher education research & development anthology*, Milperra, NSW: HERDSA.

Roberts, G., 2002. *SET for success: the supply of people with science, technology, engineering and mathematics skills*, London: HM Treasury.

van Schalkwyk, S., Cilliersa, F., Adendorffa, H., Cattella, K. and Hermana, N., 2013. Journeys of growth towards the professional learning of academics: understanding the role of educational development. *International Journal for Academic Development*, 18(2), pp.139–151.

Smith, J., 2010. Forging identities: the experiences of probationary lecturers in the UK. *Studies in Higher Education*, 35(5), pp. 577–591.

Sorcinelli, M.D., Austin, A.E., Eddy, P.L. and Beach, A.L. (eds), 2006. *Creating the future of faculty development: learning from the past, understanding the present*, Bolton, MA: Anker Publishing.

Svinicki, M.D., McKeachie, W.J. and Nicol, D., 2011. *McKeachie's teaching tips: strategies, research, and theory for college and university teachers*, Belmont, CA: Wadsworth.

Timmermans, J.A., 2014. Identifying threshold concepts in the careers of educational developers. *International Journal for Academic Development*, 19(4), pp. 305–317.

Werner, J.M., 2014. Human resource development ≠ human resource management: so what is it? *Human Resource Development Quarterly*, 25(2), pp. 127–139.

Part II

Designing and delivering quality higher education development

Higher education development is a complex function in universities. It operates in a range of ways, depending on the university and needs of the particular learning community. The scope and level of activities can vary greatly, as the following chapters will illustrate. In some cases, the developer may act as a program designer and coordinator, in others, an adviser and consultant. Many will fill a range of roles depending on the need, client and urgency of the identified focus. At present, this multiplicity is challenging for many individuals who move into the developer roles with well-established professional capabilities in their core disciplines, but limited expertise in their new role.

This section of *Developing Academics* is designed to assist those working as developers, whatever their specialist focus. It provides detailed guidance on the roles, strategies and principles that might be employed. Chapter 3 outlines how the different services might be structured. Chapter 4 provides a broad perspective on the range of roles and functions that might be integrated into HED services. Chapter 5 explores models and guidance on the different levels of influence that can be achieved by developers, from whole of organisation to customised support. In Chapter 6, the range of roles that might be encompassed in delivering these outcomes is outlined, along with some guidance on how these roles may need to be negotiated. Chapter 7 offers broad guidance on the design and delivery of engaging learning experiences. In Chapter 8, the design, delivery and management of successful programs is outlined. Chapter 9 then explores the complex context of leading institutional transitions and change. Chapter 10 concludes Part II with an exploration of two critical areas of the HED service: the provision of consultancy services to address unique, client-focused concerns; and strategies to support and interact with the executive and senior leaders.

This section provides a foundational overview of the key strategies that can be used by developers to encourage effective academic learning and enhanced organisational functioning. Those seeking support from HED groups will gain assistance in clarifying the types of support services they might anticipate. Academics working with external stakeholders who wish to enrich their engagement methodologies are particularly advised to read these chapters. While the target groups are different, the principles will be similar. Executive sponsors and supervisors of higher education development centres or leaders will also find this part to be helpful in framing their expectations and requirements.

Chapter 3

How higher education development operates in university and college settings

As outlined in Chapter 2 higher education developers emerged in response to a growing concern at the complexity of academic work and the limited efficacy of unstructured, informal learning. Many developers were initially drawn from the faculties, attracting those who were passionate about their roles or perceived to model the desired behaviours and outcomes to be encouraged. For the most part, these developers drew on their own professional knowledge to identify models and principles to inform their practice.

The growth of the field has been most pronounced in learning and teaching, where a large body of knowledge now supports new generations of university teachers. However, the role and function of development services that support learning and teaching vary greatly and depend on the particular institution and its structures (Sorcinelli *et al.* 2006). While most focus on providing support for university teachers, the scope of services may also encompass management of online learning and delivery, oversight of learning innovation and excellence initiatives, evaluation of educational quality and/or guiding and supporting curriculum or instructional reform. If the developers are academics or filling academic-related or para-academic appointments (Macfarlane 2011), they are likely to experience the pressures of maintaining a credible research track record.

Research development is a relative newcomer, having emerged as the stakes relating to research became more critical. University research services, which were initially set up as administrative supports for grant management and ethical compliance, have moved into a more supportive focus, with the goal of encouraging academics to develop their research capacities. The last decade has seen a growth in research and scholarly commentary relating to the skills academics and researchers need to be successful in their research practice. This has stimulated a range of programs and services to support research optimisation. However, interviews with university leaders across several nations revealed deep uncertainty regarding building an effective and high-impact development strategy to increase research capacity (Debowski 2012b). The major emphasis has related to establishing and supporting the role of the research developer. These individuals are often experienced researchers who have moved into assisting others to develop their capabilities. They generally offer a depth of experience in undertaking research, building networks and collaborations and in gaining funding. The recent development of the Vitae Career Framework for Researcher Developers (CFRD 2016) has offered helpful guidance to those working in this specialist area, especially with respect to doctoral or early career researchers.

Human resource management services in universities generally carry responsibility for the broad-based development of staff in universities, including academics (Debowski 2012a). The changing nature of universities has generated increased focus on support for career management and leadership development of academics (Debowski and Blake 2007). In tandem, university change agendas, which largely target academic communities, have necessitated the strengthening of organisational development services to support the dynamic and critical shifts in academic structures, activities and outcomes (Schroeder 2011). Human resource development specialists can oversee many different elements of academic learning, including support for organisational development, leadership, change management or career management. They may be responsible for developing organisational systems or structures relating to academic career paths and/or performance measurement of academics. In most cases, these professionals will be qualified in organisational development or human resource management but with limited or no direct experience of working as an academic or in academic communities. They can be quite isolated even within their human resources community, as their work is more adaptive, external and relationship-oriented compared with other elements of human resources (Werner 2014).

This brief overview highlights three challenges that the field faces:

- Higher education developers are diverse, possessing very different backgrounds and capabilities.
- They may be expert in their substantive field, but not in higher education development theory and practice.
- Their roles can be quite variable, depending to some extent on the ways in which their employers have conceived each service.

Despite these differences, it is important to note that they are all designed to enhance academic capabilities and functioning across their diverse institutions.

The location of HED service groups

There are two primary locations for HED units: central or faculty. In general, centrally located services will carry three main responsibilities:

- to deliver basic developmental services to meet the identified needs of the core community, as defined by the university or sponsors;
- to provide specialist support and guidance at point of need to support specific members of the university;

- to facilitate increased knowledge and understanding of the best practices that underpin the field (Sorcinelli *et al.* 2006).

Central services are normally housed within the administrative division of the university. Teaching and learning might be positioned under the executive leader responsible for educational outcomes. Those supporting research may report to a member of the research executive. Human resource development, on the other hand, may be located within human resources or university administration. Thus, the types of services or priorities for each of these groups can be strongly influenced by the strategic goals and priorities of their administrative environment and sponsor's requirements.

In addition to centralised HED services, it is likely that faculties, research centres or institutes may host local development services or functions. These roles emphasise the cultivation of collective capabilities pertinent to the specific academic community, and may carry responsibility for key change initiatives. These local positions are advantaged in that the relationship between the developer and the stakeholders is readily established and maintained. On the other hand, there is considerable risk of becoming isolated, with only a limited view of the broader context in which development work functions. Ideally, some connection with central colleagues is desirable to provide enrichment and knowledge exchange.

Higher education development units

Universities will frequently position their development activities within a centre, institute or as part of a broader cognate area (Sorcinelli *et al.* 2006). The purpose, goals and priorities of each higher education development unit (HEDU) can vary markedly from others in comparable universities (Gibbs 2013). They are shaped by three key influences: the executive sponsor who oversees their ongoing direction and performance; the HEDU leadership, which determines many critical priorities and services; and the needs of the learning community.

In some universities, there may be multiple HEDUs, each reporting to different executive members. There may be limited interchange across these groups, and potentially, very limited comparability in the services and practices that are delivered. This can create notable challenges for university stakeholders, as they may need to undertake considerable forensic research to determine which is the best provider for a particular need. Segregated centres may also find it difficult to collaborate or work cohesively on complex, multi-faceted stakeholder challenges.

There are examples of holistic or integrated development services in which all or composite elements of the HED function are co-located and co-managed. This option offers both advantages and challenges. The staffing of these centres can be very diverse, integrating academics and professionals, thus offering considerable breadth of expertise. These centres may report to multiple members of the executive, who may each possess different ideas about the key priorities and approaches to pursue. The funding for holistic centres of this nature may be harder to negotiate unless a key sponsor is a strong advocate. Despite these logistical challenges, the emergence of the various development groups into one HEDU can generate many innovative and responsive approaches and reduce the challenges for the academic communities in sourcing the right support. Amalgamated groups also increase economies of scale and support knowledge exchange.

Core portfolios supported by HED services

Universities and colleges are generally guided by their executive leaders. The president or vice-chancellor draws on the support of a number of experienced executive members to ensure particular elements of the institutional plan and strategy are achieved. Executives generally focus on three key issues:

- ensuring their institutions are sustainable and competitive;
- positioning their academic practices and activities to build reputation and impact across the broader national and international community;
- seeking ways to introduce improved or innovative practices, or encourage large-scale reform (Middlehurst 2013).

To achieve these large outcomes, it is necessary to have a reliable and talented team that can respond to the changing foci and perceived needs. Over the last decade, HE developers have become critical parts of the implementation group that translate and articulate the vision of their senior leaders. Effective support is predicated on having good access to the executive and the necessary resources to enact the required program of activities. Thus, the achievement of strategic HED outcomes to support institutional goals is based on a strong alliance and interchange across the two levels. This is also the case for developers who are reporting to a dean or decentralised leader.

Types of services offered by HED providers

There are numerous services that HED providers can offer to their community. These will partly be determined by executive, sponsor and constituent expectations and partly by the capabilities of those performing the roles. The following list illustrates some of the diverse ways in which academics can be supported by HED services:

- provision of workshops and seminars on core knowledge or skill areas, emerging issues or problem-based support to address an identified need;
- development of cohort based, long-term programs to facilitate capacity building;
- design of web-based learning platforms and the associated educational services;

- development of organisational systems, policies and strategies to facilitate improved academic performance, context or outcomes;
- coordination of organisational change initiatives (local or institutional);
- provision of diagnostic assessment and coaching services;
- development of resources, websites and other educational resources;
- academic-related project management and delivery;
- scholarly investigation of institutional problems/questions;
- review and feedback provision on academic capabilities or performance (e.g. teaching or leadership);
- development of evaluative or measurement systems;
- publication of scholarly papers on professional issues or specialist knowledge areas;
- working in partnership with stakeholders to resolve complex problems;
- promotion of new institutional strategies or systems to the university.

It can be seen that the range of services and activities is very wide ranging. There are few HED providers who would span all of these. Instead, they tend to build a selective portfolio that best supports the population being served (Gibbs 2013). However, as this book will illustrate, it is important to ensure the choice of services and products is reflective of institutional need rather than developer preference.

HED sponsors

There will be many elements of HE development work that rely on sponsors: senior and influential individuals who fill important roles in advocating, championing, guiding or commissioning development work (Lieberman 2011). They may sit on the executive or be a dean or research leader. Their involvement with HED activities might be sporadic or sustained, possibly including the commissioning of specific services such as guiding institutional reforms or customised programs.

The presence of multiple sponsors with varying degrees of insight and differing perceptions of the HE developer role generates some additional complexities that will need to be consciously monitored. The HED leader may need to employ a range of approaches to reflect the requirements or working style of each sponsor, and will need to monitor each initiative being delivered. The goal is to build long-term, valued relationships with each sponsor based on trust and respect.

A feature of HED work is the emergence of new sponsors as new leaders are appointed or different needs are identified by existing leaders. The guidance of new sponsors can assist in building robust and enduring relationships. They benefit from early guidance on:

- how HED operates;
- the best approaches to achieve their identified priorities;

- the time frames that can be required to engage academics and encourage shifts in practice;
- the costs attached to delivering the agreed services;
- regular feedback on progress and evidence of success.

In exchange, the HED team will anticipate that:

- Their sponsor is a strong advocate for the agreed initiative/s.
- The team or leader can gain ready access to the sponsor to discuss progress and planning.
- The necessary funding is offered to support a timely completion of the project or service delivery.

The role of the HED leader

The HED leader is a key figure in setting up the higher education development service for success. Acting as a bridge between the executive, sponsors, other HEDUs, constituents and external groups, they need to be well attuned to the different expectations that are being levelled at their team. They play a key role in building productive and respectful relationships; securing sponsorship in order to deliver the agreed services (Lieberman 2011) and building a high-performing and professional team while ensuring that the services are known, valued and accessed by their key consumers. Thus, the role of HED leader has both internal and external functions that need to be fulfilled. This multi-faceted role draws on their specialist knowledge, leadership, management and entrepreneurial expertise, as well as the capacity to communicate and build linkages across the community. Part of their responsibility is to ensure the service is perceived to be an authoritative source of guidance on academic development matters.

At the same time, HED leaders will often continue to practice as developers, contributing to projects, programs or other initiatives that require their high-level expertise. Their roles may be more coordinative or directive in nature, but their engagement in the core services can be an important way to maintain robust relationships with their constituents. Ongoing involvement in development work also enables monitoring of the university culture and identification of emerging issues. In some universities, the HED leader may also continue to fill academic posts in a faculty or within a scholarly centre, further bifurcating their focus. While this may make the role more challenging, it also offers an opportunity to stay connected to the academic world and build credibility as an active academic.

HED challenges

This brief overview highlights a number of contextual elements that can impact on the efficacy and outcomes of the HED service. Developers in these service groups are likely to encounter some or all of the following challenges:

- *Demonstrating and maintaining professional credibility*: A first condition for success in these roles is the ability to act with credibility and authority. Academics have little discretionary time to participate in development activities. They will choose to engage if they feel the development experience will support their goals and the developer is of a suitable calibre. Their assessment of a developer's credibility may be based on a range of factors, including the developer's academic or professional standing from their previous cognate field, their reputation and representation of their knowledge when interacting with clients, and their professional grounding in the HED strategies and approaches.
- *Building the necessary capabilities*: Being an excellent teacher or researcher is a valuable precursor to moving into HE development roles, but is insufficient to support the complex work of HED. Developers need to acquire an understanding of adult and HED learning theory, develop professional capabilities that support the development of academics and cultivate adaptive and responsive approaches to support the diverse academic contexts they will encounter. This is a complex boundary-spanning role that will stretch and extend developers in many ways. Sorcinelli *et al.* (2006) conducted an intensive study of faculty developers, finding that the majority possessed limited experience in educating academics, but had expertise in their cognate discipline. This can make the entry into higher education development very challenging, given new developers require a new professional theory base and repertoire to complement their initial disciplinary base.
- *Developers may interpret their roles in a variety of ways*: Without a clear framing of the HED service and its performance metrics, the definition and selection of roles and activities can be largely driven by the individual. While this may be seen as acceptable, it can create some confusion for those seeking assistance and may reduce the effectiveness of the services delivered. Further, it can generate gaps in the range of activities being covered.
- *Self vs service*: Developers who fill academic posts may find themselves somewhat torn: can they build and maintain a credible academic record while also providing a high-quality service to their university colleagues? This is made particularly difficult when developers are seconded from faculties for a period of time and then returned to their substantive roles. As academics, they will need to maintain a competitive scholarly track record while also building HED capabilities and supporting the substantive work of the HED service.
- *Competition between HED groups*: Unfortunately, the partitioning of service groups under different executive sponsors can lead to silos and competition rather than collaborative approaches. Each group may scope and manage their functions and priorities quite differently, particularly if their key foci are driven by their sponsors. Different development philosophies and imperatives can lead to highly divergent practices that impede collaboration. HED leaders and teams may also impede knowledge transfer across these groups, aiming for divergence rather than convergence (Debowski 2011).

- *Being visible*: A key challenge that has emerged over the last decade is the capacity to guide good practice in universities. The increased array of senior roles at the university executive level has reduced the capacity of some HED services to be heard and understood by influential university leaders. This competition for space and influence has made HED more challenging, as it requires careful management of messages, promotion of the services and education of key sponsors. In effect, we have seen a politicisation of the HED space that needs to be managed much more consciously and effectively.
- *Being adaptable*: There have been instances over the last decade or so of HED centres being phased out or revamped to better suit the shifts in institutional priorities (Debowski *et al.* 2012). A factor that possibly influences these institutional decisions may relate to how the centre is perceived or valued by those who have the power to deploy funds and staff. The capacity to identify and respond to shifts in strategic priorities can be an important factor in ensuring the ongoing sponsorship of the service and its activities.

Conclusion

Higher education development is a broad church: it is eclectic in nature, drawing from all three sub-disciplines of research, teaching and organisational/leadership development to enable effective support for academic learning and development. Each of these fields offers different and complementary insights that ensure the support that is offered will be fit for purpose, engaging and responsive to the complex contexts in which academics work. Chapter 4 unpacks the key principles that support this discipline, providing an important set of foundational guidelines for any person working in this area no matter the specialisation.

References

CFRD, 2016. The Vitae Career Framework for Researcher Developers. Available online at www.vitae.ac.uk/researchers-professional-development/practical-resources-for-researcher-developers-1/the-vitae-career-framework-for-researcher-developers-cfrd/introduction-to-the-vitae-career-framework-for-researcher-developers-cfrd

Debowski, S., 2011. Emergent shifts in faculty development: a reflective review. In J.E. Miller and J.E. Groccia, eds, *To improve the academy: resources for faculty, instructional, and organizational development*, Vol. 30, San Francisco, CA: Jossey-Bass, pp. 306–322.

Debowski, S., 2012a. Applying learning and organization development principles to specific organizational contexts: the higher education development experience. In W.J. Rothwell, R.K. Prescott, J. Lindholm, K.K. Yarrish, A.G. Zaballero and G.M. Benscoter, eds, *The encyclopedia of human resource management*, Vol. 3, San Francisco, CA: Pfeiffer, pp. 23–33.

Debowski, S., 2012b. *Strategic research capacity building: investigating higher education researcher development strategies in the United Kingdom, United States and New Zealand*, Winston Churchill Memorial Trust Fellowship report, Canberra,

ACT: Winston Churchill Memorial Trust. Available online at www.churchilltrust.com.au/media/fellows/2011_Debowski_Shelda.pdf

Debowski, S. and Blake, V., 2007. Collective capacity building of academic leaders: a university model of leadership and learning in context. *International Journal of Learning and Change*, 2(3), p. 307.

Debowski, S., Stefani, L., Cohen, P. and Ho, A., 2012. Sustaining and championing teaching and learning: in good times or bad. In J.E. Groccia, M.A. Al-Sudairy, and W. Buskist, eds, *Handbook of college and university teaching: a global perspective*, Thousand Oaks, CA: SAGE Publications, pp. 125–142.

Gibbs, G., 2013. Reflections on the changing nature of educational development. *International Journal for Academic Development*, 18(1), pp. 4–14.

Lieberman, D., 2011. Nurturing institutional change: collaboration and leadership between upper-level administrators and faculty developers. In C.M. Schroeder, ed., *Coming in from the margins: faculty development's emerging organizational development role in institutional change*, 1st edition, Sterling, VA: Stylus Publishing, pp. 60–76.

Macfarlane, B., 2011. The morphing of academic practice: unbundling and the rise of the para-academic. *Higher Education Quarterly*, 65(1), pp. 59–73.

Middlehurst, R., 2013. Changing internal governance: are leadership roles and management structures in United Kingdom universities fit for the future? *Higher Education Quarterly*, 67(3), pp. 275–294.

Schroeder, C.M. (ed.), 2011. *Coming in from the margins: faculty development's emerging organizational development role in institutional change*, 1st edition, Sterling, VA: Stylus Publishing.

Sorcinelli, M.D., Austin, A.E., Eddy, P.L. and Beach, A.L. (eds), 2006. *Creating the future of faculty development: learning from the past, understanding the present*, Bolton, MA: Anker Publishing.

Werner, J.M., 2014. Human resource development ≠ human resource management: so what is it? *Human Resource Development Quarterly*, 25(2), pp. 127–139.

Chapter 4

The higher education development service framework

A notable feature of higher education development (HED) services is their variety and variability. There are many different ways that each service might be designed, depending on the executive expectations, capabilities of the HED group, target audience and desired impact. This chapter offers a broad framework as to the key functions that HED services generally fulfil. It illustrates the diversity of options that might be integrated, and highlights the importance of defining the HED identity, purpose and priorities. The development of a clear framework to support the design and management of the HED service ensures there is clarity as to who is being supported and how that support is delivered.

The focus of higher education development services

HED services are likely to fulfil the following purposes:

- increase the capacity of the university to achieve its goals and priorities through the effective contribution of academics;
- encourage widespread understanding of the university's goals and priorities across the academic community;
- facilitate the development of academics throughout their career transitions and role shifts;
- support the successful adoption and performance of academic functions across the university;
- encourage the sharing and dissemination of good practice across the university;
- encourage appropriate behaviours and standards that support a high-functioning university and its disparate communities;
- cultivate effective leadership behaviours and principles;
- ensure academics are suitably prepared for their roles, responsibilities and obligations;
- provide expert advice and support to the executive and other university leaders with respect to their specialist portfolios;
- further the field through scholarly output, research and dissemination, as appropriate.

The scope and focus of the delivered services will be influenced by the mission of the HED group. Many will be specialised, focusing on research, teaching or leadership, while some will encompass all three. Similarly, the nature of the development appointments may influence the type of work that is undertaken. Developers who hold faculty/academic positions, for example, will be expected to combine their research and scholarship activities with their service delivery roles. Those in faculty-based appointments may hold a more eclectic array of responsibilities determined by their faculty, compared with developers located in a centralised service.

Framing the HED focus

Baume and Baume (2013) suggest that academic development may become redundant as academic communities take more ownership of their own capacity building. Certainly, local support for development and sponsorship are critical functions of academic groups, as this book will illustrate. Unfortunately, there is also considerable variability in the levels of leadership across any university, with HED services offering an important alternative source for those seeking guidance and support. A second advantage offered by these services is their specialist knowledge concerning academic capacity building, particularly as new methodologies and approaches emerge. A third advantage is the ability of the HED service to act in a transformative role, interacting across many levels of the institution and with key individuals (Blackwell and Blackmore 2003). This broad scope of possibilities opens many ways that each service might frame its activities. A challenge for any HED service is clarifying the scope of activities so that the activities can be appropriately balanced and prioritised. Figure 4.1 illustrates the various stakeholders that are likely to be supported by the HE developers.

The particular focus and prioritisation of support for these respective groups will be determined by a number of factors. The HED service will draw guidance from the wider HED community, models and practices that have been employed in the institution or elsewhere, or from key stakeholders. Institutional strategy will be a key concern. Where major reforms are taking place, the emphasis may largely focus on the mission-critical activities that must be supported and in some cases, guided (Baker *et al.* 2015; Moses 2012). New centres or services are likely to be strongly attuned to the requirements of their senior stakeholders as they establish sponsorship and relationships. Successful positioning of the service across these stakeholder groups will be influenced by the relationships that are established and the degree to which the service can be adaptive and responsive to new cues and demands (Brown *et al.* 2015). There is evidence of some tension between the need to provide centralised support on identified learning priorities and the provision of negotiated support within local academic communities (Boud and Brew 2013; Loads and Campbell 2015). Certainly, the engagement, impact and effectiveness of localised learning is more powerful. More people will participate and the learning transfer can be more fully accomplished. However, if this is the

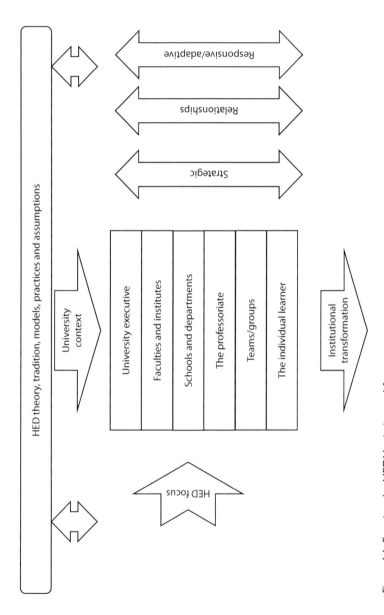

Figure 4.1 Framing the HEDU mission and focus.

only level of concentrated activity, the HEDU runs the risk of being invisible within the broader university and building an imbalanced service that privileges certain stakeholders or communities.

The capacity to be adaptive and responsive is an important element in building a successful HED service (Boyd *et al.* 2015). Many universities are moving toward the mapping of academic capabilities and promotion of strategic priorities. The HED service may be a critical contributor to these activities, helping to shape policy and/or implementation. The capacity to absorb new initiatives and priorities will require careful consideration of overall strategy to ensure the balance remains appropriate. Resilience in the face of rapid strategy shifts will also be needed (Brew and Cahir 2014). In some cases, the HEDU may need to negotiate and reposition the focus of a project or role, taking a stronger stance as knowledgeable authority to ensure the best outcomes are achieved for the target community (Di Napoli 2014; Gosling and Turner 2015; Handal *et al.* 2014).

Service and client: the HED identity

In the past decade there have been numerous incidents of HED groups being dissolved, amalgamated or restructured to better suit the needs of their university (Debowski *et al.* 2012; Fraser and Ryan 2012). These decisions are fraught with considerable angst and distress. There are many examples of developers transferred to full-time academic roles, made redundant, changed from academic to professional appointments or moved into faculty positions as in-house developers. In some cases, the core activities may be shifted to a user pays model, or the delivery of programs is moved to an external provider model. There has been very little investigation of the triggers or motives for these changes, although institutional concern for maximising value for investment is certainly an underlying factor.

Centralised university functions are generally funded "off the top" of the university budget; their budget allocation is an overhead to which all areas of the university contribute. In most cases, these funds will have been drawn from the income being generated by academics and researchers through their teaching and research activities. In essence, the academic communities underwrite the provision of HED (and other) core services in return for assistance in improving their performance and functioning. Thus, HED service groups are primarily set up as expert service providers to guide academic capacity building and enhance institutional outcomes. Ideally, they will work in partnership with their constituents, providing in-depth expertise that complements the practice wisdom of their colleagues (Bamber and Stefani 2015).

Service is a large, encompassing concept. It relates to the range of activities and forms of intervention that are offered to the university community. As service groups, HED units need to focus on what matters and to ensure the types and quality of service are fit for purpose, offered in a timely and professional manner and add value to the institutional outcomes. Some of the key services that might be delivered include programs, workshops, events, blended learning, evaluation services, reviews and reports, coaching, diagnostic services or policy and system design (Schroeder 2015). The choice and prioritisation of different activities will be determined by the university or sponsor mandate; the expectations of the key stakeholders; the capabilities and capacity of the HED group to deliver; the funding that supports the HED functions; and the willingness of university members to engage with the proffered activities. However, it must be emphasised that service does not imply subservience. The HE developer has an obligation to offer expert, specialist guidance to support optimal outcomes for their constituents. This can be a challenge in some cases (Peseta 2014), but is an important principle to be recognised by all parties.

In this book, for ease of reference, academic users of the HED service are described as "clients." This term is purposely used to reflect the nature of the HED relationship with academics and academic communities. These services generally operate on a premise of providing effective, relevant and desirable services that will attract participants and facilitate enduring and sustainable partnerships across the university community. It recognises that university staff *choose* to engage with HED services. The HED service must do more than simply exist; it needs to maintain a conscious focus on whether it is delivering the right type of support to its constituents to encourage their enhanced performance as well as addressing the needs of critical segments of the university clientele. However, the term "client" does not imply subservience. They are not always right. In fact, in many cases, the "client" may require considerable guidance to better understand the optimal support that might be needed. However, this term does encourage consideration as to how the HED service can add value that is recognised by recipients of these activities. It also encourages deeper consideration of the stakeholders and what they anticipate from their HED services. This is particularly critical when working with executive and senior leaders.

The positioning of university members as clients can generate considerable discussion and reaction from HED staff. Some may argue that this is not the core function of those appointed to higher education development roles. They may see themselves as colleagues, with some specialist knowledge that can be accessed and shared at point of need. This reactive model, which has been evident in some settings, emphasises the role of the developer as an expert advisory source that is accessed on request. Others recognise the need to build strong proactive approaches to their activities, encouraging deeper and more enduring relationships with key groups and individuals (Brown *et al.* 2015). This stance recognises that the success of the service is partially dependent on the sustainable connections that are established with university members and leaders.

The notion, then, of HED groups as service providers brings with it certain assumptions:

- The HED priority is to ensure university functioning is enhanced through the services that are offered.

- The service is relevant, valued and delivered to a high standard.
- The institutional goals are reflected in the service that is designed and delivered.
- Service users are offered a consistent and high-quality interaction with the HED providers.
- There is clear understanding as to the scope and nature of the service.
- The mode of delivery is appropriate to the user, institutional expectations and capacity of the service.
- Its funding is predicated on high performance and effective delivery.

Potential HED services

Different stakeholders will perceive and interact with the HED service in different ways. In some cases, they may come to the service seeking specialist assistance. In others, the service will seek to attract and engage them with their offerings and services. Leaders are likely to desire support that best matches their particular challenges or needs. An effective HED service will endeavour to deliver on these varied expectations, within the staffing and funding boundaries. Table 4.1 illustrates the range and diversity of services that may be offered to different clients across the institution.

The envisioning of HED delivery as services that support the goals of key client groups or stakeholders emphasises the need to be responsive and measured in the priorities that are identified. The executive, deans and heads are key clients: they have significant influence over budget allocations, can be strong advocates for new programs or services that might be delivered and also promote the service to many different university members. Part of the HED landscape is to ensure these members are kept informed of activities and outcomes and are brought into the various activities at appropriate points. Desirably, they will see strong mutual benefit between their goals and the services being delivered by the HED group/groups. In addition, as key stakeholders, they may seek adaptation of the services to better match their desired outcomes. The challenge for the HED service is to support those requests as responsively as possible, whilst also overseeing a range of core services that are foundational activities. The development of strong, respectful relationships with those key clients is an important mechanism to ensure ongoing viability and valuing. Thus, the integration of client-based and service-focused principles can greatly assist the positioning and escalation of the HED functions across the university echelons.

Core and customised services

HED services generally comprise *core services*, that are offered on a regular basis to support critical learning outcomes of key groups and *customised services* that are less predictable and generally negotiated at point of need. Core services include workshops and support activities that are offered on a routine basis each year to

Table 4.1 Potential HED services offered to university clients

Client group	Services the HED might provide	Factors to consider
University executive	• Actively support and/or implement the strategic goals and priorities of the executive through the delivery of programs, events, resources, projects or dissemination activities. • Identify and map prospective support activities that can increase the reach and the impact of the executive agendas. • Prepare reviews and reports on critical issues that are emerging, with recommendations for action to be taken. • Build strong lines of sponsorship with the relevant executive member for key initiatives. • Encourage alignment and integration of executive messages and priorities across the university community. • Develop specific activities, programs or events that support key agendas, as required. • Coordinate institutional inductions or orientations relating to increasing academic capacity to deliver expected outcomes. • Review/develop improved organisational systems, processes or policies to facilitate enhanced academic capacity or outcomes.	• Does the executive understand the nature, purpose and potential of HED development activities? • Is the executive willing to sponsor proposed/established initiatives? • Is there good consonance between the HED functions and activities and the executive priorities? Do they team up well? • Are the communication channels effective and accessible?
Deans/executive directors	• Support the development of high-performing, highly functional faculties or directorates through the provision of effective programs, workshops or strategies. • Provide specialist advice on matters relating to the HED portfolio and its implementation. • Deliver programs or support to facilitate the development of high-functioning leaders and leadership communities. • Design and deliver bespoke programs as requested. • Review, evaluate and develop customised services, if required. • Assist with building capacity of faculty/directorate staff in delivering allied services. • Encourage knowledge sharing to support critical activities or groups.	• Are deans/directors aware of the HED service and its activities? • Do they require customised support, or is generic support sufficient for their purposes? • Are they willing to invest funds in HED support to meet their identified needs? • Does the HED service have capacity to deliver customised/additional support?

Role	Activities	Questions
Heads of school/ departments/ research institutes/ directors	- Induct and support new heads to ensure they are aware of their responsibilities and how they might access assistance to review, enhance or promote academic capacity building. - Provide leadership support for heads, including access to targeted programs or activities being offered by the HED service. - Work with senior leaders within the school/department/ institute/directorate to support high-quality delivery of key agendas and activities. - Provide support to assist the development of local cohorts or strategic priorities, as negotiated with the head. - Maintain regular dissemination of key issues and events to all heads. - Support the regular interaction of all heads to enable knowledge sharing and exploration of key issues. - Facilitate the interaction of heads and their senior staff with key university leaders. - Diagnose key issues/challenges that require HED support and develop appropriate interventions or services to assist with managing the challenge.	- What do heads know about the HED service and its functions? - How are new heads supported in building their leadership capabilities? How long must they wait for this support? - How can the HED service build a strong relationship with so many leaders and their groups? - How might requests for assistance from different leaders/academic communities be prioritised? - Are there key elements of the HED service that would be better delivered locally instead of centrally? - How is HED funding managed? Will schools need to offer a co-contribution for customised services?
Associate deans/program coordinators and others in influencing roles, i.e. without significant resources or authority	- Develop guidelines and learning activities to support the induction and successful role delivery of those in influencing academic roles. - Encourage exchange and learning across this community through network meetings, peer learning and mentorship. - Provide linkages to university policy, processes and systems. - Convene regular learning events and activities. - Identify common challenges and design supportive activities to facilitate their management.	- How can the HED service support the role and outcomes of leaders who seek to influence key agendas? - How can the HED offer helpful guidance to new incumbents when there is regular turnover in these roles and their specific functions may vary considerably in depth and scope?

(continued)

Table 4.1 Continued

Client group	Services the HED might provide	Factors to consider
Academics and researchers	• Identify key capabilities that benefit from HED support and Design suitable approaches to facilitate academic and researcher Development. • Develop and deliver meaningful, engaging and productive learning experiences to meet the needs of the relevant community across the spectrum of experience. • Map, evaluate, research and/or disseminate new insights into HED matters.	• What do academics and researchers want/need? • How will they see the value of these offerings and make time to attend? • What types of offerings will offer the best outcomes for the learner and the institution? • Are the offerings of high repute and high quality?
Professional staff	• Support interaction between academics and professional staff who fill key roles in HE activities. • Encourage stronger understanding by academics of the different professional roles and functions that support their academic roles and outcomes. • Draw on the guidance and insight of professionals who work across HED functions. • Integrate deeper understanding of the broader institutional activities and services in HED offerings. • In some institutions the HED service may also carry responsibilities for the professional development of all staff.	• Are the lines of communication respectful, informed and connected? • Is there potential for collaboration to address complex issues? • What do other professional groups know of the HED activities and their priorities? • Do professionals refer people to the HED service? • Does the HED service refer people to professional services areas?

encourage widespread and consistent institutional capabilities and competencies across the community. These might include institutional induction and orientation programs; learning activities to support identified core capabilities that university staff are expected to apply and demonstrate (e.g. teaching, research or leadership); guidance on institutional practices (e.g. academic promotion); and support for strategic institutional priorities. They will generally provide a predictable, foundational suite of support that can be scheduled into the annual development cycle. Often many of these activities will be advertised as part of a yearly calendar, allowing people to predict and plan their development strategy ahead of time. These options may be integral to regular performance review discussions.

Workshops, seminars and online courses are often used as vehicles for these offerings, as they can be readily booked, repeated if demand is high and ensure core institutional capabilities are developed across the community. The program of offerings may include long-standing options that are recognised as critical to effective functioning in a university setting (e.g. cultural competence; teaching basics; postgraduate supervision). It may also integrate new offerings that address emergent learning priorities that are broadly applicable across the community (e.g. rollout of new systems; changes to academic promotion requirements). These provisions will often encourage self-enrolment, and support those who seek to learn and develop new capabilities. This is a core part of the HED service and will be valued by those who are keen to enhance their functioning and career prospects.

Customised services are those that support a specific, localised developmental need. These services often require highly intensive, long-term, sophisticated strategies. Developers who work in this space are likely to employ a range of high-end skills to help the client map their needs, plan suitable interventions and then implement a series of learning experiences that will support the desired shifts in capabilities, outcomes or culture. They will fill the role of consultant, providing expert advice and designing customised solutions in conjunction with the client. In other instances, there may be a need to develop a targeted program to assist a high-priority group or strategic need. This form of support can be highly influential but needs to be carefully negotiated and designed to ensure it does achieve the desired impact.

Targeted support

The provision of a generic suite of offerings is often complemented by more targeted offerings that are pitched to the needs of identifiable, strategically critical groups within the university. Groups likely to be identified include: early career academics and researchers who are developing their foundational skills, knowledge and support communities; talented academics ready to launch to a new level; leaders of core institutional priorities, appointed heads and other leaders who are responsible for the translation of university policy into practice; mid-career academics who are moving toward more senior appointments or roles; particular schools or faculties who have been identified as being at risk; and groups that are experiencing substantial organisational change or restructures. These groups generally have access to intensive program delivery, additional services and specialised support, to ensure they are well able to address their next challenges.

Few HED services can support all worthy target groups at the same time. Prioritisation of the groups and frequency of support will be judged on the following:

- What impact does this group have on the university's capacity to deliver its core strategic priorities?
- Are there high-priority groups that would benefit from enhanced capabilities?
- Which groups are most at risk of not meeting university expectations if they are not offered targeted and relevant support?
- Are there risks to the institution and university community if the group's knowledge and capabilities are not developed or enhanced?
- Is there evidence of issues/institutional risks emerging due to poor performance/behaviours or attitudes by this group?

It is likely that a range of approaches will need to be employed, including designing a rotation of intensive programs for smaller but strategically important groups or negotiating the hiring of external experts to assist.

The dilemma of individualised support

There has been increasing pressure on HED groups to increase their impact and influence across their university communities. A particular dilemma that emerges in building service models that are cost-effective and responsive to critical needs is the provision of support to individual learners. Those who have worked in development roles for some years will recall the "old days" where one-on-one support was a core service and offered to any who wished to seek assistance. This might have related to grant seeking, teaching portfolios, business planning or any number of things. This form of just-in-time support is highly valued by those seeking assistance, but costly in terms of the developer's time. There has been a move toward limiting this form of support, given the many demands on developers. However, there may be instances where this close assistance is warranted. The developer might, for example, consider the following:

- What have they attempted prior to seeking help? Learners should make an effort to address their learning need before asking for assistance.
- How will support for this individual contribute to the larger priorities that are being serviced? (For example, is the learner likely to be an advocate to others? Could this person teach others and extend the influence from this learning process?)

- Can the individual find guidance through other, readily accessible sources?
- Is this a common problem? Could additional support be offered through more efficient avenues (e.g. through a Wiki, FAQ, seminar)? Can the individual be encouraged to find others who would like to learn, so that a mini workshop could be offered to a group? (This will also increase the support that will be found back in the work group and facilitate learning transfer.)
- Could they be directed to an existing seminar or workshop?
- Can they be supported by colleagues in their own community?
- Is the need "mission-critical"? If the support is needed to progress core institutional strategies or support a key member of the university or target group, it may warrant the time commitment. If it is more about the individual's own basic capabilities, it may be necessary to suggest another avenue of support (e.g. a coach).
- Is there potential to encourage more mentorship, peer learning or knowledge sharing across the community? In many cases, people with suitable expertise and knowledge may be in the local community, but not visible or known to the potential mentee. The developer in that situation might act as a broker, linking the individual to local support.
- Is there capacity to assist, or will this impede the delivery of other key activities?

The decision to embrace or limit assistance of this nature is another element of the service definition that needs to be undertaken. While individualised guidance is valued, it needs to be balanced against pragmatic concerns for increasing impact and influence across the university community.

Modes of delivery

A challenge facing many HED services is the desire to provide just-in-time support to learners, but within existing resources. The widening choices of delivery modes have opened up some valuable avenues to offer online support in conjunction with face to face delivery. Online courses have become a part of many institutional offerings, particularly when all staff must undertake familiarisation with core systems or protocols. Unfortunately, their motivation and desire to undertake these learning programs may be quite low, particularly if participation is compliance driven. This can result in a tokenistic effort, just as it might with students who are being forced to complete hurdle learning. The careful design of the online program and associated infrastructure can build more engagement to some degree. Blended learning offers a more socialised and integrated mode of online support, combining online delivery with a follow-up face-to-face workshop. The learner is provided with rapid access to well-developed online resources with workshop-based support that offers social interaction, peer learning, contextual applications, and/or interaction with key leaders/models.

Features of high-quality service delivery

From this initial exposition it can be seen that the design of a HED service operates under a number of assumptions:

- It needs to be highly strategic and well positioned in terms of its purpose and functions. These may be adapted and evolve over time as different sponsors enter the university and the institutional priorities shift.
- The service may comprise a range of core and customised services to meet both generic and specialised learning needs.
- It will be necessary to clearly define the scope and target groups to be emphasised.
- The expectations of the executive and sponsors need to be well understood and respected when mapping and delivering the key services.
- The principles of service will need to be well articulated and consistently applied by all members of the HED team.
- The design of the service will encompass a variety of approaches and delivery modes.

Conclusion

The broad framing of HED services needs to be carefully considered and calibrated to meet the expectations and needs of the various stakeholders. Recognising that it is a service that should add expertise and value to the academic communities that are funding its support creates a stronger understanding of the relationship between HED services and their clients. However, each service will be likely to map a different array of functions and priorities in response to the expectations of its particular stakeholders, ideally reflecting a mix of core and customised forms of support. The capacity to be adaptive and responsive ensures the HED group will continue to be valued and relevant to those who are being supported.

References

Baker, V.L., Lunsford, L.G. and Pifer, M.J., 2015. Systems alignment for comprehensive faculty development in liberal arts colleges. *To Improve the Academy*, 34(1–2), pp. 91–116.

Bamber, V. and Stefani, L., 2015. Taking up the challenge of evidencing value in educational development: from theory to practice. *International Journal for Academic Development*, pp. 1–13. Available online at DOI: 10.1080/1360144X.2015.1100112

Baume, C. and Baume, D., 2013. The birth and death of academic development? *Innovations in Education and Teaching International*, 50(4), pp. 384–387.

Blackwell, R. and Blackmore, P. (eds), 2003. *Towards strategic staff development in higher education*, Maidenhead, Berkshire: Society for Research into Higher Education and Open University Press.

Boud, D. and Brew, A., 2013. Reconceptualising academic work as professional practice: implications for academic development. *International Journal for Academic Development*, 18(3), pp. 208–221.

Boyd, D.E., Baudier, J. and Stromie, T., 2015. Flipping the mindset: reframing fear and failure to catalyze development. *To Improve the Academy*, 34(1–2), pp. 1–19.

Brew, A. and Cahir, J., 2014. Achieving sustainability in learning and teaching initiatives. *International Journal for Academic Development*, 19(4), pp. 341–352.

Brown, M.K., Ralston, P.A.S., Baumgartner, K.B. and Schreck, M.A., 2015. Creating a supportive teaching culture in the research university context: strategic partnering and interdisciplinary collaboration between a teaching center and academic units. *To Improve the Academy*, 34(1–2), pp. 234–269.

Debowski, S., Stefanie, L., Cohen, M.W. and Ho, A., 2012. Sustaining and championing teaching and learning: in good times or bad. In J.E. Groccia, M.A. Al-Sudairy, and W. Buskist, eds, *Handbook of college and university teaching: a global perspective*, Thousand Oaks, CA: SAGE Publications, pp. 125–142.

Di Napoli, R., 2014. Value gaming and political ontology: between resistance and compliance in academic development. *International Journal for Academic Development*, 19(1), pp. 4–11.

Fraser, K. and Ryan, Y., 2012. Director turnover: an Australian academic development study. *International Journal for Academic Development*, 17(2), pp. 135–147.

Gosling, D. and Turner, R., 2015. Responding to contestation in teaching and learning projects in the Centres for Excellence in Teaching and Learning in the United Kingdom. *Studies in Higher Education*, 40(9), pp. 1573–1587.

Handal, G., Lyckea, K.H., Mårtenssonb, K., Roxåc, T., Skodvina, A. and Solbrekkea, T.D., 2014. The role of academic developers in transforming Bologna regulations to a national and institutional context. *International Journal for Academic Development*, 19(1), pp. 12–25.

Loads, D. and Campbell, F., 2015. Fresh thinking about academic development: authentic, transformative, disruptive? *International Journal for Academic Development*, 20(4), pp. 355–369.

Moses, I., 2012. Views from a former vice-chancellor. *International Journal for Academic Development*, 17(3), pp. 275–277.

Peseta, T.L., 2014. Agency and stewardship in academic development: the problem of speaking truth to power. *International Journal for Academic Development*, 19(1), pp. 65–69.

Schroeder, C., 2015. Unpacking and communicating the multidimensional mission of educational development: a mission matrix tool for Centers of Teaching and Learning. *To Improve the Academy*, 34(1–2), pp. 20–62.

Chapter 5

The role of the higher education developer

Chapter 4 explored the broad types of HED services that might be offered to university clients. The delivery of high-impact, valued services will be contingent on each individual developer and the way their role is enacted. Success will be predicated on the use of a diverse range of approaches and methodologies to provide proactive and adaptive support that effectively reflects the learning population's needs and requirements. In this chapter, core approaches that developers are likely to employ are reviewed. It will be seen that the development of a diverse repertoire of professional skills and practices will enable appropriate support in diverse contexts. This review will also illustrate the importance of guiding new developers toward a nuanced understanding of their roles and context.

The higher education development role

The HED role is a particularly creative and adaptive niche in universities. It operates across both predictable and liminal spaces and can evolve in a range of directions, depending on the individual, the institution and the development paradigm. A core platform is the provision of planned, engaging, relevant and educative learning experiences that facilitate academic capacity building and effectiveness across the institution. In addition, there is potential to work deeply within faculties or with leaders to help them shape enhanced academic communities, or to specialise in particular areas (e.g. early career learning and teaching or research) (Boud and Brew 2013). The demand for this form of strategic support is expanding with our emerging understanding of academic capabilities and leadership impact. It is increasingly recognised that the support of a developer can be an important mechanism to build informed strategies and identify optimal courses of action. Where the environment is particularly complex, the integration of someone who brings a different professional knowledge base, new ideas and models, and the capacity to share good practice from other university enclaves can be invaluable (Sherlock 2012). Ideally, the developer will work in both core and negotiated areas, although this may be more likely to occur with those filling more senior development roles. Negotiated support is complex work requiring a nuanced understanding of academics, their world and their challenges.

The contribution of the developer is four fold: first, they support the ongoing development of academic skills and capabilities to build institutional capacity; second, they encourage socialised learning across academic communities, facilitating the transfer of new skills, peer learning and knowledge sharing; third, they promote research-informed innovation and engagement; fourth, they create the environment for deep learning by the participants, encouraging them to explore their own motivations, strategies and goals as part of their learning journey.

The opportunity for the developer to work across this span of possibilities is dependent on two things. First, their capacity to relate and build viable, respectful connections with their clients and communities will be critical. Trust is a key factor in linking with academics: they anticipate developers who are expert, knowledgeable, trustworthy, respectful and adding value. Second, the developer's capacity to deliver on agreed outcomes is paramount. Reputation is the most important currency a developer brings to the role. Their track record in delivering high-quality, fit for purpose outcomes that enhance academic capabilities and outcomes will be a key factor in generating further referrals, repeat engagements and the opportunity to work more deeply within the communities. Word of mouth will be a strong mechanism for building this reputation and influence. The capacity to be adaptive and responsive to the learning community's needs underpins successful establishment of both reputation and trust (Boud and Brew 2013).

The multi-faceted developer

The HE developer needs to be multi-faceted, employing a number of methodologies to support the ongoing enhancement of academics and their work environment (Timmermans 2014). The diversity of these approaches is illustrated in Table 5.1, which offers a definition of each mode of working, along with some considerations as to where and how these might be appropriately applied. These approaches are not mutually exclusive. In some cases, they may be entwined closely to offer a layered approach to complex learning contexts.

As can be seen, this is a diverse repertoire and requires a range of sophisticated skills. The necessary capabilities are explored next.

Core capabilities of HE developers

University clients will anticipate a highly professional service from their HED colleagues. First, they will look for substantial professional grounding in the developer's specialist area of focus. The capacity to draw on authentic examples and knowledge and prior experience in the cognate area is a benefit. The developer will need to be familiar with the lexicon of the university and the academic world. They will require a knowledge of the university structures, policies, politics and practicalities. This ensures accurate contextualisation of any learning.

Table 5.1 Higher education development approaches and applications

Approach	Description	Applications
Educator	The primary function of a developer is to ensure high-quality learning experiences are offered and that the learners can source appropriate guidance at point of need. The developer is responsible for designing and delivering an experience that encourages higher order learning, reflection, feedback and encouragement to apply the key learning principles to the participant's practice. This can be offered across a range of formats.	• workshops • seminars • programs • online and blended learning • web-based sources • organisational change processes • piloting and testing of systems • self-help guides and resources.
Consultant	As an in-house consultant, the developer brings deep knowledge of the university context and experience in working with similar communities. Negotiated development will normally require a period of discussion and review to determine the real issues that require support. The agreed support will normally be designed in consultation with the client and may integrate a staged sequence of activities (Savage 2012).	This approach is often employed to support one-off, unique needs and is often requested by deans and heads.
Expert Adviser	The developer offers expert guidance on their professional field of knowledge, drawing on research and their expertise to provide in-depth and relevant research-informed guidance (Sherlock 2012).	• committees • advisory groups • institutional projects • organisational renewal or reform.
Evaluator/Analyst	Effective development is predicated on a clear assessment of the user needs and identification of any contextual elements that may impact on learning. Evaluation and analysis supports development activities at both the initial phase of planning and the final phase of evaluation and review (Swanson and Holton 1999).	• pre- and post-tests of learning outcomes • assessment of institutional context and culture • reviews of emerging issues or opportunities.

Diagnostician	There are complex elements of academic work (e.g. leadership, teaching skills) that benefit from the mapping of existing capabilities or behaviours and feedback provision. As diagnostician the developer can evaluate and debrief the individual with respect to the agreed area of learning focus. This can be a powerful cue to support subsequent learning. This role may require additional training in specialist tools (Cummings and Worley 2015).	• 360 degree reviews (normally related to commercially designed tools/services) • multi-source feedback • teaching observations • assessor • core component of a cohort-based program offering portfolio reviews.
Coach	There will be times when an individual may need more intensive support and guidance on the core skills that they need to acquire. Coaching assists in mapping how the skills will be acquired and provides guidance, feedback and support through the learning and application process (Rogers 2012).	• possible component of a cohort-based program • may be used to support leaders during complex challenges • may be offered to staff at risk or experiencing difficulties.
Observer	This support combines diagnostic and coaching components. It is often employed when an individual seeks evidence of their performance and guidance on how to improve their approach. The observer will draw on a range of indicators, monitoring the way the individual approaches their activity, and may map these practices onto a capability framework or checklist (Weade and Evertson 1991). This will then be discussed with the individual, and strategies to address identified problems will be explored. The guidance of peer observation partnerships may be part of this support (Bell 2005; Crisp et al. 2009).	• classroom teaching • chairing of meetings or groups • skill development support • communication skills • system or process skills.
Facilitator	Facilitators frame learning experiences to encourage deep reflection and engagement by the participants (Wilkinson 2012). Their goal is to build collective insights and understanding, as well as encourage individual learning and adaptation of the learning activities to their own practice. The role adapts to the needs of the group and may be less scripted than other forms of group management. These roles also benefit from the capacity to read and respond to the group and its needs.	• cohort-based programs • reflective learning activities • negotiated programs • focus groups • action learning projects.

(continued)

Table 5.1 Continued

Approach	Description	Applications
Policy/System Developer	The design of organisational systems, policies and protocols that support academic activities, learning or outcomes can be part of the development function. This may relate to the inception and design of inaugural systems or practices, or may be more maintenance/operational in focus. The role may include the development of policies and guidelines (Hill 2014), related manuals, consultation with stakeholder groups and implementation support. It may also include the conducting of pilots and the sourcing of feedback from key stakeholders.	• rollout of new student evaluation or online learning systems • academic performance and review systems • oversight of the institutional learning management system • learning analytics • online portal • staff or student e-portfolios • website design and development • online programs and services.
Project Manager	There will be a range of projects that require careful oversight. Some occur on an annual rotation, requiring oversight and management through project members, timelines and budgets. Others may be commissioned by the executive, and may relate to key innovations that are being introduced. In many cases, they may require widespread consultation and canvassing of stakeholder input, regular reporting to the sponsor and coordination of advisory groups and stakeholders (Linger and Owen 2012).	• strategic projects • annual orientation programs • large-scale events e.g. leadership summits • launches of new initiatives • HE program oversight • evaluation and review of the HED service and its outcomes • conferences or forums • thematic weeks.
Learning Partner	The developer brings their expertise to the learning context. So too, do the participants. Each experience will offer an invaluable opportunity to confirm, adapt or enrich the developer's understanding of the learning domain and the way it can be negotiated in an academic setting (Brown et al. 2014).	• This approach is a valuable form of reflection and professional review across most activities.

Network Broker	Academics value the chance to meet their colleagues to discuss issues and expand their professional contacts. The network broker provides support by coordinating the calendar of meetings, possibly arranging speakers, and hosting the event (Debowski and Blake 2007).	• heads • research leaders • women • mentoring alumni.
Scholar and/or Researcher	Developers who hold academic appointments will be expected to undertake scholarly or research-related activities to support their role. These practices may be linked to the HED functions and priorities and can assist with building a credible evidence base (Boyer 1990; Brew 2010; Laird and Ribera 2011; Weaver et al. 2013).	• HED issues • tests of new methodologies or approaches • mapping the needs of particular target groups • testing the efficacy of programs.
Event Coordinator	Developers may coordinate many events: from small, intimate gatherings, to large-scale events that might include breakout sessions, canvassing of input from stakeholders and/or residential components. The ability to plan, promote and manage the event with efficiency, professionalism and aplomb will be critical (Fenich 2015; Goldblatt 2011).	• retreats • senior leadership events • induction, orientation and other forms of institutional events • information sessions • institutional rollout of new systems, policies, requirements.

The background of the developer is only one part of the professional identity that will ensure success in delivering high-quality and well-regarded learning experiences. Effective developers also need to expand their repertoire to support the boundary-spanning role they now fill.

Some of the key capabilities that underpin successful development work include:

- The ability to communicate effectively with diverse audiences, including senior academics, using a range of media (verbal, written and formal reporting modes).
- The capacity to design engaging, informative and relevant learning experiences for diverse academic learners, with particular concern for maximising reflective learning, beneficial learning outcomes and socialised learning experiences, while minimising wasted time and unproductive demands.
- Sophisticated analytic and diagnostic skills to map the learning needs of target audiences or communities, and to identify the most appropriate mechanisms for assisting those needs.
- Effective relationship management capabilities to enable the development of strong partnerships with key clients, enduring associations with stakeholders and productive interactions with highly diverse participants.
- The capacity to present persuasive cases and to negotiate sponsorship with key stakeholders or clients.
- Effective time and priority management capabilities to successfully straddle the diverse functions and demands that will need to be filled. This includes pre-planning of key events and programs to ensure they are well positioned for success.
- Persuasive and effective presentation design and delivery capabilities that will engage the audience and encourage their full participation.
- High-level evaluative and reporting skills to build clear evidence of development impact and garner support for new initiatives.
- Political competence to ensure services and delivery are attuned to the institutional values, priorities and context (Johnson 2008).

In effect, these capabilities reflect another professional repertoire that overlays the foundational discipline or previous grounding that the developer brings to the role. Both are necessary for successful interactions with the academic community.

Critical development competencies

Because developers will primarily interact with academics, they will need to demonstrate high standards of performance. If the developer is aiming to guide their colleagues toward higher levels of learning and outcomes, they will be expected to demonstrate similar standards in their own professional roles. The following competencies will be essential for those working in development roles.

Relationship management

Relationships are a foundational core for development work. The developer will need to build strong connections with their participants and with the different stakeholders across the university. Essential to the development role is the establishment and maintenance of diverse networks. This will be predicated on the capacity to build a deep and respectful understanding of the academic world and its complexities. The range of disciplines, roles and faculty structures will need to be explored, allowing informed discussions about the particular challenges that must be addressed. This knowledge will enable robust discussions and questioning of some underlying assumptions. The relationships that are established will assist in securing sponsorship and engagement for new initiatives, as well as providing expert advice and contextual information. Established relationships offer an important litmus test for ideas, and provide a major channel for exploring emerging issues.

Effective relationship management relies on a number of principles:

- Clients should feel they can trust the developer to respect confidences.
- Regular interchange and contact maintains the connections.
- The developer seeks to learn as well as offer support through these relationships.
- The interchanges are respectful, valuing and recognising the complexities of the academic world and context.

Diagnostic, evaluative and analytic skills

Many of the developer roles draw on diagnostic, evaluative and analytic processes. Diagnostic processes are commonly employed at the start of the learning design, encouraging a deep investigative focus on the problem context, the learner needs, the historical context and the potential options that might be considered (Holten *et al.* 1997; Swanson and Holton 1999). Key questions to be addressed include: What is the real issue? How can it be addressed? Are there other issues emerging? Diagnostic work may include the use of commercial tools (such as group decision-making tests, leadership reviews); data from institutional systems (e.g. student outcomes); or interviews with key clients or groups. Prior research and scholarship may also assist in mapping some options to be considered.

Evaluation monitors the impact and effectiveness of development activities, ensuring that the community's needs are being suitably supported. In addition, it can assist in surfacing critical issues that are not yet recognised by the university or the community itself. The evaluative process may integrate a range of phases and tests to see if the learning intervention has achieved the desired outcomes. The sophistication of the evaluation process will vary according to the complexity of the program or learning intervention. In most situations, in-depth evaluation will relate to prolonged learning activities (e.g. programs) where learning transfer is more likely.

Analytic skills are required to make sense of the data and results that are generated. The developer will need to employ a range of analytic processes to assess the results and determine what they mean. The integration of longitudinal measures and statistical analyses may be important for reviewing program outcomes. The capacity to clearly document the interpretation will support successful acceptance of the reports.

Communication skills

Development work relies on excellent communication skills. First and foremost, the developer needs to be an articulate, competent presenter, capable of guiding diverse groups through complex activities. An ability to articulate clear learning goals and engage learners by framing the activities in a motivating way provides a strong foundation for learning. It is important to have the capacity to ask probing questions and to summarise discussions that have been occurring so that the key learning points have been captured and reinforced. While verbal skills are important, this skill also needs to be associated with professional presentations and a high level of literacy. The capacity to use presentation software in a sophisticated and attractive way will support strong user engagement.

Written competence will also be essential. These roles encompass the preparation of guidelines to target groups, promotions, reports, instructional materials, and possibly, online learning programs. The capacity to write in a clear, highly articulate and persuasive manner ensures the messages are high impact. Reporting is likely to be directed toward senior sponsors, and will need to be presented as a professional executive communication. The provision of evidence and substantiation of statements will need to be well integrated. High-level mastery of word processing and other professional tools will communicate a professional image.

Associated with communication skills is the ability to listen and understand other points of view. Development roles are investigative, sourcing input from many stakeholders and mapping emergent issues or ideas conveyed by those individuals. Active listening, with its focus on asking probing questions to elicit more information, will be an important part of this process. Conversely, summarising and checking that the perceived information is correct will also be required, particularly if the next step is providing expert guidance or designing customised support.

Group management skills

Good developers need to be confident in managing the dynamics of their learning communities. The key to this part of the role is to design activities that encourage interaction but in a managed and facilitative way. Most development sessions will incorporate a range of activities and interactions. There will be numerous options that might be employed, including small group discussions, structured exercises, paired discussion, panel discussions, rotating activities and group debriefs. They require clear instructions to participants and sufficient time to achieve the outcomes or desired consensus. If a plan is not working well, the developer needs to be sufficiently confident to abort the process and move the group to a new task.

While many activities will be relatively simple to design, large events will require quite sophisticated skills in thinking through the logistics of moving large groups, preparing a range of programming options and thinking creatively about ways to make the event enticing and focused on learning and development (Bunker and Alban 2006). The ability to integrate reflection, deep learning and a range of experiences will increase the valuing of the event and its outcomes. Similarly, those who are designing programs will need to operate across multiple levels of learning, with many activities filling a range of purposes in this dynamic learning setting.

Developers need to be confident in monitoring and safeguarding the learning context as a place of security and respect. They may have to corral participants who contribute too often and create the right space for more reticent members to feel confident about engaging. Setting up clear expectations at the start of a session and ensuring that bullying, belittling or excessive argumentation is quickly addressed is most important. This can be particularly challenging if the focus is on guiding complex and highly emotional discussions about issues that are of great importance to those attending. Organisational changes and challenges to academic work contexts, for example, can generate very strong emotions. In these situations, it is helpful to have considered the likely risks or challenges and to prepare suitable plans to combat potential situations. The facilitator will need to appear confident and assured in the face of opposition.

New developers can benefit from shadowing experienced colleagues and working with others as they design particular programs or activities. Good models are invaluable in encouraging high standards and providing exemplars from which principles may be developed.

Learning design

Each session that a developer presents requires a careful learning plan or curriculum. These provide a clear sense of what the learning experience is designed to accomplish, the learning outcomes and experiences that the participants will take from their attendance, and a detailed consideration of the activities and timing. This then supports planning, marketing and evaluation of the event. The quality of this pre-work will largely determine the success of the delivery. Forward planning and consideration of ways to create innovative and meaningful learning experiences is an important part of this role. This is explored in Chapters 6 and 7.

Self-management

The HED role offers diversity, high autonomy and creativity. However, it can also be frenetic, demanding and high pressure at certain periods in the academic cycle. Success in this field is predicated on being self-managing, resilient and organised. Some of the principles that can support good outcomes in these roles include:

- Integrating self-reflection and review, as well as monitoring personal responses, processes, outcomes and performance to ensure the role is effective, balanced and sustainable.
- Taking the time to play with ideas and options before settling on a particular approach. Each activity should be fresh and original in its look and feel.
- Planning well ahead, with careful scheduling of timelines and milestones to ensure all information, communications and design components are developed well before the deadlines.
- Preparing a plan that can be used as a refresher just before the session.
- Integrating relationship management into the planning, ensuring that meetings with target groups and stakeholders are scheduled well ahead.
- Completing the design of any resources or sessions well ahead of the schedule to allow for any unforeseen demands that may arise.
- If other developers or administrators are assisting, ensuring that they are clear about their responsibilities. (And ensure they have completed their contributions well ahead of time and to a high standard.)
- Keeping fit: this role will require high energy and the capacity to perform for extended lengths of time.
- Employing task lists and calendars to keep on top of multiple projects.
- Ensuring long-term career goals are also supported, despite the pace and demands. This is particularly critical for those who fill academic appointments and need to integrate research and scholarship as part of their substantive role.

Establishing a professional identity as a developer

When a person comes into the development sphere, they bring their past identity and strategies with them. The transition from academic to developer requires considerable renegotiation of one's identity (Little and Green 2012). The shift to this new role and positioning can be quite daunting: working with academics can be challenging and fearsome. They do not tolerate fools and will judge newcomers quite quickly. There is little latitude in development work for poor delivery, and issues will need to be explored sooner rather than later to ensure that the new developer can move toward confident competency in the minimum time.

The first 6 months need to be strongly supported (DiPietro 2014; Kensington-Miller et al. 2012). A detailed orientation as to the role and expectations might include shadowing of other developers as they plan and coordinate activities; observation of learning programs and sessions; participation in activities as a learner; visits to key stakeholders to learn about their roles and expectations; and participation in meetings and planning sessions. A mentor can assist in exploring some of the complex facets of this world. The provision of a critical friend to sit in on sessions and offer guidance on group management, learning design or identified issues would also support those who are inexperienced.

In addition, the supervisor will need to provide helpful support in reframing the developer's sense of identity. Developers may find it takes some time to feel at ease in this niche: they will draw on their background knowledge and capabilities, but may no longer be seen as current in that area. Conversely, their current role may feel a little tenuous and vulnerable in the early phases. Feelings of inadequacy need to be acknowledged and recognised by those who are more experienced.

A particular challenge exists for those filling academic positions. The renegotiation of research and scholarship to fit into this new role requires discussion and consideration by the supervisor and the incumbent. What will be researched? How will time be made to research and write up findings? What funds are available for conferences? Which conferences will be supported? If they are academic appointees, what outcomes will the individual need to demonstrate when seeking promotion in the future? What type of evidence should the individual source? Thus, it will be important to follow a similar process of acculturation to that offered to academics within faculties. Role clarity and a clear sense of direction will assist in determining the best approach to melding academic and developer expectations.

Conclusion

The role of the higher education developer is creative and demanding. It requires high-level organisational skills, the capacity to manage diverse relationships, good communication skills and sound evaluative capabilities. In addition, the developer is likely to build a range of approaches and applications to ensure each session or service is fit for purpose. This extended repertoire will take time to develop, and will benefit from exploration of strategies with other colleagues. Importantly, the development of a strong identity underpins successful role enactment. Good developers are assured, confident and adaptive in their approaches.

References

Bell, M., 2005. *Peer observation partnerships in higher education*, Milperra, NSW: Higher Education Research and Development Society of Australasia (HERDSA).
Boud, D. and Brew, A., 2013. Reconceptualising academic work as professional practice: implications for academic development. *International Journal for Academic Development*, 18(3), pp. 208–221.
Boyer, E.L., 1990. *Scholarship reconsidered: priorities of the professoriate*, New York: Carnegie Foundation for the Advancement of Teaching.
Brew, A., 2010. Transforming academic practice through scholarship. *International Journal for Academic Development*, 15(2), pp. 105–116.
Brown, M.K., Ralston, P.A.S., Baumgartner, K.B. and Schreck, M.A., 2015. Creating a supportive teaching culture in the research university context: strategic partnering

and interdisciplinary collaboration between a teaching center and academic units. *To Improve the Academy*, 34(1–2), pp. 234–269.
Bunker, B.B. and Alban, B.T., 2006. *The handbook of large group methods: creating systemic change in organizations and communities*, San Francisco, CA: Jossey-Bass.
Crisp, G., Sadler, R., Krause, K.L., Buckridge, M., Wills, S., Brown, C. and Brougham, B., 2009. *Peer review of teaching for promotion purposes: a project to develop and implement a pilot program of external peer review of teaching at four Australian universities*, Adelaide, South Aust.: University of Adelaide and Australian Learning and Teaching Council.
Cummings, T.G. and Worley, C.G., 2015. *Organization development and change*, 10th edition, Stamford, CT: Cengage Learning.
Debowski, S. and Blake, V., 2007. Collective capacity building of academic leaders: a university model of leadership and learning in context. *International Journal of Learning and Change*, 2(3), pp. 307–324.
DiPietro, M., 2014. Tracing the evolution of educational development through the POD Network's Institute for New Faculty Developers. *To Improve the Academy*, 33(2), pp. 113–130.
Fenich, G.G., 2015. *Planning and management of meetings, expositions, events and conventions*, Boston: Pearson.
Goldblatt, J.J., 2011. *Special events: a new generation and the next frontier*, 6th edition, Hoboken, NJ: Wiley.
Hill, M., 2014. *Policy process: a reader*, Hoboken, NJ: Taylor & Francis.
Holten, E.F., Seyler, D.L. and Carvalho, M.B., 1997. Toward a construct validation of a Transfer Climate Instrument. *Human Resource Development Quarterly*, 8(2), pp. 95–113.
Johnson, L.K., 2008. Sharpen your political competence. *Harvard Business Review*, February 27, 2008. Available online at hbr.org/2008/02/sharpen-your-political-compete-1
Kensington-Miller, B., Brailsford, I. and Gossman, P., 2012. Developing new academic developers: doing before being? *International Journal for Academic Development*, 17(2), pp. 121–133.
Laird, T.F.N. and Ribera, T., 2011. Institutional encouragement of and faculty engagement in the scholarship of learning and teaching. In J.E. Miller and J.E. Groccia, eds, *To improve the academy: resources for faculty, instructional, and organizational development*, San Francisco, CA.: Jossey-Bass, pp. 112–125.
Linger, H. and Owen, J. (eds), 2012. *The project as a social system: Asia-Pacific perspectives on project management*, Clayton, Vic: Monash University Publishing.
Little, D. and Green, D.A., 2012. Betwixt and between: academic developers in the margins. *International Journal for Academic Development*, 17(3), pp. 203–215.
Rogers, J., 2012. *Coaching skills: a handbook*. Maidenhead: Open University Press.
Savage, D.A., 2012. Human Resource transformation: the internal consulting role. In W.J. Rothwell and G.M.B. Benscoter, eds, *The encyclopedia of human resource management*, San Francisco, CA: Pfeiffer, pp. 287–297.
Sherlock, J., 2012. The HR transition to strategic partner: the rarely discussed identity challenges. In W.J. Rothwell and G.M.B. Benscoter, eds, *The encyclopedia of human resource management*, San Francisco, CA: Pfeiffer, pp. 161–172.
Swanson, R.A. and Holton, E.F., 1999. *Results: how to assess performance, learning, and perceptions in organizations*, San Francisco, CA: Berrett-Koehler.

Timmermans, J.A., 2014. Identifying threshold concepts in the careers of educational developers. *International Journal for Academic Development*, 19(4), pp. 305–317.

Weade, G. and Evertson, C.M., 1991. On what can be learned by observing teaching. *Theory Into Practice*, 30(1), pp. 37–45.

Weaver, D., Robbie, D., Kokonis, S. and Miceli, L., 2013. Collaborative scholarship as a means of improving both university teaching practice and research capability. *International Journal for Academic Development*, 18(3), pp. 237–250.

Wilkinson, M., 2012. *The secrets of facilitation: the SMART guide to getting results with groups*, new and revised, 2nd edition, San Francisco, CA: Jossey-Bass.

Chapter 6

Foundational principles of higher education development

It is widely recognised that most academics spend far more time on their academic work than a normal working week allows (Bexley *et al.* 2011). The life of an academic is pressured: there is very little space to add discretionary activities into the busy schedule of teaching, research, leadership and other roles. It can be hard to find time to reflect, experiment or learn new skills when there are so many other commitments on the never-ending list. Further, there is the need to squeeze in family responsibilities and personal goals. Developers need to work within this noisy space, helping academics to find the motivational focus to attend to their long-term developmental needs and learning priorities. This chapter explores some of the key principles that encourage academics to prioritise their learning and development. It emphasises the need for HE development to be learner-centred, acknowledging and accommodating the challenges that are inherent to academic learning.

The academic learning context

There are many factors that can facilitate or impede academics' participation in their own development:

- *The intrinsic motivation of the individual is a key predictor of a willingness to engage in learning and development* (Kruglanski *et al.* 2000; Latham and Locke 1991; Ryan and Deci 2000): people who are keen to learn and develop their capabilities will be more likely to seek ongoing opportunities to achieve their identified learning goals. In some cases, individuals may be keen to learn how to do things correctly as they are means-focused (Touré-Tillery and Fishbach 2011).
- *Goals are clearly mapped and articulated*: The identification of clear learning goals or priorities greatly assists in setting up development plans and strategies (Kruglanski *et al.* 2000; Latham and Locke 1991). These goals may be guided by institutional performance expectations, performance reviews and career ambitions via external comparators or standards, or through self-reflection and review.

- *Learning needs or gaps have been identified*: Where the individual has a clear sense of learning gaps that need to be addressed, there is more likelihood of seeking a mechanism to address this perceived need. The identification of learning needs or gaps can be self-managed or externally guided. Individuals who monitor their own performance may identify areas of performance or skill that fall below their personal expectations. Academics who map their careers and identify key goals to progress their aspirational targets are likely to establish a clear understanding of learning areas that will assist their long-term priorities. Mentoring and discussions with supervisors can also offer insights into new areas of development. The university may offer guidance through frameworks and explicit standards/performance cues. This can ensure there is a realistic understanding as to what is expected of the individual, encouraging the identification of discrepancies between existing capabilities and desired outcomes.
- *The learner is located in a supportive and learning-orientated work environment*: The context in which one works plays a key part in determining the importance of learning and development. People who are located in positive and encouraging learning environments that value ongoing development will be more likely to participate in activities (Holten *et al.* 1997). The types of messages that are conveyed will be highly influential in judging whether it is acceptable or desirable to take time away from the desk to learn. Unfortunately, there will be certain sections in universities where time away from the office or laboratory is perceived to be "goofing off." In these settings, the learner will require strong fortitude to go against the prevailing culture.
- *There are opportunities to test and apply the learning on returning to the workplace*: Learning transfer describes the process of taking newly acquired knowledge, skills or capabilities to the workplace and applying them into ongoing practice (Choi and Roulston 2015). There are many factors that can impact on the capacity to transfer learning. Collegial and supervisor encouragement to integrate and test new ideas and skills will play a critical part in determining an individual's willingness to trial new practices (Holten *et al.* 1997). This is an important consideration for developers who are increasingly asked to demonstrate the impact of their work on academic performance and practices (Stefani 2011) In some cases, an expansion of focus to promote learning priorities into faculties, schools or departments may be necessary.
- *Learning opportunities are well-matched to the perceived learning need*: While an academic may identify a particular learning need, they will then look for very targeted support that is well matched to their perceived requirements. This may be sought from peers, mentors, models and guides within the faculty, or through the formal channels of HED services. In some cases, it will require access to multiple sources, and ongoing feedback. For example, developing skills in grant writing may draw on grant writing workshops, a viewing of sample applications, meetings with mentors and feedback on draft

applications. In some cases, the individual may need to source additional forms of support such as coaching.
- *The learning opportunity reflects the academic context and high-priority areas of development*: The academic context is particularly unique in the types of roles that people play and the performance that is expected of each individual. Academics are generally keen to participate in learning that is fit for purpose, acknowledging and mapping the particular challenges that are endemic to their roles. Generic offerings are likely to be less well received (although they may have particular value and will be accessed if this benefit is clearly explained).
- *The learning opportunity is efficiently managed and perceived to be a good investment of time*: A key consideration for academics is the level of time required relative to the perceived benefit. This analysis will guide the decision to commit to a particular task. When planning a learning opportunity then, it is important to plan efficient but worthwhile activities to enable substantial outcomes for the participants in the time allocated.
- *The learning process requires a suitable level of effort*: Given this consideration, it is also important to focus on the key learning outcomes and how they may be achieved. Workshops are quite targeted in the outcomes to be delivered, normally operating as contained learning settings that do not require follow-up activities. Programs, on the other hand, may require additional work and reflection beyond the designated scheduled sessions. (See p. 105 for a description of these activities.)
- *The developer is respected for their knowledge, expertise and "value-adding"*: A key factor in determining whether to participate in academic development or not is whether the developer presenting the activity is respected and valued for their expertise, delivery and overall credibility. There is little leeway in this regard: a poor experience with a developer can affect future choices as to participation.
- *The timing of the learning opportunity is well-suited to academic rhythms* (Burdick et al. 2015): The planning of learning opportunities is quite challenging. They need to be scheduled at periods outside peak periods, avoiding the start and end of term, school holidays and public holiday weekends.
- *The learning context encourages interchange, socialisation and peer networking* (Isaac et al. 1999): A challenge for many academics is that they are quite isolated and tend to mingle only with their close associates. This can reduce their openness to different ways of working in universities and the possibilities of linking with colleagues from other disciplines. The opportunity to interact, explore and debate issues with colleagues offers an important chance to socialise and network with others. It also encourages reflection and the enhancement of social capital for all learners (Tomozumi-Nakamura and Yorks 2011). Given the busy lives most academics lead, this can be an important added benefit from attending an activity, and can increase its perceived desirability.

Foundational principles of HED 69

These are just a few of the influences that may impact upon the attraction of proffered learning opportunities to academics. The goal then, is to create highly enticing and engaging development options that deliver:

- significant value in terms of learning benefits and insights;
- an enjoyable and stimulating learning experience;
- an opportunity to learn from and with other peers;
- current and relevant guidance and approaches;
- efficient delivery, but with time for reflection, review and adaptation to their own work context.

Designing meaningful academic learning experiences

Getting academics in the room is a key achievement! Keeping them there requires careful consideration of the design of the learning experience and the core outcomes and processes to be integrated. The following list articulates some of the key principles of academic learning that will ensure a positive response from participants, and hopefully, encourage them to return for future offerings. Their advocacy and promotion of positive learning experiences to their colleagues will further raise awareness across the academic population.

1. *The content is research-informed, relevant and authentic.* Academic learners will watch for guidance that will support their immediate needs and help them address identified learning gaps or priorities. The offerings will need to be fit for purpose, providing a credible and sound overview from which they can take away useful insights, models, principles or practices that are application ready. The integration of research-informed content is helpful, as it assures them that they are being offered verifiable and well-considered guidance.
2. *The guidance and insights are of a suitable breadth and depth.* Academics are intelligent people who are looking for rich ideas and insights that can enhance their own professional capabilities and knowledge. They seek learning that offers sufficient breadth to increase their professional repertoire and skills as well as enhanced depth of understanding of key learning principles. Opportunities to test, reflect, consolidate and adapt these principles can assist in building and applying interpretive frameworks.
3. *The learning design integrates opportunities for participants to explore their ideas with other participants.* Much of the learning that takes place will be between participants. The capacity to *socialise* the learning space, enabling the sharing of ideas, good practice, case studies, experiences and reflections on their learning or issues is an important benefit from attending a session. This rich dynamic is one of the particular benefits of taking time away from a busy workspace. The design of each session needs to provide suitable avenues for these interactions. The challenge is to corral the conversation

so that it remains on-topic and focused, rather than discursive. Participants won't be looking for a talk-fest that has little direction; they are there for a purpose.

4 *Models and exemplars are explored/profiled.* When people learn, they seek evidence that they are capable of transforming their practices into the desired state. A key influence will be seeing people comparable to themselves demonstrating success in the desired behaviours (Bandura 1997). This vicarious experience of success encourages them to envisage themselves in the same context. When designing academic learning, it can be useful to integrate academic models that explore their experience. Panels or other forms of case studies also assist in building stronger self-efficacy around the learner's goals.

5 *The activities fit into a broader scaffolding of academic careers, university strategy and other contextual frameworks.* The embedding of learning into a broader contextual framework can greatly assist the learner in thinking through the implications of their new knowledge or skills. The integration of contextual framing provides an important window beyond the individual's own local experience. The developer is well placed to see the broad trends across the institution, to share key priorities and approaches that are evident across the university. Integration and translation of these can assist the participants in better understanding the broader university context. Similarly, encouraging learners to consider how this new learning will contribute to their long-term career goals can increase motivation. In some cases, it will be helpful to link the session to other frameworks or contexts, such as faculty or sectoral trends.

6 *The individual is offered time to reflect and apply the concepts to their own context.* Reflection is a critical skill that is sometimes under-developed in academics. The tendency to respond to immediate demands can reduce the capacity to take a step back and see the larger picture. There are many models of reflection that can be applied, but most operate from the key principles of self-knowledge, evaluation and review of the individual's actions and consequences, as well as identification of learning points and action plans to effect identified changes (Moon 2004). This is an important meta-skill that needs to be encouraged in academics and will serve them well as their world continues to shift rapidly and in unexpected directions. An important part of this process is the development of stories or narratives to make sense of the learning that has surfaced (Jones 2011). Kligyte (2011) demonstrates the value of "transformation" narratives which build progressive reflections to encourage deeper understanding of the academic role.

7 *The articulated outcomes are delivered.* When a prospective participant reviews the advertised learning opportunity, they will assess their interest based on the promoted learning outcomes. The activity needs to be well matched to that overview. It is, to some extent, the contract that has been offered. Clear, accurate and realistic articulation of the intended outcomes therefore

needs to be provided. A short three-hour session, for example, is likely to be awareness-raising more than transformational in its impact.
8 *The presenter is knowledgeable and respectful of the academic context.* There is a particular challenge in working with academics. They are very conscious of their unique identity and contextual complexities. Effective developers are those who are keyed into these challenges and appreciate the difference between other work settings and the environment in which academics operate. There will be times when it is necessary to challenge some of the prevailing orthodoxies and encourage fresh thinking about some of these difficulties. There is no denying that it is helpful to have worked as an academic and to have directly experienced some of these elements first-hand. However, this is not essential; rather, the key is to understand and empathise with the lived context of academe. Talk to people, ask them questions; listen carefully to the discussions that are being had in the room; and aim for a well-informed approach that acknowledges that the academic world is relatively unique. On the other hand, there will be many issues and principles that have universal application, and it is important to encourage academics to avoid being too insular.

This section has illustrated the strong interdependency between well-designed learning experiences, informed and credible developers and committed, engaged learners. All three play a key role in creating powerful, transformative learning.

Learning formats

The format of a learning activity will vary, depending on the particular learning goals to be accomplished. There are a vast array of approaches to support adult learning (Martin *et al.* 2014), with the following frequently employed. The selection of a particular approach should be determined through consideration of the desired learning outcomes, context and audience.

Key factors to consider when choosing one of these options include:

- Who is the target audience? What are they seeking to learn or develop? Will this format be a good match for their capacity to participate, willingness, availability and perceived needs?
- What are the key learning outcomes and experiences to be integrated? Is this format suitable?
- How transformative is the learning? Is it focused on information, knowledge building, skill enhancement or development? Does it require opportunities for reflection, practice, feedback and consolidation? How much time, reinforcement and/or support will the participants require?
- Who is being educated and/or influenced? Just the learner? Their community? Their leaders? All of these?

Information sessions

Information sessions are designed to impart information in a structured and coordinated manner. They are normally short in duration (e.g. one hour), aiming to capture the largest audience possible. They can be an efficient way to share critical information that needs to be disseminated, while allowing time for questions and discussion across the audience. These sessions can be particularly critical when major changes are occurring, as they ensure members feel they have been kept informed and are able to verify facts and understanding.

Seminars and conferences

Again, these sessions are often focused on sharing knowledge and providing a forum for people to learn from experts. Seminars are traditionally designed with limited audience participation, relying instead on formal presentations to guide the program. However, they may encompass time to reflect and consider how the new insights might apply to the participant's own practice. The passivity of the audience means that few will shift their practice as a result of attending, although the experience may open up reflection, critique and ongoing consideration of new ideas or practices. Thus, they can act as a valuable stimulus toward learning or professional enhancement in addition to knowledge sharing.

Workshops

A core service offered by developers is the design and delivery of workshops. These can be defined as a planned set of structured learning activities designed to encourage learning, reflection, practice and action planning. Workshops may be of varying duration, from several hours to a day or two, facilitating enhanced understanding and, in some cases, adaptive practices. Workshops are the most popular mechanism employed by developers, as they are contained, attractive to academics and focused on a particular learning goal. They can be attended without ongoing commitment to other activities, and may be repeated as required. They can also be offered across campuses or into faculties with minimal challenges or setup costs. While most are centralised offerings, negotiated workshops can be designed to support the needs of specific work communities.

Workshops are sometimes dismissed as being "dislocated, individualised and decontextualized" (Loads and Campbell 2015). This is certainly a challenge for developers that must be avoided. Well-designed workshops that reflect the principles articulated earlier in this chapter will offer creative, enticing spaces for participants to explore their ideas, reflect and socialise their learning. Many academics will need access to these offerings, as their own work communities may lack the necessary sponsorship and support that facilitates learning. A potential risk is that each workshop operates with the same basic design, leading to a perception of a formulaic design that fails to support the particular learning focus. Thus, while a core practice of many developers, it is important to recognise that workshops need to be carefully planned and presented in a way that ensures each appears as original, authentic and relevant to the learner/learners.

Online learning

In recent years, there has been a major shift in enabling learning access for academics. There are two key challenges: the first is providing sufficient depth and guidance in as efficient manner as possible, and the second is the offering of support as "just-in-time" learning. Many academics wait until they are in critical need of new skills or support before seeking assistance. Consider, for example, preparation for being a research supervisor; learning to recruit, select and supervise a graduate research assistant once funding is awarded; developing a promotion application; and so on. The necessity for these types of skills often only surfaces when the work roles demand it. However, the provision of face-to-face support at the point of need is unrealistic. This has stimulated considerable focus on developing online support for academics so that they can obtain assistance in a timely, efficient and helpful manner. The support may consist of online courses, guides, tools, checklists, samples and case studies. In some cases, the material may include assessment tasks or activities.

Online offerings can be developed in-house to support the priorities and contexts specific to a particular university, or externally sourced (with, possibly, capacity to customise components). While some of the offerings may be compulsory (e.g. research integrity or selection panel training), many are designed to support an individual learning need. They offer well-structured, sequenced learning and can be accessed repeatedly if the learner is keen to do so.

This form of learning encourages wider access to key learning opportunities and supports the development of skills across larger numbers of learners. A key challenge, however, is the support provided to the isolated learner who is working through the material. Did they have questions? How deeply did they engage with the content? Did the material make sense? A further difficulty relates to encouraging academics to engage with these resources in the first place. The capacity to provide support is more challenging when the learner is remote and potentially exploring the materials asynchronously.

"Just in time" support may integrate interactive technologies, including FAQs, Wikis, blogs and other forms of online guidance. The co-production by learners is greatly facilitated through these mechanisms. This has been little explored in the HED literature, but has considerable potential when working with complex innovation or iterative learning processes (London and Hall 2011; McPherson et al. 2015). Key to this form of guidance is ensuring the technology is easy to access and user-focused.

Blended learning

Blended learning is an important complement to face-to-face sessions, and offers an added benefit in that participants can return to the online material later to further review it at point of need. It combines the strengths of online learning with the benefits of facilitated support. In this format, participants undertake preparatory work online before attending a workshop that encourages deeper application of skills, reflection and discussion with other colleagues. The integration of models and exemplars can further contextualise the material. This has proven to be a powerful amalgamation of the strengths of workshops and online learning. The timing of the online participation and workshop attendance needs to provide sufficient leeway for busy academics to prepare, while also ensuring the review/application session is timely.

There are several elements that need to be successfully managed to ensure this approach works. First, the learners need to have completed the online component before attending the subsequent workshop. It is very challenging to facilitate a group and encourage deep discussions if attendees also include people who are totally unfamiliar with the material. This can be very frustrating for those who have come well prepared. Assiduous communication and reminders, along with clear expectations as to the preparatory process are critical in order to get people involved. It also helps to advise them of the likely amount of time that they will need to allocate for pre-work. Clear messages and expectations will assist. Second, those presenting the workshop component need to complement, not duplicate, the material that was covered in the online offering. If guest presenters or experts are being included, they need to be well inducted into this learning mode, aiming for complementing rather than duplicating the online learning coverage. Third, all elements of the experience need to offer authentic, relevant and engaging learning experiences. Thus, the design and delivery of these forms of learning, while offering great advantages, also need to be well coordinated and managed to ensure maximum value and impact. The length of the workshop session also needs to be carefully considered. If participants have already committed a number of hours to their online preparation, they will prefer to have focused and efficient reflective debriefs.

Group facilitation

While workshops are an important vehicle for individuals to learn and develop new capabilities, they are best suited to acquiring professional practices and core competencies that are generically applicable to the university audience. However, there will be times when a more targeted approach is desirable, for example, when team learning is the focus (Raes *et al.* 2015). As future chapters will outline, this can often be required when complex, multi-faceted challenges such as structural change, innovation or major reforms need to be addressed (Popova-Nowak and Cseh 2015). It is here that facilitation becomes very important. Facilitation is a highly sophisticated development strategy that integrates adaptive designs to suit a group's learning needs. It encourages intensive reflection and the critiquing of ideas and may generate considerable emotions across the participants. While some of the activities and exercises may be similar to those integrated into workshops, they will be designed to suit the particular issue being explored and the learning community. Thus, these bespoke sessions require very skilled facilitators who can read the audience, adapt and delve into emerging issues, and challenge emerging assumptions, where necessary. These sessions may span a series of events or a sequence of days to encourage shifts in culture, practice and principle. A key outcome of group facilitation is to reach a degree of consensus. This can be challenging, especially when academics are the core audience! However, the capacity to work with cognate groups in a disciplinary context, where communal views and perspectives can be explored, challenged and acknowledged is a powerful learning tool (Krause 2014; Roxå and Mårtensson 2015).

Programs

While workshops and online learning offer valuable guidance on skills and capabilities that can inform academic practice, the enhancement of self-efficacy, attitudes, critical capabilities, career strategy and leadership dispositions will require considerably more time to consolidate and build new capabilities and insights. To this end, programs offer important support to facilitate more embedded multi-faceted learning outcomes and to encourage strong learning transfers. Many programs are structured with an initial residential component to support the development of high trust and to ensure core principles are well consolidated. The residential also provides the necessary vehicle to ensure participants are highly motivated to commit to subsequent program components.

Programs are generally designed to support a specific cohort of participants who will be expected to commit to the full suite of activities over a prolonged time frame (e.g. 6 months or a year). Program offerings may relate to a specific role that participants undertake, such as teaching, research or leadership, or could support broader needs, such as mentorship or career management. The program structure supports the development of certain themes that can be revisited and encourages the testing of ideas and principles in the real work setting in the intervening times. It can integrate diagnostic tools and models that can be debriefed effectively and may also integrate tasks to be undertaken over the course of the program. Some include action learning projects that are implemented across the program, providing an invaluable opportunity to test ideas and evaluate program outcomes. Programs might incorporate mentorship, shadowing of more senior leaders, opportunities to visit various settings, coaching and other forms of support where needed.

However, these powerful learning forums require considerable planning and negotiation. Additional funding to support residential components, expert facilitation, food and other costs will be required. This normally means that only a few programs will be provided in any given year, and they may be rotated across a few years. They are recognised as powerful sources of learning, however, and are generally very well received by academics who wish to build their deeper learning outcomes (see Chapter 8 for a more detailed overview of program design).

Communities of practice

Networks and communities of practice are particularly critical to those who are building new roles or establishing foundational knowledge (Remmik *et al.* 2011). An informal, highly socialised learning context occurs when communities convene to explore their practice (Hughes *et al.* 2013). The opportunity to meet with colleagues to talk about real issues and share knowledge, problems and strategies builds significant bonds across the learning community (Calderwood and Klaf 2015). These have been used successfully by many HE developers (Houghton *et al.* 2015; Kennelly and McCormack 2015; Pharo *et al.* 2014). They have the capacity to generate alternative learning communities that provide support, even when an individual is located in less encouraging work contexts (Tovar *et al.* 2015).

Conclusion

This chapter has outlined the many considerations that support the good design of HED learning opportunities. It highlights the criticality of harnessing academic interest and engagement by ensuring the proffered learning opportunities are relevant, enticing, suitably matched to the learning scope and authentic in their focus. Each learning opportunity needs to be carefully designed, with consideration of the intended audience, the desired learning outcomes and the range of experiences to be integrated.

References

Bandura, A., 1997. *Self-efficacy: the exercise of control*, New York: W.H. Freeman.

Bexley, E., James, R. and Arkoudis, S., 2011. *The Australian academic profession in transition: addressing the challenge of reconceptualising academic work and regenerating the academic workforce*, Melbourne, Vic.: Centre for Studies in Higher Education.

Burdick, D., Doherty, T. and Schoenfeld, N., 2015. Encouraging faculty attendance at professional development events. *To Improve the Academy*, 34(1–2), pp. 367–405.

Calderwood, P.E. and Klaf, S., 2015. Mentoring within a community of practice for faculty development: adding value to a CTL role. *To Improve the Academy*, 34(1–2), pp. 290–318.

Choi, M. and Roulston, K., 2015. Learning transfer in practice: a qualitative study of medical professionals' perspectives. *Human Resource Development Quarterly*, 26(3), pp. 249–273.

Holten, E.F., Seyler, D.L. and Carvalho, M.B., 1997. Toward a construct validation of a Transfer Climate Instrument. *Human Resource Development Quarterly*, 8(2), pp. 95–113.

Houghton, L., Ruutz, A., Green, W. and Hibbins, R., 2015. I just do not have time for new ideas: resistance, resonance and micro-mobilisation in a teaching community of practice. *Higher Education Research and Development*, 34(3), pp. 527–540.

Hughes, J., Jewson, N. and Unwin, L. (eds), 2013. *Communities of practice: critical perspectives*, 2nd edition, London: Routledge.

Isaac, J.D., Sansone, C. and Smith, J.L., 1999. Other people as a source of interest in an activity. *Journal of Experimental Social Psychology*, 35(3), pp. 239–265.

Jones, A., 2011. Seeing the messiness of academic practice: exploring the work of academics through narrative. *International Journal for Academic Development*, 16(2), pp. 109–118.

Kennelly, R. and McCormack, C., 2015. Creating more 'elbow room' for collaborative reflective practice in the competitive, performative culture of today's university. *Higher Education Research and Development*, 34(5), pp. 942–956.

Kligyte, G., 2011. Transformation narratives in academic practice. *International Journal for Academic Development*, 16(3), pp. 201–213.

Krause, K.-L.D., 2014. Challenging perspectives on learning and teaching in the disciplines: the academic voice. *Studies in Higher Education*, 39(1), pp. 2–19.

Kruglanski, A.W., Thompson, E.P., Higgins, E.T., Atash, M.N., Pierro, A, Shah, J.Y. and Spiegel, S., 2000. To 'do the right thing' or to 'just do it': locomotion and assessment as distinct self-regulatory imperatives. *Journal of Personality and Social Psychology*, 79(5), pp. 793–815.

Latham, G.P. and Locke, E.A., 1991. Self-regulation through goal setting. *Organizational Behavior and Human Decision Processes*, 50(2), pp. 212–247.

Loads, D. and Campbell, F., 2015. Fresh thinking about academic development: authentic, transformative, disruptive? *International Journal for Academic Development*, 20(4), pp. 355–369.

London, M. and Hall, M.J., 2011. Web 2.0 support for individual, group and organizational learning. *Human Resource Development International*, 14(1), pp. 103–113.

McPherson, M., Budge, K. and Lemon, N., 2015. New practices in doing academic development: Twitter as an informal learning space. *International Journal for Academic Development*, 20(2), pp. 126–136.

Martin, B.O., Kolomitro, K. and Lam, T.C.M., 2014. Training methods: a review and analysis. *Human Resource Development Review*, 13(1), pp. 11–35.

Moon, J.A., 2004. *A handbook of reflective and experiential learning: theory and practice*, London: Routledge-Falmer.

Pharo, E., Davison, A., McGregor, H., Warr, K. and Brown, P., 2014. Using communities of practice to enhance interdisciplinary teaching: lessons from four Australian institutions. *Higher Education Research and Development*, 33(2), pp. 341–354.

Popova-Nowak, I.V. and Cseh, M., 2015. The meaning of organizational learning: a meta-paradigm perspective. *Human Resource Development Review*, 14(3), pp. 299–331.

Raes, E., Kyndt, E., Decuyper, S., Van den Bossche, P. and Dochy, F., 2015. An exploratory study of group development and team learning. *Human Resource Development Quarterly*, 26(1), pp. 5–30.

Remmik, M., Karm, M., Haamer, A. and Lepp, L., 2011. Early-career academics' learning in academic communities. *International Journal for Academic Development*, 16(3), pp. 187–199.

Roxå, T. and Mårtensson, K., 2015. Microcultures and informal learning: a heuristic guiding analysis of conditions for informal learning in local higher education workplaces. *International Journal for Academic Development*, 20(2), pp. 193–205.

Ryan, R.M. and Deci, E.L., 2000. Intrinsic and extrinsic motivations: classic definitions and new directions. *Contemporary Educational Psychology*, 25(1), pp. 54–67.

Stefani, L. (ed.), 2011. *Evaluating the effectiveness of academic development: principles and practice*, New York: Routledge.

Tomozumi-Nakamura, Y. and Yorks, L., 2011. The role of reflective practices in building social capital in organizations from an HRD perspective. *Human Resource Development Review*, 10(3), pp. 222–245.

Touré-Tillery, M. and Fishbach, A., 2011. The course of motivation. *Journal of Consumer Psychology*, 21(4), pp. 414–423.

Tovar, M., Jukier, R., Ferris, J. and Cardoso, K., 2015. Overcoming pedagogical solitude: the transformative power of discipline-specific faculty learning communities. *To Improve the Academy*, 34(1–2), pp. 319–344.

Chapter 7

Delivering high-quality experiences
The HED toolkit

The previous two chapters have highlighted the diversity of roles and functions that the HE developer might integrate into their regular roles. At the heart of these activities is the need to match what is delivered with what the participants or clients need or want. The capacity to provide high-quality, highly relevant experiences and services will ensure the service is well used, highly valued and likely to build increasing influence and visibility over the years. Ideally, it will be seen as the key avenue for support when capacity building, quality enhancement or shifts in strategy are being envisaged.

To achieve this positioning, core activities need to be professionally conceived, implemented and managed. This chapter offers detailed guidance on the design and delivery of learning experiences, using workshops to illustrate the key principles. The nature of facilitation is explained, clarifying the role of the facilitator in building an environment that encourages academics to optimise their participation and outcomes. Different forms of group work and broad learning design are also outlined, highlighting the diversity of approaches that might be employed.

The design and delivery of effective learning experiences to support academic development is predicated on development experiences that are rich in reflection, challenge, interaction and enjoyment. Achieving these outcomes requires three things:

- expert facilitation to ensure participants remain engaged, actively learning and reflecting, and at ease with other learners;
- a good design for the learning experience that integrates appropriate and well-contextualised learning opportunities;
- a learning community keen to participate and learn.

Each of these will be explored in this chapter. The skills of the facilitator are identified as a key element of this triad, as they will ensure creative and innovative approaches to achieve the identified learning goals.

The role of facilitator

There are many ways in which facilitation enables effective learning (Wilkinson 2012). The goals of facilitation are to:

- ensure participants are offered relevant, accurate and meaningful guidance on their learning needs, context and application of the concepts;
- encourage individuals to fully engage with their learning experience;
- support deep learning, where the learner is testing and applying the concepts and ideas with a view to integrating this information into their own professional or personal schema;
- enable socialised learning spaces that are productive, constructive, interactive settings, encouraging focused discussion and exploration of individual contexts;
- manage complex or contentious interactions;
- adapt the activities to explore emerging, unanticipated issues at point of need;
- support a range of learning experiences and interactions, including individual reflection, small group discussions and large group debriefs;
- increase the learner's confidence in interacting with their learning community and the broader university context;
- encourage engagement with the university and its mission.

While facilitators may be expert in the content being explored, they are primarily functioning as a guide to the learning group, providing a scaffold and support structure that enables participants to build confidence and familiarity with the area being explored. In effect, facilitators are knowledgeable tour operators: they are expert in choosing an optimal path to reach a desired destination, and are responsible for creating an environment that helps the traveller achieve the best familiarisation possible in the time frame available. They are responsible for setting up an experience that recognises the limitations of the learner/s, ensuring their time is well deployed and enjoyable. Thus, the facilitator role is to provide a series of learning experiences, questions and cues that encourage engaged and active learners.

Facilitation is a core competency for any developer, although it will be applied in different ways, depending on the context in which the facilitator operates. Workshops or short duration learning activities require effective facilitation to increase the power and impact of the experiences. Even where the focus is primarily on information dissemination, the presence of a facilitator can increase the effective management of questions, discussion and exploration of possible applications. This technique will be used extensively when designing customised learning experiences or programs, as these activities provide greater opportunity to surface underlying issues and resolve them over a period of time.

Facilitation tips and techniques

The best facilitation seems effortless: in many cases, it may seem unplanned and fluid, adapting to the learners and their needs, and then steering them into productive learning. However, this appearance can be deceptive: good facilitation is often the product of considerable reflection and scenario planning to prepare for a range of eventualities. While there may be a planned sequence of interactions, the facilitator can adapt and accommodate emergent needs as required. Facilitation is therefore a multi-layered process that incorporates:

- implementing the intended design of the development activity to ensure it progresses in a timely and effective manner and reaches an agreed outcome;
- monitoring the participant responses to address key issues;
- encouraging deep reflection and engagement through the use of perceptive questions, reviews of participant deliberations, adaptive tasks that take advantage of emergent discussion and real case studies from the participants;
- ensuring the group is building social and cultural competence in their interactions with each other (Berardo and Deardorff 2012).

In essence, the facilitator is doing much more than implementing a planned activity; they encourage positive but challenging learning experiences, guide constructive interactions and support adaptive learning outcomes. When designing any learning activity, then, it is helpful to consider how facilitation might enhance the learning experiences and outcomes.

The next part of this chapter explores the design of the actual learning experience.

Clarifying the intentions of the development activity

In thinking about the design and delivery of a learning activity, it is important to first clarify its purpose and function. For example, the experiences may be focused on enhancing capabilities, processes, outcomes or institutional functioning. They might encompass:

- the development of robust and well-balanced academic/research identities;
- the ongoing development of the academic with respect to desired capabilities, skills or knowledge;
- support to encourage the learner/s to apply new ideas and practices to their own work settings;
- increased capacity of the individual to relate to, and interact with, their university, school, discipline or colleagues in a productive and constructive manner;
- awareness of institutional policies, practices or avenues of support;
- the growth of collegial interaction across different communities and levels;
- the identification of improved approaches to address complex issues;

- more effective practices and applications to support the core academic activities;
- the provision of models and exemplars to support goal setting and the calibration of standards and expectations;
- talent management of high-potential academics and researchers;
- peer learning;
- action learning (where the learner seeks to address real problems in authentic contexts, and reflects on their learning outcomes).

This list is not exclusive: there are many other intentions that sit behind development work. In many cases, the intended benefits may encompass a number of these elements. It is important to carefully consider the purpose prior to focusing on how these intentions might be achieved.

Designing high-quality learning experiences

The design (and delivery) of well-planned and professionally delivered learning and support experiences encourages a range of outcomes for the participants. For example, they may enhance the individual's skills, knowledge, capabilities, confidence, and/or capacity to critique or reflect on their learning experiences. Participation may support learning transfer and the development of clear learning goals (Latham and Locke 1991) that can be pursued after the learning activity. There are a number of considerations that need to be explored in the design phase to ensure this influence is generated.

Every learning opportunity is different. The developer will need to triangulate across user expectations/needs, the key learning goals or outcomes to be achieved and the capacity to deliver the intended plan in the time and resources available. When commencing the design process some of the questions that might be asked include:

- *What is the desired outcome?* The learning goals will inform the duration, nature and experiences that are integrated. Do the learners need to explore and apply complex skills? Do they need to be informed about something that has changed? Is the goal relating to changing cultures or group practices?
- *What past experiences or pre-conceptions are the participants likely to bring to the session?* This is an important consideration. If there is a concern for shifting perceptions and ideas from past attitudes, time will be needed to unpack those assumptions and encourage new ways of viewing the particular context or practice. These shifts cannot be accomplished in a short engagement. In fact, they may require several progressive explorations of the ideas before there is readiness to adapt.
- *What do the learners bring to this activity?* Many participants in these sessions will bring considerable experience and knowledge that is worth sharing and capturing. The developer needs to be attuned to this background knowledge

and to consider how it might be harnessed through the events. The representation of the developer as the sole expert will reduce the power of the session and may limit the rich perspectives that could have been offered by other participants. Their testing of the ideas or principles in their real contexts can also create some robust discussion as to whether some adaptation of institutional practice or policy will be necessary.

- *Are there critical activities to integrate?* This can assist in thinking about the purpose and time commitments.
- *How much time will they be willing to commit?* The value of the learning experience will be assessed by the potential participants before they will be willing to engage. They will judge the time demands against the perceived benefits. Sometimes, a shorter segment can act as an appetiser or tester to stimulate interest or trial the broad design.
- *How much time and funding is available for this activity?* Many sessions will need to match the existing time and resources that are available. This does not mean the activities will be low quality, but it may require some more creative thought as to design, locations and any funding requirements. (If there is a clear need to develop a more intensive, costly option, it may be necessary to seek a sponsor who sees the merit of the concept. Efforts to recruit a sponsor can quickly show if the ideas are in tune with the needs of the community at this stage.)
- *What has been learnt from past, similar events?* Participants are generally encouraged to provide feedback, but this needs to then be acted on. It is important to review and learn from the evaluation and feedback of past events. The goal is to design and deliver enhanced versions upon each new iteration.
- *Is there value in soliciting input from other developers?* The collective input from other colleagues can offer considerable richness in thinking through plans and ideas. It can also assist with identifying some potential resources that might be shared or adapted. In some groups, there may also be a resource repository or samples of other offerings that can stimulate some interesting ideas. While these can be helpful, the framing of the experience around the learners and their expectations or needs remains paramount.

Step 1: Develop a preliminary plan

A written plan can help to clarify underlying assumptions and the practicality of the conceived design. Table 7.1 provides an overview of the information that can be helpful at this stage of the design process.

The mapping of this broad design offers a useful test to see if the ambitions are achievable in the space available and with the intended audience. It can be used for subsequent communication with the target audience or clients. It helps to affirm that the offering is interesting, enticing, well-considered, realistic and achievable. This first draft is likely to need revising and tightening as the planning progresses. For example, the design of a particular learning activity may reveal

Table 7.1 Learning design plan template

Title of proposed activity	Design a title that attracts attention, is clear as to the focus and will entice the reader further. Will the intended audience understand and relate to it?
The target audience	Outline the types of participants who are likely to find attendance helpful. Test your assumptions by answering the following questions: • Who will benefit from this activity? • Why is attendance of value to them? • What do they bring in terms of pre-knowledge and experience? • Will it be pitched at the right level?
Description	Develop a 100-word overview of the intended session, outlining the purpose and value of the activity: • Why is this activity being offered? • How will participants benefit from coming? • How does this activity complement other offerings? Will it offer different experiences? What makes it exciting and valuable?
Learning outcomes	List the key learning goals to be emphasised, e.g. *After participating in [name of activity], participants will have developed*: • *the capacity to ….* • *further confidence in ….* • *enhanced skills in ….* • *an awareness of ….* These goals need to be clear and realistic, offering a good preview of what can be gained from attendance. Avoid over-promising.
Key learning foci	Outline the key topics or areas that will be covered. Check that the sequence and flow of the learning focus makes sense and offers good coherence. What story does it tell?
Duration	How long will the activity be? Will it be a single or multiple sessions? Is the timing and schedule viable for the intended audience?
About the presenter/facilitator	Provide a short paragraph that confirms the expertise and background of the presenter.

more time is required to allow rich discussion and consolidation of the developed insights, and as a result, fewer activities might be integrated.

Step 2: Designing the learning activities

From this broad draft, it is then possible to move into thinking about the different activities that may be incorporated into the session. There is a broad architecture that is commonly applied to professional learning activities. This is explained in Table 7.2.

Table 7.2 Framing the learning experience

Element	Purpose	Points to cover
Welcome	Introduces the facilitator, broad structure and intent of the session.	• introduce self and role; • outline the key purpose of the session; • explain how it will assist the learners and the key areas of focus you will be exploring; • highlight the learning benefits that are likely to be achieved; • outline the role that participants will play in the learning process.
Introductions/ ice-breaker	Encourages the participants to meet and learn a little about each other.	If the group is small, there is benefit in hearing a little about each individual, what they bring to the session and what they hope to gain from it. Make a note of where each sits and their key experiences as these can be linked through the session. If the group is more than 15, encourage introductions in small groups for about 10 minutes. Ice-breaker exercises may also be employed for high-energy interactions (Tucker 2007).
Context setting	Helps the participants to put aside their other concerns and focus on the learning activity. Cues them into key challenges that may be addressed through the session. Helps to build more connections with each other. Increases their awareness of the diversity of contexts to be found across the university.	This exercise encourages reflection on past experience and the sharing of insights across pairs or the group. It also focuses the attention and keys the individual in at their own stage of understanding. Different options include using a checklist, sharing scenarios or experiences, identifying the most common challenge each group has encountered, picking the worst example of bad practice to share back to the larger group or collectively building the key issues that they have experienced.
Concept/ learning point	Frames a learning point, providing an exposition of the key principles, ideas, issues that the learner will need to explore.	Integrate short and focused expositions, offering clear guidance on the key learning points or concepts that the learner will benefit from considering or integrating. The exposition might be offered by the facilitator, an expert source, a panel of peers or be sourced from the participants themselves.

(continued)

Table 7.2 Continued

Element	Purpose	Points to cover
		If the concept is skill related, modelling of the process should be integrated. A clear summary of the key points or principles should be offered.
Exploration	Opens the opportunity to explore and test the concept with respect to its application to the learner.	If the learning experience is likely to uncover threshold concepts that require significant effort to transform or integrate into mental schema (Kiley and Wisker 2009; Land 2011; Meyer and Land 2005), this stage might incorporate several activities that explore the principles from different angles. These might include: • practice and feedback application; • scenario discussion; • test case of one participant's context; • self-review of past-practices and identification of what was missing and/or well done.
Reflection	Provides a space to consider how this affects the learner's own practices and to identify ways this could apply to their own context.	This can be a short self-reflection or a discussion with colleagues. Participants can be encouraged to write down key reflections to clarify their thinking.
Application	Helps the learner to identify the key steps that need to be taken to integrate this learning point in their existing practice. Supports the learner in applying the principles or ideas e.g. by redeveloping an existing document or building an initial plan for implementation.	The process of transferring learning to the real world is the most complex phase of the learning process. In this stage, the participants are encouraged to think about how they will apply this to their own context. This phase can also open up discussion of issues that might emerge when doing so. This phase of the learning process might also be undertaken after the learning session. In that case, consider how individuals will be supported and offered feedback on their efforts.

This cycle of Learning Point, Exploration, Reflection and Application may be repeated several times over the course of the workshop session. A variety of formats and experiences is desirable.

Wrap up	Provides an opportunity to summarise and check that participants have drawn helpful insights from the session and are ready to apply their learning and insights.	This may be undertaken as a summary by the presenter, a group checklist of key points they feel were most valuable, a paired discussion or a personal reflection. If there are follow-up activities, remind participants of the requirements and dates. Each participant might be asked to describe their overall impression or outcomes with one or two words. This can provide a quick check as to their state of mind.
Follow-up to support application and adaptation	Supports the learning transfer process, ensuring the intention to integrate the new skills or practices remains active.	Many workshops deliver content and leave participants to apply and test the ideas in isolation. This is high risk, as it can result in low adoption. Increased support through the application and adaptation phase can encourage participants to stay focused and motivated. A supportive follow-up message to encourage integration of their learning might be considered, providing some guidance on how they might manage the application of this process. The integration of a user-group, webpage or follow-up session provides important assistance and is an efficient way to support the learner. The development of succinct tips, procedures or other resources that can be accessed at point of need will also be a valuable support strategy.

Note that this format includes many opportunities to share and explore issues with colleagues who are attending. Effective learning experiences that support collegial interactions encourage networking and associations with colleagues beyond one's immediate circle. The participants will build a broader view of the university and its workings, source useful models of good practice and enjoy opportunities to develop some ongoing friendships and collaborations. Many of these outcomes are contingent on the facilitation approaches that are employed. There is a delicate balance between offering interactive learning segments and ensuring the discussion or activities remain on-task and productive.

Step 3: Plan the learning space and related accompaniments

The design of successful learning activities is predicated on having an appropriate space that is conducive to participant interaction, discussion and dynamic activities. In some situations, it may be necessary to use fixed spaces (e.g. lecture theatres). This will constrain some of the choices, but can still enable paired or adjacent discussion across rows. Development centres may have their own dedicated spaces, which is particularly useful in reducing the amount of transportation of items to venues. However, there will be many times when the facilitator travels to a venue arranged by others. It is important to provide guidance on the facility requirements in detail to ensure the space is appropriate to the intended activities.

The ideal setting for a facilitated activity includes:

- mobile tables and chairs to enable adaptive layouts of groups to suit the focus, including the capacity to set up the room as "café style," i.e. with 4–6 people per table;
- a spacious room that allows easy movement between groups, and, possibly, the capacity to set up different group layouts (e.g. café style tables and circles of chairs) while also supporting easy vocalisation across the whole group and a feeling of intimacy;
- suitable technology or capacity to integrate any necessary equipment;
- good lighting, suitable heating or cooling control and minimal noise from adjoining rooms or areas;
- wall display space;
- access to flip charts or other mechanisms to record discussions;
- capacity to cater in, or near, the room;
- easy access to toilets;
- WiFi access.

In addition, there will be a range of resources that will be needed at each table, depending on the particular plan. These might include:

- paper and pens
- large flip chart paper or self-adhesive poster paper
- post-it notes for brainstorming activities or mapping exercises

- textas or markers
- scissors, sticking tape or glue sticks
- highlighters
- poster putty.

Most facilitators will maintain a portable resource kit that can be transported at point of need.

Providing online support

The desire to increase the reach and accessibility of development options has encouraged the provision of online and blended learning options. The development of support that can be accessed when one needs it is highly desirable. There are various options that might be integrated, including:

- development of in-house programs using the university's learning management system or a commercial product;[1]
- licensing of programs developed by other universities (e.g. Graduate Certificates in learning and teaching);
- purchase of commercial packages that may enable customisation and adaptation of relevant segments;
- development of Wikis or webpages that support key skills, capabilities or concepts;
- the development of customised manuals, guides and frameworks to provide personalised support;
- the sharing of templates or resources that will assist with applying the capabilities that are being promoted;
- development of collaborative programs with other universities.

This extension beyond face-to-face delivery has a number of benefits, including the flexibility of providing just-in-time support. However, there are a number of challenges that will need to be considered:

- Is the material positioned at the right level for an academic audience?
- How will the learner find out about these offerings?
- What inducements encourage ongoing engagement? Is there some form of recognition of completion?
- How much contextual information does the material offer? That is, does it recognise the specific university context or challenges that this particular community may need to address?
- Is there strong encouragement to apply, test and receive feedback on the particular capabilities being promoted?
- Is there potential for the learner to share and interact with other colleagues in either a virtual or blended learning group?

- Is the material of a high quality and engaging for those who enrol?
- Is it easy to use and navigate?
- Are enrolments and completions easy to monitor?
- Are the options being sourced by potential learners?

While these sources are useful adjuncts to the core program being offered, they need to be promoted, regularly evaluated and supplemented to ensure they remain fit for purpose. University websites are generally opaque, making it very hard to find particular resources through searching. The development service needs to develop a regular mechanism to promote the options through marketing and targeted promotion to particular constituents.

Online programs are likely to have a shelf-life of two to three years before needing updating and revising. The resources in a shared repository will need to be regularly reviewed for currency and value. Thus, there is quite a focus on custodial oversight of these resources. They need to be monitored for uptake and value. The contextualisation of externally provided programs will also need to be planned well ahead. The experience of the *Future Research Leaders Program*, a collaborative initiative undertaken in Australia, for example, highlighted the challenge of translating and customising generic content into institutional contexts.[2] Similarly, if a program is designed to be blended, the complementary integration of the workshop component needs to be very carefully designed and planned. Ideally, it will offer further enrichment and contextualisation and encourage translation of the online instructional concepts to the learner's own particular setting.

Attracting and supporting the participants

Of course, there is little benefit in designing great activities if no one participates. The development of a persuasive marketing blurb to stimulate interest and encourage enrolments will greatly assist. Marketing information might address the following questions: Why is this important? Who is it intended for? What will they gain from attendance? What are the particular benefits? If the activity has been offered before and gained good reviews, these might also be shared. The title needs to be enticing, grabbing the reader's attention and encouraging them to continue reviewing the information.

Workshops and one-off development events can take time to generate a reputation and recommendations from past participants. It is not unusual to have a small take-up in the first run of a new offering. This can be valuable as a trial run, particularly if verbal feedback from the participants is sought. However, the ultimate goal is to increase participation to encourage stronger learning across the university, ensuring activities are relevant and that there are economies of scale.

The promotional process generally operates as a multi-pronged strategy. An advantage in university settings is the possibility of sending marketing information to all staff via email. However, it will need to be well managed to ensure messages from HED groups are limited in number but high in impact. Note too, that university email lists may exclude a large number of staff who are sessional or casual appointments or not employed by the central university authority. Thus, this is only a partial solution. A request to disseminate information through key faculty contacts can increase the catchment, particularly if the offering is highly applicable to their community. A well-designed, online searchable calendar is essential. Development information may also be linked to core academic capability frameworks if they are employed, linking suitable offerings to specific learning goals.

Attrition rates of academics booked for a session can be high: many participants will start to re-assess their commitment as their emergent workloads become more evident closer to the booked session. Their development may be relegated to second place in the face of pressing immediate concerns or crises. Registrant losses can be very frustrating, particularly when others were unable to secure a place in the session. Once a participant has enrolled, it can be helpful to ensure they have noted the activity in their calendar by sending an electronic calendar confirmation. An SMS or email reminder a day before can assist. Small motivational communications to follow up on the initial blurb can also be helpful. For example, if an academic was planning to attend a Time Management workshop, a friendly email a week before, providing guidance on some of the issues that could be monitored in the coming week, would be highly motivating. This type of pre-cueing requires pre-planning, but is readily integrated into the planning for the activity at the same time as it is being designed. A short cueing exercise of this nature demonstrates the need to attend and motivates the learner to address some of the challenges that are evident.

Follow-up after the event encourages people to test and transfer their learning into their own professional practice. If there were key learning points from the session, these might be uploaded onto a webpage. There may be other resources or associated programs that are useful to explore. Some of the participants might have resources or ideas to share and they will need the stimulus of the facilitator to share these with colleagues. Some participants may also seek additional guidance on their own particular context. If their difficulties surface unanticipated issues that are likely to be common, the preparation of some additional tips or guidelines, and their promotion to other participants, can be helpful. These processes offer important reinforcement and encouragement to move into the application of these ideas or actions.

Further, an underlying and important part of this consolidation process is to encourage the participants to look for a mentor, peer mentor or models within their own communities. The capacity to build support and guidance from within the local environs will increase the traction and capacity to apply new ideas.

From this overview, it can be seen that workshops and online support all benefit from strong ownership and support by the facilitator. Each experience has the potential to shift practice, but needs to be framed, marketed and supported appropriately.

Dilemmas and potential issues

There are a number of dilemmas that can emerge in the development context. A few are listed below.

Make it short!

Developers will occasionally be advised that academics and researchers have little time for development and therefore, the sessions need to be short. While it is important to ensure the time spent in sessions is highly efficient, the push to make them short(er) is based on an assumption that the key outcome to be generated is information dissemination. The capacity to outline the types of processes that will be included, and the broader experiences that will be encouraged, can reduce this form of pressure. The appropriate time required to facilitate a high-quality experience should be the key priority. However, if lengthy sessions are planned, it will be important to justify and monitor that this is a reasonable use of precious time. It is also possible that some economies of scale might be achieved through pre-reading, work-based applications after the workshop or small group work that allows more customised selection of topics to suit the participants.

Consistency or creativity?

This chapter has encouraged a creative and learner-centred design process that emphasises the need to be flexible, adaptive and strongly targeted on what is most needed. This can result in highly diverse offerings across a development group. While this can be refreshing and invigorating to participants, there is also a need to ensure a consistent look or feel is offered across the HED service. Templates, a repository for outlines and/or resources and regular meetings across the team can be valuable mechanisms for sharing good practice and encouraging a "branded" approach to the development process. However, an insistence that all workshops operate according to an established formula is highly inappropriate. Participants will feel that each session is the same and the creative energy of the developer can be compromised.

University capability frameworks

A notable new trend in the sector is the development of academic capability frameworks that outline the types of activities and roles that academics should demonstrate at different levels of appointment. These are often linked to the identification of core competencies that underpin successful performance of a role (Bobe and Kober 2015; Coates 2010; Lieff *et al.* 2013; Vilkinas *et al.* 2009) providing a useful framing for development activities. Universities have begun to map the expected capabilities of their academic staff as part of their performance enhancement drives. These articulated frameworks can offer an important device to increase academic/researcher focus on developing their skills and insights. It can be useful to map the current repertoire of HED offerings against the framework. Is there good balance? Are the workshops well suited to support these capabilities? Are there gaps in the learning support being offered?

On the other hand, the utility of particular frameworks needs to be assessed. Capability frameworks are not always research informed. They may have been devised by an internal group with little consultation. Thus, it is important to give these instruments a quick litmus test before aligning the development strategy tightly with them. Will they resonate with academics? Will they enhance academic performance? (Note too, that these frameworks should operate as guidelines: each academic will need to determine the roles and path that best suit their identity, strengths and goals.)

Conclusion

This chapter has provided some guidance on the design and delivery of effective and enticing learning experiences. It highlights the value of building advanced facilitation skills and monitoring the three factors that will ensure success: the quality of the developer; the standard and appropriateness of the learning design and delivery; and the mechanisms that encourage the participants to enrol, be fully engaged, well prepared and ready to apply their learning upon returning to their work area.

Notes

1 See, for example, the range of courses available for academics from Epigeum at //www.epigeum.com/our-courses/
2 See: https://go8.edu.au/programs-and-fellowships/go8-future-research-leaders-program

References

Berardo, K. and Deardorff, D.K. (eds), 2012. *Building cultural competence: innovative activities and models*, Sterling, VA: Stylus Publishing.
Bobe, B.J. and Kober, R., 2015. Measuring organisational capabilities in the higher education sector. *Education+Training*, 57(3), pp. 322–342.
Coates, H. and Australian Council for Educational Research., 2010. *VET leadership for the future: contexts, characteristics and capabilities*. Camberwell, Vic.: ACER Press.
Kiley, M. and Wisker, G., 2009. Threshold concepts in research education and evidence of threshold crossing. *Higher Education Research & Development*, 28(4), pp. 431–441.
Land, R., 2011. There could be trouble ahead: using threshold concepts as a tool of analysis. *International Journal for Academic Development*, 16(2), pp. 175–178.
Latham, G.P. and Locke, E.A., 1991. Self-regulation through goal setting. *Organizational Behavior and Human Decision Processes*, 50(2), pp. 212–247.

Lieff, S., Banack, J.G.P., Baker, L., Martimianakis, M.A., Verma, S., Whiteside, C. and Reeves, S., 2013. Understanding the needs of department chairs in academic medicine. *Academic Medicine*, 88(7), pp. 960–966.

Meyer, J.H.F. and Land, R., 2005. Threshold concepts and troublesome knowledge (2): epistemological considerations and a conceptual framework for teaching and learning. *Higher Education*, 49(3), pp. 373–388.

Tucker, J., 2007. *The ultimate icebreaker and teambuilder guide*, Monmouth, OR: Western Oregon University.

Vilkinas, T., Leask, B. and Ladyshewsky, R., 2009. *Academic leadership: fundamental building blocks*, Strawberry Hills, NSW: Australian Learning and Teaching Council.

Wilkinson, M., 2012. *The secrets of facilitation: the SMART guide to getting results with groups*, new and revised, 2nd edition, San Francisco, CA: Jossey-Bass.

Chapter 8

Program development and management

Universities face an ongoing challenge in building and maintaining institutional capacity to deliver on their mission and priorities, relying heavily on high-performing academics for many of these outcomes. Those who move into formal roles as part of their career progression also face considerable learning as they transition to a new identity and set of responsibilities. Development programs are a valuable mechanism to support these foci. They encourage alignment with the university's targets and priorities, building cadres of capable leaders and academics to help move the university's priorities forward. The investment in a program can reap many returns on that initial funding and is a strong motivational outcome for those who participate.

This chapter explores the broad design of academic development programs, illustrating the importance of integrating forward planning, sponsorship, evaluation and a clear focus as to the program's purpose. Examples of specific programs are provided in Part III of this book.

Development programs

Academic development programs are sustained, structured sequences of learning experiences that enable the development of reflective, academic, leadership and/or career capabilities to support current and future roles. They may target a particular facet of the academic role (e.g. research, learning and teaching or leadership) or may emphasise a more holistic view of the academic context (e.g. early career or gender). Programs may also be designed around the needs of a specific university community, such as a school or faculty.

While workshops fill a particular need for well-contained and defined learning, the capacity to promote a broader suite of academic competencies that support the exploration of academic identity, role shifts and complex challenges benefits from the intensive focus offered by programs. They encourage participants to take ownership of their careers, actions and outcomes, promoting a stronger sense of personal agency. When designing programs, it is important to create sufficient space for reflection and testing of complex ideas, enabling transformational learning rather than competency-based skill building (Brooks 2004).

Development programs have a number of substantively different features to those found in workshops or short learning opportunities. These are outlined in Table 8.1.

It can be seen that programs offer a more expansive palette and support the exploration of complementary issues or capabilities. The focus on a defined and somewhat homogenous cohort allows deeper exploration of issues that are likely to be experienced across the entire group. The discussions can be much more intensive, and support the cultivation of high trust across the learning community. Key themes and ideas can be explored progressively across program activities and longer time frames, and in a more constructive learning environment that is conducive to reflection, testing and application. The increased hours of contact also encourage participants to build a stronger sense of collective identity. Individuals who have attended programs of this nature often build a strong collective allegiance that supports ongoing engagement, collaboration, innovation and knowledge sharing with their peers (Debowski and Blake 2007). Thus, programs can offer considerable benefits to the participants, despite the need to devote substantially more effort and time. Programs allow the development of multiple learning frames, including the exploration of identity, institutional context, career management, mentorship and self-awareness as key components of academic success. These are consistent requirements across all academic levels, reflecting the ongoing challenges of melding new insights into current and emerging roles and responsibilities.

Table 8.1 A comparison of workshops and programs

Feature	Workshops	Programs
Purpose	Designed to explore a specific facet of the learning domain	Designed to support complex learning across a range of related areas
Duration	Normally spans a few hours to a day	Spans a series of sessions, lasting up to a year
Participants	Often diverse and unpredictable Normally self-selected, based on an identified learning need	Cohort-based Selected according to specified criteria or parameters
Learning activities	Short duration, generally emphasising readily digestible learning points	May be staged and progressively developed, including the use of themes or motifs across activities May include out-of-session activities, e.g. action learning projects or portfolio development May incorporate multi-source feedback as part of the program

Types of programs

There are many types of programs that might be offered:

- *Foundational programs for learning and teaching* generally target those in their first years of an academic appointment, focusing on the development of research-informed teaching capabilities to design, deliver and manage good quality courses (Kandlbinder and Peseta 2009). They may include assessable components which can be accredited.
- *Foundational programs for research* often support early career researchers. Typical foci might include collaboration, research project management, leading research teams, translation and dissemination of research and building mentorship support (Browning *et al.* 2014).
- *Leadership programs* emphasise the development of a leadership identity and repertoire. They often include a range of support strategies including multi-source feedback to increase self-awareness of leadership impact (King and Santana 2010; Markham *et al.* 2014). Heads of schools or centres, research leaders, teaching leaders or faculty leaders with responsibility for strategic agendas are often supported through these mechanisms (Debowski and Blake 2007; Vilkinas and Ladyshewsky 2012; Vilkinas *et al.* 2009). However, there is increasing support for building a stronger focus on leadership at early career level to set up good foundational capabilities earlier in the career.
- *Women's programs* assist women in building effective career strategies and mentorship support within a political environment (Madsen 2012; Tessens *et al.* 2011).
- *Writing retreats* are often intensive events designed to provide dedicated space and support to encourage academic writing and increased productivity (Grant 2008). These programs generally include guidance from expert sources and peer support.
- *Faculty programs* are designed to support the enhancement of key capabilities across an identified group. They may span the full range of academic practices, target specific capabilities or faculty priorities or be designed to support talented staff (Debowski 2007).

The scope and focus of development programs may be informed by the institutional priorities or the identified needs of particular segments of the university community (Kelsch and Hawthorne 2014; Wolverton *et al.* 2005). In some cases, it will be necessary to undertake a needs analysis to determine the target group characteristics and their development priorities. Institutional evidence may already demonstrate the need to support high-priority groups or encourage capability enhancements.

Possible program features

Programs allow a depth of exploration that is unlikely to be achievable in a workshop. The following list illustrates the features that can be integrated into this learning mode:

- 2-3 day intensive foundational programs to explore core principles, bond the participant cohort and scaffold key learning principles;
- multi-source or 360-degree reviews and debriefs (Boud and Molloy 2013; King and Santana 2010);
- breakout discussions;
- problem-based or issues-based learning;
- action learning (Cho and Egan 2010; Gunn and Lefoe 2013; Sofo *et al.* 2010);
- mentor support (American Association 2010; Debowski 2013; Sawatzky and Enns 2009);
- shadowing of senior leaders;
- group projects;
- simulations;
- learning portfolios;
- fieldwork visits;
- application and testing of capabilities, followed by debriefing and feedback;
- individualised coaching to support the transfer of the learned capabilities (Beattie *et al.* 2014; Jones *et al.* 2015; Rogers 2012).

Program management

The planning of a program can be quite prolonged, requiring considerable custodianship as sponsorship, funding, participants, contributors and the program are all developed. The following sections explore a number of management practices that can assist in designing and delivering high-quality offerings.

Getting started

The first hurdle for a program is gaining provisional funding for its delivery. The design of a new program relies on the perceived need: that this target group will benefit from additional support. The search for funding to support additional programs that have been offered previously can be greatly assisted by evidence of success and impact, including affirmations from past participants or examples of innovations that emerged from attending the program. Participant assessment of the program quality will also be persuasive if presented in a professional and analytical manner. In some cases, the funds will need to be sought from a competitive funding source, competing against other worthy bids. In others, the funds will be obtained through the agency of a senior sponsor, such as the executive member responsible for a key portfolio. There will be some instances where the need has been identified by sponsors and a proposal is sought. Whatever the path to funding, developers will need to be clear about the benefits and capability enhancements that the proposed program/s will offer. A clear business case documenting the design and intended outcomes will assist the executive, dean or other identified sponsors in assessing the value.

Program proposals need to be well articulated and accurately costed. In effect, they are grant proposals, requiring a clear account of the goals, intended cohort, need for the program and the reasons for particular expenditure items. For example, leadership programs will generally integrate multi-source reviews. These will be a major expense, as will coaching if it is offered. A clear justification for the use of these services, and some evidence of their impact from research or past participants, assists funding requests. If the sponsor has been exposed to other successful programs, they will be confident that the outcome will justify the expenditure. Programs may require considerable advocacy and justification where support is less assured.

The planning cycle

Many universities plan their program schedule in the year prior to delivery. This allows them to seek the necessary sponsorship from university sources. If many groups require program support, it may be necessary to rotate program offerings across a 2- or 3-year cycle. The frequency of offerings will also depend on the size of the population that is likely to access the proposed program/s. Early career academics and researchers are more numerous, and likely to be very keen to develop critical skills to further their careers and performance. Programs targeting this level are likely to be offered frequently. The core foundational programs relating to teaching or research, for example, need to be offered each semester and ideally might encompass more than one cohort. Even so, the number of new academics entering the university can exceed the capacity to supply program support. An emerging option is the provision of blended learning programs that explore the core capabilities with associated in-house sessions to apply the capabilities. However, this can reduce some of the strength of program delivery, particularly with respect to cohort identity and engagement. Thus, the choice of how and what to target needs to be carefully considered.

There is quite a long lead time in program planning compared with workshops. This is partly because of the need to source funding, plan complex sequences of learning events, organise venues, as well as recruit and select the cohort. Advance marketing and publicity to build interest may also be required. It is not unusual to commence the planning process at least a year ahead, and to initiate recruitment 6 months out of the commencement so that the academic participants can ensure their work calendars mesh with the program schedule.

Consultation and research

The goal of program design is to develop an approach that offers the most complete, integrated and impactful experience possible. Various sources can assist with this concept building. First, a review of published guidance on successful programs and the professional development needs of the target group is very helpful. Unfortunately, many of the reports of programs are primarily anecdotal and descriptive, rather than truly evaluative, so they may only offer ideas rather than validation. Benchmarking against comparable programs offered by other universities can fill this gap, providing significant guidance from colleagues who have developed useful models, methods or designs that have worked well with similar cohorts. These investigations provide a sound basis to build a broad shape and concept map of the program and its intended outcomes.

This initial concept design can then be taken out for further consultation with key stakeholders. This input process may take the form of group or individual meetings, reviews of past feedback from participants and discussions with other expert sources in the university. The input will assist in identifying other components for consideration and any risks or issues that may need to be addressed. Importantly, these consultation processes also increase broader understanding of the proposed program and its value.

Drawing on these inputs, a draft proposal can then be prepared to take forward for sponsor consideration and/or funding requests.

Program sponsorship

The development of a relationship with a sponsor assists in many ways. First, it provides an important signal that the program is valued and matters: the sponsor will be likely to attend the first session and help to set the context for the program's importance. They will be keen to be part of its success and to hear about the experiences of participants. A concluding event or dinner, where they can hear the anecdotes and affirmations of participants, can confirm the investment was a good one. Sponsors may also offer guidance on suitable candidates, suggest useful facets to integrate into the planning, or lobby other colleagues to endorse the program. In return, they will need to be kept informed of progress and provided with a summary of the key outcomes.

If a sponsor is not readily identifiable, an alternative path is through an advisory group comprised of representatives of key stakeholder constituents. Their input on the planning ensures the program concept has been tested and validated before funds are sought. They offer additional benefit as advocates for the program.

Costing the program

Preliminary costing of the program should be as detailed as possible, reflecting the particular funding model of the university. For example, if the development staff are already an accepted overhead, a lead developer who manages (and possibly facilitates) the program will be cost neutral. In other institutions, development time must be accounted for or the program cost might be charged back to each participant's work centre. In that case, the time spent developing and delivering the program will need to be estimated and reconciled.

Full costing of programs encourages stronger accountability, control over costs and more active consideration as to the desirable size of the program and the outcomes it generates. Some of the costs that might be considered include fixed costs (per overall program) and variable costs (per participant; see Table 8.2 for an outline of these breakdowns). This initial scoping will help to verify the overall costs and their management. If funds are tight, for example, a cheaper venue or the payment of a co-contribution levy by participants might be considered. The size of the cohort might be adjusted if some variable costs are substantial and need to be controlled. In some cases, they may need to be adapted to enable the program to run on less funding than initially scoped.

Program scheduling

The planning process operates at several levels. First, the actual program schedule needs to be mapped out to determine the commitment that will be required of the participants. They will need to perceive the demands to be reasonable and manageable. A common design option integrates several intensive days of participation at a start-up program phase, followed by half or full day sessions regularly spaced. The depth of coverage and scope of focus will determine whether the program runs over 3, 6 or 10 months. The rhythm of the university cycle

Table 8.2 Program costing

Fixed costs (per program)

- Facilitator or expert sources fees
- administrative support
- room and equipment hire
- external reviewer to evaluate the program outcomes
- equipment or developer transportation costs (e.g. if to a remote location or for equipment to be relocated)
- stationery costs. (e.g. flip-charts, mints or refreshments, other materials)

Variable costs (per head)

- Accommodation
- catering
- participant resources (e.g. folders, printing of handouts, pens, activity resources)
- team building sports or activities provided by residential sites
- multi-source or 360-degree review services
- coaching fees
- specialist support (e.g. recording of micro-teaching or media presentations)
- participant transportation costs.

might also determine whether the program spans academic years or is contained within a year. A heads program, for example, is often best commenced outside the academic cycle. This might mean launching it in one academic year and completing it in the next. Given the program comprises a cohort, a regular schedule where events occur in a predictable slot is desirable. The successful candidates will be better able to regularly attend the program. A predictable and uniform scheduling will greatly assist in negotiating timetables and commitments.

At another level, the program planning will also require detailed scheduling. There will be a number of program management processes to be anticipated, including approvals, recruitment and evaluation activities. The recruitment process will occur a number of months beforehand, particularly if successful candidates are asked to undertake some form of self-review as part of their preparatory processes or need to sequester time from their teaching schedules to attend. Integration into the university's funding, marketing and approvals processes may increase time frames. Pre-planning will enable careful consideration of administrative needs and facilitate booking of venues well ahead of time.

Program recruitment

After funding approval, the broad design and identification of the target population have been achieved, the next step is to recruit the candidates. Different programs will employ different methods. For some, the recruitment may be through open nomination, encouraging individuals to self-select. In other cases, there may be a particular group that is being targeted through invitations or as part of a talent pool. The channel for entry needs to be carefully considered: there are strong messages that will be sent, based on who is offered access and who is not. This may need considerable thought to ensure it does not have unfortunate repercussions.

There is considerable value in encouraging senior leaders and heads to assist with the recruitment phase: their engagement will increase their knowledge of the program and increase their sponsorship of staff who enrol. However, it is unwise to rely on this method alone. Unfortunately, some people who might have appreciated being invited to attend may miss out through this form of invitational approach. Further, different heads or leaders will approach this opportunity with varying degrees of application and alacrity. A direct mailing to each potential candidate will ensure all hear about the opportunity.

Program design

The program design may be progressively enriched once the initial scoping has been undertaken. However, the detailed design and breakdown of the program should be completed early to check that the times allocated for different components will work, the resources allocated will be sufficient, and the intended scope is suited to the target audience. The plan can further assist in identifying key people who might contribute as experts, and to ensure they are scheduled in well ahead of time. The planning will need to be reviewed and critiqued on a regular basis as the program develops. It may become evident that particular approaches need modifying or that key issues have emerged that will require addressing. While programs offer flexibility for this adaptive development, few changes should be made once participants have enrolled.

The program is likely to include an orientation session to set up the cohort. This will be particularly critical if participants need to undertake some form of review prior to starting formally within the full program. In this tuning session, participants can be offered an overview of the program philosophy, an opportunity to explore their mindset and experiences, as well as guidance on what will be expected of them. The chance to meet and learn about each other also provides a valuable introduction to the cohort. If there is no need for pre-work, this component might be folded into the launch of the program.

The launch is an important time. It is intended to motivate the participants and to set up the program parameters and expectations. It may include some motivational or positioning talks by key leaders (including the sponsor) and can offer participants time to learn about each other. The framing of the core principles, procedures and learning goals will provide important guidance to members. This familiarisation phase may integrate some of the meta-learning elements, such as mentorship and reflections on identity.

The core program, which may last 2 or 3 days, featuring off-campus intensive immersion experience, aims to provide a strong foundation, encouraging deep interaction with peer participants, the development of trust across the group and the establishment of the core foundations and principles that will be carried through the program. Expectations and requirements of the group will need to be clearly mapped out, including the need for full participation, inclusiveness, respect and confidentiality. Peer learning partners might be set up during this phase.

The opportunity to commence with a residential component can greatly assist the program in establishing the learning community, trust and more intensive engagement with the program content and messages. A venue that is around one hour away from the campus allows for those who critically need to return to do so, while acting as a deterrent to others. There will be some in the cohort who are unable to stay the night (e.g. due to personal obligations), but most will relish the chance to be fully present in this way. The dinner together allows rich conversations and sharing to occur and will help to build real connections across the group. It will also be possible to integrate exercises, group work and interim reading as part of the evening. This intensive learning time can be counterpointed by recreational, team or experiential activities. Each offers an important source of insight that can be debriefed and further discussed.

Subsequent sessions might employ a thematic focus, providing additional opportunities to reflect, learn, test and critique ideas and models. However, there should be an ongoing series of motifs and themes that help to meld the program into an integrated learning sequence. Programs will further enable considerable group work, paired discussions and creative problem solving.

The final component of the program will normally be a finale event that encourages summative reflection, evaluation and further planning to take the outcomes forward. This may include a presentation to key stakeholders and the sponsor, or a finale dinner to celebrate the event. A review of the program and the learner's outcomes offers valuable guidance on the benefits, potential enhancements and future possibilities that have emerged.

Post-program support may include the brokerage of a network of program alumni (Debowski and Blake 2007; Gunn and Lefoe 2013). Many participants will be keen to continue their socialised learning in partnership with their peers. Another alternative is to encourage communities of practice (Nagy and Burch 2009; Pyhältö et al. 2009; Viskovic 2006; Warhurst 2008). These groups form out of a common interest and convene regularly to explore issues of common concern. They may be self-organising (chaired and convened by group members) or facilitated and supported by a developer.

Interviews with participants

The facilitator will be a key presence throughout the program. Familiarisation with each participant and their learning goals, context and challenges can greatly assist in framing the program and drawing in support for each person. A pre-interview with each successful candidate encourages a personalised introduction to the participant, program and facilitator. This can assist in checking that the participant is emotionally ready for a program and has the necessary capacity to attend fully. These meetings can be scheduled soon after the selection process is complete, assisting in setting up the participant for the program. The facilitator will also have more capacity to integrate identified challenges and concerns of participants into the final program. Topics that might be discussed in this individual consultation might relate to the participant's background, work context and learning goals.

Multi-source reviews

An understanding of one's own motives, behaviours, responses and impact is strongly encouraged by attendance at programs. Feedback is an important mechanism to help the individual frame these insights and identify learning goals (Boud and Molloy 2013). The inclusion of multi-source or 360-degree reviews is particularly critical for those who are exploring how their roles and behaviours impact on others (Tornow and London 1998).

The provision of feedback about oneself needs to be carefully and confidentially managed (King and Santana 2010). The feedback provider needs to be experienced and qualified in managing these interactions, and the information should be offered in a setting where an individual can take time to reflect and consider the guidance offered. Multi-source reviews generally require at least 6 weeks to canvass input from contributors, develop the reports and debrief the participant. While debriefs can also be done in a group setting, leadership reviews are likely to uncover a variety of strengths and vulnerabilities in the group (Bergman *et al.* 2014), and it is better to offer some confidential framing before the results are then used in the program setting. These reviews will take up to two hours and may require a further follow-up session for those who received confrontational or unexpected feedback.

A key principle in the use of these tools is to ensure the results remain confidential to the individual. They are a development tool. They should not be released to a third party as they operate in a similar manner to mentoring. If the individual chooses to share or release the evidence, that should be their choice. This confidentiality will be fundamentally important in setting up these reviews.

Reflective activities

The capacity to critique and reflect on one's practice, values and disposition is an important part of program participation. Programs can encourage deep reflection and self-review through regular discussions, activities or more substantive components that support the application of the learning into real work settings.

Mentorship may be incorporated as either an optional or integrated element. The provision of a mentor through the program can facilitate reflection and will support a deeper understanding of the ways the program is enhancing professional and personal perspectives (Muir 2014). The mentoring discussions offer intensive one-on-one support, encouraging deep reflection and review. Where this component is included in the program, there is merit in providing guidance to mentors prior to commencement. Ensuring they are familiar with the program goals and foci will enable more contextualised support for the mentee.

Portfolios encourage participants to build their own mental schema around key learning elements and to apply that understanding into their professional activities. The translation of intention to action is greatly encouraged through portfolio activities, particularly if they are then debriefed in a subsequent program session or with a mentor. Portfolio activities may integrate feedback seeking from mentors, colleagues or supervisors, or action learning activities.

Action learning projects are undertaken in the work context, and may require a substantial length of time to develop, implement, test and review. They too, offer sound opportunities to reflect and apply the guidance from the program. These projects can be undertaken in groups or individually. They might, for example, relate to curriculum development or review, implementing improved research strategies and testing their efficacy or applying new leadership approaches to resolve issues.

Program evaluation

Development programs are funded on the assumption that they will make a substantive difference to the participants and, ultimately, to the university (Martineau and Patterson 2010). They provide an invaluable opportunity to learn, grow, advance and morph into a more confident, assured and competent academic, researcher or leader. However, the evidence of this impact is often poorly mapped or not even collected at all. This makes it much harder to secure further funding or to argue that a program has made a difference.

It is recommended then, that programs integrate an evaluation strategy that monitors behavioural and attitudinal changes over the course of the program. The evaluation might encompass pre- and post-test components, capability assessments, evaluations of performance and an exploration of the participant's learning context. Capability assessments might be followed-up after 6 months to explore changed professional practices in the ensuing time. A survey of supervisors might further triangulate these results. Portfolios or projects over the program duration also offer further evidence of outcomes (see Chapter 21 for more detail on program evaluation).

The evaluation data validates the learning design and its effective support for capacity building. It may be shared with key stakeholders and, potentially, a broader audience. Care for participant confidentiality is imperative. When collecting data of this nature, it will be critical to secure ethics approval for these evaluations, since the results are likely to be shared and may also contribute to ongoing research about program impact. There is further potential to benchmark and share program designs within the institution or further afield, which may draw on the evaluation outcomes (McCauley-Smith *et al.* 2015).

Conclusion

Programs require significant investments of university funding, participant commitment and development resources. They are pinnacle events that can make a profound difference to the participants. The opportunity to work with a cohort over a course of time provides an ideal setting to encourage deep learning, capability enhancement and identity formation. Successful programs are predicated on considerable forward planning and sponsorship. The design process is likely to integrate a range of additional support strategies and learning modes to encourage stronger reflection and self-awareness. The integration of evaluation to monitor learner outcomes and program impact is an important facet of program preparation and management.

References

American Association for the Advancement of Science, 2010. *Building relationships: mentoring, collaborating, and networking*, Washington, D.C. Available at: sciencecareers.org/booklets.

Beattie, R.S., Kim, S., Hagen, M.S., Egan, T.M., Ellinger, A.D. and Hamlin, R.D., 2014. Managerial coaching: a review of the empirical literature and development of a model to guide future practice. *Advances in Developing Human Resources*, 16(2), pp. 184–201.

Bergman, D., Lornudd, C., Sjöberg, L. and Von Thiele Schwarz, U., 2014. Leader personality and 360-degree assessments of leader behavior. *Scandinavian Journal of Psychology*, 55(4), pp. 389–397.
Boud, D. and Molloy, E. (eds), 2013. *Feedback in higher and professional education: understanding it and doing it well*, London: Routledge.
Brooks, A.K., 2004. Transformational learning theory and implications for Human Resource Development. *Advances in Developing Human Resources*, 6(2), pp. 211–225.
Browning, L., Thompson, K. and Dawson, D., 2014. Developing future research leaders: designing early career researcher programs to enhance track record. *International Journal for Researcher Development*, 5(2), pp. 123–134.
Cho, Y. and Egan, T.M., 2010. The state of the art of Action Learning Research. *Advances in Developing Human Resources*, 12(2), pp.163–180.
Debowski, S., 2007. Finding the right track: enabling early career academic management of career, teaching and research. In G. Crisp, ed., *Enhancing higher education, theory and scholarship; Proceedings of the 30th HERDSA Annual Conference*, 8–11 July 2007, Adelaide, Australia, Sydney: HERDSA, pp. 138–149.
Debowski, S., 2013. Creating fertile learning spaces: mentorship strategies to support academic success. In S. Frielick, N. Buissink-Smith, P. Wyse, J. Billot, J. Hallas and E. Whitehead, eds, *Research and development in higher education: the place of learning and teaching*, Auckland, New Zealand, pp. 113–123.
Debowski, S. and Blake, V., 2007. Collective capacity building of academic leaders: a university model of leadership and learning in context. *International Journal of Learning and Change*, 2(3), p. 307.
Grant, B., 2008. *Academic writing retreats: a facilitator's guide*, Milperra, NSW: Higher Education Research and Development Society of Australasia.
Gunn, C. and Lefoe, G., 2013. Evaluating action-learning and professional networking as a framework for educational leadership capacity development. *International Journal for Academic Development*, 18(1), pp. 45–59.
Jones, R.J., Woods, S.A. and Guillaume, Y.R.F., 2015. The effectiveness of workplace coaching: a meta-analysis of learning and performance outcomes from coaching. *Journal of Occupational and Organizational Psychology*. Available online at https://eprints.worc.ac.uk/id/eprint/3655
Kandlbinder, P. and Peseta, T., 2009. Key concepts in postgraduate certificates in higher education teaching and learning in Australasia and the United Kingdom. *International Journal for Academic Development*, 14(1), pp. 19–31.
Kelsch, A. and Hawthorne, J., 2014. Preparing new faculty for leadership: understanding and addressing needs. *To Improve the Academy*, 33(1), pp. 57–73.
King, S.N. and Santana, L.C., 2010. Feedback-intensive programs. In E. Van Velsor, C.D. McCauley and M.N. Ruderman, eds, *The Center for Creative Leadership handbook of leadership development*, San Francisco: Wiley, pp. 97–124.
McCauley-Smith, C., Williams, S.J., Gillon, A.C. and Braganza, A., 2015. Making sense of leadership development: developing a community of education leaders. *Studies in Higher Education*, 40(2), pp. 311–328.
Madsen, S.R., 2012. Women and leadership in higher education: learning and advancement in leadership programs. *Advances in Developing Human Resources*, 14(1), pp. 3–10.
Markham, S.E., Smith, J.W., Markham, I.S. and Braekkan, K.F., 2014. A new approach to analyzing the Achilles' heel of multisource feedback programs: can

we really trust ratings of leaders at the group level of analysis? *The Leadership Quarterly*, 25(6), pp. 1120–1142.

Martineau, J.W. and Patterson, T.E., 2010. Evaluating leader development. In E. Van Velsor, C.D. McCauley and M.N. Ruderman, eds, *The Center for Creative Leadership handbook of leadership development*, San Francisco, CA: Wiley, pp. 251–284.

Muir, D., 2014. Mentoring and leader identity development: a case study. *Human Resource Development Quarterly*, 25(3), pp. 349–379.

Nagy, J. and Burch, T., 2009. Communities of practice in academe (CoP-iA): understanding academic work practices to enable knowledge building capacities in corporate universities. *Oxford Review of Education*, 35(2), pp. 227–247.

Pyhältö, K., Stubb, J. and Lonka, K., 2009. Developing scholarly communities as learning environments for doctoral students. *International Journal for Academic Development*, 14(3), pp. 221–232.

Rogers, J., 2012. *Coaching skills: a handbook*, Maidenhead, Berkshire: Open University Press.

Sawatzky, J.A.V. and Enns, C.L., 2009. A mentoring needs assessment: validating mentorship in nursing education. *Journal of Professional Nursing*, 25(3), pp. 145–150.

Sofo, F., Yeo, R.K. and Villafane, J., 2010. Optimizing the learning in action learning: reflective questions, levels of learning, and coaching. *Advances in Developing Human Resources*, 12(2), pp. 205–224.

Tessens, L., White, K. and Web, C., 2011. Senior women in higher education institutions: perceived development needs and support. *Journal of Higher Education Policy and Management*, 33(6), pp. 653–665.

Tornow, W.W. and London, M. (eds), 1998. *Maximizing the value of 360-degree feedback: a process for successful individual and organizational development*, 1st edition, San Francisco, CA: Jossey-Bass.

Vilkinas, T. and Ladyshewsky, R.K., 2012. Leadership behaviour and effectiveness of academic program directors in Australian universities. *Educational Management Administration and Leadership*, 40(1), pp. 109–126.

Vilkinas, T., Leask, B. and Ladyshewsky, R., 2009. *Academic leadership: fundamental building blocks.*, Strawberry Hills, NSW: Australian Learning and Teaching Council.

Viskovic, A., 2006. Becoming a tertiary teacher: learning in communities of practice. *Higher Education Research & Development*, 25(4), pp. 323–339.

Warhurst, R.P., 2008. 'Cigars on the flight deck': new lecturers' participatory learning within workplace communities of practice. *Studies in Higher Education*, 33(4), pp. 453–467.

Wolverton, M., Ackerman, R. and Holt, S., 2005. Preparing for leadership: what Academic Department Chairs need to know. *Journal of Higher Education Policy and Management*, 27(2), pp. 227–238.

Chapter 9

Facilitating organisational change and transitions

Universities are highly dynamic, changeable contexts where structures, functions, key priorities and systems can be subject to major transformation and reconfiguration in efforts to improve institutional outcomes. Some reforms are driven by external factors, such as changes to government policy or funding, while others may be more institutionally determined, with the intention of enhancing university functions, such as student learning (Styron *et al.* 2015). A change in senior leaders is likely to stimulate a vast array of initiatives that are aimed at improving university outcomes. If the executive has been extensively revamped, each new leader is likely to generate a range of change initiatives. They may also hope for quite rapid turnarounds on development, design and delivery of those innovations.

During these transitions, it is particularly important to understand how people respond to change and the forms of support that they will appreciate receiving. Many can feel quite distressed about impending shifts to organisational practices and priorities, particularly if their role, positioning or personal understanding of their own activities requires adjustment. In some cases, the changes may have limited impact, requiring minor adaptations to mindset or practice. In many cases, the planned adjustments can be quite significant. Some common areas of change within universities, for example, have included:

- budget reductions or changes to funding models, which may result in workload changes, redundancies, new roles and responsibilities, or changes to education or research activities;
- staffing changes to reflect shifts in student demand;
- reviews of current practices, groups or services;
- restructure of academic faculties;
- new educational priorities, branding or curriculum reforms;
- changes to performance standards, expectations or performance assessment practices.

These all impinge on the individual's context and sense of security. While some will see the changes as great opportunities to put new innovations in place, there will be others who feel considerably threatened by any disruption to their traditional practices. For academics, the sense of anxiety may be heightened by the need to maintain teaching and research activities in the face of change. Teelken (2012) notes that the level of academic engagement with key initiatives can be tokenistic, pragmatic or marginally compliant. This superficial commitment to reforms can lead to highly inconsistent adoption and risks to long-term enhancements.

At times like these, the leadership of groups is particularly critical, requiring considerable focus, reassurance, direction-setting and repositioning of the group's activities. There may be much time spent on consultation and decision-making to help turn the community toward new approaches or paths that will affect the necessary changes. Failure to acknowledge and manage the transition process can result in considerable damage to the community's well-being, trust and engagement (Bridges 2009). This can result in lowered productivity, higher turnover, stress and ill-health. These all impact on both research and teaching quality and outcomes.

The HED service can provide considerable support through these processes (Schroeder 2011a). A vast array of roles might be filled. Having sufficient influence to guide the initial planning and thinking of a major reform is a particular asset (Van Note Chism 2011). Neame (2013) notes the importance of adapting the development orientation to suit the particular context and audience. Guidance for leaders as they navigate their community through innovations or reforms; identifying and addressing issues which may arise; effecting good communication; facilitating consultation processes; helping to map new designs, systems or processes; and evaluating the integration of new changes are just some of the roles that might be undertaken. Some of this work may be commissioned by the executive (e.g. system redesign or roll-out of new initiatives) while other activities may assist particular communities. There may be opportunities to steer creativity and innovation, guiding new thinking and approaches to institutional problems (Loewenberger 2013). While each developer may have a different specialism (e.g. teaching, research or leadership), the principles for supporting and guiding these changes are similar. In effect, the developer can provide a sense of balance and perspective that may be missing from those emotionally embroiled in the transition process.

Understanding transitions

Bridges (2009) has provided considerable insight into the ways that people respond to change initiatives. His recognition that the transition phase is a major time when leadership must be strongly supportive and in evidence has built an important foundation for many leaders. He maps three phases of change: Endings; The Neutral Zone and New Beginnings. Endings is a highly emotive time, associated with grief, denial, anger and many other emotional responses. The feelings of rejection and hurt can be marked and can lead to many behaviours that are quite destructive. People will need time to relinquish their strong attachment to the past and the practices they have consolidated. This initial phase can be very lengthy for some, particularly if they are largely disempowered from any consultative or decision-making processes. Those who have had some opportunities to influence the processes may feel more attuned to the changes.

Over time, these feelings should diminish and the individual, Bridges argues, moves toward The Neutral Zone, where options and opportunities can be explored and tested. This can be a very creative space as new paths and ideas emerge. At the same time, there may still be resentment, stress and anxiety as new processes are trialled. Workloads may be higher as new systems or requirements are introduced. There may also be considerable scepticism about the change and its likely benefit. From this, the individual moves toward the consolidation phase of New Beginnings, where they embed their new practices. This can be a time of great energy and enthusiasm.

Leaders and facilitators need to be attuned to the different responses that are likely to be found in any one group. Some will transition quickly to the new context while others will stay attached to the past for a very long time. Leaders will need to provide guidance and support using a range of different strategies:

- empathy and acknowledgement of the individual's feelings and emotions;
- information and regular communication to help people explore the options and implications;
- guidance on the implications of different options;
- encouragement to be involved and provide input;
- leadership in engaging the community with the intended reforms.

There may be times when the leader also feels disempowered, alienated and marginalised through the reform process. New policies and systems that seem to be at a dissonance to the institutional mores and cultures, for example, can be difficult to accept and advocate to other colleagues. In this situation, it will be necessary to work through these issues before moving back into the leadership role. The leader is pivotal in providing assurance and a sense of optimism to the community (Kotter 2012). Understanding the rationale for the change is a helpful part of this process.

Culture as part of change

The impact of culture, attitudes and values on acceptance of change and its implications also needs to be understood. University staff bring considerable passion and commitment to their work. They like to feel valued and to be part of the solutions that are generated. They hope to have a workplace that is congenial, supportive and sensible in how it operates. The disruptiveness of change can be quite confronting, particularly if it is dealt with in a peremptory or arbitrary manner. Academics, accustomed to having considerable autonomy and self-determination, may find change particularly confronting if they view the decisions as hard to fathom or impracticable. This can result in considerable backlash. Schein (2010) recognises the importance of building alignment across the different layers of the organisation, arguing that it is important to mesh the values that guide people, the directives communicated and enacted through the systems, policies and processes, and the models, guidance and messages generated by senior leaders. This consistency reduces confusion and mixed messages that can further muddy the change setting. Schein's work has great implications for leaders at all levels: the identified paths need to be sensible and well articulated; they need to be consonant with the dominant values and beliefs that people possess; and the introduced systems and processes should be reflective of those same principles.

In many universities, this alignment may not be reflected in reform initiatives, particularly if a range of messages are being conveyed by different leaders across the university. Consider, for example, the need to promote learning and teaching priorities if academics are being judged and measured solely on their research performance. This dissonance can cause considerable friction and unease across the academic community. The dominant discourses can determine the degree to which academics feel connected with the desired reforms (Quinn 2012).

Planning and leading reforms

The process of leading and guiding reforms has been strongly influenced by Kotter's work on leading change (Kotter 2012). His eight-step model offers some practical guidance on the steps that will assist in bringing people along a major transition cycle. Table 9.1 offers an adapted and customised approach that supports the university context, identifying tips and principles to guide leaders through the various transition phases. Column 3 of the table illustrates some of the ways the HE developer might support leaders through these processes. The extent of that involvement will be contingent on the way in which the HED service has established its role as change agent/change partner (Jamieson *et al.* 2012; Schroeder 2011b; Schroeder 2011c; Sherlock 2012; Sutherland 2014). Note too, the emphasis on aligning messages with the university context and communicating with constituents throughout the process.

The communication strategy

Transitions require extensive communication, incorporating individual consultation, large group meetings and written guidance. As part of the transition, it is recommended that a communication plan be developed to clarify the purpose and timings of messages that will be conveyed.

Key points to be considered relate to the following questions:

- Which stakeholder groups need to be kept informed?
- What are their particular communication needs (e.g. to be informed, consulted, provide approval)?

Table 9.1 Leading and facilitating university transition processes

Stage	Leader guidelines	Developer support
Clarify the need for change	• Review the evidence and the perceived need for change, including the fit with university priorities and emerging challenges. • Identify potential options and the implications of each. • Identify any good examples that you can draw from other institutions. What have they done differently? • Source expertise to test any assumptions or modelling; identify colleagues who have had similar challenges and make contact with them. • Build the case and evidence. • Confirm with upper management that there is support to take this approach.	• If requested, prepare a scoping paper, drawing on research and other universities to document options and implications. • Link the leader to other colleagues who might be able to offer mentorship or guidance. • If the change will affect many groups, set up a webpage and group discussion board to facilitate interchange across similar leaders.
Build the narrative and case for change	• Why is the status quo unsustainable/unsuitable? • What will happen if we stay the same? • What are the drivers for change? • What benefits might we gain from changing? • Who is likely to be affected? How? • What are the main outcomes we will have to achieve?	• Coach the leader/s on articulating their narrative and vision.
Establish the transition team	• Identify key people to recruit to the transition team, seeking diversity (seniority, gender, location) and possibly, someone who may oppose the change, as they will help to identify potential risks that must be ameliorated. • Share the narrative and case for change with the team. • Clarify areas of concern and build these into the narrative. • Determine the roles each will play during the transition, drawing on their skills and strengths. • Establish the vision and messages across the transition team, emphasising why the change is necessary.	• Provide guidance on building a strong transition team. • Facilitate the inaugural planning meeting of the transition team to help them build a common focus and strategy. • Support the development of a clear vision that can be readily articulated, shared, promoted and consistently viewed by all stakeholders.

(continued)

Table 9.1 Continued

Stage	Leader guidelines	Developer support
	Be clear about: • the reason for the change; • the aim of the process; • the level and scope of change; • the likely time frame; • risk management strategies to avert or mitigate adverse consequences.	• Link the leader/s to other service groups that might be able to assist during this process, if this is of value.
Engage the community	• Consider Bridges' Transition phases and the different approaches that may be needed. • Allow sufficient time for consultation. • Provide a clear narrative around the change and benefits. • Build a sense of urgency for action. • Establish clear communication channels. • Contact key representatives of your constituents and canvass their input and support. • Undertake wide consultation, possibly with different staff-groups, providing a clear timeline as to the planned schedule. • Set up a website for staff to view and contribute to. • Encourage innovative ideas. • Clarify and address any emerging issues that might create risk. • Confirm the way forward. • Remove any cultural or structural barriers that discourage engagement with the change process. • Empower people to act and take responsibility for the changes. • Be open and transparent: provide full disclosure on relevant matters (e.g. finances). • Establish effective communication channels. • Encourage the transition team to share and explore the change messages with their colleagues. • Meet regularly with the transition team to review any emergent issues. • Provide regular updates to staff on the consultation processes.	• Prepare the leader and team members for likely responses or challenges. • Support the leader and their team in their consultation roles. • Guide the transition team with respect to understanding and managing the responses of the community. • Assist with developing a clear communication strategy. • Facilitate public meetings and forums to enable discussion, including the generation of other ideas or strategies to be considered. • Assist with analysing key themes or issues from the consultations.

Phase	Actions	Support
Confirm the change and process	• Determine the agreed path and key outcomes to be emphasised, based on the consultations and advice provided. • Prepare a clear summary of the decision and ensure this meets with senior management approval. • Meet with staff to share the final vision and to explore the implications for their roles and work context. • Outline the intended timeline and key stages to be followed. • Meet with any staff who will be particularly affected. • Provide written guidance to all staff confirming this information.	• Provide support for the leader during the consultation and decision-making phase. • Facilitate the staff consultation session to communicate the outcomes. • Provide guidance to the transition team on managing a transition project.
Implement the agreed process	• Set up a transition implementation team. • Identify milestones and progress points. • Initiate staff training and support if required. • Maintain communication channels and share progress. • Continue consultation and regular review. • Build a strong positive energy around the reform/s.	• Facilitate the planning session of the transition implementation team. • Assist with identifying and programming training and support for the community or team as required. • Assist with consultation strategies as required.
Celebrate the wins	• Monitor the progress and quality of the outcomes. • Identify the progressive wins and milestones that are achieved. • Acknowledge early adopters and contributors. • Engage your sponsors in any celebratory events. • Reiterate the benefits and value of the change.	• Provide guidance on measuring and evaluating the outcomes and impact of the change process. • Provide independent evaluator support to measure outcomes.
Monitor the change outcomes	• Review the change strategy and targets. Are they achievable / realistic? Do they need to be adapted? • Adjust plans as required. • Monitor staff well-being and morale. • Check that processes and systems are well embedded. • Identify any implementation challenges that must be addressed. • Adapt the plans to address these challenges. • Is more training or system enhancement required?	• Assist with reviewing staff morale and responses to the change via interviews, surveys or focus groups. • Provide guidance on system / process enhancement as appropriate. • Evaluate the impact of the training and any evidence of further skill gaps to be addressed.
Evaluate the change impact and process	• Evaluate the outcomes of the intervention. Has it achieved the desired outcomes? • Evaluate the change process and any lessons learnt. Map a set of guidelines for the next transition.	• Assist with the evaluation phase if required. • Facilitate a group review of the change experience and lessons learnt. • Update tips and points on leading transitions to share with other leaders.

- When would they need to be involved?
- What level of information will they require?

Good communication strategies benefit from:

- a consistent message;
- two-way communication, with the feedback integrated, respected, and where appropriate, acted on;
- appropriate approaches for the purpose (e.g. face-to-face vs written or group);
- shared responsibility for communication across the transition team and other senior staff;
- honesty and full disclosure;
- an openness to feedback.

Good consultation encourages stakeholders to clarify concerns and contribute their ideas. The use of a facilitator for complex consultations can be most important, particularly if emotions are high. Well-managed consultative approaches offer considerable benefits, including:

- effective participation by all staff;
- increased staff commitment and engagement;
- consistent messages and shared understanding;
- early identification of problems or issues;
- two-way communication;
- harnessing the innovation and contributions of members;
- reducing the likelihood of disruptive influences;
- supporting the education/guidance of staff;
- reducing the stress related to uncertainty and mixed messages;
- maintaining morale and staff commitment.

Rollout of institutional initiatives

There will be times when the HED service is the primary service for the rollout of new systems or policies that may substantially impact on the university activities and its functioning. These might include: mandated teaching approaches; performance review or evaluation systems; research metric and reporting systems; quality assurance practices; or many other systemic requirements. When this occurs, the developer will need to apply many of the leader-based strategies outlined in Table 21.1. The following pointers offer some more specific guidance to ensure successful delivery of the initiative across the full university community.

Plan the rollout strategy

- Identify the key stakeholders who will be affected by these reforms. What issues are they likely to raise? What concerns will they have?

- Build a strong narrative and case for the reform, addressing potential issues that may be raised.
- Prepare a draft plan for release and promotion of the reform.
- Prepare a draft communication to be sent to all staff by the sponsor.
- Develop models and examples to illustrate what the reform will look like in practice.
- Consider how the reform might need to be adapted for different university groups or contexts.
- Identify any questions or issues that are likely to be raised at staff forums, and ensure there are suitable answers available.
- Prepare a website and FAQs to address likely questions. Update this when new questions arise.
- Identify how the success of the reform will be evaluated and commence the baseline data collection.
- Develop a communication strategy and plan well ahead for leader consultation/implementation review sessions.

Manage the rollout

- Organise a leadership forum to explore the reform and likely implications. Invite attendees' inputs and suggestions.
- Share any raised issues with the sponsor, with recommendations as to how they might be managed.
- Visit faculties and centres, promoting the system and answering any questions.
- Prepare a follow-up briefing note for senior leaders, outlining the steps undertaken, and the next phases of implementation, including review meetings.
- Manage the project implementation, providing regular updates to all stakeholders.
- Keep track of the planning time frames and ensure these are maintained.
- Schedule regular project meetings to keep everyone focused and to identify emergent risks. Is there slippage? Are the outcomes what was intended? Are there emergent problems that should be addressed?
- Identify and address problems quickly.
- Support leaders with local consultation sessions or project implementation workshops as required.

Evaluate the rollout implementation and impact

- Invite regular feedback on the implementation and its impact.
- Evaluate the project delivery and its outcomes.
- Undertake evaluative processes to review stakeholder responses to the change and any issues that have arisen.
- Identify successes and map the narratives about those successes. Build an evidence base as to what has been achieved.

- Undertake a debriefing meeting with your team to explore how the process operated. What was learnt? Would you do anything differently?
- Prepare the sponsor report.

It can be seen that the process remains focused on building strong, persuasive messages, developing the leadership/communication channels to enable consistent approaches, two-way communication and ongoing refinement of the process. However, it will be a complex process as the stakeholders are likely to span all levels and areas of the university.

Determining the consultation strategy

There will be various phases of consultation for large or significant reforms. Those that have significant consequences for peoples' work activities, careers or well-being need to be highly consultative. In other situations, they can be more dissemination focused. Table 9.2 provides further guidance on the choice of consultation strategy, outlining some considerations when planning community engagement.

The HE developer as provocateur, agent of change, partner in arms or anarchist

As representatives of the university, developers fill an important role in translating institutional reforms to the wider community (Moses 2012). They are expected to encourage engagement and adoption of key initiatives. The HED literature has been quite active in exploring the challenges that HE developers may face in working in these transitionary spaces (Di Napoli 2014). The question of neutrality is an intriguing one, as efforts to sit on the fence are likely to be difficult and poorly received by key stakeholders. Rathbun and Turner (2012), for example, suggest the need to develop a clear stance that is ethical, intentional and reflective. However, this is not always a comfortable space to be in. Institutional reforms may be poorly conceived or simply not attuned to the needs of the population. There are important accounts of developers who have disagreed with the paths being taken by their institutions (Szkudlarek and Stankiewicz 2014; Wouters *et al.* 2014) or broader agendas (Gosling 2009; Handal *et al.* 2014). This has caused them considerable angst as they grappled with the path to take. The HE developer will need to consider where they sit on the agency paradigm (Debowski 2014). These decisions can have significant consequences for future relations with key leaders or for the reputation of the HED service as a whole.

Conclusion

Change and transitions are now integral parts of university life. However, the process of guiding transitions is made more complicated by the likelihood of

Table 9.2 Consultation strategy considerations

Principle	Points to consider
Plan your communication strategy	Ensure that the process is clearly outlined, planned and followed.
What is the purpose?	Is it intended to inform people about policy, planning or decision-making on which they will have little influence, or is the consultation designed to seek feedback or stakeholder input?
Is the consultation restricted to information dissemination or open to input from contributors?	Restricted consultation limits input from the audience, primarily inviting comments on draft recommendations or conclusions. Open consultation will seek input including the generation of ideas, soliciting input and building diverse perspectives. This form of consultation will require more time for debate and idea generation, and may require various permutations of consultation.
Who should be consulted?	Identify all relevant stakeholders. Encourage diverse perspectives. Aim for opportunities for all stakeholders to be present or heard.
Where and when should the consultation take place?	Seek central, accessible venues. Schedule times that will encourage full participation. Offer multiple options to enable participation.
Information sharing	Good information increases understanding, encourages informed contributions and greater ownership of ideas, and reduces misinformation. Make sure the information is comprehensible, accurate, informative, meaningful and accessible. Release the information in good time. Ensure correct messages are being shared.
Format of the consultation	Plan the consultation to suit the identified purpose. Multiple options might be employed, including a website, online commentary, discussion document or public forum. Facilitated discussions, focus groups and large group techniques e.g. Open Space or World Café approaches (Bunker and Alban 2006) open up good spaces for input.
Timeline	Allow enough time for consultation, feedback and potentially, more consultation.
Process clarity	Provide clear guidance on the purpose, schedule, procedure, intended use of inputs and the dissemination plan.

multiple changes that simultaneously impact on the same community. For academics and researchers who must also manage their ongoing roles in teaching and research, this can be particularly disconcerting. There is a clear onus on the executive, leaders and developers to make the processes smooth, reasonable and manageable. Careful consideration of the benefits and optimal approach should be seen as an essential precursor to any initiative. Suitable consultation that allows interchange of ideas and adaptive learning will further support a constructive shift to more advanced outcomes. As this chapter also notes, there is a responsibility to monitor the outcomes and ensure the initiative was successful in achieving its goals. Communities that are forced to weather ill-conceived and poorly planned reforms will become jaded and unsupportive, which can have dire long-term consequences. This chapter has offered well proven techniques that will increase the engagement and commitment of academics and university communities generally. It has also illustrated the ways a HE developer can add considerable support and value.

References

Bridges, W., 2009. *Managing transitions: making the most of change*, 3rd edition, revised and updated, Philadelphia, PA: Da Capo Press.

Bunker, B.B. and Alban, B.T., 2006. *The handbook of large group methods: creating systemic change in organizations and communities*, San Francisco, CA: Jossey-Bass.

Debowski, S., 2014. From agents of change to partners in arms: the emerging academic developer role. *International Journal for Academic Development*, 19(1), pp. 50–56.

Di Napoli, R., 2014. Value gaming and political ontology: between resistance and compliance in academic development. *International Journal for Academic Development*, 19(1), pp. 4–11.

Gosling, D., 2009. Educational development in the UK: a complex and contradictory reality. *International Journal for Academic Development*, 14(1), pp. 5–18.

Handal, G., Lyckea, K.F., Mårtenssonb, K., Roxåc, T., Skodvina, A. and Solbrekkea, T.D., 2014. The role of academic developers in transforming Bologna regulations to a national and institutional context. *International Journal for Academic Development*, 19(1), pp. 12–25.

Jamieson, D.W., Eklund, S. and Meekin, B., 2012. Strategic business partner role: definition, knowledge, skills, and operating tensions. In W.J. Rothwell and G.M.B. Benscoter, eds, *The encyclopedia of human resource management*, San Francisco, CA: Pfeiffer, pp. 112–128.

Kotter, J.P., 2012. *Leading change*, Boston, MA: Harvard Business Review Press.

Loewenberger, P., 2013. The role of HRD in stimulating, supporting, and sustaining creativity and innovation. *Human Resource Development Review*, 12(4), pp. 422–455.

Moses, I., 2012. Views from a former vice-chancellor. *International Journal for Academic Development*, 17(3), pp. 275–277.

Neame, C., 2013. Democracy or intervention? Adapting orientations to development. *International Journal for Academic Development*, 18(4), pp. 331–343.

Quinn, L., 2012. Understanding resistance: an analysis of discourses in academic staff development. *Studies in Higher Education*, 37(1), pp. 69–83.

Rathbun, G. and Turner, N., 2012. Authenticity in academic development: the myth of neutrality. *International Journal for Academic Development*, 17(3), pp. 231–242.

Schein, E.H., 2010. *Organizational culture and leadership*, 4th edition, San Francisco, CA: Jossey-Bass.

Schroeder, C.M. (ed.), 2011a. *Coming in from the margins: faculty development's emerging organizational development role in institutional change*, 1st edition, Sterling, VA: Stylus Publishing.

Schroeder, C.M., 2011b. Embedding centers in instutional strategic planning. In Schroeder, ed., *Coming in from the margins: faculty development's emerging organizational development role in institutional change*, 1st edition, Sterling, VA: Stylus Publishing, pp. 260–272.

Schroeder, C.M., 2011c. Faculty developers as institutional developers: the missing prong of organizational development. In Schroeder, ed., *Coming in from the margins: faculty development's emerging organizational development role in institutional change*, 1st edition, Sterling, Va: Stylus Publishing, pp. 17–46.

Sherlock, J., 2012. The HR Transition to strategic partner: the rarely discussed identity challenges. In W.J. Rothwell and G.M.B. Benscoter, eds, *The encyclopedia of human resource management*, San Francisco, CA: Pfeiffer, pp. 161–172.

Styron, R.A., Michaelsen, L.K. and Styron, J.L., 2015. Implementing a university-wide change initiative. *To Improve the Academy*, 34(1–2), pp. 194–233.

Sutherland, K.A., 2014. Academic developers as partners in change, scholarship, and reflection. *International Journal for Academic Development*, 19(3), pp. 159–161.

Szkudlarek, T. and Stankiewicz, Ł., 2014. Future perfect? Conflict and agency in higher education reform in Poland. *International Journal for Academic Development*, 19(1), pp. 37–49.

Teelken, C., 2012. Compliance or pragmatism: how do academics deal with managerialism in higher education? A comparative study in three countries. *Studies in Higher Education*, 37(3), pp. 271–290.

Van Note Chism, N., 2011. Getting to the table: planning and developing institutional initiatives. In C.M. Schroeder, ed., *Coming in from the margins: faculty development's emerging organizational development role in institutional change*, 1st edition, Sterling, VA: Stylus Publishing, pp. 47–59.

Wouters, P., Clement, M., Frenay, M., Buelens, H. and Gilis, A., 2014. Avoiding compliance and resistance through collaboration? A Belgian teaching portfolio case. *International Journal for Academic Development*, 19(1), pp. 26–36.

Chapter 10

A delicate alliance

Establishing effective relationships with university executives and senior leaders

Successful HE development benefits from the establishment and maintenance of viable relationships between the HE developer and university leaders who sponsor, advocate and commission developmental support. They will generally elect to work with a HED developer when they have identified a strategic reform need, and/or see the service as providing valued support to their role or community. These perceptions of the HED service will often be informed by their own past experience with the HED representatives or similar services. The challenge for developers, then, is to build the reputation, associations and presence across the university so they are the first source of support that comes to mind. Central to this outcome is the delivery of a high-quality, fit for purpose guidance and support system that ensures optimal outcomes. In some instances, this may require considerable political acumen to guide the leader's expectations and assumptions toward viable paths.

This chapter therefore focuses on a particularly critical facet of the HED activities: providing strategic and customised support to the most senior members of the university. It explores the nature of the consultancy role which underpins these interactions, offering guidance on how the HED service can provide appropriate and responsive support to senior leaders, while ensuring advice is professional, well informed and fit for purpose.

The consultancy process

The executive and senior leaders will generally seek assistance from the HE development service to address an identified need. Such needs might relate to strategic consultations, institutional reforms, customised programs, facilitation of change transitions, specialised services (e.g. coaching) or institutional projects. Where the need is problem-based, leaders may be unsure as to the causative factors, simply recognising that there is an issue that needs to be resolved. In other cases, they may have a clear sense of the outcome to be delivered, but with limited consideration as to the best process to follow in achieving this ambition. The provision of in-house consultancy services requires a methodical and professional approach to clarify an agreed path. The following steps can assist in achieving this consensus.

Clarify the real issue/s

First, the developer needs to clarify what is really happening. While the client may affirm that "x needs to be fixed," this is not always correct. Careful questioning, interviews with other key stakeholders and evaluation of various sources of evidence can reveal a different issue that may require attention. The problem may be multi-faceted and require a range of interventions. Thus, the first stage of consultancy work is to ensure the real issues and needs have been clearly identified. This should be explored with the client before moving on to the next stage.

Confirm the agreed process, costs and scope

Following confirmation of the identified needs to be addressed, the scope of work, processes and costs (if any) can be negotiated. The role of the developer as a consultant, partner and/or facilitator may require clarification. The development service may have limited resources and may need to clarify the scope of work that is feasible, or the additional support that may be required from the client's resources. The leader may benefit from additional coaching, support or guidance in addition to the identified intervention focus. This might be discussed at this stage.

Map the options

There may be a range of approaches that might be considered. The client should be offered options that are well aligned with the desired outcomes, the community that will be involved, the capacity to deliver on the promised activities and the time that is available. The readiness of the leader and their community to embrace the recommended option/s will need to be considered. It may be necessary to commence with a context-setting phase before moving into a stronger implementation strategy. The options should be discussed in full, including any likely demands on the leader and their community. Agreement on the final path needs to be obtained before commencement.

Document the preferred option with respect to timelines, roles, costs and outcomes

Confirm agreement as to both timelines and resources before the implementation is commenced, including the role of the leader in supporting the initiative. If activities, venues or project elements are to be organised by the client's team, provide clear guidance on the requirements to avoid any confusion. Confirmation via email offers a useful record.

Maintain regular communications and catch-up meetings during the implementation phase

This complex close work requires the development of trust, regular interaction and ongoing monitoring of impact. Regular interchange via phone, email or face-to-face chats can be an important element of building strong and robust partnerships.

Work together to solve any issues

As the consultant, the developer is helping the client achieve their goals. If issues emerge, the resolution needs to be in partnership, ensuring the solution is suited to that environment and culture.

Review and monitor outcomes

It is likely that negotiated development work will require regular updating and adaptation as the implementation occurs. The capacity to review, adapt and refine the plan is readily managed when a close relationship has been established.

It can be seen that the developer can play a key role in guiding the conception, planning, implementation and evaluation of many institutional enhancements. However, considerable care needs to be taken to ensure the recommended choices and methods are effective and that the desired outcomes are achieved. A willingness to start at the client's level of development that encourages them to test, explore, experiment and ultimately master the processes is essential. The capacity to guide these journeys in a respectful and adaptive way will greatly contribute to the building of powerful and enduring relationships. Clarity of purpose and communication facilitates the development of robust relationships.

However, as the next section illustrates, working with university leaders carries some challenges and can generate considerable reflection on the role and impact of the HE developer in the politicised echelons of a university.

Supporting senior leaders

Scans of the HE development literature show that there has been little discussion of the practices that can support effective interactions with the executive and other senior leaders (Van Note Chism 2011). First, it is important to note that the majority of interactions with these members will relate to unique service provision that is negotiated by them, customised to suit their needs, and unlikely to be replicated elsewhere in the university. This means that the HE developer will primarily fill a consultancy role in these interactions, with the senior leader being the client. The key to successful relationships is to ensure each client's needs and expectations are addressed. With the shifting context for higher education, these will often be focused on improving efficiencies, developing or refining products (e.g. curricula, policy), systems or services, supporting quality enhancement or assurance, or facilitating enhanced community outcomes. The developer is likely to focus on three things: clarifying what is needed; designing a suitable strategy to support the desired enhancements or innovations; and implementing the agreed support (Jamieson *et al.* 2012).

Senior leader expectations and interactions

The executive and deans have particular expectations that they must meet, especially with respect to achieving notable advancements in university strategy, profiling, performance and reputation. They may also have strong concern for engaging leaders and the faculties with identified reforms. These leaders will be drawing on many support services to help them achieve their goals. They will anticipate alacrity in responding to a request; strong alignment with their priorities; timely management of agreed reforms; a smooth and uncomplicated process; and regular progress updates. Their role in the negotiated process is likely to be focused on providing an initial brief, approving a proposed path (and possibly, funding), and monitoring reports and updates. They will be pleased to have evidence of the success and take-up, and may appreciate opportunities to publicly sponsor events or celebrations.

Developers will need to prioritise senior leaders' requests and ensure they are delivered to the best possible standard. This is not necessarily easy to accomplish. Some of the following possible complexities may emerge:

- There is insufficient clarity as to what is required or should be delivered.
- It is unclear who is the main sponsor.
- There are mixed messages emanating from different individuals.
- The development strategy is being conveyed by a third (or fourth) party and therefore becomes skewed.
- The desired path is not the optimal or recommended one.
- There is misunderstanding by the sponsor as to some basic principles that should be reflected.
- The expectations as to timelines and integration are unrealistic.
- The planning excludes piloting and testing of the concept before full implementation.
- Insufficient funding is being provided or the interventions are expected to be delivered within the basic generic HED funding.
- There is little understanding about the HED development process and how it operates.

The preparation of an initial scoping document that outlines options and recommendations can ensure effective framing of the initiative. It can guide the leaders through a rational consideration of the ways their goals might be accomplished. This may be the only time the developer can influence that formative stage of decision making, so the research and professionalism of the document needs to be readily apparent. The scoping paper might feature:

- a clear description of the project brief;
- the goals and intended outcomes to be achieved;
- existing research, models or other sources of guidance that might assist in framing the project;

- potential options and a brief outline of their pros, cons and implications;
- issues to be considered (timelines, costings, staffing, piloting);
- recommendations, including next steps.

Ideally, the developer will be offered an opportunity to talk through this document. In some cases, this won't occur, and instead, it will be necessary to work through a spokesperson, who will need a thorough briefing. Once the go-ahead is received, a full project plan should be prepared to ensure that all relevant parties are clear on the scope and focus of the activities. The inclusion of an evaluation plan will ensure a good evidence base is captured. The provision of regular reports and careful management of the project and expectations will be essential. Regular updates, examples of wins or successes that can be profiled and the pursuit of optimal, practicable outcomes will assist in demonstrating strong responsiveness. If there are particular issues that will need to be addressed, investigate them, prepare a report on the issue/s and offer ideas as to how they might be ameliorated.

Some inherent tensions in the role of HED development

> You can only dance as fast as the music is playing...

The HE developer faces some particular challenges in seeking to be influential and a key source of guidance to those who make institutional decisions. The last 15 years have seen an interesting shift in the positioning of development services. Once offering key advice to the most senior university levels, now they are often required to work through intermediaries to get messages through (Gibbs 2013). A distal or ill-defined link between the HE developer and those with power can cause considerable frustration and difficulty if the HE developer is tasked with guidance of large-scale reform or wishes to promote new ideas.

A frustration for many developers is that their passion and desire to make their institutions exemplary models of best practice can be greatly impeded by the willingness of key leaders, communities or individuals to come on the same journey (Peseta 2014). While there may be clear evidence as to the need and critical urgency of the desired initiatives, they will be doomed to failure unless the university community, sponsors or some early adopters can be persuaded to join the crusade. The developer may have a very clear view of the risks to the institution if these issues are not addressed, but unless others also see these challenges, they are unlikely to be seen as a high priority. This can cause immense personal frustration, particularly if there has been considerable investment in mapping the problem. This particular scenario can be quite frequently experienced: the developer, as an expert in their chosen area of HED service, has a sound knowledge of practices being enacted in other institutions, the research around this practice and the ways in which it will benefit the university and its goals. The challenge is to communicate these insights and engage leaders who possess power and influence.

There is evidence of concern about the positioning of the HE development function in terms of its marginality, habitation of liminal spaces, and the need to be chameleons (Green and Little 2013; Kensington-Miller *et al.* 2015; Little and Green 2012). These conversations recognise both the potential and the risks in being out of the traditional locations where decisions and policy are made. While the positioning of HED groups offers considerable potential for working creatively and adaptively across the university, it is first necessary to be included in conversations or to be invited to participate in key initiatives (Van Note Chism 2011).

Credibility, expertise and authenticity in terms of the advice and guidance being offered is essential to the HED role, particularly when engaging with senior leaders. However, timing the development of persuasive and evidence-based messages, and the capacity to build allies, sponsors and champions, will also be important strategies to achieve the necessary reach and influence (Loewenberger 2013). Opportunities to engage with senior university leaders often draw on the capacity of the HE developer to be a consultant, ally, expert adviser, partner or co-investigator (Sherlock 2012). Implicit in these roles is the recognition that each party brings particular expertise, knowledge and insights to discussions. The developer is not the only expert in the room. While they may have particular insights to offer, the negotiated solution may be adaptive and somewhat pragmatic, accommodating particular contextual challenges or limitations. A willingness to work within this adaptive space is critical to building good partnerships and outcomes.

The quote at the start of this section was from a colleague when I first commenced in this field. Keen to get things moving, I was frustrated at the time it was taking to engage others in reforms that were clearly necessary! One of the challenges of working within the mid-tiers of university management is the need to work through and with others, rather than simply ordain that something should happen. Many desired innovations may take several years to gestate before surfacing as an institutional priority. In the first instance, the seeding of ideas about what might be feasible or needed may be all that is possible. Over time, these ideas can be canvassed with a range of people, encouraging their testing of the practicality of the proposals in this particular university context. In some cases, these respondents may identify problems or barriers that were not anticipated. This is one of the challenges that developers sometimes experience. They need to ensure their ideas and proposals are realistic, viable and credible. Close knowledge of the academic/research context can assist with initial testing, but its acceptance and embrace by those at the coalface will be the best litmus test. Over time, if the proposal has merit, a groundswell of advocates may emerge. This can result in another challenge for the developer: the idea that was initially touted by them is likely to resurface as the brilliant idea of another individual. This is part of the inherent development tension, with many ideas seeded but often attributed to later advocates. Recognition of the HED influence can be minimal, despite the immense effort that may have gone into the initial investigations and lobbying. However, if this is perceived to be evidence of successful impact, it can be regarded as a highly successful, *embedded* outcome.

If there are difficulties in gaining sponsorship for ideas or even being invited to be involved in discussions or initiatives, it may be important to review the stance and philosophy that is being pursued by the HED group. There may be discord between the agenda that developers wish to pursue and the more pragmatic, grassroots concerns that may drive senior leaders (Golding 2014; Moses 2012; Schroeder 2011). The capacity to reflect and support strategic priorities as part of the development service will be critical. The past demise of HED groups may be linked to their poor alignment with the shifts in institutional strategy, leadership or priorities (Van Note Chism 2011; Debowski *et al.* 2012). While the quest to seek excellent outcomes (as perceived by the developer) is most important (Rathbun and Turner 2012), it must also be grounded in a degree of pragmatism, recognising that development work operates as a partnership. If senior leaders have little interest in taking a proposal forward, there is little likelihood of success, and potentially, continuing to pursue the topic may increase the risk of being marginalised. This can be particularly hard for developers whose research focus is tied into achieving sponsorship for particular strategies or agendas. On the other hand, the integrity and courage to speak "truth to power" (Peseta 2014) is a professional responsibility. Leaders need to know that they are receiving the best advice possible, even if it does not accord with what they wish to hear. Of course, there are different ways to convey this information. Gibb (2013), for example, notes that there is an ongoing difficulty in having high ideals but being marginalised or being influential but lacking integrity. The importance of building a sound evidence base (McAlpine and Amundsen 2012) and drawing on research, evaluation, practice wisdom, and judgement (Bamber and Stefani 2015) can increase the power of the advice.

Thus, the inherent tensions in the development role often relate to a desire to be a major change agent and the perceived expert, while recognising the need to operate within a collegial but managerial context (Neame 2013). The HE developer is likely to be one of several sources of guidance to senior leaders, with other stakeholders also seeking to influence the agenda, solutions and approaches that are likely to be taken. Ultimately, the key concern is that enhancements have been initiated and successfully embedded. The role that the developer plays may be multi-faceted and variable, reflecting the dynamic contexts in which they operate. Their expertise may be more subtly influential and possibly, less visible to others.

Indicators of a healthy client-focused executive service

To ensure an effective interface with senior leaders then, the HE development service will need to be:

- sensitive to the political context and complexities that riddle senior leadership levels;

- adaptive and responsive to the different needs and expectations of the various clients or client groups;
- capable of recommending or implementing innovative approaches that are fit for purpose and best suit the context and limitations that may be evident;
- strongly (and visibly) aligned to the institutional needs, priorities and strategies;
- open to facilitating and implementing stakeholder solutions;
- keen to broker good ideas and collaborations across different stakeholders;
- willing to be an indirect agent of reforms, if necessary.

Conclusion

Service provision to more senior members of the university offers considerable potential to make a substantive difference to institutional outcomes and encourage good practice. However, the negotiation of an agreed project or process can be quite political and unpredictable, as many voices may be influencing the decisions. The HE developer can build more certainty around this work by ensuring any presentations or proposals are well informed and highly professional, and that there is good alignment with the client's own goals and priorities. The establishment of an authoritative, reliable role that delivers on agreed activities will put the service in a good position to be valued and relied on by these senior leaders.

References

Bamber, V. and Stefani, L., 2015. Taking up the challenge of evidencing value in educational development: from theory to practice. *International Journal for Academic Development*, pp. 1–13. Available online at DOI: 10.1080/1360144X.2015.1100112

Debowski, S., Stefanie, L., Cohen, M.W. and Ho, A., 2012. Sustaining and championing teaching and learning: in good times or bad. In J.E. Groccia, M.A. Al-Sudairy, and W. Buskist, eds, *Handbook of college and university teaching: a global perspective*, Thousand Oaks, CA: SAGE Publications, pp. 125–142.

Gibbs, G., 2013. Reflections on the changing nature of educational development. *International Journal for Academic Development*, 18(1), pp. 4–14.

Golding, C., 2014. Blinkered conceptions of academic development. *International Journal for Academic Development*, 19(2), pp. 150–152.

Green, D.A. and Little, D., 2013. Academic development on the margins. *Studies in Higher Education*, 38(4), pp. 523–537.

Jamieson, D.W., Eklund, S. and Meekin, B., 2012. Strategic business partner role: definition, knowledge, skills, and operating tensions. In W.J. Rothwell and G.M.B. Benscoter, eds, *The encyclopedia of human resource management*, San Francisco, CA: Pfeiffer, pp. 112–128.

Kensington-Miller, B., Renc-Roe, J. and Morón-García, S., 2015. The chameleon on a tartan rug: adaptations of three academic developers' professional identities. *International Journal for Academic Development*, 20(3), pp. 279–290.

Little, D. and Green, D.A., 2012. Betwixt and between: academic developers in the margins. *International Journal for Academic Development*, 17(3), pp. 203–215.

Loewenberger, P., 2013. The role of HRD in stimulating, supporting, and sustaining creativity and innovation. *Human Resource Development Review*, 12(4), pp. 422–455.

McAlpine, L. and Amundsen, C., 2012. Challenging the taken-for-granted: how research analysis might inform pedagogical practices and institutional policies related to doctoral education. *Studies in Higher Education*, 37(6), pp. 683–694.

Moses, I., 2012. Views from a former vice-chancellor. *International Journal for Academic Development*, 17(3), pp. 275–277.

Neame, C., 2013. Democracy or intervention? Adapting orientations to development. *International Journal for Academic Development*, 18(4), pp. 331–343.

Peseta, T.L., 2014. Agency and stewardship in academic development: the problem of speaking truth to power. *International Journal for Academic Development*, 19(1), pp. 65–69.

Rathbun, G. and Turner, N., 2012. Authenticity in academic development: the myth of neutrality. *International Journal for Academic Development*, 17(3), pp. 231–242.

Schroeder, C.M., 2011. Recentering within the web of institutional leadership. In Schroeder, ed., *Coming in from the margins: faculty development's emerging organizational development role in institutional change*, 1st edition, Sterling, VA: Stylus Publishing, pp. 273–292.

Sherlock, J., 2012. The HR transition to strategic partner: the rarely discussed identity challenges. In W.J. Rothwell and G.M.B. Benscoter, eds, *The encyclopedia of human resource management*, San Francisco, CA: Pfeiffer, pp. 161–172.

Van Note Chism, N., 2011. Getting to the table: planning and developing institutional initiatives. In C.M. Schroeder, ed., *Coming in from the margins: faculty development's emerging organizational development role in institutional change*, 1st edition, Sterling, VA: Stylus Publishing, pp. 47–59.

Part III

Academic capacity building

This part of the book explores the ways in which academics progress from novices to experts across their different areas of responsibility. The foundational capabilities that support this transition are explored, extending beyond the traditional foci of research, teaching and leadership to encompass additional factors that ensure academic acculturation, performance and career progression. Academic identity, collegiality and engagement are examined, illustrating the increasingly complex learning and performance environment in which academics function. This broad review encourages a more holistic understanding of academic work and its positioning within university contexts. The chapters explore how leaders and HE developers can support academic enhancement. Various strategies and more formalised development approaches are outlined, illustrating the value of building a multi-faceted array of support initiatives.

In Chapter 11, the evolving construction of academic identity is explored, illustrating the critical influences that can impact on the individual's perceptions and articulation.

Chapter 12 then examines the ways in which prospective academics might enter academe, highlighting some of the particular risks that new academics now face. This chapter maps the key forms of support that can assist these newcomers.

Chapter 13 explores the under-discussed notion of collegiality and culture, highlighting the importance of working in constructive work settings that provide the right context for learning. Implications for leaders and developers are explored.

Chapter 14 then examines the different ways in which academics extend their impact and reach to both the university and the broader community, emphasising the importance of building relationships and connections across the academic role and its component functions.

In Chapter 15, the process of moving from novice researcher to research leader is mapped. This is further explored in Chapter 16, where the forms of support and guidance that assist research capability enhancement are examined.

A similar approach is taken in Chapters 17 and 18, which explore teaching and learning capabilities and their development.

Chapter 19 examines the complexities of leadership in academic worlds, mapping the different ways that academics move into influencing roles. This is complemented by Chapter 20, which explores the different ways in which leadership can be developed within the university.

This part of the book will assist developers, academic leaders and academics in guiding academic strategy and capability enhancement.

Chapter 11

The evolution of academic identity

Academics are strongly influenced by their sense of identity. However, unlike many professions where there is a clear view of what the role and career trajectory are likely to encompass, academe is a complicated construct that evolves over time and can be reshaped by different experiences, influences and choices (Dowd 2005; Ylijoki and Henriksson 2015). Over the course of an academic career, there can be many different identities that are tested, adopted and refined as experience, contextual forces and circumstances forge different paths. In some cases, there are also conflicting identities that must somehow be integrated. This chapter outlines some of the ways in which academic identity operates, and the different processes by which identity constructs are shaped. It demonstrates the critical importance of being attuned to these insights when working as a higher education developer or leader, as each participant's identity will guide their commitment, engagement and motivation. Mentors can also play a key role in guiding self-reflections on identity.

Why be an academic?

There are many factors that encourage people to engage in academic work. Consider, for example the following ambitions:

- contribute to the nation's productivity agenda;
- leave a legacy in your discipline;
- establish a name as a leading commentator in your field;
- build a high-level profile as a researcher;
- gain patents and other forms of intellectual excellence;
- promote better practice in your discipline/the sector/your specialist role;
- obtain stable employment;
- access a reasonable income;
- be recognised as a leading figure in the discipline;
- enjoy opportunities to learn and grow;
- undertake rich and meaningful work;
- work in an innovative and engaging employment context;

- encourage students;
- make a difference to society;
- work flexibly;
- operate in a research-rich setting;
- acquire new skills and capabilities;
- build a world-wide reputation;
- gain opportunities to write and publish;
- move into academic leadership;
- work with community groups;
- move into consultancy roles;
- find time to think, play with ideas and innovate.

When offered this list, a group of academics will each choose a different combination of motivators: some will seek an opportunity to make a difference, while others may be more focused on becoming known as an expert. Others will be passionate about their teaching and helping new generations to learn and grow. For some, the mystique of academe prevails, encouraging them to seek a contemplative and innovative space where they can transition to more expert forms of thinking and acting. The alluring thing about academic work is that it does offer considerable scope for all of these ambitions to be achieved. The way an individual shapes their foci and priorities will be influenced by these broad intentions. These subjective measures of career success are driven by what matters to the individual (Arthur *et al.* 2005) and may transcend employment in any one institution or role.

In his seminal work, *Flourish*, Martin Seligman (2011) argues that people thrive when they are able to engage in activities that support:

- positive emotions and outlook
- opportunities to be fully engaged and immersed
- relationships that are supportive and important
- meaningful work
- the capacity to achieve and build credible outcomes.

Seligman's model emphasises the importance of establishing an environment that allows the individual to pursue what is important to them, and to be successful in a way that is appropriate to their needs, goals and talents. This model is particularly well suited to academics, who tend to work as self-managing, autonomous individuals. They are responsible for directing their work tasks to meet the necessary outcomes, but in a manner that best suits them. The formation of a clear identity that is motivating, affirming and fulfilling is an important part of this subjective determination of success. Drawing on their particular goals, needs and perceptions, each individual is likely to develop a personal set of success metrics that is motivating and meaningful. In her study of early career academics, for example, Sutherland (2015) identified life satisfaction, contribution to society, freedom, job satisfaction and influencing students as subjective factors that were very important to early career academics. The capacity to integrate one's own desires and sources of fulfilment greatly assists in building robust and resilient self-conceptions that can be sustained across many different career experiences.

Measuring academic success

While individual academics may seek these intrinsic indicators of success, there are many other forces that determine what matters with respect to academic work. Objective or external metrics of success are also influential in guiding an academic's priorities and foci. Stupnisky *et al.* (2015) identified research productivity and teaching success as two key sets of metrics that are used to signify academic success. However, the challenge that is clearly visible across the sector is the strong reliance on these outcome-based measures to the exclusion of other, more distal and attitudinal components. These "objective" forms of success (Arthur *et al.* 2005) are allied with increased prestige or power, and are normally the key indicators that universities draw on for career recognition or advancement. They operate as significant drivers of sponsorship, feedback, rewards, recognition and ongoing employment. In recent years, research productivity has been particularly influential, given its readily accessible outcome measures relating to publications, grant funding, student research completions, number of citations and research impact (Sutherland 2015). Teaching indicators, on the other hand, are less readily "quantifiable," hard to compare and more subjective in the definition of performance. They are likely to draw on process measures, such as student evaluation scores, or competitive awards to signal suitable outcomes (Sutherland 2015). Other, more embedded outcomes and activities, such as leadership and relationships that are central to long-term academic success, are less likely to be valued or recognised (Debowski 2010). This dissonance between self and institutional values can generate discord for the individual (Boyd and Smith 2016).

The academic career cycle

Academics face a complex world when they enter academe. For the most part, they are melding disciplinary-knowledge and a competency base, which may have been developed over many years, to a highly specialised level. While some may continue to practice their professional skills (e.g. as a clinician) (Kumar *et al.* 2011), many will seek to move into ongoing employment as a dedicated academic. A particular challenge is the accommodation of new inputs and messages about what defines success. The individual can find it challenging to either adopt a new framing of their identity or adapt and meld new cues with their previously well-established identity (Boyd and Smith 2016; Duffy 2013). For some, this is a simple transition process, while others may find it much harder to achieve a balance (Levin and Shaker 2011; Smith 2010). The sociocultural cues from the discipline can be a strong influence (Krause 2014), particularly for more mature academics who retain a strong allegiance to their field of knowledge (Martimianakis and Muzzin 2015). Institutional messages about the key roles and activities that academics must prioritise have resulted in increasing tension between the desired (personal/professional) state and the required state of play for many academics (Billot 2010; Gonzales *et al.* 2014; Shin and Jung 2014). This is particularly challenging for those new to academe, as they must somehow make sense of conflicting sources of guidance, including feedback from students and the desire to be seen as an excellent teacher (Gale 2011; Rowan 2013). A key challenge is the hybrid nature of academic identity: each individual will draw on a range of sources of guidance to create meaning that is distinctly unique. This makes it harder to extrapolate from existing models and to emulate the path of others (Feather 2014).

Academic careers can be categorised into three phases: early career, mid-career and senior. These stages are signalled by transitions to more senior roles and titles, and are largely managed by the respective universities through their selection and promotion practices. A traditional career path is to enter as an early career academic and then transition to more senior roles. However, there is increasing variation in the possible paths one might pursue and the ways in which a career might be mapped. The diversity of the academic fraternity must also be noted: an early-career academic can be older, while some junior academics experience stellar career trajectories to the professoriate. Similarly, not all academics choose to pursue career progression: some plateau at a certain career level (by choice or circumstance), where they may focus on lateral development rather than hierarchical career progression. The divergent paths that lead academics toward their roles make it hard to build a consistent demographic profile. Despite this, we can identify a few key characteristics of each phase.

The early career academic

Early career academics (ECAs) are generally deemed to be academics or researchers who completed their doctoral studies within the last 5–7 years and are filling entry-level positions. In some cases, ECAs may embark on their career while completing their doctoral studies or may be appointed because of their other professional credentials, without a doctorate. Thus, the doctorate is only one of the markers, and may not be relevant to someone who brings significant professional know-how to their role. However, those coming into academe without this qualification may feel they are "imposters" who lack the necessary credentials compared to colleagues who have travelled a more predictable path (Hutchins 2015; Knights and Clarke 2014). ECA levels of appointment can be quite diverse, ranging from casual tutor, assistant lecturer, teaching or research fellow or assistant, assistant professor, graduate assistant or lecturer. They are generally regarded as newcomers to the sector who are still finding their way and building the capabilities and identity necessary for their career.[1]

The ECA period is one of acclimatisation, requiring the individual to develop a range of skills and capabilities that are necessary for successful academic performance. The following lists the basic competencies that underpin successful integration as an early career academic:

- possesses a clear understanding of the required role, performance standards and outcomes;
- builds effective relationships and networks;
- writes and publishes academic papers;
- establishes a clear path of research that demonstrates a sustained progress;
- conducts research in a timely and well planned manner;
- supervises research students, ensuring the timely completion of their research;
- designs and delivers good quality educational programs and experiences that support student needs and the curriculum requirements;
- reflects on and evaluates their teaching to identify improvements and further development;
- possesses a good knowledge of the university, sector and disciplinary contexts;
- communicates effectively across a range of media and forums.

This is a very vulnerable time for many ECAs who are employed through short-term contracts, as casual staff or on an occasional basis (Cummings and Finkelstein 2012). Junior academics have become a flexible workforce, with many working in temporary or precarious roles that lack long-term security (Kimber 2003). This volatility reduces the ease of developing the core capabilities that will more readily support a transition into tenured or longer-term appointments. At a time when they should be able to access important development and support, many ECAs are on the periphery, regarded as a disposable workforce that does not need development.

ECAs face many challenges at the acclimatisation stage as they seek to establish and consolidate a clear academic identity. In this early phase, access to career opportunities may be strong determinants of the type of identity that an individual establishes. If, for example, tutoring roles are the primary source of employment, an ECA may experience strong pigeon-holing as a teacher. Others may be directed toward research-intensive roles that are less teaching oriented. The guidance of significant people (e.g. mentors and supervisors), types and access to support, career opportunities, and the prevailing culture will strongly influence the academic roles and identity that are pursued. A challenge that many encounter is mapping a long-term vision and a set of priorities while working in contexts that are focused on immediate exigencies. In these settings, ECAs may find themselves working intensively, but without the development and consolidation of a credible track record that will help them transition past the ECA hurdle. At a minimum, ECAs need to build a scholarly profile that includes research papers where they are the lead or sole author, and, possibly, evidence of capable teaching. This may be sufficient to get them into a further role. Ideally, they will need to show a more comprehensive suite of capabilities that evidences strong foundations in academic performance and practices. Without this evidence, it is possible that the individual will remain in ECA limbo.

This is also the time when ECAs need to demonstrate they are worthy of ongoing employment. Many universities operate lengthy probationary periods, where the performance of the academic is closely monitored, to assess whether they show the potential to be a valued long-term employee (Fitzgerald *et al.* 2012; Kehm and Teichler 2013). In the US, the process of achieving tenure is a very challenging and uncertain period, although the expectations and cues are well understood. In other nations, the confirmatory process is also lengthy, often requiring a probationary time of 3–5 years before the employee is confirmed for a continuing appointment. In this highly critical and competitive context, it is essential that the early career academic is familiar with the expectations and the norms of performance. Good mentoring and sponsorship are important in managing this candidature phase (Foote and Solem 2009; Haynes 2010).

The mid-career academic

Mid-career academics (MCAs) are those who have progressed to the next level of employment beyond the base-entry point or pre-tenure phase. Many academics move to this level within the first ten years of their university appointment, often through promotion from the base ranks or as a result of the tenure process. While they have successfully evidenced a capacity to perform the basic academic functions of teaching and research, they now face a key identity transition: moving from being a junior academic to an independent, well profiled academic who demonstrates leadership capacity.

This is an important phase in the academic journey. The individual is faced with some key decisions: continue to progress as a traditional teaching/research academic, or move into a more specialised focus in research or teaching? Transition to leadership and administration roles where the individual's talents are much needed? Transition to an allied or different discipline? Each of these paths is likely to be available, encouraging some soul searching as to where one best fits. There may be other factors to be considered: status, personal concerns (e.g. family responsibilities), emerging recognition of one's talents, a potential fast-track career path to more senior roles, a serendipitous set of circumstances. These and many other considerations need to be weighed up.

Whatever the path, the MCA will need to focus on further expanding and strengthening their capabilities and outcomes to remain competitive and future-proofed. Some of the additional competencies that will need to be developed or consolidated include:

- the establishment of a range of collaborative linkages with other colleagues, universities or sectors;
- the capacity to build professional relationships and collaborations that have longevity;

- the ability to develop, manage and lead teams and projects;
- the capacity to undertake scholarship relating to one's teaching;
- leadership of innovations and key initiatives;
- engagement with external stakeholders;
- increasing scholarly impact from publications, keynotes and other research-related activities (Watermeyer 2014);
- the capacity to gain funding to support research.

While these capabilities build on the initial ECA scaffolding, they now take a more intensive focus on building reach, influence and impact. The MCA needs to leverage off their strengths and to increase momentum, generating more and improved outcomes across their portfolio.

For some MCAs, this transition from novice to independent academic can be a major stumbling block on their academic journey. The support offered to MCAs is less accessible, and the roles may have increased in complexity and scope. Increased use of research metrics and a focus on performance outcomes has encouraged institutions to closely analyse the productivity of their professoriate. While many MCAs are successful and progressive academics, others may have struggled to maintain their profile and outputs for a number of reasons, including the roles they have assumed. In some cases, MCAs may struggle to progress their ongoing identity as researchers. For example, the research focus may require renewal following an initial burst of doctoral research publications. If there has been a long gap between publications, there can be reduced confidence to write and build a credible flow of work. In this situation, the MCA may become more at risk, perceived by university administrators to be research-inactive, and in some institutions, surplus to requirements.

Thus, the mid-career phase is a pivotal point in academic career management. This is a time when many individuals feel alienation, frustration and confusion as the roles they previously enjoyed offer less satisfaction and meaning (Morison *et al.* 2006). This loss of career trajectory and focus can be termed "middlescence," signalling that the individual needs to re-engage with their purpose, focus and identity. There can be many reasons for this loss of connectedness, including: limited adaptation and regeneration of the initial ECA skills; an absence of feedback and guidance on performance standards and requirements; poor career guidance or mentorship; minimal acquisition of new skills; continued attachment to more junior practices/identity and standards; or an unwillingness to admit that one is not coping. The risk for the silent MCA who is not progressing is increasing: it is now much harder to stay invisible and just keep doing what one has always done.

Thus, at this stage of academic careers, it becomes imperative that the individual builds a robust identity that has clarity, focus and direction. They need to progress their initial ECA identity to a more sophisticated, nuanced interpretation. The shift from being a good employee to a leader of academics, teams, projects, initiatives or other institutional priorities is a major transition point that is increasingly seen as an indicator of potential for the next stage. However, the adoption of these important roles also brings further challenges in forging a strong, integrated identity (Holt *et al.* 2013). At this stage, the MCA needs to be adaptive and flexible, able to critique potential career options and choose a path that complements their own professional and personal needs, strengths and potential. To achieve this, it is necessary to have a clear understanding of the broader institutional and sectoral context.

The senior academic

"Senior" academics are defined as those who have attained professorial status or who carry responsibility for large portfolios. The transition to senior academic has been little discussed, although there is considerable concern for articulating the nature of successful academic leadership and its enactment (Macfarlane 2012). The entry route to the senior ranks is not always straightforward, with women often experiencing more challenges in achieving recognition, or indeed, an invitation to be considered for senior roles (Van den Brink 2011). For many, the achievement of professorial or reader status is a final stage, while, for others, it is a launching pad into more senior roles, such as associate dean, dean, provost or a named chair.

Senior academics are expected to move into quite complex leadership roles in research, teaching or administration. They will need to be effective chairs of committees, working parties, reviews and other forms of evaluative activities. They play a key role in setting the tone and culture of their particular communities and in determining how the next generation will fare. At this stage, many will assume formal roles of authority. Heads of school or departments carry some of the more complex roles that academics may assume. They will have oversight of large groups and budgets, and will be charged with making significant decisions that have both operational and strategic implications. Their oversight of academic and professional groups will require different forms of governance and they may need to lead large reforms. Many heads are appointed for a specified period of time (e.g. 3 or 5 years) on a rotating basis. It has been recognised that the shift from colleague to a more senior position, then back to colleague, carries considerable challenges, as tough decisions can carry consequences for long-term relationships with colleagues in the future. The rapid shift in identity from colleague to authority figure can therefore prove difficult for some.

Universities have experienced some challenges in keeping senior academics engaged after they have achieved their aspirational professorial target. The lure of promotion is no longer there, and there may be a reluctance to overtly manage more senior colleagues. Despite these difficulties, there is increasing concern for delineating the roles that more senior academics should play. Universities are developing explicit performance expectations and role statements to provide clearer guidance on the roles and activities that academics need to fulfil. They are also moving toward redundancies as one means of managing more senior academics who are deemed to be underperforming (Blackham 2015). Thus, even senior academics are working in a more volatile environment where they need to read the cues and be prepared to be adaptable and future-proofed. There is also concern for the disenfranchised professoriate, with many of the intellectual functions once delegated to professors now assumed by growing numbers of executive leaders (Macfarlane 2012). Thus, there is considerable work to be done in supporting the enhancement of academics across the entire career cycle.

Identity challenges and dilemmas

There are other factors and experiences that will also influence the identity that an individual builds and nurtures. With new disciplines, it can take time to establish the key characteristics and expectations of academic fraternities. This can be a challenging time, as the individual may experience some conflicting messages about standards, parity and rivalry with competing knowledge paradigms (Levin and Shaker 2011; Smith 2010). Those moving into academe from doctoral studies may also find it difficult to transition from their student identity to that of colleague, professional or expert. This can be even more pronounced for students who are employed part-time or as international appointees (Fotovatian and Miller 2014; Teeuwsen et al. 2014). Those who move to other countries can experience considerable tension between their established identities and the experiences or expectations of their new environment (Austin et al. 2014; Chapman et al. 2014; Szelényi and Rhoads 2013). This can be particularly exacerbated by the uncertainty associated with contract appointments that are regarded as short-term.

It is important that the academic develops a sense of identity that is true to their values, goals and beliefs. However, this is being increasingly challenged as universities build stronger framing of academic work and institutional assessment of value (Winter and O'Donoghue 2012). This can pressure individuals to "edit" their identities, removing any outcomes, skills or history that is seen as peripheral or of little value (Hyland 2011). This excision of self is a risk, as the efforts to conform and limit one's talents to those officially prescribed can increase the perceived tension between personal and prescribed personas. This can lead to an increasing differentiation between public and private scripts, with this dissonance challenging the well-being of the individual (Martimianakis and Muzzin 2015).

A further risk that is now emerging is the difficulty of building a coherent and authentic identity when employment opportunities are pushing the individual in a certain direction. This is particularly relevant to early-career academics who may need to accommodate different requirements to maintain their employability (Gale 2011; Levin and Shaker 2011). Those who move across disciplines or into specialised/new roles will also need to re-engage with a more holistic view of themselves in order to integrate these new experiences (Nyhagen and Baschung 2013). As the individual establishes a successful niche, new opportunities may also emerge, requiring further adjustment (Jain et al. 2009). The individual may wish to explore, for example, the challenge of melding the role of researcher with entrepreneur as research moves toward commercialisable outcomes. The different experiences of women in building their career and support base has also been highlighted as another complicating factor that needs to be more carefully monitored (Crimmins 2016).

Supporting identity and career development

Figure 11.1 illustrates the different identity and career influences which may guide an individual as they progress their careers. Early-career academics often

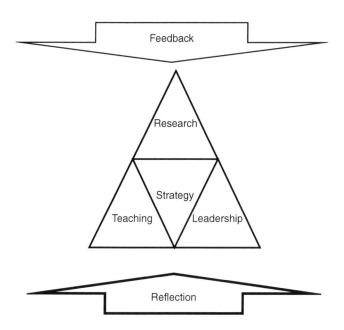

Figure 11.1 Academic identity influences and enablers.

identify serendipitous factors, such as opportunity or sponsorship, as having a pivotal influence on their choices and paths. Mid- to senior-level academics are likely to point to more strategic, intentional sources that have required their personal agency and ownership. The transition of the individual from *being influenced* to *influencing* their identity and career is an important part of transitioning from novice to senior academic. However, as the following chapters will illustrate, this progressive self-realisation benefits from a positive leadership community and the support of effective developers.

Building a coherent narrative

There are considerable risks for academics who fail to build a sense of their holistic academic identity. The articulation of a nuanced narrative is an important process that assists the academic in resolving conflicts and tensions. Narratives are stories that explain the individual's journey, illustrating how the different stages, decisions, outcomes and experiences have contributed to the whole self. They assist in building a strong sense of self-determinism and self-esteem (Levin and Shaker 2011). These narratives can take time to construct, and will require ongoing reconstruction.

The capacity to develop, articulate and critique persuasive narratives is a foundational skill for every academic. They will be expected to put forward clear cases that outline how they have progressed their career, teaching, research, leadership or all of these, as part of their efforts to be recognised and rewarded in the university system. Grants and award schemes will also require powerful substantiation to show how the individual has developed a well-articulated and successful strategy to further their career or goals. Probation, annual reviews, promotion, recruitment and specialised roles also rely on well-articulated narratives. Unfortunately, this is an often under-developed element of academic identity management.

Mentors, sponsors, reviewers, supervisors and higher education developers all play important roles in helping academics articulate and test their identities. Opportunities to voice the perceived identity and to map the paths that have been taken are valuable tests to ensure the individual is evolving in an authentic, considered and strategic manner. Regular identity reviews with an interested audience can also help to verify key assumptions about systemic requirements and expectations.

Some key questions that will assist people in reviewing and enhancing their identities and career narratives include:

- How have you arrived here? What were the key influences and milestones that you have experienced?
- What is important to you? What do you want to be known for?
- How will you make a difference to the discipline, university or sector?
- What are your long-term aspirations? How are you planning to achieve these?
- What are your strengths and talents? How are they used in your current role?

- What are your key achievements to date?
- How have you grown over the last three years? Can you see evidence of increased capabilities and skills? If not, why not?
- Are you happy? Does academic work give you joy? If not, why not? Can you change the things that are a problem?
- What are the main goals you have aimed to achieve? How have you approached achieving those goals?
- How have you balanced your different role components?
- What are the challenges or difficulties you have encountered? How have they influenced you? How have you resolved or addressed them?
- Where do you plan to go next? Are you on the right path or is it time to look at different options? What are your key strategies to make your goals a reality?
- Do you have a mentor? How has your mentor assisted? Could you be more active in seeking guidance and support?

These questions open up considerable reflection and provide a valuable basis for mentoring, orientation and ongoing career-strategy discussions.

Conclusion

From this overview, it is clear that academic identity is a transient yet progressive construct. Each role and experience that an academic encounters offers a new lens through which the individual can review and map their skills, capabilities and potential. Identities need to be regularly tested and adapted to form increasingly nuanced interpretations of one's emerging academic role and context. It is particularly important to develop skills in articulating and critiquing evolving identities and narratives. These act as academic road maps and need to be well framed to facilitate desired outcomes.

Note

1 There are different conventions for naming academics. This book will employ the UK tradition of retaining the title of professor for those who have achieved the highest levels of academic standing. The use of the terms early and mid-career will help to differentiate the particular groups being referred to.

References

Arthur, M.B., Khapova, S.N. and Wilderom, C.P.M., 2005. Career success in a boundaryless career world. *Journal of Organizational Behavior*, 26(2), pp. 177–202.

Austin, A.E., Chapman, D.W., Farah, S., Wilson, E. and Ridge, N., 2014. Expatriate academic staff in the United Arab Emirates: the nature of their work experiences in higher education institutions. *Higher Education*, 68(4), pp. 541–557.

Billot, J., 2010. The imagined and the real: identifying the tensions for academic identity. *Higher Education Research & Development*, 29(6), pp. 709–721.

Blackham, A., 2015. Managing without default retirement in universities: a comparative picture from Australia. *Legal Studies*, 35(3), pp. 502–531.

Boyd, P. and Smith, C., 2016. The contemporary academic: orientation towards research work and researcher identity of higher education lecturers in the health professions. *Studies in Higher Education*, 41(4), pp. 678–895.

Chapman, D., Austin, A.E., Farah, S. and Ridge, N., 2014. Academic staff in the UAE: unsettled journey. *Higher Education Policy*, 27(1), pp. 131–151.

Crimmins, G., 2016. The spaces and places that women casual academics (often fail to) inhabit. *Higher Education Research & Development*, 35(1), pp. 45–57.

Cummings, W.K. and Finkelstein, M.J., 2012. *Scholars in the changing American academy: new contexts, new rules and new roles*, Dordrecht: Springer.

Debowski, S., 2010. Leading research in an evolving world: implications for higher education development, policy and practice. In *Research and development in higher education: reshaping higher education*, Melbourne, Vic.: HERDSA, pp. 213–222.

Dowd, K.O., 2005. The career life of academics: boundaried or boundaryless? *Human Relations*, 58(6), pp. 699–721.

Duffy, R., 2013. Nurse to educator? Academic roles and the formation of personal academic identities. *Nurse Education Today*, 33(6), pp. 620–624.

Feather, D., 2014. Defining academic – real or imagined. *Studies in Higher Education*, pp. 1–14.

Fitzgerald, T., Gunter, H. and White, J., 2012. *Hard labour? Academic work and the changing landscape of higher education*, Bingley, UK: Emerald Group.

Foote, K.E. and Solem, M.N., 2009. Toward better mentoring for early career faculty: results of a study of US geographers. *International Journal for Academic Development*, 14(1), pp. 47–58.

Fotovatian, S. and Miller, J., 2014. Constructing an institutional identity in university tea rooms: the international PhD student experience. *Higher Education Research & Development*, 33(2), pp. 286–297.

Gale, H., 2011. The reluctant academic: early-career academics in a teaching-orientated university. *International Journal for Academic Development*, 16(3), pp. 215–227.

Gonzales, L.D., Martinez, E. and Ordu, C., 2014. Exploring faculty experiences in a striving university through the lens of academic capitalism. *Studies in Higher Education*, 39(7), pp. 1097–1115.

Haynes, K., 2010. *Analysis of university reports on career development and transferable skills training (Roberts) payments*, Newmarket Suffolk, UK: The Professional and Higher Partnership Ltd.

Holt, D. *et al.*, 2013. Leading at the coal-face: the world as experienced by subject coordinators in Australian Higher Education. *Educational Management Administration and Leadership*, 41(2), pp. 233–249.

Hutchins, H.M., 2015. Outing the imposter: a study exploring imposter phenomenon among higher education faculty. *New Horizons in Adult Education and Human Resource Development*, 27(2), pp. 3–12.

Hyland, K., 2011. The presentation of self in scholarly life: identity and marginalization in academic homepages. *English for Specific Purposes*, 30(4), pp. 286–297.

Jain, S., George, G. and Maltarich, M., 2009. Academics or entrepreneurs? Investigating role identity modification of university scientists involved in commercialization activity. *Research Policy*, 38(6), pp. 922–935.

Kehm, B.M. and Teichler, U., 2013. *The academic profession in Europe: new tasks and new challenges*, Dordrecht: Springer.

Kimber, M., 2003. The tenured 'Core' and the tenuous 'Periphery': the casualisation of academic work in Australian universities. *Journal of Higher Education Policy and Management*, 25(1), pp. 41–50.

Knights, D. and Clarke, C.A., 2014. It's a bittersweet symphony, this life: fragile academic selves and insecure identities at work. *Organization Studies*, 35(3), pp. 335–357.

Krause, K.-L.D., 2014. Challenging perspectives on learning and teaching in the disciplines: the academic voice. *Studies in Higher Education*, 39(1), pp. 2–19.

Kumar, K., Roberts, C. and Thistlethwaite, J., 2011. Entering and navigating academic medicine: academic clinician-educators' experiences. *Medical Education*, 45(5), pp. 497–503.

Levin, J.S. and Shaker, G.G., 2011. The hybrid and dualistic identity of full-time non-tenure-track faculty. *American Behavioral Scientist*, 55(11), pp. 1461–1484.

Macfarlane, B., 2012. *Intellectual leadership in higher education: renewing the role of the university professor*, New York: Routledge.

Martimianakis, M.A. and Muzzin, L., 2015. Discourses of interdisciplinarity and the shifting topography of academic work: generational perspectives on facilitating and resisting neoliberalism. *Studies in Higher Education*, 40(8), pp. 1454–1470.

Morison, R., Erickson, T. and Dychtwald, K., 2006. Managing middlescence. *Harvard Business Review*, 84(March), pp. 78–87.

Nyhagen, G.M. and Baschung, L., 2013. New organisational structures and the transformation of academic work. *Higher Education*, 66(4), pp. 409–423.

Rowan, L., 2013. What price success? The impact of the quest for student satisfaction on university academics. *International Journal of Pedagogies and Learning*, 8(2), pp. 136–150.

Seligman, M.E.P., 2011. *Flourish*, North Sydney, NSW: Random House Australia.

Shin, J.C. and Jung, J., 2014. Academics' job satisfaction and job stress across countries in the changing academic environments. *Higher Education*, 67(5), pp. 603–620.

Smith, J., 2010. Forging identities: the experiences of probationary lecturers in the UK. *Studies in Higher Education*, 35(5), pp. 577–591.

Stupnisky, R.H., Weaver-Hightower, M.B. and Kartoshkina, Y., 2015. Exploring and testing the predictors of new faculty success: a mixed methods study. *Studies in Higher Education*, 40(2), pp. 368–390.

Sutherland, K.A., 2015. Constructions of success in academia: an early career perspective. *Studies in Higher Education*, pp. 1–17. Available online at DOI 10.1080/03075079.2015.1072150

Szelényi, K. and Rhoads, R.A., 2013. Academic culture and citizenship in transitional societies: case studies from China and Hungary. *Higher Education*, 66(4), pp. 425–438.

Teeuwsen, P., Ratković, S. and Tilley, S.A., 2014. Becoming academics: experiencing legitimate peripheral participation in part-time doctoral studies. *Studies in Higher Education*, 39(4), pp. 680–694.

Van den Brink, M., 2011. Scouting for talent: appointment practices of women professors in academic medicine. *Social Science and Medicine*, 72(12), pp. 2033–2040.

Watermeyer, R., 2014. Impact in the REF: issues and obstacles. *Studies in Higher Education*, 41(2), pp. 1–16.

Winter, R.P. and O'Donohue, W., 2012. Academic identity tensions in the public university: which values really matter? *Journal of Higher Education Policy and Management*, 34(6), pp. 565–573.

Ylijoki, O.H. and Henriksson, L., 2015. Tribal, proletarian and entrepreneurial career stories: junior academics as a case in point. *Studies in Higher Education*, pp. 1–17. Pre-publication copy. Available online at DOI: 10.1080/03075079.2015.1092129

Chapter 12

Entering academe

The increasing volatility of the higher education sector has had unfortunate consequences for those seeking a foothold in academic careers. Notably, the stability of senior academics who hold continuous or tenured appointments has led to a decreased turnover of senior staff (May *et al.* 2011). This has put pressure on limited university budgets as their staffing costs continue to escalate. This would not be an issue if the sector was stable and predictable. Unfortunately, it is not. Uncertain funding, unpredictable student demand, rising costs and an increasingly competitive sector all necessitate cautious management of the staffing complement, given that it is generally the largest budget expenditure in universities. The economic downturns of the last decade have forced strong oversight of budgets and expenditure and a recognition that there must be sufficient flexibility, to be agile and adaptive if shifts in student demand or research funding occur.

As a consequence, we have seen a much less generous employment setting for early career academics and researchers. They will often be employed on part-time or casual contracts, and may find themselves filling a series of short-term appointments (Kimber 2003). There is much less surety about gaining an academic appointment, with approximately half of doctoral graduates likely to achieve an academic or research post (McAlpine 2010). They are precarious employees, evidencing high work uncertainty and insecurity, limited control over work intensity and flows, minimal industrial protection, as well as limited and disrupted income streams (Rodgers and Rodgers 1989). For the majority of aspiring academics, it will be necessary to show very high potential or a strong track record of experience and research before securing ongoing employment. This can be particularly challenging when casual appointment periods are short, strongly focused on the immediate role and provide little sponsorship to assist in building the requisite skills or outcomes. Some institutions also act as gatekeepers to developmental opportunities: restricting access to staff who hold longer-term appointments.

This emerging context raises two key issues that universities need to consider: first, how can we best prepare doctoral students and postdoctoral staff as competitive, high-talent candidates who can progress to viable academic careers? Second, how can universities provide the right development and support to facilitate successful transition into academic careers by new staff?

The aspirant academic/researcher

There are many different paths into academe. One of the most common is via completion of a higher education research degree, such as a doctorate. However, other paths include entering as an experienced professional; assuming a teaching role; transitioning from a research role to an academic role; or filling a particular specialist niche. Each avenue is predicated on showing evidence of potential capacity and established capabilities. This is putting increased pressure on aspirant academics to better plan their career preparation in advance, so that they appear competitive and desirable. It also places the onus on universities and their development groups to ensure better support for research students to prepare them for multiple futures.

Future proofing the doctorate

Across the world, there has been considerable discussion as to the nature and purpose of doctoral programs (Blaj-Ward 2011; Lee and Danby 2012; McKenna et al. 2014; Walker et al. 2008). The basic premise of a research degree is that the student will develop a rich and in-depth professional grounding that enables them to make an original and substantial contribution to their field of knowledge (Burton et al. 2009). Traditionally, the evidence of this knowledge and capability rested in the final thesis or equivalent products stemming from the research. In recent years, however, there has been considerable debate as to the role a doctoral program should play in:

- preparing the candidate for successful completion of their research;
- grounding them in the key capabilities to secure an academic position (if so desired or available);
- preparing them for teaching roles (Simon and Pleschová 2012);
- providing a suitable grounding in interdisciplinary research (Frodeman 2010);
- supporting their transition toward working in or with industry (Borrell-Damian et al. 2010);
- increasing the impact and outcomes of their research (Nurius and Kemp 2014).

These pressures to reform the doctoral approach and focus have forced a deeper consideration of the pedagogical underpinnings, desired learning outcomes and program approaches that will best support more holistic and future-focused outcomes.

A key benefit of this debate is the recognition that doctoral candidates need stronger grounding in the transferable skills that ensure they are employable, no matter the career path they select. However, the desired professional repertoire grows ever larger, reflecting an increasing concern for providing a sound grounding in key capabilities that are required by academics, professionals and researchers. For example, students will benefit from the following as part of their doctoral training:

- An *induction and orientation* that clarifies the purpose and focus of their research program and the generic skills they should be gaining. This guidance acts as an important form of acculturation, offering a clear message as to the expectations and performance outcomes that will be expected. This is particularly important for those who may enrol in hybrid (Mu *et al.* 2014) or remote programs where university engagement may be less frequent.
- Guidance on cultivating a *strategic career* that reflects their strengths, goals and aspirations to support their long-term goals and ambitions. A realistic understanding of potential career paths and their requirements is an important part of the early candidature period. Those who wish to enter academe, for example, benefit from a clear understanding of the research track record that they should develop during their candidature.
- The development of high *ethical capabilities*, particularly with respect to performing responsible research. Many universities are introducing compulsory programs for doctoral candidates to ensure they are clear about their research obligations. This understanding also extends to their rights as authors and the protocols that guide good research practice.
- Skills in obtaining *funding* or writing grants. This capability signals that the individual is able to clearly articulate their research and map the real costs of those activities.
- *Grant and research project management* (Debowski 2012). This professional capability is particularly valued in industry, but is also essential for good research management (De Grande *et al.* 2014).
- The development of effective *networking and collaborative* capabilities. The capacity to build robust and respectful relationships with a range of stakeholders (including industry, academic, research, community and political groups) is an essential skill for professionals and academics (Debowski 2012). The ability to interact across a global arena is of great value, along with a sensitive approach to the international context in which research operates (Wellington *et al.* 2012). The ability to work in a transdisciplinary context is also becoming increasingly important (Frodeman 2010; Lee and Danby 2012; Woods *et al.* 2014).
- Communication of the research outcomes through *publishing and dissemination* across various media platforms.
- Accessing *teaching* experience during the research candidature. This offers an important opportunity to build some evidence of teaching potential, seek student feedback and learn some basic educational practices (Simon and Pleschová 2012).
- A more advanced capability that may be encouraged for those hoping to move to industry or postdoctoral roles which relates to *leadership and management*.

The capacity to manage a team or guide the outcomes of others can be a valuable asset when looking for roles after graduation.

There are many other skills and capabilities that are being identified for inclusion in a doctoral program. The challenge is balancing the mix of knowledge production, broad-based professional and transferable skill development, as well as career positioning. The integration of a broader, more targeted curriculum necessitates careful planning of learning activities and the monitoring of both short- and long-term outcomes. It also requires well-advised mentoring and support to ensure the individual can develop professional skills and a research track record while still progressing their research. Central to these outcomes is a clear understanding of career management and the realities of academic work and employment. The active engagement of the student in managing their development plan provides foundational career strategy skills. The increasing restrictions on doctoral completion time frames further challenge students who take longer to move toward their doctoral identity and more sophisticated self-management capabilities.

As a result of these increasing expectations on doctoral programs, many universities have moved toward a more structured, capability-focused curriculum that encourages these additional competencies. In the United Kingdom, Centres for Doctoral Training have encouraged a strong shift toward thinking differently about the outcomes a doctoral program should achieve. They have encouraged increased engagement with industry and provided an important conduit for future careers for many of the candidates. Certainly, there is no question that novice academics who have received a solid grounding across these various capabilities will be in a better position to move into academic or professional work. This major shift in focus from apprenticeship to developmental program puts additional pressure on academic supervisors to play a stronger role in acting as mentors and sponsors to assist planning for the future as well as guiding the doctoral research. The shifts in expectations and standards also pressures universities to provide effective developmental programs and support. These programs are likely to necessitate multiple modes of delivery to reach all candidates.

Transitioning to academe from doctoral studies

The completion of the doctorate is one rite of passage; the next is entering academe. As noted earlier, the transition to academic work can be highly competitive and unpredictable. There are many factors that will impact on this successful entry: the individual's mobility, track record, profile, sponsorship and just being in the right place at the right time may all play a part in setting up a fortuitous opportunity. In other circumstances, individuals may find it necessary to build a patchwork career base, meshing different employers and roles together to form a whole. The experience can offer rich connections with potential employers in the future, although this is a precarious approach to an academic career if it continues for a long period.

Tenure track

The most desirable path to academe for many is via the tenure track or continuing appointments. These positions allow the individual to learn and develop their capabilities through teaching and research until they are deemed to be tenurable. This provides an important measure of security and encourages strong identity formation: the individual is connected with a cognate group and is part of the broader discipline, faculty or department. There will be opportunities to learn and develop, and ready access to models, mentors and funding to support their plans. While the first years may be difficult, requiring considerable acculturation, most will find themselves part of a broader professional network. The achievement of tenure necessitates a very focused emphasis on university standards and expectations. There is also a delicate balance between illustrating the capacity to function as an independent researcher and someone who collaborates. For some, this can generate some very confused mixed messages as to what is really important. A mentor is a critical success factor while navigating these first few years. However, network participation, career management and mentorship can be hard to initiate in this very complex working world. Guidance from leaders and/or HE developers can provide a crucial bridge for these practices.

Research-focused roles

Many early career academics commence their careers as postdoctorates (Akerlind 2005; Chen *et al.* 2015). These roles are normally as part of a research team or via a grant and are for a set period of time. The experience can set up individuals for a very successful career, supporting gaining grants, building a profile, setting up teams and establishing a research identity. The capacity to fund oneself and the team from competitive funding can be very stressful, particularly where funding sources are limited. The pressure to fund one's research has become a major focus for most Western nations in recent years, and this has necessitated even more sophisticated capabilities with respect to gaining sponsorship. It has also pushed a stronger focus on collaboration and industry linkages. Those wishing to pursue a purely research-focused career will therefore require considerable resilience, fortitude and capacity to forge sustainable and productive partnerships with a range of parties. They will also need to build a program of research that shows progressive strengthening of outcomes (Debowski 2010).

A key challenge that is often evident when postdoctorates meet to talk about their experiences is the diversity of cultures in which they operate. Postdoctorates come into their roles hoping to be given opportunities to develop grants, publish, build their networks and increase their impact, thereby ensuring they are well-positioned for their next career opportunity. However, this is dependent on the calibre of leadership within their team. Too many will depart from their contracted role much worse off than when they entered. They will be less competitive, pigeon-holed and invisible (McAlpine 2010). While some may be ill-suited to the tough world of research, others struggle with ungenerous supervisors who see them as fodder, readily replaceable and expendable. Again, they need to be supported by mentors and to be strategic careerists. It is concerning, too, to see how powerless university human resource management services are in dealing with toxic cultures or bullies. The high turnover of particular research groups is rarely monitored or addressed. This can have real career consequences for junior members of research teams.

An interesting career path that has emerged for many researchers is that of research manager, who ensures effective oversight of projects or programs of research. After completing one or two postdoctorates, this can be an enticing channel to pursue: it keeps the researcher in the world of knowledge production, but with a little more predictability and control. Another option that some researchers pursue is the shift to research development, which also draws on this real experience to inform the guidance they provide to their university community.

Teaching-focused roles

A third academic career avenue is through teaching-focused appointments. We have seen an increasing diversification of university career paths, as institutions better articulate the types of activities that need to be funded and managed. The establishment of teaching specialist roles has been welcomed by passionate individuals who wish to make a difference to student learning. These academics may fill important roles, including coordinating service- or work-integrated learning (Ferns 2014), large teams or innovations.

Conversely, a new academic who is offered a teaching-focused role will be likely to carry substantial teaching and coordination duties. These can be quite onerous, particularly if a large number of tutors must be coordinated. They may be extensively involved in setting up programs, delivering online courses or overseeing other key educational priorities. Those who are very competent may find that they continue in these roles for many years. However, this can have considerable consequences if the desired path is to transition to a teaching-research appointment. The capacity to build a credible and competitive research track record that supports the desired career shift may prove difficult to achieve unless sponsorship and guidance is provided.

Those who are teaching-focused in casual, unpredictable roles will be even more challenged due to their limited time and access to resources which would allow them to undertake research, attend conferences and build a notable presence in the field (Percy *et al.* 2008). There is considerable risk that this could be a long-term, tightly confining role that offers little sponsorship or security. Instead of following a research track, the individual may find that they are juggled according to student demand each semester. In many cases, universities will pay by the hour for teaching, thereby limiting the presence of these individuals on campus to face-to-face teaching only, and providing little access to infrastructure and community, including development opportunities. Building a long-term career will be increasingly challenging as the individual becomes less competitive over time.

Entering academe from the professions

Universities are particularly fortunate in that they often attract professionals who have led a full and rich career into the academic world. While they are "new" academics, they are highly experienced, well-regarded experts who bring a wealth of knowledge to their role. They are well-attuned to the professional world and its expectations of graduates, and may act as important links to external groups. However, they now face a very different world in which different measures of status and success are employed. They may lack a doctoral qualification, having built other credentials more suited to their previous field. They may have never undertaken research. They may not be experienced teachers. They are likely to be very unprepared for the extreme workloads that will be necessary in the first few years as they find their way and build their curricula, identity and credible outcomes (Eisenberg 2011; Lanzon *et al.* 2012; Sabel and Archer 2014; Tong *et al.* 2014). In the case of clinicians, they must straddle two very demanding professions.

For some professionals, the entry into a new academic career is a wonderful, engaging and fulfilling experience. They are valued for their rich insights and enhance the curriculum and student experience with real-world experience. They may bring new perspectives to research and move into a strong niche that fully deploys their experience. Others may find it harder to be a newcomer whose experiences are perhaps less valued. The ability to write in a scholarly way and identify a viable research niche may also prove challenging, as these are new skills that require considerable perseverance in the developmental phase. In some cases, the university may appoint the individual at a very junior level; signalling that they regard the past roles as insignificant. These experiences can all lead to considerable insecurity on the part of these new careerists. It is even more challenging if they continue to practice in their professional space and work as a part-time academic: the duality of the roles can put considerable pressure on their available time and capacity.

Facilitating the growth of the new academic

From this overview, it can be seen that the entry into academic work can be smooth or fractured. It may set the individual up for success or failure. The role that departments, supervisors and universities play in facilitating successful capabilities and strategies can be a major factor in determining the outcome. Some strategies that can greatly assist newcomer academics include:

- a comprehensive orientation program that provides a clear overview of the institution, its policies, employment practices and standards;
- an effective local induction into the role and its requirements, with resources to be provided and support to be offered;
- orientation mentors who can explain the culture, protocols and work practices (Debowski, 2012);

- clear guidance on role expectations and performance standards;
- encouragement to map and implement a career strategy into regular activities (McAlpine *et al.* 2013);
- access to developmental and training opportunities (with casual staff paid to attend), particularly with respect to learning about systems and core policies;
- support for the individual to meet with other new colleagues;
- mentorship to guide career planning and capability development (Debowski 2012; de Janasz and Sullivan 2004);
- career development support that spans all elements of the role, rather than isolated components (Adcroft and Taylor 2013);
- sponsorship of the individual into the relevant networks and opportunities to further their career;
- guidance on the importance of participating in networks and development opportunities despite feeling busy;
- support to develop reflexive approaches to identity formation, career management and goal setting (Mathieson 2011);
- regular meetings with the supervisor to discuss issues, questions and strategy;
- monitoring of well-being and staff satisfaction over the course of time.

Conclusion

The transition to academe requires a reformation of academic identity and focus. This shift can greatly undermine an individual's confidence and may even lead to feelings of being an "imposter" who is insufficiently qualified to be there (Hutchins 2015). The support and guidance of experienced academics and a well-articulated higher education development service can make a substantial difference to encouraging a successful career path, enhanced capabilities and assurance upon entering academe. Of particular importance is increasing access to development and support for those who are employed in precarious roles.

References

Adcroft, A. and Taylor, D., 2013. Support for new career academics: an integrated model for research intensive university business and management schools. *Studies in Higher Education*, 38(6), pp. 827–840.

Akerlind, G.S., 2005. Postdoctoral researchers: roles, functions and career prospects. *Higher Education Research & Development*, 24(1), pp. 21–40.

Blaj-Ward, L., 2011. Skills versus pedagogy? Doctoral research training in the UK Arts and Humanities. *Higher Education Research & Development*, 30(6), pp. 697–708.

Borrell-Damian, L., Brown, T., Dearing, A., Font, J. Hagen, S., Metcalfe, J. and Smith, J., 2010. Collaborative doctoral education: university-industry partnerships for enhancing knowledge exchange. *Higher Education Policy*, 23(4), pp. 493–514.

Burton, C.R., Duxbury, J., French, B., Monks, R. and Carter, B., 2009. Re-visioning the doctoral research degree in nursing in the United Kingdom. *Nurse Education Today*, 29(4), pp. 423–431.

Chen, S., McAlpine, L. and Amundsen, C., 2015. Postdoctoral positions as preparation for desired careers: a narrative approach to understanding postdoctoral experience. *Higher Education Research & Development*, 34(6), pp. 1083–1096.

Debowski, S., 2010. Leading research in an evolving world: implications for higher education development, policy and practice. In M. Devlin, J. Nagy, and A. Lichtenberg, eds, *Research and development in higher education: reshaping higher education*, 6–9 July, 2010, Melbourne: HERDSA, pp. 213–222.

Debowski, S., 2012. *The new academic: a strategic handbook*, London: Open University Press.

De Grande, H., De Boyser, K., Vandevelde, K. and Van Rossem, R., 2014. From academia to industry: are doctorate holders ready? *Journal of the Knowledge Economy*, 5(3), pp. 538–561.

Eisenberg, M.J., 2011. *The physician scientist's career guide*, New York: Springer.

Ferns, S. (ed.), 2014. *Work integrated learning in the curriculum*, Milperra, NSW: Higher Education Research and Development Society of Australasia.

Frodeman, R. (ed.), 2010. *The Oxford handbook of interdisciplinarity*, Oxford: Oxford University Press.

Hutchins, H.M., 2015. Outing the imposter: a study exploring imposter phenomenon among higher education faculty. *New Horizons in Adult Education and Human Resource Development*, 27(2), pp. 3–12.

de Janasz, S.C. and Sullivan, S.E., 2004. Multiple mentoring in academe: Developing the professorial network. *Journal of Vocational Behavior*, 64(2), pp. 263–283.

Kimber, M., 2003. The tenured 'Core' and the tenuous 'Periphery': the casualisation of academic work in Australian universities. *Journal of Higher Education Policy and Management*, 25(1), pp. 41–50.

Lanzon, J., Edwards, S.P. and Inglehart, M.R., 2012. Choosing academia versus private practice: factors affecting oral maxillofacial surgery residents' career choices. *Journal of Oral and Maxillofacial Surgery*, 70(7), pp. 1751–1761.

Lee, A. and Danby, S. (eds), 2012. *Reshaping doctoral education: changing approaches and pedagogies*, Milton Park, Oxfordshire: Routledge.

McAlpine, L., 2010. Fixed-term researchers in the social sciences: passionate investment, yet marginalizing experiences. *International Journal for Academic Development*, 15(3), pp. 229–240.

McAlpine, L., Amundsen, C. and Turner, G., 2013. Constructing post-PhD careers: negotiating opportunities and personal goals. *International Journal for Researcher Development*, 4(1), pp. 39–54.

McKenna, H., Keeney, S., Kim, M.J. and Park, C.G., 2014. Quality of doctoral nursing education in the United Kingdom: exploring the views of doctoral students and staff based on a cross-sectional questionnaire survey. *Journal of Advanced Nursing*, 70(7), pp. 1639–1652.

Mathieson, S., 2011. Developing academic agency through critical reflection: a sociocultural approach to academic induction programmes. *International Journal for Academic Development*, 16(3), pp. 243–256.

May, R., Strachan, G., Broadbent, K. and Peetz, D., 2011. The casual approach to university teaching: time for a re-think? In K. Krause, M. Buckridge, C. Grimmer and S. Purbrick-Illek, eds, *Research and development in higher education: reshaping higher education*, HERSDA: Gold Coast, Australia, pp. 188–197.

Mu, K., Coppard, B.M., Bracciano, A.G. and Bradberry, J.C., 2014. Comparison of on-campus and hybrid student outcomes in occupational therapy doctoral education. *American Journal of Occupational Therapy*, 68(Supplement 2), p. S51.

Nurius, P.S. and Kemp, S.P., 2014. Transdisciplinarity and translation: preparing social work doctoral students for high impact research. *Research on Social Work Practice*, 24(5), pp. 625–635.

Percy, A., Scoufis, M., Parry, S., Goody, A., Hicks, M., Macdonald, I., Martinez, K., Szorenyi-Teishi, N., Ryan, Y., Wills, S. and Sheridan, L., 2008. *The RED report, recognition–enhancement–development: The contribution of sessional teachers to higher education*, Sydney: Australian Learning and Teaching Council.

Rodgers, G. and Rodgers, J. (eds), 1989. *Precarious jobs in labour market regulation: the growth of atypical employment in Western Europe*, Geneva, Switzerland: International Institute for Labour Studies.

Sabel, E. and Archer, J., 2014. 'Medical Education Is the Ugly Duckling of the Medical World' and other challenges to medical educators' identity construction: a qualitative study. *Academic Medicine*, 89(11), pp. 1474–1480.

Simon, E. and Pleschová, G., 2012. *Teacher development in higher education: existing programs, program impact, and future trends*, Hoboken, NJ: Taylor & Francis.

Tong, C.W., Ahmad, T., Brittain, E.L., Bunch, T.J., Damp, J.B., Dardas, T., Hijar, A., Hill, J.A., Hilliard, A.A., Houser, S.R., Jahangir, E., Kates, A.M., Kim, D., Lindman, B.R., Ryan, J.J., Rzeszut, A.K., Xivaram, C.A., Valente, A.M. and Freeman, A.M., 2014. Challenges facing early career academic cardiologists. *Journal of the American College of Cardiology*, 63(21), pp. 2199–2208.

Walker, G.E., Golde, C.M., Jones, L., Bueschel, A.C. and Hutchings, P., 2008. *The formation of scholars: rethinking doctoral education for the twenty-first century*, San Francisco, CA: Jossey-Bass.

Wellington, J., Pitts, S. and Biggs, C., 2012. *Becoming a successful early career researcher*, London: Taylor & Francis.

Woods, K.V., Peek, K.E. and Richards-Kortum, R., 2014. Mentoring by design: integrating medical professional competencies into bioengineering and medical physics graduate training. *Journal of Cancer Education*, 29(4), pp. 680–688.

Chapter 13

Academic collegiality and service

There is an inherent contradiction in the messages that academics receive. On the one hand, they are encouraged to be generous team players, constructively orientated and service active. This creates a strong platform for a range of critical activities that universities need to accomplish in order to function (Shattock 2010). On the other hand, academics are pushed to perform and to be high achievers, demonstrating individual excellence and differentiating themselves from the crowd. This can encourage narcissistic, selfish and even anti-social behaviours. It can increase competitiveness, a reluctance to share and an unwillingness to spend time on administration and other "unmeasured" activities (Cipriano 2011). Where the leader lacks concern for others, it becomes increasingly problematic, particularly if they fail to sponsor and advance their subordinates or protégés (Saltmarsh *et al.* 2011). These leadership styles can generate high turnover, including the attrition of good potential employees from the sector, and may also incur considerable costs through ill-health, complaints and loss of productivity (Gilbert *et al.* 2012; Schyns and Schilling 2013). Poorly behaved individuals also provide a highly visible model as to the dominant behaviours that will be accepted.

Collegiality has long been regarded as a foundational characteristic of universities. It describes the cordial relationships that operate between colleagues across an institution (Cipriano and Buller 2012). Collegiality entails working with others to achieve a common purpose and respecting the different contributions that others make. Rowland (2008) takes this a step further, suggesting that collegiality also encompasses "intellectual love," a desire to exchange, share and interact with others to promote learning and knowledge. This point of view argues that collegiality is therefore a critical foundation for both teaching and research, and indeed, broader engagement within the university. Academic work is knowledge-based, encompassing regular interchange across colleagues. Universities are highly interactive, relying on trust and respect to build sustainable and productive relationships across all levels of the institution and beyond. An academic is therefore expected to reflect collegial practices on a daily basis, in their personal exchanges, formal committee work and management of roles and responsibilities. This concept of collegiality also implies a willingness to take responsibility for the collective outcomes of the work group and/or the university.

There is strong recognition that the consensus-based structures of universities, and their dependence on academic contributions, necessitate widespread collegial contributions to collective work. However, as Cipriano and Buller (2012) note, the difficulties in articulating what these behaviours mean and look like makes it hard to explore and guide people toward improved approaches. Even so, they note that in the United States, collegiality, or the lack of it, has influenced legal judgements on employment or dismissal decisions (Cipriano and Buller 2012).

Collegiality has been under considerable threat as university governance and practices have become more centralised and managerialistic (Burnes *et al.* 2014; Fredman and Doughney 2012). It can be argued that universities have themselves exacerbated the problem through their ongoing quest for high academic performance. Consider, for example, the reliance on research metrics to determine the value of an academic. Given the direct linkage to rewards, recognition and sanctions, it builds a very powerful message to all academics: *If you don't demonstrate research competence/excellence, then your other activities will not compensate for this lack.* Messages that promote these individualistic behaviours can undermine many practices that encourage collegiality and collective effort (Rowland 2008). Zabrodska *et al.* (2011) suggest that this is one of the causes for bullying, that incivility in the neoliberal university can be attributable to performativity and the pressure to produce. However, this implies that academics are simply being acted on, not acting, in these settings.

Many individuals would take it as a given that they should act in an ethical, respectful and inclusive way toward their colleagues and contribute to the university beyond what is being assessed through formal mechanisms. Unfortunately, this is not universally understood or reflected in real behaviours (Stupnisky *et al.* 2015). Academics will encounter a range of conflicting messages and cues from their colleagues, their university reward and recognition systems and their supervisors. They may experience bullying or mobbing (group action against an individual) (Keim and McDermott 2010; Metzger *et al.* 2015). Talented academics may be located in a community that encourages mediocrity, where they may be marginalised, or where group systems and rewards are adapted to increase support for the mediocre majority (Hermanowicz 2013).

The challenge of guiding academic behaviour has prompted universities to clarify what is meant by collegiality, including, for example, as a specific academic expectation to be reviewed annually. However, many universities have grappled with this concept and, as a result, have left a void that makes the promotion of civil communities more difficult, given the lack of articulation and guidance. In this chapter, then, a description of collegiality is offered, with guidance on the role that different actors in the university might play in promoting these productive behaviours. It will also be shown that this is a joint responsibility between university leaders at all levels, the HE developer and the individual themselves. In tandem, the particular role of service to the university will be explored. This is often under-recognised in terms of its educative and generative function for the individual and the university generally. Again, there are many messages that percolate around service. In this chapter, it will be shown to be an important apprenticeship for leadership and engagement. The fundamental need to encourage a more engaged, contributory professoriate as the next generation moves into the sector will be emphasised.

Unpacking collegiality

The notion of being an academic colleague carries with it a number of underlying assumptions. At the most fundamental level, collegiality can be described as the contribution the individual makes to the workplace community and a positive working environment. Embedded in this statement is the assumption that the individual will:

- apply ethical and respectful approaches to all aspects of their work;
- collaborate with others in teams, working groups, school or institutional settings;
- demonstrate honesty, integrity, empathy, respect and tolerance in dealings with others;
- influence people's behaviour and decisions in effective and constructive ways;
- model cultural competence by building productive relationships with students and staff from diverse cultures and backgrounds;
- support the development of others through the provision of sponsorship, mentoring and/or coaching;
- actively reflect, promote and implement relevant equal opportunity and work-based health and safety legislation, policies and practices and, if established, the university's own Code of Conduct.

Underpinning these attributes is the capacity to manage one's own behaviours, actions, responses and attitudes. Academic work requires considerable self-knowledge, including an accurate assessment of one's strengths, personal approaches to work and limitations. Equally, there is also a need to be adaptive and flexible, to persevere and be resilient, to learn from challenging experiences and to seek ongoing learning about oneself. The capacity to differentiate one's own behaviours and those of other actors when dissecting problems is particularly helpful in difficult work contexts (Field 2010). Inherent in this foundational base is a willingness to seek and act on constructive feedback. This responsiveness is a strong foundation for future success.

The capacity to model emotional, social and cultural intelligence is also critical to a successful academic career (Ang and Dyne 2015; Boyatzis *et al.* 2015). Relationships are the foundation of academic work. Few academics succeed in isolation: most need to collaborate, work in teams and ultimately, lead productive, effective groups. The ability to engage with and contribute to constructive formal and informal processes across diverse university groups is essential. This requires additional skills that may need to be consciously developed over time, including the capacity to listen, communicate, reflect and provide feedback. The ability to guide emotional or crucial conversations where there is strong engagement by all parties, for example, will be a particularly valuable capability (Patterson 2012). Avoidance of conflict can lead to much larger issues over time. Thus, an ability to act with integrity, courage, respect and good judgement is also an important element of ensuring a strong collegial setting.

The development of these basic foundational capacities flows to more complex roles that most academics will later assume as part of their teaching, research or leadership roles. For example, they will find themselves encouraged to:

- engage with and contribute to the work of the discipline, school, institute, and/or university;
- effectively lead groups to improve the quality and outcomes of teaching, research or other administrative activities;
- develop and mobilise networks or teams of colleagues to solve key challenges;
- form and maintain collaborative relationships or partnerships within the university, regionally, nationally and/or internationally;
- effectively negotiate links and partnerships with industry, government and community, regionally, nationally and globally.

Inherent in these interactions is the capacity to be adaptive, tailoring interactions and responses in a way that matches the community, role and purpose that is being supported. To be successful in achieving these complex outcomes, the academic needs to possess a nuanced understanding of the university governance structure, systems, policies and processes. They will need to reflect the necessary protocols, ensuring they are representing the university and their profession in a constructive, positive and professional manner. Those who collaborate will benefit from developing a shared purpose and an ethical approach to contribution (Adler *et al.* 2011).

Thus, collegiality is a complex but critical facet of academic behaviour that helps to sustain the university setting as a desirable, effective and productive workplace (Shattock 2010). It ensures the individual can seek help from other colleagues when required, and means that those in need are being looked out for. It is the foundational principle of mentorship and sponsorship and encourages each person to seek ways of enhancing the culture and the lived experience of each colleague.

The non-collegial academic

Despite the promotion of collegiality as a desired virtue in academic spheres, there is considerable evidence of individuals and communities that behave badly (Beckmann *et al.* 2013; Wright and Hill 2015; Zabrodska *et al.* 2011). There is insufficient space to explore these issues in detail. However, three factors may be highlighted for consideration. First, as previously noted, the institutional and leadership cues will strongly predict the cultural mores and practices that are favoured. Failure to recognise, value or promote collegiality sends a strong message as to what matters (Schein 2010). Gedro and Wang (2013) illustrate the power of encouraging community engagement to address non-collegial behaviours.

There are academics who simply lack the personal insight or willingness to consider how their behaviours impact on others. Their emotional or social intelligence can be quite under-developed, and they may be quite ignorant of broader perceptions of their behaviours (Boyatzis *et al.* 2015). The concept of academic freedom, for example, can be wrongly employed to justify being argumentative, aggressive, bullying and dismissive of others (see Gappa *et al.* 2007). An absence of feedback will encourage these behaviours to continue.

And there are others who are conscious manipulators of the politics and the context for their own personal gain. Sociopathic behaviour does occur in universities and in some institutions is encouraged (Babiak and Hare, 2006). Where checks and balances are not in place, universities find it particularly hard to address dysfunctional behaviour if the perpetrator is a highly celebrated, successful senior staff member. The public nature of the review process and the general outcry that can generate from clamping down on these behaviours can encourage avoidance of the issue. On the other hand, staff are increasingly aware of the fact that dysfunctional behaviours are detrimental to their well-being and are encouraged to name and act on them (Field 2010). In the meantime, many individuals may have been harmed, along with the university's reputation as a desirable workplace. Thus, an absence of policies and guidance on collegiality is a recipe for major crises later, and can decrease productivity and morale. It is important to act on these uncivil behaviours early, as a later section will outline.

Service: an undervalued component of university activity

University performance and outcomes are strongly reliant on the contribution of academics to achieve their outcomes. Employee engagement describes the individual's emotional and cognitive support for achieving university outcomes and the behaviours and effort they expend on enacting those commitments (Shuck 2011). In a university, this is often described as service.

Many universities are explicitly promoting service activities as an important function of academic work. Service is normally perceived as encompassing additional roles that the individual undertakes to support strategic or operational university activities. Universities are dependent on academic involvement in these activities. Without academics, many important functions could not be undertaken. Their involvement in committees, student advisory services, developmental projects, innovations and liaison, for example, are essential to the ongoing enhancement of university services and practices. There are numerous ways for service to be enacted, from simple participation in student open days, information sessions or other activities, through to more dedicated roles, including as coordinators, committee chairs or working party membership. Promotion, annual review and probationary processes may all require evidence of an individual's contribution to their university's service activities.

Service is a facet of academic work that can sometimes be viewed as an imposition on university staff. Mamiseishvili *et al.* (2015), for example, found that mid-career academics were notably less satisfied with their service roles and recognition of their contributions compared with early career academics and senior professors. This may be due to the limited recognition of service as an integral component of academic work, particularly by more senior academics who have been reared in a different era of the academy. In a recent session with academic performance advisers, for example, one senior academic noted that she told her junior colleagues to "pick any committee and make sure you don't have to do anything: it doesn't count: you just have to show that you have sat on something." Interestingly, other senior advisers at that meeting rejected this statement, noting that there is a real need to make a difference through the service one offers.

In reality, service offers an important learning environment for developing the many capabilities that support teaching, research, leadership and engagement. As representatives of their university, it is important that academics acquire an understanding as to how their institution operates and functions. Their capacity to articulate and relate to their employer's strategic priorities encourages better representation of the university to external groups. Further, service roles are a valuable mechanism for building a strong institutional profile and identity as a result of increased interactions with administrators, executive leaders and colleagues from across the institution. The academic will see different models of committee management, gain access to a diversity of networks and potentially be offered access to some exciting and different roles. Participation on committees and other formal decision-making forums offers guidance on how groups can be effectively chaired and guided toward productive outcomes and processes. The capacity to communicate and engage with diverse communities and participants supports future engagement activities beyond the institution. Increased political competence will stand the individual in good stead as they move into more senior roles (Johnson 2008). Without this grounding, it becomes much harder to assume a position of authority with confidence. Thus, service can be a valuable apprenticeship as the academic moves toward more formal university or external roles.

However, institutions can be insatiable in their desire to have academics enact service roles. It is important that these service contributions be balanced and contribute to the ongoing development of the academic. Each role should encourage the acquisition or consolidation of key capabilities that will support the advancement of the academic toward leadership and engagement roles. For the most part, the choice of service roles will be determined by the individual. There will be many options from which to choose. These might relate to teaching, service or broader administrative roles. The avenues for service may be opportunities that are open to all, or more finely attuned to the academic's particular talents and strengths. Ideally, each new service role that is undertaken should complement and extend the experiences gained from previous activities. While the initial roles may be primarily participatory in nature, over time, the nature of service will progress toward leadership activities and the guidance of others. This growth in influence and authority offers an important foundation to facilitate the development of the critical capabilities that also support external engagement. Of course, there will be some academics who choose to continue to enact service within their university as their primary target. They recognise the importance of continuing to promote university strategy to further the core goals of the institution.

The non-contributory academic

Despite the benefits of being and encouragement to be service-focused, there remain many disengaged academics who are largely invisible when volunteers are sought, or when groups come together. There can be many reasons for this. They may:

- be under considerable pressure to meet deadlines;
- be highly stressed due to workloads;
- need to manage their time commitments within constrained schedules (e.g. family duties or dual employers);
- carry a large substantive workload;
- have been strongly advised by colleagues to remain disengaged;
- find the environment critical, hostile or unsupportive;
- be seeking promotion and do not feel service is a key facet of the portfolio they are consolidating;
- already have a large administrative role that is being managed;
- have burnt out;
- work remotely;
- see few examples of good service models;
- not see any valuing of service or collegiality;
- have been affected by work members who model very dysfunctional behaviours;
- have not experienced highly collegial settings.

It can be seen that there may be many different reasons for apparent non-collegiality. First, the environment itself may discourage engagement, reflecting a focus on "What's in it for me" rather than "What can I offer to others?" In these dysfunctional contexts, the tendency is to stay as invisible as possible, with the goal of being safe and protected from the depredations of difficult colleagues (Shuck 2011; Shuck and Rose 2013; Shuck et al. 2015). Feelings of insecurity and threat may be strong, generating high levels of anxiety. Volunteering or moving into roles that can include some risk can be seen as very unsafe. In these settings, service is likely to be hard to encourage and difficult to undertake.

The second cause may relate to workload and capacity. Individuals may be keen to assist, but unable to find the necessary time to devote to the activities. When under stress, the tendency is to focus on critical priorities. This pressure may be further escalated through the existing ways in which roles are allocated, and, for newcomers, a lack of support with reduced workloads as they build institutional knowledge and experience. It is ironic that many new academics are also put into key service roles that might readily be filled by more experienced colleagues (Stupnisky *et al.* 2015). Where possible, service roles that are educative and help to set up contextual knowledge rather than add arduous workloads offer a valuable orientation into the work environment.

Strategies to encourage collegiality and service

Efforts to encourage collegiality and service are best undertaken at five levels: university, local group, supervisor, individual, and developer (Burnes *et al.* 2014; Cipriano 2011; Clarke and Reid 2013; Gilbert *et al.* 2012; Schein 2010). Strong alignment across all five will ensure consistent messages are received and assure the individual that adaptation to reflect these cues is safe and desirable. If they are not in sync, there will be increased dissonance, and less willingness to fully engage with these desirable practices, particularly if they are portrayed by some colleagues as career limiting.

University strategies

It is reassuring to see the growth in university strategies to support a constructive, collegial environment and increased service activities. These have included:

- stronger enunciation of values as part of the institutional rhetoric;
- clear valuing of collegial and service-related activities in performance, probation and promotion reviews;
- modelling of collegial values at more senior levels, including respectful treatment of more junior staff;
- establishment of clear Codes of Conduct, including defining bullying and its various characteristics;
- establishment of an ombudsman to deal with complaints;
- improved processes and protocols to handle staff concerns about non-collegial behaviour;
- surveys of institutional culture on a regular basis to assist with identifying groups or communities or cohorts at risk;
- the encouragement of a constructive and supportive leadership culture, including articulation of values, leadership attributes and the provision of development programs;

- effective policies and support for those who are evidencing distress;
- prompt action on reported environments/individuals that are evidencing dysfunctional tendencies;
- annual review of turnover, sickness and complaints statistics for each organisation unit in the institution, and investigation of causes for those that are showing distress;
- investment in coaching and related support for leaders who are demonstrating less constructive behaviour;
- funding to support leaders in guiding their communities toward more constructive, collegial cultures;
- recognition and awards for those who have demonstrated a significant commitment to the enhancement of the institution or their community as part of their service contribution;
- acknowledgement of individuals who have provided support and guidance to others as mentors;
- promotion of mentoring and recognition of mentoring as a key element of university service and collegial activity.

Of particular importance is the modelling by senior leaders of desirable, constructive attributes. Generosity and the enactment of collegial behaviours will be visible to the university members, and serves to encourage their replication.

Local group strategies

The immediate environs in which one is located has a profound impact on the way an individual will engage with their work setting. In a research team, there is considerable reliance on the senior researcher to ensure equity, fairness and generosity is reflected in the decisions and messages that are conveyed. Departments and schools also exert considerable influence and modelling of dominant cultures through their selection practices (Cipriano 2015), actions, policies, anecdotes and stories that are shared and enacted across the group (Schein 2010). The culture that is enacted will have a strong influence on the individual's choices and priorities. Communities that reflect a strong commitment to collegial approaches will encourage this in newcomers. Those that are less reflective of these values are likely to experience more difficulty in building a collegial setting. The workload policies and mechanisms by which newcomers are supported will also play a part in determining how the culture is perceived and responded to. To build a strongly collegial setting, the following might be considered:

- build some explicit and well-articulated statements concerning the values and collegial behaviours that are encouraged and desired;
- develop clear guidelines for induction of new staff and ensure they are implemented, with a discussion of the desired behaviours to be evidenced;
- ensure senior leaders model these behaviours;

- explicitly promote collegial behaviours in staff meetings, retreats and other public forums;
- provide helpful guidance on career choices, including service-related choices to new or early career academics;
- ensure early career staff are offered support as they develop their political competencies and career strategy;
- encourage all staff to consider how their messages impact on those new to university work;
- identify and promote success stories that highlight the types of behaviours that are desired and encouraged;
- integrate service awards into annual recognition schemes;
- identify staff who are at risk or finding it hard to act collegially and provide support, coaching, feedback and other forms of guidance;
- address poor behaviour promptly;
- develop programs to support new academics and academic leaders to assist their effective adoption of desired behaviours;
- establish regular group meetings with staff to whom you have delegated performance review responsibilities' to establish clear expectations, explore desired messages and behavioural expectations, and encourage an equitable and high-quality experience;
- encourage peer networks and meetings of cohort groups if the department or group is large, dispersed or isolated.

Supervisor strategies

The supervisor has a particularly critical role in setting up expectations and facilitating the ongoing development of their direct reports. In academic settings this can be complicated if the span of reports is large. This has often led to a disconnect between the worker and the putative "boss." It is not uncommon for an academic to have only one discussion about performance each year, and often, with a third party, not the direct supervisor. In this situation, there is considerable risk that no one explores collegiality or service with the academic. Instead, the short, annual discussion will be focused on evidencing performance with respect to research and teaching. This sends a very strong message as to what matters.

Supervisors, then, need to consider carefully how they might better guide the expectations and strategies of their people, even if the span of control is large. Some possible approaches include:

- ensure that every new appointee is offered a comprehensive induction, including a discussion around values, behaviours and expectations;
- provide clear guidance on career strategies, including the selection of service roles and their integration into work plans;
- develop regular catch-up meetings with new staff, possibly as a group;

- monitor early warning signs and meeting with staff before the problems escalate;
- provide effective feedback on behaviours or problems that are likely to impact on the individual, their colleagues or their career outcomes;
- develop skills in coaching and mentoring to ensure the support offered is appropriately positioned;
- liaise with reviewers who have been delegated responsibility for the provision of performance feedback to ensure collegiality and service are explored.

Individual strategies

The best of intentions from other levels can only succeed if the individual is committed to acting in a constructive and collegial manner. Each person will need to be conscious of their actions and impact, and to consider how these are reflective of the dominant values that are evident across the institution. Academics are well advised to develop a strong consciousness around their professional practices and to monitor how they engage with others. An understanding of collegiality and service and the role they play in supporting the university and their own careers will be important in building a professional identity that supports their career advancement. Key to these processes is a willingness to seek feedback, reflect, observe and monitor the impact of specific behaviours. Of great importance is considering how one can make a difference rather than simply passively "ticking boxes" to demonstrate service activity. Active engagement and effective use of one's talents and capabilities will increase the overall potential and future positioning of the academic as a person of value. In some instances, individuals may have to rein in their tendency toward service roles: an over-developed sense of obligation or desire to fill in the missing areas of support can lead to career penalties if service becomes the primary work focus. Thus, achieving a good balance is important.

Developer strategies

Another influence in universities will be the developers who encourage and explore desirable practices and behaviours. Whether focused on research, teaching, leadership or a composite of all three, it is important to recognise that these values and attributes are essential to the long-term success of each person and the institution as an employer of choice. To this end, the developer can assist in this process by:

- ensure these elements are integrated and addressed in their workshops and programs;
- open up discussions of difficult cultural problems in a safe setting;
- follow up identified issues with participants to check that they are clear about their options and choices;

- consider different ways these issues might be approached or addressed through their services and activities;
- identify systems, services or inconsistent processes that need to be reviewed or enhanced;
- encourage alignment across institutional, leadership, work-group and individual levels of activity;
- facilitate interaction with good models and exemplars who illustrate the value of supporting these good practices;
- identify, clarify and address non-collegial behaviour in facilitated sessions;
- alert the university services or leaders as to emergent issues that may need to be further explored if they are systemic rather than isolated occurrences.

The HE developer is more likely to see and hear of poor behaviour as they interact with hundreds of people across a range of sessions. They will witness the impact of these practices on individuals and may be approached to offer guidance on managing these difficult dynamics. It is important to act on identified issues. This would normally take the form of a confidential discussion but may draw on expert advice from other sources.

Conclusion

Collegiality and service matter. They are foundational processes that encourage the development of critical academic attributes and encourage an environment that is conducive to growth and transformation. Institutional policy and messages are particularly powerful in encouraging or discouraging these behaviours. It is evident that there is considerable work to be done in establishing a strong and consistent message across all levels of the university. Modelling of good practice from the executive level down is particularly important, as is the lived culture within each work group. This chapter has been designed to articulate and frame discussions relating to these processes, and will assist leaders, developers and individuals in reviewing the roles they play in building collegial academic communities.

References

Adler, P., Heckscher, C. and Prusak, L., 2011. Building a collaborative enterprise. *Harvard Business Review*, July–August, pp. 94–101.

Ang, S. and Dyne, L.V., 2015. *Handbook of cultural intelligence*, Hoboken, NJ: Taylor & Francis.

Beckmann, C.A., Cannella, B.L. and Wantland, D., 2013. Faculty perception of bullying in schools of nursing. *Journal of Professional Nursing*, 29(5), pp. 287–294.

Boyatzis, R.E., Gaskin, J. and Wei, H., 2015. Emotional and social intelligence and behavior. In S. Goldstein, D. Princiotta, and J.A. Naglieri, eds, *Handbook of intelligence*, New York: Springer, pp. 243–262.

Burnes, B., Wend, P. and By, R.T., 2014. The changing face of English universities: reinventing collegiality for the twenty-first century. *Studies in Higher Education*, 39(6), pp. 905–926.
Cipriano, R.E., 2011. *Facilitating a collegial department in higher education: strategies for success*, 1st edition, San Francisco, CA: Jossey-Bass.
Cipriano, R.E., 2015. Collegiality as a fourth criterion for personnel decisions. *The Department Chair*, 25(4), pp. 21–22.
Cipriano, R.E. and Buller, J.L., 2012. Rating faculty collegiality. *Change: The Magazine of Higher Learning*, 44(2), pp. 45–48.
Clarke, C. and Reid, J., 2013. Foundational academic development: building collegiality across divides? *International Journal for Academic Development*, 18(4), pp. 318–330.
Field, E.M., 2010. *Bully blocking at work: a self-help guide for employees and managers*, Bowen Hills, Qld: Australian Academic Press.
Fredman, N. and Doughney, J., 2012. Academic dissatisfaction, managerial change and neo-liberalism. *Higher Education*, 64(1), pp. 41–58.
Gappa, J.M., Austin, A.E. and Trice, A.G., 2007. *Rethinking faculty work: higher education's strategic imperative*, 1st edition, San Francisco, CA: Jossey-Bass.
Gedro, J. and Wang, J., 2013. Creating civil and respectful organizations through the scholar-practitioner bridge. *Advances in Developing Human Resources*, 15(3), pp. 284–295.
Gilbert, J.A. *et al.*, 2012. Toxic versus cooperative behaviors at work: the role of organizational culture and leadership in creating community-centered organizations. *International Journal of Leadership Studies*, 7(1), pp. 29–47.
Hermanowicz, J.C., 2013. The culture of mediocrity. *Minerva*, 51(3), pp. 363–387.
Johnson, L.K., 2008. Sharpen your political competence. *Harvard Business Review*, February 27, 2008. Available online at hbr.org/2008/02/sharpen-your-political-compete-1.html
Keim, J. and McDermott, J.C., 2010. Mobbing: workplace violence in the academy. *The Educational Forum*, 74(2), pp. 167–173.
Mamiseishvili, K., Miller, M.T. and Lee, D., 2015. Beyond teaching and research: faculty perceptions of service roles at research universities. *Innovative Higher Education*, pp. 1–13. Available online at DOI: 10.1007/s10755-015-9354-3
Metzger, A.M., Petit, A. and Sieber, S., 2015. Mentoring as a way to change a culture of academic bullying and mobbing in the humanities. *Higher Education for the Future*, 2(2), pp. 139–150.
Patterson, K. (ed.), 2012. *Crucial conversations: tools for talking when stakes are high*, 2nd edition, New York: McGraw-Hill.
Rowland, S., 2008. Collegiality and intellectual love. *British Journal of Sociology of Education*, 29(3), pp. 353–360.
Saltmarsh, S., Sutherland-Smith, W. and Randell-Moon, H., 2011. 'Inspired and assisted', or 'berated and destroyed'? Research leadership, management and performativity in troubled times. *Ethics and Education*, 6(3), pp. 293–306.
Schein, E.H., 2010. *Organizational culture and leadership*, 4th edition, San Francisco, CA: Jossey-Bass.
Schyns, B. and Schilling, J., 2013. How bad are the effects of bad leaders? A meta-analysis of destructive leadership and its outcomes. *The Leadership Quarterly*, 24(1), pp. 138–158.

Shattock, M., 2010. *Managing successful universities*, 2nd edition, Maidenhead, Berkshire: Open University Press.

Shuck, B., 2011. Four emerging perspectives of employee engagement: an integrative literature review. *Human Resource Development Review*, 10(3), pp. 304–328.

Shuck, B. and Rose, K., 2013. Reframing employee engagement within the context of meaning and purpose: implications for HRD. *Advances in Developing Human Resources*, 15(4), pp. 341–355.

Shuck, B., Rose, K. and Bergman, M., 2015. Inside the spiral of dysfunction: the personal consequences of working for a dysfunctional leader. *New Horizons in Adult Education and Human Resource Development*, 27(4), pp. 51–58.

Stupnisky, R.H., Weaver-Hightower, M.B. and Kartoshkina, Y., 2015. Exploring and testing the predictors of new faculty success: a mixed methods study. *Studies in Higher Education*, 40(2), pp. 368–390.

Wright, M. and Hill, L.H., 2015. Academic incivility among health sciences faculty. *Adult Learning*, 26(1), pp. 14–20.

Zabrodska, K., Linnell, S., Laws, C. and Davies, B., 2011. Bullying as intra-active process in neoliberal universities. *Qualitative Inquiry*, 17(8), pp. 709–719.

Chapter 14

The engaged academic

Academics are increasingly expected to demonstrate engagement and impact as part of their overall outcomes. *Engagement* describes the outreach and collaborative activities that academics undertake with other individuals, university groups or external stakeholders who seek to draw on their academic expertise. It supports the integration and translation of knowledge and practice beyond the university environment (Sandmann 2008; Sandmann *et al.* 2008). *Impact* can be defined as the capacity to extend the influence and reach of one's research beyond academia, particularly through contributing to the enhancement of the economy, society, culture, national security, public policy or services, health, the environment, or quality of life. This enactment of scholarship to encourage public good has long been recognised as an important function of academic work (Boyer 1990).

Teaching and research rely on enduring relationships and interactions with diverse groups and stakeholders. Teaching activities may be framed around students learning in authentic settings through work-integrated or service learning, practitioners exploring their professional practice, visits to community groups and various forms of fieldwork (Lieberman 2014). Similarly, much of the research conducted by universities relies on community participation, partnerships with industry, government or other groups, and regular interaction with policy holders, the media and other interested parties, locally, nationally and internationally. Thus, the interpretation of engagement can be focused on many different activities, such as:

- supporting the institutional outreach strategies;
- guiding learning innovations that draw on community and industry input/collaboration;
- translating research to a broader audience and promoting its translation into policy, practice or innovative applications;
- working with their discipline to further its goals, including sitting on boards, committees, working parties, conference planning committees or panels;
- advising government and other key groups on policy or review initiatives;
- working with community groups to support their needs.

Perkmann *et al.* (2013) suggest that engagement is partly driven by the need to access resources and strengthen the foundational support for research. Holland (1999) also notes further benefits, such as prestige, support for educational outcomes, increased access to funding and the expansion of reputation. In addition, universities gain referred prestige from these activities. Engagement advances research on community issues or needs, drawing on the collective knowledge of more diverse contributors and ensuring this co-creation achieves wider dissemination through the relevant communities (McNall *et al.* 2009).

There are numerous ways in which engagement can be interpreted and enacted. The opportunities and options are more than any one individual can fulfil. The challenge, then, is to choose wisely. Each academic may take a slightly different focus, partly driven by their own interests and expertise, and partly guided by their school, faculty or university needs and priorities, and in some cases, the available opportunities that emerge. There is considerable benefit in aligning engagement strategies with overall career focus, goals and directions. The capacity to meld engagement foci with teaching, research or leadership emphases can act as a multiplicative factor, consolidating and enhancing the overall impact being achieved.

For many academics, the first experience of engagement is likely to be associated with teaching activities that link students to work-based learning experiences or service-learning (Holland 1999). This provides a structured focus and enables the development of core skills in communicating and engaging with external stakeholders. As academics become more expert in their chosen field/s of knowledge, their influence and impact are likely to grow and they will become increasingly connected with external parties. Recognition as a subject-matter expert will generate invitations and opportunities, stimulating further connections and networks within and beyond the university. These activities or roles may sometimes be formally assigned (e.g. designing a work-integrated learning program or seeking community input on a school initiative) or may be more closely aligned to the academic's own professional interests or pursuits (e.g. working with disciplinary groups, sitting on a board or contributing to a policy review).

Choosing engagement foci

Engagement generally encourages the development of long-term, sustainable relationships with core groups or contacts. These connections promote progressive profiling and reputational enhancement, the development of enduring relationships and leadership opportunities. Thus, academics need to think strategically about the path/s they will pursue. It may make sense to test several avenues to see how each operates, but ultimately, it will be necessary to dedicate attention and effort to one or two paths that offer the best return to both the academic and their constituents. Again, it is important to have a clear narrative and connection with the overall identity and goals that the individual seeks to pursue through their academic career.

Figure 14.1 illustrates the different ways engagement might be focused. Universities may direct academic engagement foci toward key groups, priorities or outcomes that support their institutional priorities. Educational engagement may stem, for example, from a school's desire to encourage students to learn more about industry. Disciplinary or inter-disciplinary investigations, sometimes around "wicked problems" (Ramaley 2014), can open up another pathway for engagement. Research projects themselves often require engagement with communities and groups to test ideas and produce knowledge. Equally, the needs of community members or stakeholders might be the drivers for engagement. More experienced academics may find that they integrate all of these foci into their engagement strategy.

The choice of focus needs to be carefully considered by each academic, as the engagement and interaction with stakeholders can be demanding and time-consuming. The questions in Box 14.1 are useful prompts for inexperienced academics as they negotiate their engagement identity and priorities. They emphasise a degree of selectivity in choosing a particular emphasis, based on one's strengths, passions, opportunities and desired or potential career path.

Successful engagement is generally directed toward building robust and respectful partnerships between parties with a mutual interest. An understanding of mutuality and reciprocity is critical: each partner needs to feel that there is equity and balance in both contributions and benefits. While academics offer their expertise and know-how, the other parties also bring considerable knowledge and insight to the relationship. The capacity to partner with other stakeholders requires sophisticated skills in being empathetic and building relationships.

Engagement also implies that the contributions of the academic make a difference. Effective promotion of core concepts or strategies to stakeholders via a range of dissemination/communication channels and their adoption into policy and practice are important translational roles. The evaluation of the resultant impact and the efficacy of the engagement activities should also be monitored as part of the academic's reflexive practices.

As Box 14.1 also illustrates, there are a number of factors that can impact on an individual's capacity to engage. The individual needs to be highly motivated, with a desire to create more in-depth involvement with relationships and academic activities. They will need the necessary capabilities to effect these practices. Opportunities to connect with suitable stakeholders also facilitate these interactions, often requiring a proactive approach to seeking suitable opportunities. The degree to which the institution and academic community value and recognise these activities will further influence the choices that are made. In the UK, for example, where impact has become a key measure of research success, a sharpened prioritisation toward engagement is evident.

However, a desire to be impactful can be unrealised if the necessary skills and capabilities are under-developed. In the final section of this chapter, the strategies to provide engagement sponsorship and support will be examined.

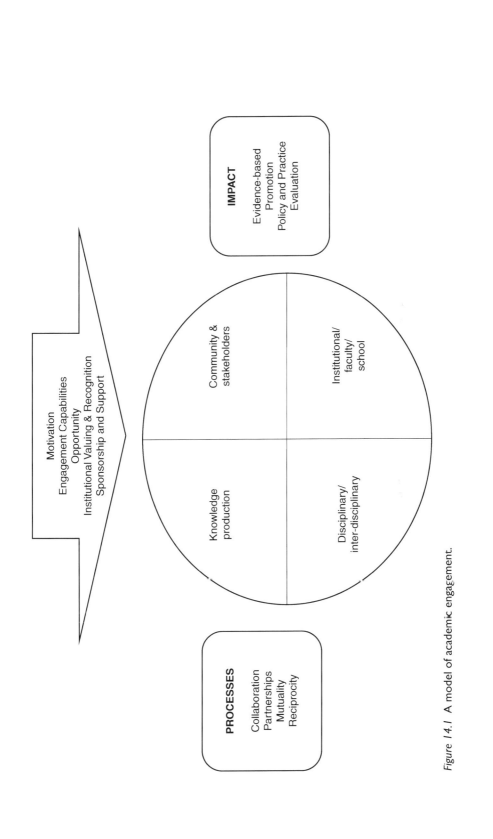

Figure 14.1 A model of academic engagement.

Box 14.1 Evaluating an engagement option

- How does this engagement path draw on your passions, skills, talent and expertise?
- What role will you play? Will it challenge you and encourage you to develop new skills and capabilities?
- Does it complement your teaching, research or leadership?
- How will it benefit society, the university, the school, and/or your career?
- What contribution will you be able to make? Are you able to add value to this area?
- What activities will you need to undertake? How much time will you need to devote? Do you have the time and energy to commit as you should?
- Will it supplement and enrich your existing professional networks?
- How does this experience build on and complement your existing profile?
- Where might this activity progress to? Does it open additional avenues for collaboration, teaching, research or leadership?
- How will you be able to demonstrate that you have made a difference by being involved in this activity?
- How will this role assist you in achieving promotion and/or recognition as an expert or leader?
- How will impact be evident? What will you need to do to achieve this impact?

Engagement skills and capabilities

Many of the capabilities that support effective teaching and research will be pertinent to engagement. However, there are some additional, more sophisticated capacities that will be required to fully capitalise on these opportunities (Duncan and Spicer 2010). These are outlined below.

Communication skills will be well tested. The academic will be communicating with more diverse communities and individuals, with different motives and assumptions. The ability to listen empathetically and to respond appropriately, with care for cultural sensitivities is essential (Hay 2008). This will require advanced capacities to interpret other points of view and negotiate agreed outcomes (Taylor and Kent 2014). The capacity to write in ways that engage different audiences has become increasingly important. Each communication benefits from tailoring to match the particular community (Cherney *et al.* 2012). Communication forums include social media (Smith and Gallicano 2015), professional communiques, the media and more formalised avenues. Engagement often incorporates the development of written communications and reports. These might include proposals, expressions of interest, executive reports, review documents, technical or industry reports and tender documents. Each requires different protocols and styles of writing. Oral communication channels will be similarly diverse, spanning the ability to work with small and large groups; work in virtual communication forums, present in international forums (with an awareness of intercultural differences) and via various media modes. The management of social media channels to effect maximum impact will also need to be explored and enacted. Thus, the capacity to articulate, present and engage with others is fundamental to extending one's influence, reach and impact. These interactive skills extend further to building a dissemination and engagement repertoire that ensures the messages are being received by the intended audience/s (Haigh 2011).

Networking skills support engagement. While some engagement opportunities may be sponsored by others, many will need to be initiated by the academic. Thus, a capacity to develop associations and connections with new individuals, groups or communities will be needed. This can be very challenging for many people: it requires resilience and confidence when moving into new circles of connection. A willingness to learn from and with others and to share one's own passions and interests opens up many potential partnerships for research, teaching and alliances.

While academics will move across many networks and communities, they will also build strong linkages to certain networks and people. Again, it will be important to determine which of those associations are the highest priority. While social media facilitates engagement and connection with many individuals, close links to certain individuals or communities require more concerted management. Thus, even networking requires some strategic planning to ensure that key contacts and linkages are regularly sustained and nurtured. These contacts need to feel that they are a high priority and valued by their colleague. This is particularly the case for those who are engaged with the academic, pursuing paths of mutual interest and obligation. Regular evaluations of networks and their efficacy assists in prioritising the most productive associations. Cross and Thomas (2011), for example, recommend analysing the health of these connections, de-layering those that are unproductive, diversifying the base to reflect the ongoing growth of the strategy and ensuring that each connection is maximised. This strategic approach emphasises the critical importance of proactively managing these relationships. Leadership of engagement strategies and inter-disciplinary connections will require considerable focus to maintain their energy and effectiveness (Ibarra and Hansen 2011; Ylijoki and Henriksson 2015).

Engagement relies on effective *relational skills*. A willingness to learn more about the other party and to integrate those insights into the ongoing conversations and processes supports effective interactions. This can be particularly important when the other individuals or groups work outside the university. Industry partners, for example, will have different rhythms, expectations, protocols and cultures that must be accommodated and respected. Community groups will bring an entirely different set of knowledge, language and traditions that will influence the way the relationship operates in terms of formality, timelines and outcomes (Debowski 2012). Academics need to bridge these differences, learning to move to the rhythms and boundaries of those different communities. Trust, open communication and an understanding of the mutual obligations that must be respected will ensure that the relationships can flourish. Recognition that all parties share ownership of outcomes and findings, as well as the role of expert, supports these productive relationships (Holland 1999).

The development of external relationships requires a range of *adaptive responses*. It is important to learn as much as possible about the stakeholder politics, decision making and cultural nuances. The language and lexicon may need to be adapted to better match the community's own practices. Key concepts and terminology, historical practices, processes, protocols and systems will need to be explored to support the academic's acculturation and adaptation. It may be necessary to produce a number of documents that will assist with negotiation, communication or reporting. These may look substantially different to those developed for in-house university purposes. Thus, the capacity to be adaptive and responsive will be important cues for success.

There will be particular times when the academic will need to mobilise the support and energy of their university colleagues to accomplish their engagement goals. This can be challenging. Academics are asked to support numerous projects or initiatives. Their capacity to allocate discretionary time to a specific project will be partly driven by the degree to which they see that work as important. Each individual will have to consider where their priorities and energy are best allocated, particularly if they too carry significant portfolios and responsibilities. The articulation of a clear vision, mutual benefits to be gained and required contribution can assist in building internal stakeholder commitment (Abele 2011). Planning and strategy should be well coordinated, including recognising and valuing the part each contributor will play and designing participatory experiences that are enjoyable or, at least, worthwhile. Thus, the capacity to be positive, persuasive and passionate about the initiative will increase engagement and commitment from other parties.

The capacity to reflect, evaluate and assess the impact of engagement strategies will enhance the overall outcomes of any initiative. Many academic projects are poorly reviewed, thereby reducing the opportunity to learn and enhance future approaches. Good examples of evaluations and impact assessments are now to be found (Bolden and Petrov 2008; Bolden *et al.* 2010). The addition of evaluative practices into the planning cycle will generate considerable benefits for the engaged academic and their constituents.

Developing engaged academics

It can be seen that engagement is a high-end academic capability. It has significant potential to increase the impact and profile of the academic and their work. However, few academics come into their role with well-honed capabilities. Most benefit from the support and sponsorship of their institution, supervisor, colleagues and developers, including through:

- clear guidance on institutional policies, valuing and recognition of engagement and impact (Britner 2012; Sandmann *et al.* 2011);
- encouragement by supervisors to map an engagement strategy as part of regular academic planning;
- collegial interchange and sharing about engagement experiences, including lessons learnt (Wenger *et al.* 2012);
- increased promotion of the science of engagement, rather than reliance on trial and error;
- opportunities to work with or shadow experienced, connected academics;
- the provision of courses or workshops on building engagement strategies;
- the development of reflective tools and guides to encourage effective design of engagement practices;
- access to experienced mentors and sponsors;
- identification of successful models willing to share their experiences and insights with other colleagues;
- opportunities to participate in capacity-building exercises;
- supportive discussions of engagement strategies and their impact as part of performance reviews;
- feedback on capabilities that need to be developed to effect successful engagement.

Conclusion

The public sphere of academic work is a very creative and dynamic field. It offers a fertile space to develop entrepreneurial, relationship and leadership capabilities. It also enables each individual to give back to society, their university, discipline, school or faculty and other stakeholders in a way consonant with their skills and abilities. Participation in engagement will be richly rewarding and inspiring, encouraging the continual expansion of capabilities, impact and influence. These capabilities support enhanced development and impact of research, teaching and leadership. They provide additional opportunities to build a strong integrated identity that encourages increased depth and breadth of knowledge, applications and impact.

References

Abele, J., 2011. Bringing minds together. *Harvard Business Review*, July–August, pp. 86–92.
Bolden, R. and Petrov, G., 2008. *Employer engagement with higher education: a literature review*, Bristol: University of Exeter.

Bolden, R., Hirsch, W., Connor, H., Petrov, G. and Duquemin, A., 2010. *Strategies for effective employer-HE engagement: defining, sustaining and supporting higher skills provision*, Exeter: University of Exeter Press.

Boyer, E.L., 1990. *Scholarship reconsidered: priorities of the professoriate*, New York: Carnegie Foundation for the Advancement of Teaching.

Britner, P.A., 2012. Bringing public engagement into an academic plan and its assessment metrics. *Journal of Higher Education Outreach and Engagement*, 16(4), pp. 61–77.

Cherney, A., Povey, J., Head, B., Boreham, P. and Ferguson, M., 2012. What influences the utilisation of educational research by policy-makers and practitioners? The perspectives of academic educational researchers. *International Journal of Educational Research*, 56, pp. 23–34.

Cross, B. and Thomas, R., 2011. A smarter way to network. *Harvard Business Review*, July–August, pp. 149–153.

Debowski, S., 2012. *The new academic: a strategic handbook*, London: Open University Press.

Duncan, S. and Spicer, S., 2010. *The engaging researcher*, Cambridge, UK: Careers Research and Advisory Centre. Available online at www.vitae.ac.uk/researcherbooklets

Haigh, N., 2011. Sustaining and spreading the positive outcomes of SoTL projects: issues, insights and strategies. *International Journal for Academic Development*, 17(1), pp. 19–31.

Hay, I., 2008. Postcolonial practices for a global virtual group: the case of the international network for learning and teaching geography in higher education (INLT). *Journal of Geography in Higher Education*, 32(1), pp. 15–32.

Holland, B., 1999. Factors and strategies that influence faculty involvement in public service. *Journal of Public Service and Outreach*, 4(1), pp. 37–44.

Ibarra, H. and Hansen, M.T., 2011. Are you a collaborative leader? *Harvard Business Review*, July–August, pp. 68–74.

Lieberman, D., 2014. The ABCDs of service-learning: who is serving whom? *Journal of Higher Education Outreach and Engagement*, 18(4), pp. 7–15.

McNall, M., Reed, C.S., Brown, R. and Allen, A., 2009. Brokering community–university engagement. *Innovative Higher Education*, 33(5), pp. 317–331.

Perkmann, M., Tartari, V., McKelvey, M., Autio, E., Brostrom, A., E'Este, P., Fini, R., Geuna, A., Grimaldi, R., Hughes, A., Krable, S., Kitson, M., Llerena, P., Salter, A. and Soberero, M., 2013. Academic engagement and commercialisation: a review of the literature on university–industry relations. *Research Policy*, 42(2), pp. 423–442.

Ramaley, J.A., 2014. The changing role of higher education: learning to deal with wicked problems. *Journal of Higher Education Outreach and Engagement*, 18(4), pp. 7–21.

Sandmann, L.R., 2008. Conceptualization of the scholarship of engagement in higher education: a strategic review, 1996–2006. *Journal of Higher Education Outreach and Engagement*, 12(1), pp. 91–104.

Sandmann, L.R., Saltmarsh, J. and O'Meara, K., 2008. An integrated model for advancing the scholarship of engagement: creating academic homes for the engaged scholar. *Journal of Higher Education Outreach and Engagement*, 12(1), pp. 47–63.

Sandmann, L.R., Thornton, C.H. and Jaeger, A.J., 2011. *Institutionalizing community engagement in higher education: new directions for higher education*, Hoboken, NJ: Wiley.

Smith, B.G. and Gallicano, T.D., 2015. Terms of engagement: analyzing public engagement with organizations through social media. *Computers in Human Behavior*, 53, pp. 82–90.

Taylor, M. and Kent, M.L., 2014. Dialogic engagement: clarifying foundational concepts. *Journal of Public Relations Research*, 26(5), pp. 384–398.

Wenger, L., Hawkins, L. and Seifer, S.D., 2012. Community-engaged scholarship: critical junctures in research, practice, and policy. *Journal of Higher Education Outreach and Engagement*, 16(1), pp. 171–181.

Ylijoki, O.-H. and Henriksson, L., 2015. Tribal, proletarian and entrepreneurial career stories: junior academics as a case in point. *Studies in Higher Education*, pp. 1–17. Available online at DOI 10.1080/03075079.2015.1092129

Chapter 15

From novice researcher to research leader

Research is a key differentiator between higher education institutions and other educational providers. A high-cost enterprise, it requires institutional investment to support research activities. Each country has developed different approaches to sponsoring and recognising research. However, there are clear similarities. Research drives university reputation and the public nature of research outcomes, quality and productivity metrics makes research everyone's business. While the nature, depth and breadth of the research activities will be highly divergent across different universities, each academic plays a part in building their institution's research identity.

Every academic needs to be an excellent researcher, but this is not an automatic process: it takes dedicated focus, time and practice to acquire the skills and capabilities that underpin research success (Orlando and Gard 2014). While many universities have articulated the outcomes and standards they expect to see demonstrated, there has been less surety in mapping the requisite skills that need to be developed to achieve these targets. This has created a duality in terms of research performance, with well-supported researchers building highly successful careers, while those in less conducive settings often left to languish.

The identification of core research capabilities[1] now provides an invaluable basis to guide each researcher through their learning and development (Evans 2011). This chapter maps the core research practices that have been identified, and the processes that support progressive transition from novice to mastery. Our understanding of these processes has continued to evolve since Gordon (2005) offered a detailed exploration of the capabilities that supported successful research, with many researchers and research groups documenting and sharing their practices and learning since then (e.g. Debowski 2012; Evans 2015).

However, as Evans (2015) notes, each researcher brings particular dispositions and orientations to their research strategy. They develop unique research identities, creating a particular profile, capabilities and alliances. Their research will vary markedly in form, methodology, impact and focus. They will range from limited to extremely talented in their research capacity (Evans 2015). There are many reasons for this variability. The individual's own talent, drive and determination is a key contribution to successful outcomes. The discipline and institution also influence what is researched and how research is carried out. The priorities that the individual assigns to research will affect the time, importance and focus that is given to research, particularly where there are other competing demands. The environment in which the academic is situated will also play a part in enabling high performance (or the opposite) (Bland *et al.* 2005).

Researcher capabilities

Six core capabilities have been identified as necessary for research mastery (CFRD 2016; Debowski 2010, 2012; Evans 2015). These relate to:

- the capacity to publish high-impact, quality research outputs;
- the ability to obtain research funding;
- effective management of the project to ensure its timely and productive completion;
- the development of collaborative alliances and relationships (Bozeman *et al.* 2013);
- the capacity to train new researchers, ensuring they complete high-quality research projects;
- the ability to lead and manage productive, effective research teams.

Additional capabilities continue to be identified. The capacity to be entrepreneurial (Sinclair, Cuthbert and Barnacle 2014), for example, is emerging as a new discussion thread.

Publishing

Academics are expected to publish scholarly publications that reflect their expertise in their chosen discipline. These publications are primarily scholarly articles that are peer-reviewed and published in high-impact journals. However, they may also include books, book chapters, refereed conference papers or creative works, depending on the discipline. There has been a strong preference toward publishing articles in high-impact journals as these are more readily cited. Box 15.1 provides an overview of the key indicators that guide assessments of a track record with respect to publications.

The ability to document and publish research is the foundational base for any academic career (Sadler 2009). The capacities to fund research, build collaborations and, indeed, stay employed, are predicated on evidence of these scholarly outcomes. These increasing expectations have raised the bar on what and how academics publish: they must build clear narratives about the purpose of their publishing and the ways in which their work adds value and worth to society generally. It is no longer enough to get something accepted; it must also be demonstrably valued by others, and preferably, adopted by others. At the same time, the pressure to publish in high-quality journals has escalated with the growth in the

> **Box 15.1 Indicators of a successful publication track record**
>
> - *A strong track record* of progressive publications that evidences their sustained, specialist expertise across a number of publications.
> - *Quality publications*, measured for some research areas by the impact factor of the journals or reputation of their publisher.
> - *High-impact publications*, that is, works that are cited and/or influential with respect to being adopted or recognised within and beyond the academy.

academic population and the push to be more productive. A top-tier journal will commonly only accept 5–10% of papers that are submitted.

The successful development and publication of academic work can be a daunting hurdle for many people. This may be due to poor doctoral preparation; limited skills in academic writing; inexperience in research or scholarly activities; an unproductive research focus; challenges in finding time to write (Gardiner and Kearns 2010); or a myriad of other reasons. Boice (1985) identified work apprehension, procrastination, dysphoria, impatience, perfectionism, evaluation anxiety and rules as further factors that can impede writing productivity. Whatever the cause, it is essential that academics address these barriers if they wish to remain in academe.

There are a range of strategies now being encouraged to assist academics wishing to enhance their productivity and publication impact. These include:

- *Building a strong research identity and depth of knowledge in a particular cognate area*: It can take some time to establish a clear focus, particularly if the individual shifts to new projects, disciplines, research groups or contributes to inter-disciplinary research.
- *Setting clear goals and priorities for publishing* (Boice 1989; Gardiner and Kearns 2010).
- *Understanding the science of writing a good paper* (Aitchison 2010; Belcher 2009; Cargill 2009; Debowski 2012; Sword 2009, 2011).
- *Writing regularly* (Boice 1990; Gardiner and Kearns 2010).
- *Seeking feedback* from mentors, peers or writing circle members.
- *Acquiring resilience in the face of rejection*.
- *Co-authoring with other colleagues*.

Academics who find their writing skills are insufficiently developed will need to address this as a critical priority. Coaches, writing retreats (Aitchison and Guerin 2014; Grant 2008), mentors, writing circles (McGrail *et al.* 2006), as well as critical readers are strategies that many have found useful.

A concern in the literature relates to the skewing of research publication practices in nations where research is assessed via national or international metrics

(Doyle and Cuthill 2015; Hughes and Bennett 2013). Researchers need to develop a coherent and well-articulated publication strategy that assists in building a strong narrative and focus to support their choices.

Funding their research

The capacity to obtain research funding is another indication of research success (Aldridge and Derrington 2012; Debowski 2012). Funding may relate to supporting a research grant or possibly, the individual's own employment through grant funding or fellowships. Access to funding can also assist researchers in gaining additional resources, attending conferences or adding further depth or efficiencies to their research projects. However, the process of writing a grant is intensive, taking, in some cases, hundreds of hours of work (Herbert *et al.* 2013). While a history of funding sources will be viewed very positively by their university and funding agencies, academics need to assess when is the right time to move into the funding game. In many cases, grant seeking is undertaken as a collaborative enterprise. This provides an ideal opportunity to explore research from a number of different perspectives, including as an inter-disciplinary endeavour. Hottenrott and Lawson (2014) note that access to funding can influence the path a researcher pursues, as might the particular orientation of the discipline (Pitman and Berman 2009).

Successful grant writing is predicated on a range of capabilities including:

- an established track record that demonstrates the expertise of the researcher/s in the proposed research area;
- identifying persuasive and attractive research projects;
- familiarity with the funding body and the grant criteria;
- designing well managed projects;
- articulating a coherent and well justified proposal;
- planning ahead to allow time for feedback and revisions;
- accurately costing and justifying project funding;
- an ability to build a clear narrative about the researcher and their suitability to research this topic.

The development of successful grants requires a persuasive and standout argument as to why the academic's research should be funded ahead of other highly competitive proposals. Submissions need to be authoritative, coherent and easy to read and have something that highlights their uniqueness and difference. Initial efforts to develop grant proposals can be greatly assisted through grant mentors; access to successful grant proposals that might be used as models; the provision of guidelines and checklists; feedback throughout the development process; and an opportunity to debrief on the research outcomes. Browning *et al.* (2014) encourage early career researchers to test grant concepts with an expert audience before they have invested too much effort and emotional attachment. This has proven to be a very successful way of reducing unproductive grant activity. Box 15.2 encapsulates the key indicators of a successful funding track record.

> ### Box 15.2 Indicators of a successful funding track record
>
> - *A progressive track record* of funding from various sources, including high-prestige funders.
> - Evidence of the capacity to gain competitive funding from a variety of funding sources.
> - Funded research with industry, government and the community.

Research project management

An expectation of funded projects is that they will be carried out professionally and with due concern for maximising the value achieved. Unfortunately, few researchers are well prepared in terms of either management skills or research management practices in particular. Research projects are complex and require careful management. Poor project management can increase the risks of non-completion, cost blow-outs, poor quality outcomes and reduced future funding opportunities. Research project management is generally poorly developed, but is now better understood as a valuable mechanism to manage the systems, progress and outputs of the project (Debowski 2012).[2]

Effective management of the research project can reduce the time academics have to spend on crises and ensures their team has a much stronger understanding of the role they should be playing in executing the project. Many researchers find it hard to focus on research management issues (e.g. planning for stakeholder engagement, reporting or communication, managing staff or identifying potential risks). A valuable tool is the *Research Project Management Checklist* (Debowski 2012), which maps the key tasks to be undertaken throughout the lifecycle of a project. This checklist, developed by researchers and professional experts to pool their shared knowledge, identifies eleven aspects of research project management that need to be carefully monitored and addressed. These include scope, time, quality, costs, research risk, human resources, communication and stakeholder management. Offering a useful list of cues, it can be used as a self-help guide for those new to thinking about their projects in a methodical way. Several research centres and universities have adopted the checklist pro forma for research projects.

Like any professional practice, the initial stages of learning how to apply management principles to research projects may feel cumbersome. However, researchers will find that their projects will achieve smoother transitions from plan to completion if these project management practices are employed. These capabilities could be introduced at the doctoral level, encouraging students and their supervisors to think more carefully about the project and its management through the research candidature process. As Box 15.3 illustrates, there are a number of ways in which research projects can demonstrate good project management.

Box 15.3 Indicators of successful research project management

- The project is completed on time and within budget.
- Publication and dissemination strategies have been successfully undertaken and completed during the project cycle.
- The team has demonstrated high performance and low turnover.
- The project has generated goodwill with stakeholders and recognition more broadly.
- All reporting and legal obligations have been successfully met.
- The project has enabled the cultivation of good relationships with stakeholders.

Collaboration

Successful researchers recognise the value of collaborating with other colleagues. Collaboration enables opportunities to engage, debate and explore ideas from a number of perspectives. It enriches and expands the researcher's potential. It also increases the likelihood of wider dissemination of any research outcomes. Evidence of collaborative capacity is recognised as one form of peer esteem as it demonstrates that other researchers value the opportunity to work with academics. Collaboration can improve the quality of the research, generating increased outputs, encouraging more citations and stimulating different insights into the research. The social benefits of collaboration are also significant, increasing energy, motivation and creativity if the right collaborators are sourced (Adams 2012; Bossio *et al.* 2014; Bozeman *et al.* 2013).

Collaborations take many forms. Academics may collaborate with researchers within their discipline or across disciplines. Their partners may be local, national or international; drawn from within the academy or beyond, incorporating industry, government agencies, practitioners or the community. The capacity to manage these complex relationships is an important capability for those wishing to move toward more senior roles.

Key skills academics require to initiate and maintain collaborations include the development of strong peer networks; the capacity to build a strong and well-articulated narrative and profile that can be readily found and interpreted by others; and the ability to manage collaborations once they are initiated. There is considerable value in assessing the benefits for all concerned parties and how each contributor will add value to the pool of talent.

It is very important to choose the right collaborator/s. However, many academics move into collaborations with limited consideration of the implications for their reputation, workload or goals. Careful evaluation of the outcomes from collaborations can assist in monitoring costs and benefits of each association. Poor choices as to collaborators can create considerable difficulties, including the need to address numerous relational crises or repair damage caused by a collaborator.

Collaboration does not occur overnight. It requires the development of connections and relationships based on trust and mutual respect. The ability to work with other colleagues in a research productive mode necessitates careful management of time and commitments. The collaborative process can also require considerable negotiation, particularly at the time of start-up where complex legal considerations and the policies relating to intellectual property and funding must be addressed. The development of a collaboration requires careful management of expectations, relationships, legalities and interactions. Collaboration leaders will also need to develop skills in managing conflict and addressing issues of poor quality. Thus, collaboration is something that needs to be undertaken with careful consideration of what will be required, the intended outcomes and the agreed obligations of each party. Box 15.4 illustrates some of the indicators that can be used to evaluate successful collaborations.

Box 15.4 Indicators of successful collaboration

- Collaborations extend across more than one project.
- There are higher impact publications stemming from the partnership/s.
- New innovations are emerging from the collaborative group.
- The partners are more productive than if they were operating as sole researchers.

Research supervision

As part of their research role, academics will be expected to successfully supervise graduate research students to timely completions. The development of a conscious supervisory style and effective practices support these outcomes (Debowski 2012; Denholm and Evans 2007; McAlpine and Amundsen 2011; Thomson and Walker 2010; Walker *et al.* 2008). The capacity to give effective feedback, offer mentorship and structured guidance and encourage broader outcomes from the research experience is all part of the supervisory role.

The role of the supervisor has evolved as research programs have transitioned to a more expansive brief (Boud and Tennant 2006; Halse and Malfroy 2010; Lee and Danby 2012; Mowbray and Halse 2010). Supervisors need to be responsive to the specific needs and goals of their students (Denholm 2006;

King and Denecke 2003). They need to ensure that they are familiar with university policies and the systems that support the student. Where problems emerge, they need to address them promptly, often in partnership with other university services. As a sponsor, they will play a key role in guiding their students toward completion of the research project, drafting, publishing, presenting papers and the building of networks to increase their presence and visibility. Guidance on career planning and preparation for employment paths is now integrated into research supervision. The capacity to give effective feedback, offer mentorship and structured guidance, as well as encourage broader outcomes from the research experience are all part of the supervisory role. Good supervisors are readily able to illustrate their achievement of the indicators outlined in Box 15.5.

Box 15.5 Indicators of successful research supervision

- Students complete their candidature within the specified institutional time frame.
- Student theses are passed with minimal or no corrections.
- There is high retention of students.
- Students transition successfully to their academic, postdoctoral or professional careers.
- Students report a positive experience with their supervisor.

Research leadership and management

A natural progression for successful researchers is the move toward leadership and management of project teams or programs of research. Research teams and groups are complicated, with team members bringing many different levels of experience into the group. There will be pressure to perform and to generate funding to sustain the group. Members may also be highly dispersed, operating as a virtual team or, possibly, working across various projects as part of a larger program of research.

Research leaders face a number of challenges, particularly in doing a lot more with a lot less in a tight time frame when expectations are high (Evans 2014; Middlehurst et al. 2009; Saltmarsh, Sutherland-Smith and Randell-Moon, 2011). Leaders may also have teams that are highly diverse in composition, ranging from graduate research students and assistants right through to experienced researchers and postdoctorates. Teams may comprise long-standing members and new contributors who need to be acculturated into their group. Thus, they require considerable grounding in leadership and management principles that will ensure the research team flourishes. (Leadership principles and practices are further discussed in Chapter 20.) There are many indicators of successful research

> **Box 15.6 Indicators of successful research leadership**
>
> - Groups of people are mobilised to achieve a designated goal.
> - Institutional, school, institute or project outcomes are achieved in a strategic and timely way.
> - A significant body of work has been generated, published and disseminated.
> - There is low turnover across the team.
> - Team members demonstrate high performance and positive career enhancement including new skills, stronger track records and greater confidence in their roles.
> - Collective group outputs reflect optimal contributions of all team members.
> - Increased collaborations, opportunities and partnerships enable the research to expand its impact, visibility and future potential.
> - Longevity of the group and research, supports an ongoing series of projects.

leadership, as outlined in Box 15.6. These relate to effective team building, achieving high-quality outcomes and ensuring the group delivers on its intended goals. Leadership requires careful attention to all of these concerns.

Conclusion

Research is the foundational base for an academic's career. However, successful research requires dedication, strategic focus, a clear understanding as to what is required to be successful and a focused professional approach. These capabilities take years to build, and will benefit from support from higher education developers, colleagues, mentors, supervisors and, in some cases, coaches, in order to achieve the transition from novice researcher to research leader. The first step in promoting improved capabilities is the articulation of the skills and capabilities that underpin research success. Fortunately, as this chapter shows, we are now better placed to unpack the practices employed by successful researchers, rather than simply requiring people to somehow intuit these practices.

Notes

1 Vitae is supported by the Careers Research Advisory Centre (CRAC) in the UK. It has played a significant role in guiding researcher development. The Research Development Framework is a comprehensive document that maps a vast array of capabilities that support good research. It maps the capabilities that underpin four domains of activity: knowledge and intellectual abilities; personal effectiveness; research governance; and organisational engagement, influence and impact. Visit www.vitae.ac.uk/rdf for access to the full framework.

2   A comprehensive online program relating to research project management can be found at http://frlp.edu.au. This program was developed in 2007 as a collaboration across eight Australian universities (the Go8). It is now available as an open access resource.

References

Adams, J., 2012. Collaborations: the rise of research networks. *Nature*, 490(7420), pp. 335–336.
Aitchison, C., 2010. *Publishing pedagogies for the doctorate and beyond*, New York: Routledge.
Aitchison, C. and Guerin, C. (eds), 2014. *Writing groups for doctoral education and beyond: innovations in practice and theory*, London: Routledge.
Aldridge, J. and Derrington, A.M., 2012. *The research funding toolkit*, London; Thousand Oaks, CA: SAGE Publications.
Belcher, W.L., 2009. *Writing your journal article in 12 weeks: a guide to academic publishing success*, Thousand Oaks, CA: SAGE Publications.
Bland, C.J., Weber-Main, A., Lund, S.M. and Finstad, D.A., 2005. *The research-productive department: strategies from departments that excel*, Hoboken, NJ: Wiley.
Boice, R., 1985. Cognitive components of blocking. *Written Communication*, 2(1), pp. 91–104.
Boice, R., 1989. Procrastination, busyness and bingeing. *Behaviour Research and Therapy*, 27(6), pp. 605–611.
Boice, R., 1990. *Professors as writers: a self-help guide to productive writing*, Stillwater, OK: New Forums Press.
Bossio, D., Loch, B., Schier, M. and Mazzolini, A., 2014. A roadmap for forming successful interdisciplinary education research collaborations: a reflective approach. *Higher Education Research & Development*, 33(2), pp. 198–211.
Boud, D. and Tennant, M., 2006. Putting doctoral education to work: challenges to academic practice. *Higher Education Research & Development*, 25(1), pp. 293–306.
Bozeman, B., Fay, D. and Slade, C.P., 2013. Research collaboration in universities and academic entrepreneurship: the-state-of-the-art. *The Journal of Technology Transfer*, 38(1), pp. 1–67.
Browning, L., Thompson, K. and Dawson, D., 2014. Developing future research leaders: designing early career researcher programs to enhance track record. *International Journal for Researcher Development*, 5(2), pp. 123–134.
Cargill, M., 2009. *Writing scientific research articles: strategies and steps*. Hoboken, NJ: Wiley-Blackwell.
CFRD, 2016. The Vitae Career Framework for Researcher Developers. Available online at www.vitae.ac.uk/researchers-professional-development/practical-resources-for-researcher-developers-1/the-vitae-career-framework-for-researcher-developers-cfrd/introduction-to-the-vitae-career-framework-for-researcher-developers-cfrd
Debowski, S., 2010. Leading research in an evolving world: implications for higher education development, policy and practice. In *Research and development in higher education: reshaping higher education*, Melbourne, 6–9 July, 2010, 33, Melbourne, Vic.: HERDSA, pp. 213–222.
Debowski, S., 2012. *The new academic: a strategic handbook*: London: Open University Press.

Denholm, C., 2006. *Doctorates downunder: keys to successful doctoral study in Australia and New Zealand.* Camberwell,Vic.: ACER Press.

Denholm, C.J. and Evans, T.D., 2007. *Supervising doctorates downunder: keys to effective supervision in Australia and New Zealand.* Camberwell, Vic.: ACER Press.

Doyle, J. and Cuthill, M., 2015. Does 'get visible or vanish' herald the end of 'publish or perish'? *Higher Education Research & Development*, 34(3), pp. 671–674.

Evans, L., 2011. The scholarship of researcher development: mapping the terrain and pushing back boundaries. *International Journal for Researcher Development*, 2(2), pp. 75–98.

Evans, L., 2014. What is effective research leadership? A research-informed perspective. *Higher Education Research & Development*, 33(1), pp. 46–58.

Evans, L., 2015. Enhancing the quality of research in Europe: theoretical perspectives on and guiding principles for researcher development. In A. Curaj, L. Matei, R. Pricopie, J. Salmi and P. Scott, eds, *The European Higher Education Area*, Cham, Switzerland: Springer, pp. 573–591.

Gardiner, M. and Kearns, H., 2010. *Turbocharge your writing: how to become a prolific academic writer.* Adelaide, SA: Flinders University.

Gordon, G., 2005. The human dimensions of the research agenda: supporting the development of researchers throughout the career life cycle. *Higher Education Quarterly*, 59(1), pp. 40–55.

Grant, B., 2008. *Academic writing retreats: a facilitator's guide.* Milperra, NSW: Higher Education Research and Development Society of Australasia.

Halse, C. and Malfroy, J., 2010. Retheorizing doctoral supervision as professional work. *Studies in Higher Education*, 35(1), pp. 79–92.

Herbert, D.L., Barnett, A.G., Clarke, P. and Graves, N., 2013. On the time spent preparing grant proposals: an observational study of Australian researchers. *BMJ Open*, 3(5). Available online at DOI: 10.1136/bmjopen-2013-002800

Hottenrott, H. and Lawson, C., 2014. Research grants, sources of ideas and the effects on academic research. *Economics of Innovation and New Technology*, 23(2), pp. 109–133.

Hughes, M. and Bennett, D., 2013. Survival skills: the impact of change and the ERA on Australian researchers. *Higher Education Research & Development*, 32(3), pp. 340–354.

King, M.F. and Denecke, D.D., 2003. *On the right track: a manual for research mentors.* Washington, DC: Council of Graduate Schools.

Lee, A. and Danby, S. (eds), 2012. *Reshaping doctoral education: changing approaches and pedagogies*, Milton Park, Oxfordshire: Routledge.

McAlpine, L. and Amundsen, C., 2011. *Doctoral education research-based strategies for doctoral students, supervisors and administrators*, Dordrecht: Springer.

McGrail, M.R., Rickard, C.M. and Jones, R., 2006. Publish or perish: a systematic review of interventions to increase academic publication rates. *Higher Education Research and Development*, 25(1), pp. 19–35.

Middlehurst, R., Goreham, H. and Woodfield, S., 2009. Why research leadership in higher education? Exploring contributions from the UK's leadership foundation for higher education. *Leadership*, 5(3), pp. 311–329.

Mowbray, S. and Halse, C., 2010. The purpose of the PhD: theorising the skills acquired by students. *Higher Education Research & Development*, 29(6), pp. 653–664.

Orlando, J. and Gard, M., 2014. Playing and (not?) understanding the game: ECRs and university support. *International Journal for Researcher Development*, 5(1), pp. 2–15.

Pitman, T. and Berman, J.E., 2009. Of what benefit and to whom? Linking Australian humanities research with its 'end users'. *Journal of Higher Education Policy and Management*, 31(4), pp. 315–326.

Sadler, D.R., 2009. *Up the publication road: a guide to publishing in scholarly journals for academics, researchers, and graduate students*, 3rd edition, Milperra, NSW: Higher Education Research and Development Society of Australasia.

Saltmarsh, S., Sutherland-Smith, W. and Randell-Moon, H., 2011. 'Inspired and assisted', or 'berated and destroyed'? Research leadership, management and performativity in troubled times. *Ethics and Education*, 6(3), pp. 293–306.

Sinclair, J., Cuthbert, D. and Barnacle, R., 2014. The entrepreneurial subjectivity of successful researchers. *Higher Education Research & Development*, 33(5), pp. 1007–1019.

Sword, H., 2009. Writing for higher education differently: a manifesto on style. *Studies in Higher Education*, 34(3), pp. 319–336.

Sword, H., 2011. *Stylish academic writing*, Cambridge, MA: Harvard University Press.

Thomson, P. and Walker, M., 2010. *The Routledge doctoral supervisor's companion: supporting effective research*, London: Routledge.

Walker, G.E., Golde, C.M., Jones, L., Bueschel, A.C., Hutchings, P. and Carnegie Foundation for the Advancement of Teaching, 2008. *The formation of scholars: rethinking doctoral education for the twenty-first century*, San Francisco, CA: Jossey-Bass.

Chapter 16

Developing research capacity

Research development is a very recent field that is still building a shape and identity within the sector (Browning *et al.* 2014; Evans 2011). As outlined in Chapter 2, there have been some key influences in shaping this development focus, mostly stemming from national and competitive pressures to build research capacity (Debowski 2012a; Gordon 2005). The public nature of research performance has acted as a considerable stimulus for action, with many faculties and research groups seeking improved ways to build their collective outcomes and impact (Bland *et al.* 2005). This creates a strong platform for research development, but also emphasises the importance of working in partnership with leaders who will strongly influence localised support for applying any new insights or skills.

Evans (2015) notes that research capacity building is multi-dimensional, supporting the development of researchers across three key dimensions: *behavioural* (the process of doing research); *attitudinal* (the perception and interpretation of research and its context); and *intellectual* (the interpretation and advancement of research). However, two additional dimensions need to be added: *socioemotional* (the capacity to productively work with colleagues and collaborators) and *strategic* (professional judgement and planning). Thus, research capacity building is likely to emphasise the following:

- the construction of a robust research identity and research strategy that supports progressive enhancement of research self-efficacy (Quimbo and Sulabo 2014), profile and impact;
- gaining competence with the key research processes (grant application writing, research design, writing and working within a research community) (Evans 2015);
- acquiring good judgement as to timing, focus and prioritisation (Evans 2015);
- clarifying the expected standards and quality that should be achieved (Evans 2015);
- enhancement of research leadership, management and collaborative capabilities (Debowski 2012b).

There will be many factors that influence the achievement of these goals, including the recognition by the individual that learning and development is a necessary part of the research journey. The feedback, support and encouragement of mentors, supervisors and other colleagues to participate in learning opportunities will be influential, as will strong advocacy from university leaders. And, of course, the provision of appropriate, useful and well-tailored support is fundamental to the researchers who are participating.

This chapter explores some of the ways that research development can be framed and offered, particularly through the agency of the research developer, who might be located within faculties, institutes, or centrally. Different development options will be explored, highlighting some of the principles and key considerations that could be factored in when designing or delivering these services. The partnership between the research developer and other capacity-building agents (e.g. leaders and the executive) will be explored in tandem.

Research capacity building success indicators

There are three primary goals to be targeted with respect to research development:

- to support and enable quality research and high productivity across the entire university community;
- to stimulate a strong research development culture in faculties, centres and institutes, and via research and academic leaders;
- to embed good research practice principles and processes in university systems and practices.

Box 16.1 outlines key indicators that test whether high-impact research development is evidenced.

Development options and strategies

Research development is a complex area of university capacity building. It is often supported by multiple agencies in the university, with different leaders keen to see certain things achieved. While some will be strongly focused on ensuring compliance (e.g. ethics and research reporting), others will be keen to encourage innovation, increased quality and productivity and emerging talent. These complementary, but somewhat different priorities, need to be reflected and embraced as part of research development.

Support for research development may require the services of different agencies and sponsors. The Research Office, reporting to the deputy vice-chancellor or vice-president (research) is likely to have key responsibilities in ensuring the research function is achieving the targets that have been set. At the same time, the critical importance of research may also encourage strong alliances with the executive member who is responsible for academic outcomes and enhancement (e.g. the provost or deputy vice-chancellor, responsible for academic matters). Human Resource professionals may be actively engaged in designing programs to support the development of complex research capabilities (e.g. career management,

> **Box 16.1 Evidence of high-impact research development**
>
> - Research capacity building is featured in institutional priorities.
> - Executive leaders demonstrate a strong commitment to encouraging research excellence across the institution.
> - Key research capabilities are identified and encouraged throughout the university.
> - Research-active staff can readily access and seek guidance, support and information to support their research.
> - An effective orientation program is attended by incoming researchers.
> - Doctoral candidates and early career researchers are assisted in building their core research capabilities.
> - A range of development strategies are employed, including workshops, programs, mentorship support.
> - Support is offered across the research career cycle, with recognition of the changing capabilities that underpin research advancement and success.
> - Faculty leaders are strong advocates of research development and capacity building.
> - Research mentorship is strongly employed across the university.
> - There is a strong culture of sharing good practice and successful models of research practice.
> - Successful researchers are actively engaged in sharing their expertise and knowledge with more junior researchers.
> - There are strong partnerships between faculty leaders, senior researchers and developers in encouraging ongoing development of research capabilities.
> - Research leaders actively engage in evaluating and enhancing their leadership strategies.
> - Research-active staff demonstrate increasing success in publishing quality, peer-reviewed scholarly publications and gaining funding.
> - Collaborations are well developed and generate high impact.
> - Research projects are effectively managed to achieve high-quality outcomes, timely completion and demonstrable outputs.
> - There is good interchange and interaction across research disciplines.

leadership, management and collaborative strategies), either as the specific target, or as a component of a more holistic support for academic development. Deans and in-faculty developers are likely to lead research enhancement strategies. The supervisor and senior staff in faculties or research groups should also play their part in building capacity through their modelling of good practice, mentorship, constructive supervision and advocacy (Bland *et al.* 2005). It is important then to clarify who is engaged in research development, what they are focused on supporting, and whether there is a need to collaborate on joint offerings or refine the range and focus being offered. Something to watch for is the assumption that someone else is ensuring coverage. It is often not the case, and may generate significant gaps in support. For example, mentorship is widely acknowledged as being a key tool for research success (Debowski 2013), but many researchers and academics lack a mentor. This is a significant risk to capacity building.

Developing the research identity, narrative and portfolio

Many people operate in the research environment with little conscious mapping of their research strategy or intentions. This can reduce their research performance, as reactive approaches can impede effort, prioritisation and the identification of suitable opportunities (MacLeod *et al.* 2012; Ito and Brotheridge 2007). Research strategy encourages the targeted development of publications, research advancement, grant seeking, collaboration and role escalation. As part of this process, individuals benefit from building a research narrative and portfolio that acts as a record of research development, documenting the individual's goals, strategies, achievements, as well as mapping areas for ongoing development. Many universities simply ask academics to document their outcomes when performance discussions are being undertaken. There is considerable benefit in encouraging the development of a research portfolio that emphasises developmental goals and progressive performance, as this will encourage deeper questions relating to research leadership, impact and long-term goals. To illustrate, the following prompts encourage considered planning of research strategy and development, encouraging individuals to be more agential in their research approach. They also provide a valuable precursor to clarifying areas that would benefit from further development.

- *Your research context*: How did you reach this point in your research career? Describe your role and responsibilities with respect to research. What aspects of the research context enhance or limit your capacity to do research? To what extent are these within your control?
- *Research philosophy*: What do you want to achieve from your research? What impact do you hope to have? Identify both long and short-term goals that can assist you to reach these intended targets.
- *Research Achievements*: Document your key achievements across the different research activities (publications, funding, supervision, collaboration, project management and outcomes, leadership). Consider how your track record evidences a growth in depth, expertise and seniority.
- *Research leadership*: Consider the roles you are playing in guiding teams, projects or programs of research. How do you manage these roles? What is your leadership approach? Is it making a difference to your team? How can you tell? What performance indicators are you using? If you are not yet leading, how can you build more opportunities to do so?

- *Research development*: From this analysis, identify any gaps or potential areas of enhancement that you would like to pursue. Map the key learning outcomes you will target in the coming year. Identify how you might address your learning needs, using courses, mentorship, experiential learning or other helpful strategies.
- *Evidence*: Build your evidence base for documenting your research outcomes and effectiveness. It may be helpful to gradually build a longitudinal dossier of evidence (e.g. progressive numbers of citations, higher degree by research [HDR] graduates, funding) that offers a clear visual picture of progress. Letters of invitation, awards and other evidence of peer esteem should also be captured in readiness for annual reviews or promotion rounds.

The development of a clear narrative and conscious insight into how a research profile has evolved provides an important foundation for productive discussions about performance and strategy. These questions are valuable for supervisors, mentors and developers.

Building research capacity

There are a range of approaches or experiences that might be integrated into research capacity building including:

- institutional reforms that promote better practice and principles;
- workshops that focus on key learning areas or skill enhancement;
- programs that facilitate deeper learning, a sustained learning experience and, possibly, cohorts of learners;
- blended learning programs that support self-directed learning at point of need, or encourage efficient skill enhancement in a supportive but efficient setting;
- negotiated, customised programs or activities designed to address a key challenge or collective capacity building;
- projects that improve the systems, policies, support or outcomes of the research agenda.

While the focus in this review will emphasise the HE developer as a dedicated resource to support these initiatives, it will be seen that this is strongly allied to the leadership and advocacy of many other leaders in the research community.

Whole of institutional reforms

Institutional reforms may be multi-faceted, focused on improving institutional outcomes through the refinement of systems, education and adoption across the institution. Many universities, for example, have introduced research metric systems that are influencing the assessment of research performance and outcomes. The developer may fulfil a number of functions in these reform processes.

- Research on other institutional models and practices may be carried out to scope the likely features, their implications and the issues to be considered.
- The development of the systems themselves may require piloting, testing and input from stakeholders.
- There may be a need to work with more senior staff to explore how research reforms and innovations may best be introduced. Their support and encouragement will need to be sought and integrated.
- Specific sessions to prepare leaders and local communities are beneficial.
- The introduction of the reform, new systems and/or related policies may necessitate a widespread rollout across the different institutional faculties, research groups and communities. The message will need to be adapted to suit each context.
- The development of FAQs, demonstration clips, manuals and ongoing information may be needed.
- Feedback on take-up and possible enhancements may be provided to the sponsor.
- Once established, the developer will need to retain a current knowledge of these basic systems and expectations, and to integrate these into ongoing workshops, programs and guidance. This will include integrating information on this new initiative in orientation programs and guidelines.

It is likely that a number of contributors will be engaged in this process. Regular meetings with all contributors can increase efficiency and ensure any emergent issues are addressed quickly.

Research capability frameworks

Universities are moving toward the clarification of the core capabilities that underpin research success (Jacob and Meek 2013; Kahn *et al.* 2012). These can be focused in two ways: as the broad roles and functions that are likely to be fulfilled; or in terms of the different competencies that support those roles and functions (e.g. team building; project management; decision-making; relationship management). The development of an institutional research capability framework may be part of a broader project, aimed at mapping all academic capabilities. It may closely align with statements of performance expectations and could be part of an institutional focus on performance and standards setting. The framework may play a fundamental role in reviewing annual performance and providing detailed feedback. It may guide promotion decisions for those pursuing an academic track. The use of frameworks can be beneficial when they act as guides and development tools. However, when used to control and tightly prescribe the focus and activities that researchers emphasise, they can reduce motivation, productivity and creativity.

The developer is likely to promote, rather than create, a framework of this nature. The guidelines can assist in exploring what is expected of researchers, and may also clarify the core expectations of researchers and research-active staff as they progress through the ranks. Frameworks of this nature can also assist in planning the annual program of workshops or seminars to support the work of researchers. A further source of guidance can be the Vitae framework (CFRD 2016), which provides some detailed analysis of competencies. In designing the program of activities, aim for those that are readily evident as critical capabilities, and where attendance at workshops or related activities can add some value. Some of these areas may be better suited to a faculty-driven approach, particularly if peer-learning and mentorship can be integrated.

Researchers will appreciate a single source of information to access guidance on what is available, rather than the need to shift across different websites and services, particularly if they are new and unfamiliar with the institutional architecture and organisational structures. If research development operates across differentiated HED groups, an alliance to map what is being covered by whom can enrich and avoid unnecessary duplication.

Supporting doctoral candidates

Research support commences with higher degree research students, particularly those engaged in doctoral studies. Traditionally, this has emphasised the completion of the research project and the demonstration of competence in designing and publishing a thesis of merit. Workshops or programs have targeted specific skills in research capabilities, but many leave students somewhat adrift in terms of career management, transitioning to research roles or moving into postdoctoral roles.

There is evidence of a shift toward designing curricula to support the transition from research student to researcher (McAlpine and Turner 2012; McAlpine *et al.* 2013). Monash University in Melbourne, Australia, for example, offers a dynamic and flexible curriculum that supports the doctoral candidate as they progress from novice researcher to pursuing a career in either academe or industry. Each year of candidature emphasises a progressive transition to the next phase of development, encouraging the student to commence planning for their post-candidature phase. Online and face-to-face workshops are offered, catering for the diverse community and multiple campuses.[1] A particular strength of this model is the link back to supervisors, who are encouraged to explore the planned development each year as part of their annual review of the students' outcomes. A further advantage of this curriculum is that it is focused on the students' imminent and career-related needs.

It is likely that doctoral support will increase in sophistication as more research on doctoral programs is undertaken (McAlpine and Amundsen 2011; McAlpine and Emmioğlu 2015; McAlpine and Turner 2012). Improved linkages between faculty-based support, which may be largely focused on disciplinary research contexts, and the centralised curriculum, which may emphasise career, team, leadership and strategy, can become significant assets for the university. This may require re-education of supervisors to ensure that they understand the changes in focus toward integrated, future-focused guidance.

Orientation and induction

The object of orientation and induction is to provide each incoming researcher with contextualised knowledge regarding institutional research and its enactment across the institution. There are four areas in which researchers new to the university need to be guided:

1 their responsibilities and obligations as researchers;
2 the services and sources of support that can be accessed;
3 the policies, standards and expectations of performance that will underpin their practice;
4 introduction to the broader research community.

An orientation into the institutional research context provides guidance on the larger environment in which the research will be conducted. Research orientation programs may be provided centrally several times per year, offering context setting to researchers who have recently joined the university. In addition, each researcher benefits from a focused induction into their particular work context, enabling familiarity with their key local contacts, particular expectations, protocols, systems and practices that will support their research work. Thus, the initiation of newcomers is a joint responsibility.[2]

The orientation is an ideal context for the executive leader of research to be profiled, particularly in terms of guiding new staff toward an appreciation of the institution's research priorities and core initiatives. Conversely, the design of the program can be greatly enhanced by avoiding numerous "talking heads." There is little value in creating a lengthy dissemination format when much of the information can be provided in a portable format that is better accessed at point of need. (This might include a checklist of compliance-related training that must be completed, highlighting the critical nature of early preparation.) This session can provide a valuable linkage between the faculties and the institutional services and strategy. The encouragement of faculty-based discussions to explore the key approaches and methods in each faculty, along with introducing key contacts and colleagues from their own faculties, is greatly valued by participants, offering a valuable chance to build linkages and learn more about their local context and priorities. Contributions of faculty representatives also increases their engagement with this important event.

A challenge for research orientations is publicising the event and gaining faculty sponsorship for attendance. The development of alliances with faculty leaders, administrators and research team leaders can improve the take-up of the sessions. Statistics indicating the percentage of new appointees who are attending can offer evidence as to relative engagement, encouraging leaders' consideration as to the preparedness of their new research staff. Monitoring of completion of compliance training can also be tied into this preparatory phase.

Encouragement to seek a research mentor (Brown *et al.* 2009; Debowski 2012b; de Janasz and Sullivan 2004; Ligon *et al.* 2011; Nakamura and Shernoff 2009; Sorcinelli 2007) and build linkages across the faculty provides important support at this stage of entry. This support is often best sponsored by faculty leaders and supervisors.

Early career researchers

Early career researcher support is likely to take three approaches. First, workshops to support core capabilities are likely to be regularly offered. These may be ½ to 1 day in duration, and commonly emphasise the core capabilities that have been identified as essential for research success. There is increasing focus on dissemination practices as part of this repertoire (Mewburn and Thomson 2013; Parr 2012). The development of workshops may be guided by a capabilities framework, institutional priorities, needs analysis of early career staff or feedback from faculties. Topics may relate to getting published, building networks, intellectual property, research project management, collaboration, research supervision and possibly, leadership of teams or projects. The workshops generally explore key principles to be followed, along with interaction with models, exemplars and expert commentators. Often, the take-up of the offerings is monitored, acting as another cue as to whether they are well judged and meeting the needs of the community. However, low enrolments might also indicate poor timing (e.g. near grant deadlines), poor communication channels or the need to create more attractive marketing information.

A challenge with regard to supporting researchers is that many will not think about developmental needs until it is quite critical. The integration of blended learning programs can offer an important transitionary learning medium as the individual can access courses to undertake when a need is identified.[3] Ensuring people are aware of this option and encouraging supervisors and mentors to promote them can greatly assist in their adoption. However, as noted previously, these benefit from the contextualisation that a follow-up workshop offers.

Early career researcher programs facilitate capacity building; exploring research identity and strategy formation; core capabilities (e.g. publishing, getting funded, collaboration, research leadership and project management); sharing good practice; supporting the initiation of mentoring; and encouraging connections with peers and exemplars. A focused encouragement to publish over the program duration is an important motivator for the participants (Browning *et al.* 2014). A very successful approach to building early career research capabilities is to situate programs in faculties (Debowski 2007). Faculty-sponsored programs attract strong interest and engage leaders in their delivery.

Generally, these programs would seek to support those with doctorates who are consolidating and extending their research capabilities and career strategies. The models and context are more disciplinary-relevant and participants are able to meet and engage with colleagues at many levels. These programs may be funded by deans, who appreciate the opportunity to guide the priorities and emphases that are incorporated. In some faculties, a dual focus across teaching and research might be integrated, acknowledging that this might be the one time many will participate.

Universities are also moving toward talent programs for high-flying early career researchers. The selection of candidates will need to be carefully managed, and ideally, should draw on the judgement of a range of research leaders from across the university. These highly competitive programs can provide an important launch pad for talented researchers who have demonstrated their capacity to build an excellent track record, including successful funding bids. The provision of a program that helps them travel to meet with international or national leaders, seed new projects or explore their emerging role as research leaders can further assist their trajectory. Multi-source feedback might be integrated to inform their leadership identity and strategies.

Support to increase writing capacity, strategy, outputs and quality is a key priority for many institutions. These can take a myriad of forms, including writing retreats, communities of practice, workshops and the provision of writing spaces[4] (Aitchison and Guerin 2014; Bastalich 2011; Cuthbert *et al.* 2009; Grant 2008; Lee and Boud 2003; MacLeod *et al.* 2012; Murray and Newton 2009; Murray and Thow 2014; Petrova and Coughlin 2012; Wardale *et al.* 2015; Weaver *et al.* 2014).

An encouragement to build enhanced mentorship strategies threads through all of these offerings. Opportunities to hear inspirational researchers talk about their careers and the provision of coaching further enriches programs. More customised support, such as guidance and feedback on grant and fellowship proposals, are further mechanisms to set up early career researchers.

Mid-career researchers

The transition from early to mid-career research brings with it new challenges. Researchers transition toward more senior roles and must progress toward leadership of teams, projects, grants, collaborations and possibly, research committees, agendas and faculty activities. They may need to escalate their research impact and influence and find themselves moving into more diverse stakeholder relationships, which often carry considerable complexity. There is evidence of more universities identifying this phase as a risky time. People can start to lose their edge, and may find it hard to generate new lines of research or transition to higher levels of responsibility. Those who remain firmly attached to their "early career" hands-on way of doing things will find it particularly hard to transition into more influential and strategic roles.

Generic workshops offer one source of support for this group. However, the titles of workshops and their descriptions need to be carefully phrased to avoid positioning them as "beginner classes." Refresher or master classes that assume some prior knowledge can be attractive, as they explore advanced techniques and strategies. These sessions greatly benefit from participant input and can be conducted a little more intensively, given the experience the participants bring with them. Mentors who wish to develop a larger repertoire to share with their protégés can also be encouraged to attend.

Problem-based workshops can provide another frame for development. Recognition that a faculty is losing its funding base due to poor grant success, for example, can generate strong interest in promoting a funding/research strategy activity. The provision of a faculty forum that explores the issue, including sharing of successful established approaches, will be a popular in-service for committed staff at all levels. Mid-career staff are likely to benefit from hearing what others are doing, and can learn in a safe, collegial environment. Ideas to stimulate more faculty strategies are likely to come forward from such sessions, and may spark some more intensive activity within faculties or the university as a whole.

Universities are now introducing tightly focused, intensive programs for mid-career researchers, providing updates on advanced research capabilities and encouraging more in-depth discussions around research identity, strategy, building impact and influence, as well as creating a sustainable and fundable track record. A large challenge for many is the willingness to take time to reflect, acquire new skills and critique one's practice. Busy people can find it hard to disengage and take a step away from being fully present in the daily routine. Strong encouragement from supervisors and leaders to build advanced skills and capabilities will be a key incentive. The positioning of research capacity building as critical for the group or institution also escalates its prioritisation.

Encouragement to reflect and review one's career and established strategies is an important part of this stock-taking process. Mid-career researchers are frequently mentor-less, and they can benefit from this gap being addressed. Institutions that promote mentorship as a critical facet of their learning and development approach will see a profound impact across all levels. If conducting a mentorship program, a refresher for mentors relating to career management, the context in which research now operates, the expectations and capabilities to be developed and their role in guiding increased strategy and career success can be highly beneficial. It is helpful to have all members of the research community reflecting similar understandings and more sophisticated insights into research strategy and impact.

Research leaders

Research leaders come in all guises, including quite junior researchers who have been successful in gaining funding and recognition for their work. They can lead teams, projects or research programs. The common factor is that they have transitioned from focusing on their own research to the enabling of collective research capacity across individuals. Three development approaches that work very well at this level are the provision of targeted workshops, research leadership programs and negotiated support.

Targeted workshops on research leadership offer more guidance on the science of research leadership, along with opportunities to explore key issues and their resolution. More senior researchers value the time to work with their colleagues and hear about different approaches. However, these workshops will need to be conducted in a different manner to those for more junior staff. They will need to offer chances to reflect, while remaining energetic, focused and productive. Co-facilitation between developers and credible research leaders can be an effective approach.

Research leadership programs can operate at either faculty or university level. Generally cohort-based, they encourage deep engagement with research leadership in conjunction with other, like-minded colleagues. The program might follow a similar path to that outlined in Chapter 8: residential, mentorship and issues-focused follow-up sessions that explore key research challenges, a multi-source review, coaching and other in-depth learning exercises. While many might argue that few leaders will come forward for an intensive activity of this nature, the reality is that many will value the opportunity to enhance their practice and to learn more about the nature of research leadership (Debowski 2010). Encouragement from their deans or leaders will encourage participation. These programs have wide-reaching influence as each leader is a touch-point for their team, providing strong modelling of research practice.

The third approach is that of negotiated support. Research leaders face many challenges as they seek to build a team, carry it through a program of research and ensure it progresses effectively to new initiatives. Leaders are seeking expert assistance more often, looking for ways to build better cultures, higher performance, greater capacity or to address emerging vulnerabilities. This negotiated support can include, for example, guidance on managing difficult members, optimising talented teams or increasing productive outcomes. Expert facilitators who can work with the leader and their group/s provide in-context learning support. They may employ many of the program-based support mechanisms, but within the specific team context. For example, the use of a multi-source review becomes more powerful if the leader is able to be debriefed and then supported in their testing of different behaviours and interventions across their team. Leaders often take these reviews further, encouraging their subordinates to undertake a similar reflective journey. This offers considerable benefit in building a common language and focus for the team's development. This form of support may require a sustained partnership for some time as preliminary activities reveal related issues that may require further exploration.

Research project groups may seek development support, focusing on different elements of their activities. Those that are working with external stakeholders or partners, for example, may seek assistance in facilitating collaborative start-ups.

Others may wish to review the efficiency or effectiveness of their established systems or processes. In these contexts, the team and leader may embark on an important journey of discovery that surfaces considerable insight about being a team, high performing and researchers.

Conclusion

This chapter has repeatedly affirmed a critical point: research development needs the support of many different leaders and faculty members to build the right culture, messages and environment to encourage high performance and aspirations. While research is touted as being important, the necessary acquisition of higher order research capabilities is less well supported and understood (Evans 2012). Leaders, mentors, supervisors, reviewers, colleagues, developers and all researchers play a part in promoting these goals. The guidance of the research developer can add considerable value to this process.

Notes

1 See: www.monash.edu/graduate-research/future-students/phd/professional-development-option
2 Some useful ideas on orientation can be found in the Future Research Leaders Program orientation module: http:frlp.edu.au
3 The Epigeum Professional Skills for Research Leaders program, for example, has been designed to support this context. See: https://epigeum.com/courses/research/professional-skills-research-leaders-2
4 The University of Massachusetts offers a range of such programs. See: www.umass.edu/ctfd/scholarly/index.shtml

References

Aitchison, C. and Guerin, C. (eds), 2014. *Writing groups for doctoral education and beyond: innovations in practice and theory*, London: Routledge.
Bastalich, W., 2011. Beyond the local/general divide: English for academic purposes and process approaches to cross disciplinary, doctoral writing support. *Higher Education Research & Development*, 30(4), pp. 449–462.
Bland, C.J., Weber-Main, A., Lund, S.M. and Finstad, D.A., 2005. *The research-productive department: strategies from departments that excel*, Hoboken, NJ: Wiley.
Brown, R.T., Daly, B.P. and Leong, F.T.L., 2009. Mentoring in research: a developmental approach. *Professional Psychology: Research and Practice*, 40(3), pp. 306–313.
Browning, L., Thompson, K. and Dawson, D., 2014. Developing future research leaders: designing early career researcher programs to enhance track record. *International Journal for Researcher Development*, 5(2), pp. 123–134.
CFRD, 2016. The Vitae Career Framework for Researcher Developers. Available online at www.vitae.ac.uk/researchers-professional-development/practical-resources-for-researcher-developers-1/the-vitae-career-framework-for-researcher-developers-cfrd/introduction-to-the-vitae-career-framework-for-researcher-developers-cfrd

Cuthbert, D., Spark, C. and Burke, E., 2009. Disciplining writing: the case for multi-disciplinary writing groups to support writing for publication by research candidates in the humanities, arts and social sciences. *Higher Education Research & Development*, 28(2), pp. 137–150.
Debowski, S., 2007. Finding the right track: enabling early career academic management of career, teaching and research. In G. Crisp, ed., *Enhancing higher education, theory and scholarship: proceedings of the 30th HERDSA Annual Conference*, 8–11 July 2007, Sydney: HERDSA, pp. 138–149.
Debowski, S., 2010. Leading research in an evolving world: implications for higher education development, policy and practice. In *Research and development in higher education: reshaping higher education*, Melbourne, 6–9 July, 2010, Melbourne, Vic.: HERDSA, pp. 213–222.
Debowski, S., 2012a. *Strategic Research Capacity Building: Investigating higher education researcher development strategies in the United Kingdom, United States and New Zealand*, Winston Churchill Memorial Trust Fellowship report, Canberra, ACT: Winston Churchill Memorial Trust. Available online at www.churchilltrust.com.au/site_media/fellows/2011_Debowski_Shelda.pdf
Debowski, S., 2012b. *The new academic: A strategic handbook*. London: Open University Press.
Debowski, S., 2013. Creating fertile learning spaces: mentorship strategies to support academic success. In S. Frielick, N. Buissink-Smith, P. Wyse, J. Billot, J. Hallas and E. Whitehead, eds, *Research and development in higher education: the place of learning and teaching*, Auckland, New Zealand, 1–4 July 2013, Milperra, NSW: HERSDA, pp. 113–123.
Evans, L., 2011. What research administrators need to know about researcher development: towards a new conceptual model. *Journal of Research Administration*, 42(1), pp. 15–37.
Evans, L., 2012. Leadership for researcher development: what research leaders need to know and understand. *Educational Management Administration & Leadership*, 40(4), pp. 423–435.
Evans, L., 2015. Enhancing the quality of research in Europe: theoretical perspectives on and guiding principles for researcher development. In A. Curaj *et al.*, eds, *The European Higher Education Area*, Cham, Switzerland: Springer, pp. 573–591.
Gordon, G., 2005. The human dimensions of the research agenda: supporting the development of researchers throughout the career life cycle. *Higher Education Quarterly*, 59(1), pp. 40–55.
Grant, B., 2008. *Academic writing retreats: a facilitator's guide*, Milperra, NSW: Higher Education Research and Development Society of Australasia.
Ito, J. and Brotheridge, C., 2007. Predicting individual research productivity: more than a question of time. *The Canadian Journal of Higher Education*, 37(1), pp. 1–25.
Jacob, M. and Meek, V.L., 2013. Scientific mobility and international research networks: trends and policy tools for promoting research excellence and capacity building. *Studies in Higher Education*, 38(3), pp. 331–344.
de Janasz, S.C. and Sullivan, S.E., 2004. Multiple mentoring in academe: developing the professorial network. *Journal of Vocational Behavior*, 64(2), pp. 263–283.
Kahn, P., Petichakis, C. and Walsh, L., 2012. Developing the capacity of researchers for collaborative working. *International Journal for Researcher Development*, 3(1), pp. 49–63.

Lee, A. and Boud, D., 2003. Writing groups, change and academic identity: research development as local practice. *Studies in Higher Education*, 28(2), pp. 187–200.

Ligon, G.S., Wallace, J.H. and Osburn, H.K., 2011. Experiential development and mentoring processes for leaders for innovation. *Advances in Developing Human Resources*, 13(3), pp. 297–317.

McAlpine, L. and Amundsen, C., 2011. *Doctoral education research-based strategies for doctoral students, supervisors and administrators*, Dordrecht: Springer.

McAlpine, L. and Turner, G., 2012. Imagined and emerging career patterns: perceptions of doctoral students and research staff. *Journal of Further and Higher Education*, 36(4), pp. 535–548.

McAlpine, L. and Emmioğlu, E., 2015. Navigating careers: perceptions of sciences doctoral students, post-PhD researchers and pre-tenure academics. *Studies in Higher Education*, 40(10), pp. 1770–1785.

McAlpine, L., Amundsen, C. and Turner, G., 2013. Constructing post-PhD careers: negotiating opportunities and personal goals. *International Journal for Researcher Development*, 4(1), pp. 39–54.

MacLeod, I., Steckley, L. and Murray, R., 2012. Time is not enough: promoting strategic engagement with writing for publication. *Studies in Higher Education*, 37(6), pp. 641–654.

Mewburn, I. and Thomson, P., 2013. Why do academics blog? An analysis of audiences, purposes and challenges. *Studies in Higher Education*, 38(8), pp. 1105–1119.

Murray, R. and Newton, M., 2009. Writing retreat as structured intervention: margin or mainstream? *Higher Education Research & Development*, 28(5), pp. 541–553.

Murray, R. and Thow, M., 2014. Peer-formativity: a framework for academic writing. *Higher Education Research & Development*, 33(6), pp. 1166–1179.

Nakamura, J. and Shernoff, D.J., 2009. *Good mentoring: fostering excellent practice in higher education*, 1st edition, San Francisco, CA: Jossey-Bass.

Parr, C., 2012. Blog-standard turn-offs for social media neophytes. *Times Higher Education*, 1 November, p. 13.

Petrova, P. and Coughlin, A., 2012. Using structured writing retreats to support novice researchers. *International Journal for Researcher Development*, 3(1), pp. 79–88.

Quimbo, M.A.T. and Sulabo, E.C., 2014. Research productivity and its policy implications in higher education institutions. *Studies in Higher Education*, 39(10), pp. 1955–1971.

Sorcinelli, M.D., 2007. From mentor to mentoring networks: mentoring in the new academy. *Change: The Magazine of Higher Learning*, November/December, pp. 58–60.

Wardale, D., Hendrickson, T., Jefferson, T., Klass, D., Lord, L. and Marinelli, M., 2015. Creating an oasis: some insights into the practice and theory of a successful academic writing group. *Higher Education Research & Development*, 34(6), pp. 1297–1310.

Weaver, D., Robbie, D. and Radloff, A., 2014. Demystifying the publication process – a structured writing program to facilitate dissemination of teaching and learning scholarship. *International Journal for Academic Development*, 19(3), pp. 212–225.

Chapter 17

From aspirant to excellent teacher

Universities place great importance on their educational mission. However, there is increasing concern that learning and teaching strategy, as effected by university leaders, can be impersonal and largely directed at outcomes, not process (Smith 2012). The prioritisation of instrumental outcomes to meet economic challenges is seen by some as compromising a focus on qualitative pedagogy (Ransome 2011). Despite these uncertainties, the promotion of student learning remains strong in the rhetoric and focus of administrators (Trapp 2012). There is more pressure to ensure educational quality and global competition for students and diminished resourcing in many nations have encouraged a stronger focus on the practices and outcomes related to teaching. Students are essential to university functioning, and in turn, effective teachers are essential to their students' outcomes and experience. Thus, teaching academics have experienced growing pressure to be high-performing, efficient and caring educators, whilst also balancing their research and other academic roles.

Like the research role, teaching is a long developmental process. The initial focus for learning will relate to demonstrating competence as a teacher. The public nature of teaching can generate considerable anxiety as to demonstrating suitable capabilities. The initial goal, then, is to develop sufficient capability to survive and, ultimately, excel. In the process, the individual teacher is likely to identify a number of dilemmas that will need to be worked through. These include the transition from being a competent to an excellent teacher; the integration of scholarship and leadership roles; the development of a sound evidence base to illustrate teaching quality and development; and the positioning of teaching in an academic career.

This chapter will scaffold some of the areas that academics may engage with in their progression as teachers.

Academics as teachers

A potential tension that is often experienced, particularly in the early academic years, is the need to focus on both teaching and research. The transition into university work can be a challenging time: teaching and research both require the development of a range of new capabilities and skills before academics will feel confident and competent. However, it is important to realise that this competence will take time to become established. The developmental process encourages a journey of self-discovery about oneself as teacher, richer insights into the student condition and an emerging understanding of the underlying principles and theories of learning and instruction (pedagogy). Ideally, it is undertaken in collaboration with others and with the guidance of mentors, models and supervisors to offer some disciplinary-based scaffolding.

Like research, the professional enhancement of one's teaching requires regular evaluation, progressive adaptation and critique of practice and outcomes. Each student cohort will pose new challenges; the curriculum will require regular enhancement; there will be a desire to improve student ratings of teaching; and resources, ideas and teaching approaches will need regular renewal. Thus, the foundational skills designed to survive in the classroom are just the first step in a career-long journey. As part of this progression, the individual teacher will need to collect and review evidence of a progressive enhancement of skills, effectiveness and impact. Promotion, probation, tenure and award processes all require clear evidence of these elements. The capacity to clearly articulate what, how and why one pursues certain pedagogies and practices is an important part of the maturation process. Each teacher will also need to locate their practice within the institutional context, demonstrating familiarity with relevant policies, systems and practices, as well as reflecting disciplinary approaches to student learning.

The development of critical, reflexive practice is particularly important for teaching. The dynamic and somewhat unpredictable role that a teacher plays requires regular testing of assumptions, methodologies and roles (Sherbino *et al.* 2014; Stoddard and Borges 2015). Regular evaluation of one's teaching and critiquing of professional practice with reference to the broader body of scholarship on teaching is an essential skill. Those who have progressed past novice status are likely to move past praxis (the application of theory to practice) into a more critical engagement and testing of the knowledge base. In some nations, this has encouraged a strong tradition of scholarly activity.

In addition, university academics may embrace educational leadership, encouraging good practice in a range of communities, including teaching teams, curriculum innovation teams, schools or departments, and faculties. This broadened capacity to influence and encourage innovation and quality outcomes can be particularly significant in generating improved practice.

Building a teaching identity

As with research, each academic will develop a personalised approach to their teaching (Trevitt *et al.* 2011). The development of their teaching identity can be informed by a number of influences. The institution is likely to present a particularly detailed overview of the priorities to be supported and the outcomes to be delivered. Graduate attributes often provide institutional signposts as to the broad outcomes students should demonstrate (Barrie 2007). Student evaluation of teaching instruments and the assessment of teaching outcomes in promotional and annual review processes are all clear indicators as to what is being reviewed and valued. In this context, the teacher is likely to build a targeted insight into what counts in terms of teaching practice. The disciplinary/local context is a strong influence on both practice and professional perspectives (Krause 2014).

However, the development of a robust teaching identity will need to progress well beyond simple adherence to these core indicators. Higher education teaching is complex, requiring nuanced judgements about teaching processes, principles and outcomes. Different disciplines promote particular approaches (Healey 2000), and the calibre and nature of the student group must also be accommodated. As the teacher progresses toward mastery and confident negotiation of roles, the shape and focus of the teaching identity is likely to shift. The capacity to articulate these concepts and to locate them in a scholarly framework offers a rich mechanism to build research-informed practice that can be confidently critiqued and explored.

The role of teacher as innovator can be somewhat fraught. Innovation brings some risk, particularly in the early phases of experimentation. Students, as the recipients of innovation, may perceive this test phase in a critical light, resulting in poor teacher ratings. The courage to push the boundaries is an important part of the role, but may need to be managed carefully. On the other hand, the quest to find better methods and approaches to student learning and outcomes is important evidence of transforming from competent to outstanding teacher.

Teaching is complex: it is a multi-faceted, interpretive professional process that draws on educational theory, established practices and the ongoing quest to develop mastery and excellence in delivering a quality outcome. The academic needs to develop a clear identity as to their purpose and role as an educator while remaining adaptive and responsive to new cues and trends that are emerging. Thus, teachers need to be adaptive, reflective, informed and scholarly. They also benefit from being articulate about their practice and praxis.

Understanding the educational context

Entry into university teaching opens up many insights as to the role of the university teacher and the contribution to be made. The following list demonstrates the areas of knowledge that might be explored by a teacher as part of that integrative process:

- *Educational outcomes*: Teachers play a key role in guiding students' development and identity. While they will be promulgating basic subject matter, they may also contribute to the students' preparation for their futures as graduates, critical thinkers (Davies 2011; Vardi 2013), intelligent citizens, ethical actors and lifelong learners. The university context offers a rich environment for enhancing the student's social, emotional, intellectual and learning capabilities. Each teacher needs to consider what educational outcomes will be emphasised through their teaching: they might, for example, seek to encourage higher order thinking, cognitive, social, emotional, values and/or professional perspectives (Barnett and Coate 2005). These considerations will be influential in shaping the teaching philosophy and design.

- *The student as learner*: University students are expected to take responsibility for their learning. The educational role, then, is to provide a pathway and clear signposts as to the knowledge, skills and process outcomes to be attained. This facilitative role requires adaptive responses by the teacher (Sadler 2012). While first year university students require more guidance on structure, self-management and problem-solving (Bone and Reid 2011), students in later years will be more self-determining (Barratt *et al*. 2011).
- *Student learning theory*: A range of theories guide our understanding of the ways that students learn at universities (Biggs 2012; Biggs and Tang 2011; Leibowitz 2009; Pepper 2010). These offer guidance on the ways in which teaching can be managed to encourage student ownership of their learning experience.
- *Student engagement*: This construct describes the degree to which a student participates and feels motivated to learn (Australian Council for Educational Research 2010; Crosling and Heagney 2009; Kuh 2005; Matthews *et al*. 2011; Schroeder 2005; Solomonides 2012). An understanding of the facilitative processes and the teacher's role provides important foundational guidance for any teacher.
- *Curriculum design*: A curriculum is a structured program of study designed to help students achieve the desired learning outcomes that have been identified for that portion of their course. Teachers are responsible for designing the activities, assessment and sequence of activities that form their curriculum. The quality of their design will have a major impact on the student experience, outcomes and engagement. The unit of study and its location in a program will also influence the nature of the curriculum, with core curricula in professional programs placing more restrictions on design and focus. Students enrolled in a capstone course, on the other hand, can be offered integrative learning that explores their cumulative understanding through participation in authentic learning projects, research, action learning, case studies, or fieldwork (Thomas *et al*. 2014).
- *Student diversity*: Students are highly heterogeneous, with diverse cultural, socio-emotional, and intellectual learning backgrounds. They may be located in different nations or on different campuses. There is considerable exploration of the need to build an inclusive, internationalised curriculum (Leask 2015; Velayo 2012) and to ensure cultural contexts are acknowledged (Sun 2012). This has been extended to recognising the educational differences that are likely to be encountered in different national systems (e.g. Ismail and Hassan 2012; Nickson 2012).
- *Instructional strategies*: Practical tools and strategies to enable confident management of the learning environment encompass a variety of approaches

to encourage student learning and participation (Hanover Research 2010; Svinicki *et al.* 2011).
- *Assessment practices*: The design of appropriate assessment activities to evaluate student learning, provide feedback on progress and encourage student reflection on their learning is an important capability.
- *Work-integrated learning*: These activities combine preparation for work placements with allocated time in real work contexts (Ferns 2014). Coordination of these units can be challenging, as students can require considerable support to adapt to busy professional settings. The development of students' professional capabilities is a particularly important outcome of these experiences.
- *Online learning*: This mode of education is now accepted as being part of the teaching context. There is considerable growth in the theory base and methodologies attached to engaging students remotely and encouraging a rich learning experience (Boettcher and Conrad 2010; Crisp 2009; Garrison 2011; Steel 2010).

It can be seen that this is a very large field of knowledge to explore and somehow extrapolate what is most suited to the discipline, specific learning context and the teacher's own particular preferences. As will be outlined in the next chapter, the provision of support and development is a critical part of navigating this very large field of knowledge and practice.

Evaluating educational effectiveness

Reflective and evaluative skills will greatly assist the development of excellent teaching. These reflections can be informed by a number of other feedback sources, including student feedback on teaching and peer review (Bell 2005; Crisp *et al.* 2009). Peers can provide different perspectives, including observing student responses and interactions. It is also helpful to build a longitudinal view of how particular units are improving, based on the different approaches and enhancements that have been implemented. Alternatively, the teacher might benchmark their teaching, reviewing how they have covered the core components compared with colleagues in other institutions. The focus on pedagogical reflection, which articulates back to learning theory and principles, encourages the teacher to reflect on their actions and plan for future actions and approaches (Winchester and Winchester 2011).

Many universities encourage the development of a teaching portfolio to illustrate teaching advancement (Trevitt *et al.* 2011). These are often employed for both summative and developmental purposes. The portfolio provides a concise and articulate account of the individual's educational journey, practice and performance. It documents the academic's teaching philosophy, progress and achievements across the different dimensions of teaching, scholarship and leadership. Sources of evidence to support those statements may be in the form of tabulated or collated summaries as well as original sources (such as award statements or testimonials from peer reviewers). As an evidence-based dossier, the portfolio provides a valuable source for review, evaluation and evidence provision when seeking awards, promotion or probation. It also supports discussions with mentors or supervisors when undertaking annual reviews.

Extending reach and influence: scholarship and research on teaching

The integration of a scholarly approach to teaching is strongly encouraged, particularly in nations like Australia and the United Kingdom (Trigwell *et al.* 2000). One component of this process is the engagement with the scholarly literature to build a research-informed approach, or praxis (Hardy 2010). This encourages academics to apply their understandings of the field and theory into their own professional practices. Praxis and reflection encourage teachers to critique their assumptions, outcomes and impact with reference to this scholarly base (Brew 2010; Brew and Sachs 2007). Kreber (2013) argues that the translation of these processes into documenting and sharing these insights as scholarly outputs enables public scrutiny and an opportunity to explore professional practice with more rigour.

Over time, the academic may contribute to this field of knowledge as a scholar and/or researcher. Scholarship of teaching and learning (SOTL) incorporates the practice of evaluating and documenting the academic's learning insights so that they may be shared with others (Trigwell *et al.* 2000). This may be based on their reflections, observations of student learning, research into student learning processes or outcomes, or documentation of the impact of certain practices. As part of these activities, the teacher might explore innovative or enhanced practices that better support student learning in their field of expertise. The capacity to evaluate, test, experiment and modify existing practices, systems or theories to better support student engagement and outcomes is an important indication of advancing skills in learning and teaching.

Developing scholarship around one's teaching can be undertaken in a number of ways such as:

- developing textbooks, models, programs, technologies or teaching resources that are tested, shared, published and disseminated;
- undertaking collaborative investigations with other colleagues who are experiencing similar challenges;
- identifying, trialling and evaluating innovative practices that enhance student learning;
- attending and/or contributing to conferences that explore teaching practices or insights;
- benchmarking with colleagues from other institutions to identify key indicators of excellence related to the field of teaching;

- building a specialist focus that contributes to the broader field of knowledge through publications and dissemination;
- seeking funding to undertake a major investigation of educational research in the design, testing and reporting of described interventions.

Leading learning and teaching initiatives and groups

Leadership of learning and teaching is the third strand of educational practice that academics will need to develop over their teaching careers. Effective leadership of learning and teaching initiatives will range across many levels and activities, potentially integrating course or unit coordination, as well as practicum or service-learning leadership roles, through to formal roles such as a director of studies, associate dean or head of department or school. These leadership roles often seek to influence direction and teaching cultures, increase the visibility and presence of learning and teaching in the university environment and position the leader as an advocate for good practice (de la Harpe and Mason 2014; Hofmeyer *et al.* 2015; Ramsden *et al.* 2007). A knowledge of university policy and directions ensures these processes are aligned and supportive of those broader imperatives. These roles will require a range of leadership capabilities (see Chapter 19).

These leadership skills will progressively develop as the individual builds confidence in articulating their pedagogical knowledge and insights and develops expertise in planning and managing learning innovations, programs and initiatives. A key factor in their success will be the ability to inspire and motivate academics to be part of these change processes (Smith 2012). An area of focus that is likely to be encountered relates to curriculum reform, which has become a common approach for universities seeking to enhance learning and teaching (O'Neill *et al.* 2014).

Assessing teaching excellence

Universities have become more concerned with monitoring the performance of their teachers. Various indicators of excellence have been identified, with the goal of encouraging high quality across the community (Chalmers 2011). Academics will be required to develop evidence of their teaching impact and progress. When assessed in sum, the teacher's evidence base will be compared with that of other academics, established benchmarks or external indicators. A challenge evident in the field is the difficulty of sourcing evidence of teaching impact, given its mediation by student motivations and characteristics, learning context and many other factors. This has made it harder for teachers to build a coherent base to support claims of being excellent teachers. For most teachers, the evidence of quality will relate to showing incremental advancement in student ratings and teaching evaluations, particularly as they relate to addressing areas of weakness or poor performance. Enhanced student learning outcomes; innovations; enhancements that have been successfully disseminated and adopted or external recognition through awards are additional sources of evidence.

Conclusion

Teachers are essential to their university, but must build many capabilities to ensure they are adaptive, effective and confident. The capacity to be self-reflective and open to new ideas and feedback will be critical to successful teaching. The development of sound teaching capabilities is a progressive process that can be greatly escalated through the support of faculty colleagues, models and mentors, familiarisation with the extant literature and opportunities to share with and learn from other colleagues. It is important to note that the foundational skills attained in the early stages of teaching are not sufficient grounding. Each individual will need to progress toward more nuanced and sophisticated insights relating to scholarship, research, curriculum design, leadership and student learning.

References

Australian Council for Educational Research, 2010. *Doing more for learning enhancing engagement and outcomes: Australasian survey of student engagement*, Camberwell, Vic.: ACER Press.
Barnett, R. and Coate, K., 2005. *Engaging the curriculum in higher education*, Maidenhead, Berkshire: Society for Research into Higher Education.
Barratt, C., Hanlon, D. and Rankin, M., 2011. Assessing the success of a discipline-based communication skills development and enhancement program in a graduate accounting course. *Higher Education Research & Development*, 30(6), pp. 681–695.
Barrie, S.C., 2007. A conceptual framework for the teaching and learning of generic graduate attributes. *Studies in Higher Education*, 32(4), pp. 439–458.
Bell, M., 2005. Peer observation partnerships in higher education, Milperra, NSW: Higher Education Research and Development Society of Australasia (HERDSA).
Biggs, J., 2012. What the student does: teaching for enhanced learning. *Higher Education Research & Development*, 31(1), pp. 39–55.
Biggs, J.B. and Tang, C.S., 2011. *Teaching for quality learning at university: what the student does*, Maidenhead, Berkshire: Society for Research into Higher Education.
Boettcher, J.V. and Conrad, R.-M., 2010. *The online teaching survival guide: simple and practical pedagogical tips*, San Francisco, CA: Jossey-Bass.
Bone, E.K. and Reid, R.J., 2011. Prior learning in biology at high school does not predict performance in the first year at university. *Higher Education Research & Development*, 30(6), pp. 709–724.
Brew, A., 2010. Transforming academic practice through scholarship. *International Journal for Academic Development*, 15(2), pp. 105–116.
Brew, A. and Sachs, J., 2007. *Transforming a university: the scholarship of teaching and learning in practice*, Sydney: Sydney University Press.
Chalmers, D., 2011. Progress and challenges to the recognition and reward of the Scholarship of Teaching in higher education. *Higher Education Research & Development*, 30(1), pp. 25–38.

Crisp, G., 2009. *Designing and using e-assessments*, Milperra, NSW: Higher Education Research and Development Society of Australasia.
Crisp, G., Sadler, R., Krause, K.L., Bruckridge, M., Wills, S., Brown, C., McLean, J., Dalton, H., Le Lievre, K. and Brougham, B., 2009. *Peer review of teaching for promotion purposes: a project to develop and implement a pilot program of external peer review of teaching at four Australian universities*, Adelaide, South Aust.: University of Adelaide and Australian Learning and Teaching Council. Available online at www.adelaide.edu.au/clpd/peerreview
Crosling, G. and Heagney, M., 2009. Improving student retention in higher education. *Australian Universities Review*, 51(2), pp. 9–18.
Davies, M., 2011. Introduction to the special issue on critical thinking in higher education. *Higher Education Research & Development*, 30(3), pp. 255–260.
Garrison, D.R., 2011. *E-learning in the 21st century: a framework for research and practice*, New York: Routledge.
Hanover Research, 2010. *Strategies for Teaching Large Undergraduate Classes*, Washington, DC: Hanover Research. Available online at www.businessand-economics.mq.edu.au/intranet/learning_and_teaching/leading_discussions_projects/Strategies_for_Teaching_Large_Undergraduate_Classes.pdf
Hardy, I.J., 2010. Teacher talk: flexible delivery and academics' praxis in an Australian university. *International Journal for Academic Development*, 15(2), pp. 131–142.
de la Harpe, B. and Mason, T., 2014. Leadership of learning and teaching in the creative arts. *Higher Education Research & Development*, 33(1), pp. 129–143.
Healey, M., 2000. Developing the scholarship of teaching in higher education: a discipline-based approach. *Higher Education Research and Development*, 19(2), pp. 169–189.
Hofmeyer, A., Sheingold, B.H., Klopper, H.C. and Warland, J., 2015. Leadership in learning and teaching in higher education: perspectives of academics in non-formal leadership roles. *Contemporary Issues in Education Research*, 8(3), pp. 181–192.
Ismail, E. and Hassan, M., 2012. Cultural contexts and curricular design in Saudi Arabia and other Middle Eastern nations. In J.E. Groccia, M.A. Al-Sudairy and W. Buskist, eds, *Handbook of college and university teaching: a global perspective*, Thousand Oaks, CA: SAGE Publications, pp. 279–292.
Krause, K.L.D., 2014. Challenging perspectives on learning and teaching in the disciplines: the academic voice. *Studies in Higher Education*, 39(1), pp. 2–19.
Kreber, C., 2013. Empowering the scholarship of teaching: An Arendtian and critical perspective. *Studies in Higher Education*, 38(6), pp. 857–869.
Kuh, G.D. (ed.), 2005. *Assessing conditions to enhance educational effectiveness: the inventory for student engagement and success*, 1st edition, San Francisco, CA. Jossey-Bass.
Leask, B., 2015. *Internationalizing the curriculum*, Milton Park, Oxfordshire: Routledge.
Leibowitz, B., 2009. What's inside the suitcases? An investigation into the powerful resources students and lecturers bring to teaching and learning. *Higher Education Research & Development*, 28(3), pp. 261–274.
Matthews, K.E., Andrews, V. and Adams, P., 2011. Social learning spaces and student engagement. *Higher Education Research & Development*, 30(2), pp. 105–120.
Nickson, R.A.R., 2012. Developing faculty for the 21st century in South Africa: building capacity through collaborative preparation programs. In J.E. Groccia,

M.A. Al-Sudairy and W. Buskist, eds, *Handbook of college and university teaching: a global perspective*, Thousand Oaks, CA: SAGE Publications, pp. 108–125.

O'Neill, G., Donnelly, R. and Fitzmaurice, M., 2014. Supporting programme teams to develop sequencing in higher education curricula. *International Journal for Academic Development*, 19(4), pp. 268–280.

Pepper, C., 2010. "There's a lot of learning going on but NOT much teaching!": Student perceptions of Problem-Based Learning in science. *Higher Education Research & Development*, 29(6), pp. 693–707.

Ramsden, P., Prosser, M., Trigwell, K. and Martin, E., 2007. University teachers' experiences of academic leadership and their approaches to teaching. *Learning and Instruction*, 17(2), pp. 140–155.

Ransome, P., 2011. Qualitative pedagogy versus instrumentalism: the antinomies of higher education learning and teaching in the United Kingdom. *Higher Education Quarterly*, 65(2), pp. 206–223.

Sadler, I., 2012. The challenges for new academics in adopting student-centered approaches to teaching. *Studies in Higher Education*, 37(6), pp. 731–745.

Schroeder, C., 2005. Building bridges for student engagement: the key to enhancing learning productivity. In J.E. Groccia and J.E. Miller, eds, *On becoming a productive university: strategies for reducing costs and increasing quality in higher education*, Bolton, MA: Anker Publishing, pp. 216–226.

Sherbino, J., Frank, J.R. and Snell, L., 2014. Defining the key roles and competencies of the clinician–educator of the 21st century: a national mixed-methods study. *Academic Medicine*, 89(5), pp. 783–789.

Smith, K., 2012. Lessons learnt from literature on the diffusion of innovative learning and teaching practices in higher education. *Innovations in Education and Teaching International*, 49(2), pp. 173–182.

Solomonides, I., 2012. *Engaging with learning in higher education*, Oxfordshire: Libri Publishing.

Steel, C., 2010. Teaching online: issues and challenges for on-campus and online distance education. In R. Cantwell and J.J. Scevak, eds, *An academic life: a handbook for new academics*, Camberwell, Vic.: ACER Press, pp. 83–96.

Stoddard, H.A. and Borges, N.J., 2015. A typology of teaching roles and relationships for medical education. *Medical Teacher*, 38(3), pp. 1–6.

Sun, Q., 2012. Learning for transformation in an international context: the implications of the Confucian learning model. In J.E. Groccia, M.A. Al-Sudairy and W. Buskist, eds, *Handbook of college and university teaching: a global perspective*, Thousand Oaks, CA: SAGE Publications, pp. 200–218.

Svinicki, M.D., McKeachie, W.J. and Nicol, D., 2011. *McKeachie's teaching tips: strategies, research, and theory for college and university teachers*, Belmont, CA: Wadsworth Publishing.

Thomas, K., Wong, K. and Li, Y., 2014. The capstone experience: student and academic perspectives. *Higher Education Research & Development*, 33(3), pp. 580–594.

Trapp, A., 2012. The changing context of learning: changes in UK higher education. In J.E. Groccia, M.A. Al-Sudairy and W. Buskist, eds, *Handbook of college and university teaching: a global perspective*, Thousand Oaks, CA: SAGE Publications, pp. 185–199.

Trevitt, C., Stocks, C. and Quinlan, K.M., 2011. Advancing assessment practice in continuing professional learning: toward a richer understanding of teaching portfolios for learning and assessment. *International Journal for Academic Development*, 17(2), pp. 1–13.

Trigwell, K., Martin, E., Benjamin, J. and Prosser, M., 2000. Scholarship of teaching: a model. *Higher Education Research and Development*, 19(2), pp. 155–168.

Vardi, I., 2013. *Developing students' critical thinking in the higher education class*, Milperra, Sydney: HERSDA.

Velayo, R.S., 2012. Internationalizing the curriculum. In J.E. Groccia, M.A. Al-Sudairy and W. Buskist, eds, *Handbook of college and university teaching: a global perspective*, Thousand Oaks, CA: SAGE Publications, pp. 268–278.

Winchester, T.M. and Winchester, M., 2011. Exploring the impact of faculty reflection on weekly student evaluations of teaching. *International Journal for Academic Development*, 16(2), pp. 119–131.

Chapter 18

Developing learning and teaching capacity

Excellent teaching is a core aspiration for most universities: their mission emphasises the delivery of quality student outcomes, building a reputation for outstanding student experiences and generating high demand from a new generation of students. Fundamental to these targets is the cultivation of great teaching across the educational workforce. However, this is challenged by the need to promote basic teaching capabilities to an extensive (and potentially casualised) workforce. This dilemma has challenged universities for some years, and is also being encountered in new nations as they seek to build teaching capacity. This chapter will explore some of the ways in which learning and teaching capabilities have been encouraged across the academy and some of the inherent challenges that continue to be evident.

Evaluating the impact of learning and teaching capacity building

There are many actors in the learning and teaching capacity-building space. Executive leaders, deans, professors and HE developers all play a role in encouraging a deeper institutional engagement with learning and teaching. HE developers support a number of these institutional actors. They are also likely to interact with a vast number of teachers as they promote the need for quality learning and teaching across the institution. What, then, would a successful approach to capacity building look like? Box 18.1 outlines some of the potential indicators of successful learning and teaching capacity building, illustrating the importance of encouraging strong alignment across the different university leaders and levels.

While no university has yet reached this level of sophistication, the explication of these indicators helps to clarify what teaching and learning capacity building comprises: it is focused on building a cohesive community that values and prioritises quality educational outcomes, with members of the university contributing toward the enhancement of student learning. In the next sections, the support that can be offered by HE developers in this process is explored.

Box 18.1 Indicators of successful teaching capacity building

- Excellent teaching is publicly valued through teaching awards schemes, performance reviews and promotion guidelines.
- Executive leaders are keen to build a strong development strategy to support quality learning and teaching.
- The student experience, learning and teaching foci are featured in core university priorities.
- There are clear capabilities mapped for excellent teaching.
- Teachers are familiar with and effectively employ university learning and teaching policies, systems and processes.
- Incoming teachers are supported by effective teaching inductions and an orientation.
- The teaching orientation is well attended by new teachers.
- Faculty leaders are strong advocates of teaching development.
- There are strong partnerships between faculty leaders, faculty developers and central HE developers in the promotion of a robust learning and teaching culture.
- There is evidence of widespread participation in learning and teaching development activities across different academic levels.
- Teaching evaluation encompasses a range of approaches.
- Peer review and teaching mentorship are well established support strategies.
- University staff produce quality, peer-reviewed scholarly publications relating to their teaching.
- Senior academics engage in further development to inform their teaching leadership roles.
- The HE developer provides support within faculties to enhance teaching capabilities, processes and outcomes.
- The university is well represented in national awards and recognition schemes.
- Student evaluations of teaching demonstrate improved outcomes.

Setting the context for excellent teaching

Learning and teaching is the most advanced field of HE development in terms of its scholarship, research, learned academies and established practices. Teachers have a plethora of resources to explore, including resources pertaining to their particular discipline and innovative practices. However, this very richness makes it hard to extract a focused and well-articulated stream of guidance to support busy and inexperienced teachers who are novices in this new professional domain. In this context, then, the developer is particularly critical in helping to build clear and efficient learning tracks to the core literature and the key principles that should underpin teaching activities.

A particular challenge that is encountered in universities is the variable importance placed on research and teaching. Institutional processes that prioritise research metrics and competitive research capabilities can significantly influence an individual's decision to participate in learning and teaching development. This creates a more fractured development environment for the developer. There will be highly committed teachers seeking support while others prioritise their research. Similarly, some academic leaders will be keen to promote a high-quality learning context for their students, while others will see research as their primary concern. Thus, developers promoting learning and teaching will need to build a strong case for the *need* for development, as well as delivering high-quality services that support academic capacity building. They need to consider how the institutional culture and messages about learning and teaching are evidenced in the policies, initiatives and recognition that teaching is afforded.

Evidencing quality teaching

The strengthening of institutional expectations as to quality teaching provides powerful messages concerning the importance of building effective teaching capabilities. Universities have been working intensively on defining excellent teaching. However, the development of quality assurance processes is challenging. Student outcomes are hard to measure and attribute to a teacher's intervention and we have not yet developed rigorous and credible measures to assess HE teaching impact and outcomes.

Regardless, there is evidence of increased efforts to promote teaching accountability (Chalmers 2011). Universities have developed stronger guidelines on what they expect of their academic and research workforce. Many institutions have developed teaching performance standards and guidelines, including explicit statements about the types of evidence that reflect teaching excellence. This has assisted in balancing the ledger to some extent and offers developers important support for promoting quality teaching. However, many of these descriptions are more input (i.e. effort or process) than outcome (student learning) focused. Further incentives can be found through teaching excellence reward and recognition schemes offered at national, discipline, university and faculty levels to acknowledge and publicly value excellent teachers, teams of teachers or teaching innovation. These are reliant on good teachers documenting their evidence and building a persuasive case as to their philosophy, methodologies and impact on student learning. This dossier approach makes judging and evaluating an individual's performance much more subjective, although peer recognition, impact across the broader profession and awards are strong indicators of excellence. Universities have also experimented with recognising schools or departments that provide exceptional educational leadership. Thus, there is a strong push to build more verifiable evidence as to teaching quality and outcomes. This remains under-researched, however, particularly in testing the validity and reliability of teaching excellence indicators.

There are many ways in which teaching is assessed as part of the regular evaluation cycle. Teachers are likely to receive feedback several times a year through student evaluations of teaching. This feedback may be institutionally managed as a regular part of the academic cycle, or may be self-initiated. Student feedback serves as an important cue to quality teaching, although it would ideally be but one source of evidence, as it can contain some biases and flaws stemming from the student characteristics, instrument design and the evaluative context. This feedback offers important guidance to teachers on their progress and can guide development plans for the coming year. The debate over who may access the results has been vigorous for many years, but the trend is toward supervisors seeing the outcomes to ensure student learning is achieved. Certainly, the capacity to view and discuss a teacher's evaluations can enrich annual review discussions and explorations of development needs. Academics who are in the probationary stage of their appointments are likely to be focused on monitoring their feedback. Productive discussions with supervisors to discuss their performance are particularly important during this stage.

Peer review of teaching has long been valued as a developmental tool to triangulate feedback on teaching (Barnard *et al.* 2015; Bell 2005; Bell and Cooper 2013; Hendry *et al.* 2014; Thomson *et al.* 2015).[1] Designed to provide intensive feedback in a confidential and supportive context, it offers an opportunity for diagnosis, feedback reflection and mapping new learning goals. This process encourages the teacher to learn through feedback and, in some cases, via dialogue and observation of others. The use of this approach is now being employed as part of promotional processes, integrating careful vetting of potential reviewers to ensure that they are themselves effective teachers, training reviewers and the development of a teaching capabilities framework to guide the review process (Crisp *et al.* 2009).[2] The move toward using these methods for summative purposes adds another form of validation that triangulates performance evidence. The training of reviewers also encourages their exploration of teaching performance indicators, further increasing capacity across the community.

Unit and program reviews acknowledge that the collective efforts of teachers responsible for any unit of teaching impacts on the final student experience. This can be valuable feedback for coordinators, and may provide some important signals as to areas requiring improvement. However, there is potential for this to be taken further, with the use of an evaluative framework to explore the group's process of delivering the curriculum, and with an opportunity for the group to explore their efficacy and effectiveness in framing the program. This is another, more authentic form of peer review, encouraging all members of the program to explore their professional agency to achieve quality outcomes.

The review and evaluation of whole curricula also informs the subsequent design, delivery and overall calibre of a program of study. External panels facilitate benchmarking and more objective quality assurance to provide extensive guidance on how programs might be further enhanced. While they operate infrequently, the information and guidance derived from these reports provide important indications as to areas that might turn into larger systemic concerns. Pressure to act on any recommendations and prompt debrief on the outcomes encourages ongoing quality enhancement and reforms.

A further environmental influence that encourages teachers to focus on their teaching practice relates to grants to support teaching innovation. These grants may be institutionally funded or may be nationally competitive. Aimed at exploring innovative approaches to enhance student learning, they support teachers who wish to test and apply new ideas and approaches. The maturation of this field has encouraged more rigorous research and evaluative methodologies as part of these bids. Much of the literature relating to higher education learning and teaching has been assisted through this sponsored support. The HE developer often fills a supportive role as critical friend, expert and collaborator in these processes.

Institutions may seek guidance on the quality of the learning environment through national surveys such as NSSE (nsse.indiana.edu) and AUSSE (www.acer.edu.au/ausse). Schemes that assess comparative institutional performance can trigger considerable reaction if teaching outcomes or reputation are at risk. They can generate major reform initiatives that spearhead significant changes in institutional priorities and support.

To summarise, leaders and the HE developer need to build some clear messages as to the ways in which a quality learning environment can be measured, interpreted and understood. They will need to be *au fait* with promotional and performance targets and are likely to be key messengers in terms of scholarship, evidence gathering, interpretation of data and promotion of good practice. The encouragement of reflective teaching will be critical, as it underpins many of these processes. These elements will inform the different services that are offered to increase the university's valuing and enactment of quality teaching. The following sections explore specific approaches that have been employed by universities, along with some suggestions for further enhancements to encourage teaching capacity building.

Starting right: the learning and teaching orientation program

Orientation programs help to promote institutional teaching priorities to new or incoming teachers. Designed to provide a quick overview of the institutional priorities, sources of support, structures and policies, these events serve to emphasise the critical part that teaching plays in the university ecology.

Successful orientation programs are attended by most newcomers and supported by faculty leaders. They stimulate positive motivations around being a teacher and encourage people to think about their educational strategy. Approaches that can assist in achieving these goals include:

- integrating a direct invitation into the letter of appointment for new staff;
- featuring the most senior learning and teaching leader who can offer an informative overview of the learning and teaching context and the role each teacher plays;
- encouraging interactive experiences, modelling some of the practices that are being encouraged across the university;
- integrating some inspirational practitioners and students to explore their experiences in the educational space;
- integrating linkages with faculty leaders or developers as part of the session;
- providing high-quality information and guides to assist those commencing, including practical support for using the learning management systems and core educational student record systems.

Many institutions now boast a number of campuses, including locations in other nations. The provision of a consistent orientation program needs to be ensured, possibly through the provision of an online orientation with a local welcome from a senior leader. The alignment of this event with a faculty-based induction creates positive reinforcement of the valuing of learning and teaching. It also increases the engagement of the newcomer with advocates and champions in the faculty, something that may increase their commitment over the long-term (Thomas *et al.* 2011) and supports the building of a discipline-based identity (Boyd 2010). The collection and analysis of attendance statistics can provide important evidence concerning university groups where staff are not engaging with this familiarisation stage. This may stimulate more leadership and sponsorship of teaching. Additional support and acculturation is needed when staff are travelling overseas to teach (Debowski 2005; Hoare 2013; Smith 2014).

Building good foundations in learning and teaching

As outlined in Chapter 17, new teachers face great challenges in working out how the higher education system works, navigating their curriculum and disciplinary expectations, as well as exploring their identity as teachers. A major concern at the start of university teaching is building familiarisation with core systems so that the teacher is ready to launch their courses. Online self-help support, workshops and faculty-based assistance all play a part in building this readiness. These assist with the immediate concerns of being "survival ready." Workshops provide an important starting point for many, offering efficient, expert guidance on how to use systems and implement key practices. These can be usefully framed around the key capability areas that are documented in institutional requirements for quality teaching. Grant and Barrow (2013) note the enduring success of the "teaching seminar." As noted in earlier chapters, academics appreciate effective and succinct support where it is well tuned to the needs of the community.

Foundational programs for learning and teaching

Entry into university teaching also requires much more extensive grounding in the complexities of design, assessment, delivery, evaluation and scholarly practice. Universities expect to see their academics move toward significant proficiency and to evidence progressive enhancement of teaching capabilities over their early years.

Learning and teaching centres have developed substantial programs to support teachers in this developmental phase. In-house cohort-based programs offer intensive support in establishing a clear teaching identity, articulating a learning philosophy and building a basic insight into the professional literature. A survey of 46 programs across Australia, New Zealand and the UK found that these programs emphasise reflective practice, constructive alignment, student approaches to learning, scholarship of learning and teaching, as well as assessment of learning outcomes (Kandlbinder and Peseta 2009; Peseta and Kandlbinder 2011).

However, the size of the cohort is generally limited to 20 to 25 participants to enable good support of each individual. This then raises a question: what happens to the hundreds who are unable to gain access to these programs? The development of blended learning options fills this gap to some extent. The University and College Teaching program,[3] for example, was designed by universities to fill an identified gap in provision. Comprising nine courses of study, participants can select the program that suits their needs. Other online programs, including video-based online programs (Johannes et al. 2013), have been introduced to increase access to professional development at point of need. When combined with regular workshops to encourage debriefs and contextualisation, these options open up considerably more access. However, they will require much stronger marketing and promotion through central and faculty communication channels, as they are likely to be self-managed and may not gain traction. Further enhancements, such as the integration of learning portfolios to map developmental progress, a mentor and accreditation of completed courses as part of a formal higher education teaching qualification could also encourage take-up.

Many universities have moved toward developing different courses or programs and providing recognition via formal accreditation as a qualification. Two approaches have been common: many Australian institutions have moved toward awarding a Graduate Certificate in Higher Education or Teaching and Learning; alternatively, accreditation by an external authority, such as the Higher Education Academy[4] or SEDA[5] can be sought (Trevitt et al. 2011). These forms of external validation have also been found to encourage experienced teachers to refresh their knowledge and skills (Butcher and Stoncel 2012; Spowart et al. 2015).

Universities would benefit from undertaking audits of their teaching faculty to explore the impact of their programs. Identifying the percentage and faculty take-up of these courses can offer an important insight into how well these approaches are influencing the university and its educational delivery. Longitudinal mapping of program graduates against those who later excel or lead may also offer some useful guidance on the eternal development questions: did it make a difference? If so, how?

A particular challenge for these programs is that the learner must ultimately return to a largely unchanged faculty context and implement their acquired skills in isolation. Faculty-based programs that integrate more engagement from faculty teaching leaders and exemplars have considerable potential to gain more traction and build stronger influence. These programs also encourage stronger responsibility for those who are working in that disciplinary context. The role of the central developer might shift toward developing the faculty leaders and development team; coordinating across faculties; and brokering good practices across these representatives.

Setting tutors and graduate assistants up for success

Universities rely on a casual workforce to undertake many aspects of teaching. However, these staff are often minimally paid and may be undertaking full-time study or work in conjunction with their educational role. They are a very critical interface with many students, and may, in large part, determine the learner's satisfaction with their university education. Their teaching capabilities can be further enhanced by a mini-program (often 1 day) where they can explore more deeply some of the underlying pedagogical framing to guide their practice (Chadha 2015). In particular, exploring techniques to enhance student learning (e.g. questioning; small group learning techniques), identifying particular approaches to suit their major disciplinary emphasis (e.g. STEM vs humanities) and assessing and giving feedback are fundamental skills for anyone moving into teaching roles. Given the limited remuneration that these teachers normally receive, they are often paid to attend the 1-day workshop. This would need to be factored into the faculty or university budget. Many of the attendees will be doctoral candidates who are keen to build sound evidence of teaching potential. The capacity to access credentialed courses will be important to them (Chadha 2015).

Supporting course coordinators

The course coordinator fills an important role in providing the scaffolding and guidance to instructors as to the standards required; the curriculum design and outcomes that should be generated; and how assessments will be moderated and reviewed. They face some major challenges: large student cohorts; multiple tutors or demonstrators; oversight of online course design and delivery; communication with students and co-teachers; and representation of the course within their faculty or curriculum groups. The coordinator will need to have an intensive knowledge of university policies and systems, and be capable of resolving complex problems. These roles require considerable dedication, organisation and relationship management.

Research on course coordinator roles has identified the importance of guiding these individuals to increase their focus on excellence and ensure the role is manageable (Holt *et al.* 2013; Ladyshewsky and Flavell 2012). The opportunity to learn from and share with others is very much valued by these busy people. A strength of programs of this nature is the diversity of perspectives that are shared. Many good ideas can be found as different disciplines and their approaches are mapped and explored through the discussions. An innovative approach that has been trialled is the engagement of students as co-creators in course enhancement (Bovill *et al.* 2011). The provision of a coordinator website where resources and templates can be shared offers further support, as would regular network meetings.

Encouraging scholarship of learning and teaching

As teachers consolidate their basic capabilities, they will start to reflect on and evaluate their approaches and perceived outcomes. This is the commencement of the transition to scholar, innovator and potentially, leader. Brew (2010; 2012) suggests that three levels of engagement can be encouraged: content, process and premise. This enables each learner to address these complex ideas at a level where they are comfortable (Trevitt *et al.* 2011). The use of student evaluations of teaching has also been found to be a productive stimulus for reflection, encouraging teachers to analyse, reflect and respond (Winchester and Winchester 2011). The capacity to undertake reflection within a disciplinary context can also assist those who are learning this intensive practice (Nsibande and Garraway 2011).

There are many ways to guide scholarship. At a basic level, engagement with the literature offers many models and examples as to how other individuals have built their research and scholarly investigations. Forums and conferences challenge and guide new insights and forms of thinking. A combination of in-faculty and intra-university activities encourages engagement and builds a stronger, visible culture (Kreber 2013). Universities may hold intensive thematic forums (such as Teaching Week) to encourage this interchange across their community, or as inter-institutional forums with rotating hosting and sponsorship. National and international conferences further enrich these insights.

The development of a complete project or paper relating to a teaching innovation or investigation benefits from progressive support of developers, mentors and colleagues. A practical mechanism that increases broader engagement and interaction across faculties with teaching scholarship and research is the provision of internships that are jointly supported by developers and faculties. This approach increases the span of influence while still offering guidance through an action learning project. When structured as a program, it can support the integration of mentorship and strong sponsorship from faculty leaders.

Scholarly writing circles offer additional support as papers are drafted (Wardale *et al.* 2015; Weaver *et al.* 2014). These might emphasise the development of papers or the preparation of award applications (Layton and Brown 2011; McCormack *et al.* 2014). However, the level of support offered to individual candidates needs to be carefully considered, as this may be a very time-consuming activity. The developer may build research collaborations with faculty colleagues, providing expertise in learning and teaching methodologies and approaches to complement the disciplinary knowledge of other colleagues. This partnership can build powerful commentary and insights relating to authentic contexts and problems and affirm the developer's credibility as a scholar and expert in their field.

Communities of practice have also gained considerable support (Hubball *et al.* 2010; Thomson 2015). Network meetings to explore themes of common interest and forums to share outcomes from published papers are further ways to generate interaction and engagement of educators as they progress their scholarship.

The HE developer role in these processes spans a range of functions. Importantly, higher education developers act as knowledge brokers, encouraging scholarship and knowledge exchange. In addition, they fill an important role as disrupters of conventional thinking, encouraging the questioning of assumptions and tradition. This can then lead to innovation and space for new insights. Their impact will be greatly strengthened by working in partnership with faculty leaders and other passionate advocates.

Guiding teaching leaders

There are numerous teaching leaders across the university. They share common concerns for encouraging academic engagement in learning and teaching, promoting innovation, ensuring quality practices and promoting the best possible support to students. These are very complex concerns, requiring considerable understanding of curriculum reform, educational design and delivery, student learning principles, leading innovation and how to facilitate cultures that are educationally focused. In many cases, these leaders will also chair award panels, committees, working parties or guide developmental projects. They may also carry responsibility for evaluating and reforming university curricula, playing a key role in promoting change and good practice.

Traditionally, these leaders have been left to do the job with little guidance or support. However, there is increasing recognition of the challenges they may encounter in engaging and maintaining energy and momentum around these matters. While some of these leaders (e.g. heads of school or associate deans) warrant an individualised induction, there is insufficient capacity to offer this to all. Instead, the provision of an occasional program that specifically explores teaching, leadership and related strategies will be highly valued. If a faculty is planning major reforms of its own, it may also seek to conduct a more targeted program to bring all core leaders into a unified approach and focus. The use of an intensive 3-day program modelled on the UK Change Academy, for example, offers considerable potential (Healey *et al.* 2013).

Deans and heads need to have a different level of engagement with educational enhancement. They will be the key architects of quality assurance and educational oversight. Their roles include sponsorship of innovation and new talent, selection of incoming leaders and the provision of educational vision and direction for the faculty or school/department. Oversight of student rankings, supply and demand, reputation and strategic positioning of the educational brand are all part of this leadership level. Their focus may be directed toward the international market as well as their specific community, as the expansion of their student population will be a key concern. On the other hand, their responsibility for current students is substantial. The development of appropriate services and structures, including acting in custodial roles for some, will have high priority. Clearly, these concerns are quite different to those that surface for distributed leaders. This form of strategic leadership also benefits from support. However, given the pressing nature of these roles, professional development will generally need to be focused, short duration and often, after hours. Forums that delve more intensively into emerging strategic concerns can gain strong support, but need to be extremely well designed, productive and focused on identifying optimal solutions to complex problems. Thus, the peer-learning context becomes particularly important for these levels. In designing forums of this nature, input from members of the target community will provide validation and assurance that the plan will be attractive to the audience. Equally, if a senior leader is struggling, the identification of a previous leader who has grappled with similar issues can offer valuable mentoring support.

Institutional reforms

There will be times when the university decides to move with a whole of institutional reform to enhance its delivery of educational services. The focus for these innovations can be quite varied. Some approaches have included: major curriculum reforms requiring redesign and re-approval of every course; the introduction of online learning as a core delivery mechanism across all courses; a focus on a particular evaluation practice; review and strengthening of internationalised curricula; and the introduction of work-integrated or service learning across courses. It is likely that these initiatives will be heavily promoted and particular targets will be set for embedding the new processes in place. Hopefully, there will be realistic expectations as to how quickly the transition will occur, but this is not always the case.

When a whole of institutional reform is being introduced, the development team is likely to be heavily involved. In addition to scoping papers, consultation and project work, they may host forums and working parties; develop new systems and policies; design manuals and guidelines; support the implementation of policies and ideas; work with faculty contacts to support the embedding of such ideas; and provide the professional expertise that is required to set up the innovations for success. This is a real opportunity for developers to shine, particularly if they are able to add value to the skills and expertise that are found in faculties. A focus on documenting the process, including mapping the earlier context, and then illustrating how the change has impacted on learning outcomes, student experiences, teacher attitudes or efficiencies, will be an enticing aspect of the role. This form of documentary evidence can be particularly helpful in positioning the HED service as a proactive, effective agent of change and reform.

The faculty–central partnership

As with other broad activities associated with HED, the linkage between faculty and central services needs to be robust, sustained and respectful. The capacity to anticipate the likely needs of different faculties, to build regular interactions with heads and deans to discuss their educational agendas, and to design fitting interventions that serve their purposes, builds an ideal context to do this work. Developers who are located in faculty roles will also need to be integrated into broader institutional discussions and agendas to ensure that they have a sound insider knowledge of the larger context and drivers. Good networking from their compatriots will increase the use of shared resources and ideas, which promotes institutional consistency.

Conclusion

The promotion of quality teaching requires a sustained effort from many different parties. The developer role can make a fundamental difference to the prioritisation of learning and teaching, and the alignment of institutional standards, policies and expectations with the lived practice within faculties. There is still considerable scope to encourage wider engagement with learning to teach and learning to lead teaching. Developers have considerable potential, but need to consider the key ways they can make a difference to the institutional outcomes, teaching leaders, the community orientation and focus on learning. In turn, leaders need to recognise the significant impact of their own practices, modelling and messages in focusing attention on excellent teaching.

Notes

1 See: www.peerreviewofteaching.org/tools/other-tools-and-templates.jsp for a useful review of projects and principles that have been employed in Australian universities.
2 See: www1.rmit.edu.au/browse/Staff/Learning%20and%20Teaching/Priorities/Peer%20feedback/Peer%20review/ for a useful overview as to how RMIT has implemented these practices.
3 See: www.epigeum.com/courses/teaching/university-college-teaching
4 See: www.heacademy.ac.uk/services/accreditation
5 See: www.seda.ac.uk/fellowships

References

Barnard, A., Nash, R., McEvoy, K., Shannon, S., Waters, C., Rochester, S. and Bolt, S., 2015. LeaD-In: a cultural change model for peer review of teaching in higher education. *Higher Education Research & Development*, 34(1), pp. 30–44.

Bell, M., 2005. Peer observation partnerships in higher education, Milperra, N.S.W.: Higher Education Research and Development Society of Australasia (HERDSA).

Bell, M. and Cooper, P., 2013. Peer observation of teaching in university departments: a framework for implementation. *International Journal for Academic Development*, 18(1), pp. 60–73.

Bovill, C., Cook-Sather, A. and Felten, P., 2011. Students as co-creators of teaching approaches, course design, and curricula: implications for academic developers. *International Journal for Academic Development*, 16(2), pp. 133–145.

Boyd, P., 2010. Academic induction for professional educators: supporting the workplace learning of newly appointed lecturers in teacher and nurse education. *International Journal for Academic Development*, 15(2), pp. 155–165.

Brew, A., 2010. Transforming academic practice through scholarship. *International Journal for Academic Development*, 15(2), pp. 105–116.

Brew, A., 2012. Teaching and research: new relationships and their implications for inquiry-based teaching and learning in higher education. *Higher Education Research & Development*, 31(1), pp. 101–114.

Butcher, J. and Stoncel, D., 2012. The impact of a Postgraduate Certificate in Teaching in Higher Education on university lecturers appointed for their professional expertise at a teaching-led university: 'It's made me braver'. *International Journal for Academic Development*, 17(2), pp. 149–162.

Chadha, D., 2015. Evaluating the impact of the graduate certificate in academic practice (GCAP) programme. *International Journal for Academic Development*, 20(1), pp. 46–57.

Chalmers, D., 2011. Progress and challenges to the recognition and reward of the Scholarship of Teaching in higher education. *Higher Education Research & Development*, 30(1), pp. 25–38.

Crisp, G., Sadler, R., Krause, K.L., Buckridge, M., Wills, S., Brown, C., McLean, J., Dalton, H., Le Lievre, K. and Brougham, B., 2009. *Peer review of teaching for promotion purposes: a project to develop and implement a pilot program of external peer review of teaching at four Australian universities*, Adelaide, South Aust.: University of Adelaide and Australian Learning and Teaching Council. Available online at: www.adelaide.edu.au/clpd/peerreview

Debowski, S., 2005. Across the divide: teaching a transnational MBA in a second language. *Higher Education Research & Development*, 24(3), pp. 265–280.

Grant, B. and Barrow, M., 2013. Fashioning docile teacher bodies? The strange space of the 'staff teaching seminar'. *International Journal for Academic Development*, 18(4), pp. 306–317.

Healey, M., Bradford, M., Roberts, C. and Knight, Y., 2013. Collaborative discipline-based curriculum change: applying Change Academy processes at department level. *International Journal for Academic Development*, 18(1), pp. 31–44.

Hendry, G.D., Bell, A. and Thomson, K., 2014. Learning by observing a peer's teaching situation. *International Journal for Academic Development*, 19(4), pp. 318–329.

Hoare, L., 2013. Swimming in the deep end: transnational teaching as culture learning? *Higher Education Research & Development*, 32(4), pp. 561–574.

Holt, D., Cohen, L., Campbell-Evans, G., Chang, P., Macdonald, I. and McDonald, J., 2013. Leading at the coal-face: the world as experienced by subject coordinators in Australian Higher Education. *Educational Management Administration & Leadership*, 41(2), pp. 233–249.

Hubball, H., Clarke, A. and Poole, G., 2010. Ten-year reflections on mentoring SoTL research in a research-intensive university. *International Journal for Academic Development*, 15(2), pp. 117–129.

Johannes, C., Fendler, J. and Seidel, T., 2013. Teachers' perceptions of the learning environment and their knowledge base in a training program for novice university teachers. *International Journal for Academic Development*, 18(2), pp. 152–165.

Kandlbinder, P. and Peseta, T., 2009. Key concepts in postgraduate certificates in higher education teaching and learning in Australasia and the United Kingdom. *International Journal for Academic Development*, 14(1), pp. 19–31.

Kreber, C., 2013. Empowering the scholarship of teaching: an Arendtian and critical perspective. *Studies in Higher Education*, 38(6), pp. 857–869.

Ladyshewsky, R.K. and Flavell, H., 2012. Transfer of training in an academic leadership development program for program coordinators. *Educational Management Administration & Leadership*, 40(1), pp. 127–147.

Layton, C. and Brown, C., 2011. Striking a balance: supporting teaching excellence award applications. *International Journal for Academic Development*, 16(2), pp. 163–174.

McCormack, C., Vanags, T. and Prior, R., 2014. 'Things fall apart so they can fall together': uncovering the hidden side of writing a teaching award application. *Higher Education Research & Development*, 33(5), pp. 935–948.

Nsibande, R. and Garraway, J., 2011. Professional development through formative evaluation. *International Journal for Academic Development*, 16(2), pp. 97–107.

Peseta, T. and Kandlbinder, P. (eds), 2011. *Higher education research & development anthology*, Milperra, NSW: HERDSA.

Smith, K., 2014. Exploring flying faculty teaching experiences: motivations, challenges and opportunities. *Studies in Higher Education*, 39(1), pp. 117–134.

Spowart, L., Turner, R., Shenton, D. and Kneale, P., 2015. 'But I've been teaching for 20 years…': encouraging teaching accreditation for experienced staff working in higher education. *International Journal for Academic Development*, pp. 1–13. Available online at DOI 10.1080/1360144X.2015.1081595

Thomas, K., McNaught, C., Wong, K.-C. and Li, Y.-C., 2011. Early-career academics' perceptions of teaching and learning in Hong Kong: implications for professional development. *International Journal for Academic Development*, 16(3), pp. 257–268.

Thomson, K., 2015. Informal conversations about teaching and their relationship to a formal development program: learning opportunities for novice and mid-career academics. *International Journal for Academic Development*, 20(2), pp. 137–149.

Thomson, K., Bell, A. and Hendry, G., 2015. Peer observation of teaching: the case for learning just by watching. *Higher Education Research & Development*, 34(5), pp. 1060–1062.

Trevitt, C., Stocks, C. and Quinlan, K.M., 2011. Advancing assessment practice in continuing professional learning: toward a richer understanding of teaching portfolios for learning and assessment. *International Journal for Academic Development*, 17(3), pp. 163–175. Available online at DOI 10.1080/1360144X.2015.1081595

Wardale, D., Hendrickson, T., Jefferson, T., Klass, D., Lord, L. and Marinelli, M., 2015. Creating an oasis: some insights into the practice and theory of a successful academic writing group. *Higher Education Research & Development*, 34(6), pp. 1297–1310.

Weaver, D., Robbie, D. and Radloff, A., 2014. Demystifying the publication process – a structured writing program to facilitate dissemination of teaching and learning scholarship. *International Journal for Academic Development*, 19(3), pp. 212–225.

Winchester, T.M. and Winchester, M., 2011. Exploring the impact of faculty reflection on weekly student evaluations of teaching. *International Journal for Academic Development*, 16(2), pp. 119–131.

Chapter 19

Leading academic communities

Academic leadership takes many forms. Early career academics may assume responsibility for projects, course coordination, student oversight, administrative roles, events or annual activities as part of their core or service roles. The transition to senior professoriate roles integrates leadership responsibilities across a range of intellectual pursuits (Macfarlane 2012). Over time, academics may move into formalised positions of authority, including head of discipline, faculties, departments or schools (Bland *et al.* 2005; Buller 2011; Wolverton *et al.* 2005); as strategic leaders for teaching and learning (Debowski 2012a; Quinlan 2011); research positions (Debowski 2010); as well as other academic functions. Thus, the nature of academic leadership is somewhat inchoate, reflecting the diverse paths that a particular individual may take.

University leaders straddle varying levels of authority and power, with those in formal roles having considerable discretion over the allocation of resources, organisational priorities and the well-being of other individuals. The presence of a toxic or dysfunctional leader can have a profound impact on the community and its cultural, productive and sustainable progress (Rose *et al.* 2015). It is likely that employee engagement will be low and stress, turnover and absenteeism will be high. Unfortunately, many universities fail to monitor the impact of poor leadership, primarily addressing its consequences rather than creating a leadership-oriented environment as part of their institutional frameworks. In this chapter, a range of perspectives will be offered, illustrating the importance of encouraging conscious, research-informed strategic leaders who are capable of building inclusive, sustainable communities at any level. The articulation of some leadership principles and features is an initial step in building this communal understanding.

Defining good academic leadership

There are some well-established principles that support good academic leadership (Avolio *et al.* 2009; Fullan and Scott 2009; Hubbard 2002; Jackson and Parry 2011; Schein 2010). They highlight the role of the leader as setting a clear vision for the future, encouraging people to subscribe to that vision; building effective strategies and paths to achieve those targets; maintaining effective oversight of the internal and the external environment; and ensuring there is good balance between the long-term goals and the well-being of the communities being led. There has also been considerable discussion on the ethical conduct of leaders and the values they bring to their role (Debowski 2012b; McCauley *et al.* 2006; Schein 2010). Thus, academic leaders carry responsibility for guiding sustainable, long-term outcomes for their portfolios, while ensuring their communities flourish in the process. In tandem, many leaders also carry management responsibilities that ensure the planning and execution of key priorities and strategies. This may necessitate careful oversight of resources (including people), costs and time management.

The development of a common framework and lexicon to explain and describe leadership and its enactment is helpful in guiding communal understanding of these behaviours (Floyd and Fung 2015). Many universities are now spending considerable time exploring the parameters of good leadership, encouraging leaders to be strategically focused, high achievement-oriented, clear about goals and priorities, capable of working constructively and productively with diverse stakeholders, employing effective communication practices and ensuring their communities are equitable and inclusive.

In addition to these applications of leadership principles, it is helpful to consider how academic leaders might be encouraged to be conscious leaders who monitor their impact on people, processes and outcomes (Middlehurst 1993; Middlehurst 2008). The formation of an informed and adaptive leadership identity contributes to the capacity to reflect, evaluate and respond to feedback. In addition, there is considerable benefit in building reflexive leadership and an evidence-based understanding of the academic context and leadership role (Bolden *et al.* 2014).

Academic transitions to leadership

Universities are recognising the importance of leadership as a necessary component of the roles that academics play. For example, many institutions have articulated the leadership roles academics might fill in readiness for promotion or probation. Initial forays into leadership might be undertaken via *distributed leadership* roles that are informal but support important university functions (Bolden *et al.* 2009; Floyd and Fung 2015; Ramsden 1998), commencing with oversight of teaching or research projects before progressing to more extended leadership of teams. In some cases, a career track that is leadership/administration focused may be pursued.

Despite the recognition and encouragement of leadership, academe does not follow a well-delineated apprenticeship to facilitate the transition into these leadership responsibilities. The assumption of academic leadership roles can be somewhat serendipitous rather than planned and anticipated, with some academics provided valuable opportunities to move into more complex work, while others are neglected. While many women will be evident in the junior leadership ranks, they will be less prominent in the more senior levels of most universities (Blackmore and Sachs 2007; Howe-Walsh and Turnbull 2016; Obers 2015), an issue that needs to be more seriously monitored and considered as part of the institutional leadership strategy. While there are many potential reasons for this absence, some evident issues relate to sponsorship, opportunity and, in some institutions, an inhospitable climate toward diverse leaders.

It is important to recognise that academic leadership is complex, unpredictable and strongly influenced by external forces (institutional, financial, student demand). The nature of the leadership context (including the temporal nature of some roles) must also be considered. The capacity to adapt, respond and reflect on each experience is a strength that leaders will benefit from building, although it will require resilience in some situations.

The adaptive academic head

Academic heads are defined as those who have formal, delegated control and authority over people, finances, university processes and the direction of an academic community. They may head departments, schools, faculties or research institutes and centres. These roles are very complex. Each head must navigate shifts in institutional strategy, politics and expectations of their community and external stakeholders while maintaining a conscious focus on helping their members flourish and achieve their full potential. The challenge of focusing on the daily minutiae while steering a strategic path requires adaptive and responsive approaches to ensure that actions and behaviours are appropriate and effective. Figure 19.1 illustrates the different emphases that an academic head is likely to incorporate in their role enactment.

There are five key foci that need to be accommodated: a strong *people-focus* offers people clear guidance on their goals, priorities and performance expectations, including the provision of effective feedback. With appropriate sponsorship and a supportive culture that ensures all members are offered equitable access to resources and opportunity, the community is able to achieve its optimal outcomes.

However, it is also necessary to ensure that the *processes* facilitate successful achievement of goals and responsibilities. The head plays a key role in overseeing the establishment and maintenance of suitable systems, policies and processes, including the disposition of available resources. Planning and monitoring of outcomes supports efficient progress and risk management. The use of consultation for major planning processes encourages collegiality and member engagement with major reforms.

Strategy is a third leadership focus. The capacity to outline and pursue a long-term vision that is both realistic, ambitious and informed by suitable environmental scanning provides a clear path for the community to follow. Other activities that underpin strategy include the optimal use of available talent,

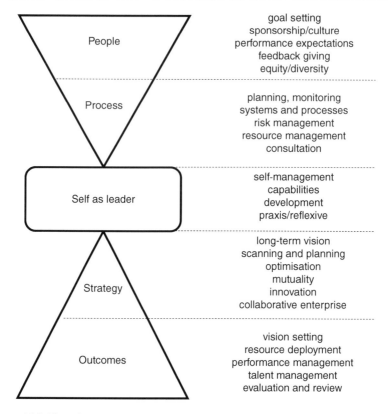

Figure 19.1 The adaptive academic head.

including encouraging innovation and collaboration to benefit stakeholders and the university.

Outcomes are often promoted as the highest priority in our universities in their efforts to increase productivity and advantage. However, these are dependent on the collective effort of all members of the fraternity. The provision of appropriate resources, a strong learning orientation to develop staff potential and regular guidance as to performance outcomes all provide foundational support to generate the desired outcomes. The evaluation and review of outcomes provides critical insight into the quality and impact of leadership. Additionally, consideration of *what* constitutes outcomes needs further debate. If the only focus is on productivity, leaders have considerable potential to create stressful and challenging work settings.

Finally, and centrally, the *leadership qualities* that are consistently employed support a vibrant, effective academic community. The leader's capacity to be self-aware and self-managing is fundamental. The development of core leadership capabilities and a willingness to apply praxis (research-informed practice) and reflexive processes (evaluation of behaviours and impact) are essential features of effective leadership (Scheffer *et al.* 2012; Shepherd 2012).

Reflection allows the leader to consider the context, their own actions, the response of their constituents and the consequences of the events that took place (van Woerkom 2004; Yeo and Gold 2011). These processes of review and evaluation provide an ideal setting to learn from and build better practices to manage the complex situations that often emerge in academic settings. It is important to recognise that leadership is a learning journey and there will be many experiences along the way that will challenge the leader and may require new skills and a different behavioural approach. Reflexive leaders review their leadership effectiveness on a regular basis to ensure that they are creating the right setting for optimal performance across their community.

A challenge for formally appointed leaders is that they oversee highly dynamic and volatile settings. Their communities can experience pressures from internal and external sources, and may need to be reformed or reviewed to accommodate new demands. This may require recalibration and adjustment of the particular leadership focus. For example, major reforms will need to emphasise strategy, people and process, with outcomes likely to be impacted for some time during the transition. Stable communities, on the other hand, can place more emphasis on outcomes and strategy. The capacity to be adaptive and reflective is a critical capability for leaders in these roles.

Evaluating effective leadership

Regular review and evaluation of their effectiveness offer a valuable insights into how academic leaders are performing. Access to peer networks, reflective tools, action-learning resources and in-house development support at point of need provide important support during this self-review process.

There are other ways in which leaders might seek feedback. First, they might monitor the team members and check how each member is faring. The well-being of a community can offer an important cue regarding the impact of the leadership style on the capacity of the members to fulfil their roles. Low productivity, for example, is often an early warning of leadership challenges; so too is turnover and absenteeism. Feedback from the group on their perceptions of leadership style and impact could be canvassed through an anonymous process such as an online survey or as part of a regular debrief after critical events. The review might be holistic or possibly focused on a particular element of the leadership role (such as meeting management skills) with feedback invited as to how it could be improved. A willingness to seek feedback in an open discussion also models reflexive leadership but the recipient must be capable of accepting and responding constructively to any feedback that is offered.

Second, academics might seek a leadership mentor who can offer experienced insights, models and suggestions on their leadership practices. These mentors are commonly those who have successfully filled a similar role. They act as an important critical friend, particularly during the formative phase of leadership as the individual establishes their identity, mode of operation and relationships with their community.

Third, individual academics might seek some professional feedback or diagnostics through a third party, such as their human resources division or an external leadership consultant. 360-degree reviews offer multi-source feedback, normally drawing on the supervisor, the individual, their direct reports and their peers or stakeholders. When correctly administered by an experienced professional, these diagnostic tools act as a critical touchstone as to how the leadership style is being experienced and perceived, offering clear indicators of both strengths and areas for development (Tornow and London 1998). More nuanced 360-tools are now available. To illustrate, the Human Synergistics Leadership Impact instrument[1] is a powerful diagnostic tool that maps the types of behaviours that the leader evidences, and the impact they have on those around them. Focused on ten key behaviours (envisioning; role modelling; mentoring; stimulating thinking; referring; monitoring; providing feedback; reinforcing; influencing; and creating a setting), it offers guidance on how to build a constructive approach to leadership. This type of guidance is sorely missing in many universities and the negligence shows in the forms of leadership that are experienced in many communities. These forms of feedback are ideally suited to headship and greatly assist those appointed to such complex roles. Academic leaders appreciate the rigour and the research that sits behind such tools.

Institutional support for good academic leadership

From this overview, it is evident that there is considerable work to be done in terms of building a comprehensive support base for academic leadership. The assumption that leaders will evolve into their roles and become competent is dangerous: leaders are responsible for large programs of activity; finances, human resources, university reputation and numerous other institutional outcomes need to be well supported and assisted throughout their tenure. Poor leadership can have disastrous consequences for the institution and the staff who sit under uncertain, indifferent or incompetent leaders (Rose *et al.* 2015). Universities' investment in their leaders can reap significant returns in terms of staff productivity, morale and reputation.

There are many strategies that can be developed to support university leaders. Some of the approaches now being introduced by far-sighted universities include:

- development of clear standards and expectations regarding leadership attributes and behaviours;
- effective supervisory oversight by more senior leaders, providing informed guidance and mentoring concerning institutional strategy and goals;
- institutional clarity in messages about culture, leadership values and attributes, along with clear modelling of those same values from the top down;

- establishment of an effective induction and orientation mechanism for those in leadership roles (including research, teaching and broader academic contexts), ensuring that they are aware of core systems, policies and protocols from the time of entry into their roles;
- access to regular reviews of leadership impact and behaviours for those in official designate roles, with expert debriefing and support;
- access to leadership mentors;
- the facilitation of leadership networks;
- regular forums on emerging issues or challenges that leaders need to address;
- institutional audits of culture to identify groups that are not thriving;
- the recognition and valuing of leadership roles and activities in probation, tenure, promotion and development discussions;
- the provision of expert in-house or consultancy services to provide just-in-time diagnostic, cultural and coaching services;
- the development of guides and tools that will support general leadership challenges;
- the sharing of best practice systems, models, tools and templates with leaders holding similar roles;
- development of online resources that can provide just-in-time guidance on leadership dilemmas;
- the provision of a one-stop website for leaders with key resources and information;
- regular visits by professional support staff to check for any new areas of need that might be supported;
- rapid action on poor leadership, either to support or address issues.

Specific approaches to encourage leadership capacity building are explored in the following chapter.

Conclusion

This chapter has offered a broad picture of academic leadership, encouraging increased focus on the articulation and sponsorship of good leadership. It can be seen that this is a whole of institutional responsibility and best operates from a coherent, well-articulated and well-considered framework. The sponsorship and modelling from the executive down is particularly valuable in setting up a strong leadership culture and expectation. The funding of HE development services to further act on this front is the other key area that needs to be considered. While much of this support could be offered through a specialist in-house organisational development group, it may also cross over into the teaching and research development service areas. Collaboration across those groups to provide a seamless support service is important. Academics need to be provided with the best quality guidance that will assist them in dealing with the many dilemmas that emerge. Above all, creating a leadership culture that is transparent, well aligned and respectful of all members can be a major point of excellence for an institution and its many members.

Note

1 See: www.human-synergistics.com.au/Solutions/DevelopingLeaders/LeadershipImpact.aspx

References

Avolio, B.J., Walumbwa, F.O. and Weber, T.J., 2009. Leadership: current theories, research, and future directions. *Annual Review of Psychology*, 60(1), pp. 421–449.

Blackmore, J. and Sachs, J., 2007. Performing and reforming leaders: gender, educational restructuring, and organizational change, Albany, NY: State University of New York Press.

Bland, C.J., Weber-Main, A., Lund, S.M. and Finstad, D.A., 2005. *The research-productive department: strategies from departments that excel*, Hoboken, NJ: Wiley.

Bolden, R., Gosling, J. and O'Brien, A., 2014. Citizens of the academic community? A societal perspective on leadership in UK higher education. *Studies in Higher Education*, 39(5), pp. 754–770.

Bolden, R., Petrov, G. and Gosling, J., 2009. Distributed leadership in higher education: rhetoric and reality. *Educational Management Administration & Leadership*, 37(2), pp. 257–277.

Buller, J.L., 2011. *Academic leadership day by day: small steps that lead to great success*, 1st edition, San Francisco, CA: Jossey-Bass.

Debowski, S., 2010. Leading research in an evolving world: implications for higher education development, policy and practice. In *Research and development in higher education: reshaping higher education*, Melbourne, 6–9 July, 2010. Melbourne, Vic.: HERDSA, pp. 213–222.

Debowski, S., 2012a. Leading higher education learning, teaching and innovation. In J.E. Groccia, M.A.T. Alsudairi and W.H. Bergquist, eds, *Handbook of university and college teaching: a global perspective*, San Francisco, CA: SAGE Publications, chpt. 17.

Debowski, S., 2012b. *The new academic: A strategic handbook*, London: Open University Press.

Floyd, A. and Fung, D., 2015. Focusing the kaleidoscope: exploring distributed leadership in an English university. *Studies in Higher Education*, pp. 1–16. Available online at DOI 10.1080/03075079.2015.1110692

Fullan, M. and Scott, G., 2009. *Turnaround leadership for higher education*, San Francisco: Jossey-Bass.

Howe-Walsh, L. and Turnbull, S., 2016. Barriers to women leaders in academia: tales from science and technology. *Studies in Higher Education*, 41(3), pp. 415–428.

Hubbard, G. (ed.), 2002. *First XI winning organisations in Australia*, Camberwell, Vic.: Wiley.

Jackson, B. and Parry, K.W., 2011. *A very short, fairly interesting and reasonably cheap book about studying leadership*, 2nd edition, Los Angeles: SAGE Publishing.

Macfarlane, B., 2012. *Intellectual leadership in higher education: renewing the role of the university professor*, New York: Routledge.

McCauley, C.D., Drath, W.H., Palus, C.J., O'Connor, P.M.G. and Baker, B.A., 2006. The use of constructive-developmental theory to advance the understanding of leadership. *The Leadership Quarterly*, 17(6), pp. 634–653.

Middlehurst, R., 1993. *Leading academics*, Buckingham, England: Society for Research into Higher Education.

Middlehurst, R., 2008. Not enough science or not enough learning? exploring the gaps between leadership theory and practice. *Higher Education Quarterly*, 62(4), pp. 322–339.

Obers, N., 2015. Influential structures: understanding the role of the head of department in relation to women academics' research careers. *Higher Education Research & Development*, 34(6), pp. 1220–1232.

Quinlan, K., 2011. *Developing the whole student: leading higher education initiatives that integrate mind and heart*, London: Leadership Foundation for Higher Education.

Ramsden, P., 1998. *Learning to lead in higher education*, London: Routledge.

Rose, K., Shuck, B., Twyford, D. and Berman, M., 2015. Skunked: an integrative review exploring the consequences of the dysfunctional leader and implications for those employees who work for them. *Human Resource Development Review*, 14(1), pp. 64–90.

Scheffer, A., Braun, N. and Scheffer, M., 2012. *Hanging the mirror: the discipline of reflective leadership*, Shelbyville, KY: Wasteland Press.

Schein, E.H., 2010. *Organizational culture and leadership*, 4th edition, San Francisco, CA: Jossey-Bass.

Shepherd, N.A., 2012. *Reflective leaders and high-performance organizations: how effective leaders balance task and relationship to build high-performing organizations*, Bloomington, IN: iUniverse.

Tornow, W.W. and London, M. (eds), 1998. *Maximizing the value of 360-degree feedback: a process for successful individual and organizational development*, 1st edition, San Francisco, CA: Jossey-Bass.

Van Woerkom, M., 2004. The concept of critical reflection and its implications for human resource development. *Advances in Developing Human Resources*, 6(2), pp. 178–192.

Wolverton, M., Ackerman, R. and Holt, S., 2005. Preparing for leadership: what academic department chairs need to know. *Journal of Higher Education Policy and Management*, 27(2), pp. 227–238.

Yeo, R.K. and Gold, J., 2011. The inseparability of action and learning: unravelling Revans' action learning theory for Human Resource Development (HRD). *Human Resource Development International*, 14(5), pp. 511–526.

Chapter 20

Developing academic leadership capacity

Throughout this book, the essential role that leaders play in setting up a university for success has been emphasised: academics fill a vast array of informal and formal leadership roles, ensuring the university can fulfil its mission. However, there are many anecdotes of poor leadership and communities that experience downturns, failure or deeply embedded toxic cultures. Academics benefit from support as they learn to lead or negotiate complex, dynamic contexts. Whether enacting informal roles within the professoriate, as formal leaders with stipulated responsibilities or as members of academic communities, they benefit from engaging with good leadership principles and practice. The capacity to reflect, evaluate and adapt when leading others, and to take responsibility for both process and outcomes, provides a strong foundation for effective leaders.

There are various approaches that universities might employ to guide leadership practices. At the worst extreme, crisis management might be the primary approach. This is not the ideal scenario for learning. Emotions will be high and the pressures to effect rapid change will be large. The leader, under considerable strain, will find it hard to reflect, test and adapt existing behaviours while putting out fires. Thus, this form of peripatetic support should ideally be occasional or rare.

Instead, the establishment of a well-designed and comprehensive suite of leadership capacity-building strategies can ensure leaders are well prepared for any contingencies (and better able to avoid crises). In addition, they will be more attuned to cultivating cultures that encourage constructive workplaces, high achievement and strong alignment across members. Thus, leadership capacity building supports individual, workplace and organisational learning (Watkins *et al.* 2011).

Leadership capacity building is supported by three key factors:

- the executive and its leadership orientation;
- the leadership community as an engaged and active leadership fraternity;
- the quality and effectiveness of the HE development service in supporting the development and enhancement of leadership capacity across the institution.

The university executive as leadership models and sponsors

Executives are formed for a specific purpose. The governing body has a strong influence over the choice of most senior leaders (such as the president or vice-chancellor) and may also guide the appointments of other senior staff (Grove 2012). The last few years have seen notable churn at the top of universities, as established leaders move on and new leaders emerge. There has been considerable focus on getting things done and turning around business models and practices. The executive can be highly energetic and keen to make things happen. However, they may not be experienced in leading at an executive level. This opens up risks for many institutions, particularly if the new appointees generate high turnover of other senior staff who hold extensive corporate knowledge. This trend can be an early warning indication that executive leaders could benefit from more intensive guidance on their new roles and leadership approaches.

The modelling of effective and constructive leadership by the executive is an extremely powerful message across the university community. However, this requires conscious leaders who draw on praxis and reflection. Uninformed leadership at this level can be particularly damaging, given the power and resources that each member wields. This is a blind spot for many executives: they are unaware of, or indifferent to, their leadership impact on their subordinates and the institutional culture as a whole. A specialised executive leadership program (which might include deans as part of the extended executive), integrating multi-source feedback and coaching, offers an important space to build a collective insight into leadership approaches and impact. While many organisations in other sectors see the provision of regular diagnostic feedback and coaching as critical to their success, the university sector has tended to be less keen on seeking feedback from subordinates or peers. Possibly, this stems back to their limited exposure to leadership development in their previous academic roles or indeed, the paucity of effective feedback through their careers. Facilitation of this personal and collective leadership journey is best supported by an external executive consultant who offers confidentiality, distance and expertise that is well tuned to the complexities of this leadership group.

The executive can sponsor leadership capacity building by:

- engaging in the process of leadership development as part of their own executive journey;
- encouraging consistent principles and standards relating to leadership practices;
- selecting leaders who reflect appropriate leadership attributes;
- advocating for good leadership and its enactment across the university;
- supporting, and actively engaging with, activities that support the leadership community, including sponsoring key events or programs;
- reflecting a coherent language and approach to being a quality leader.

The leadership community

The leadership community is extensive, ranging from those who are distributed leaders, i.e. working in their substantive academic roles while executing leadership responsibilities (Bolden *et al.* 2009; Floyd and Fung 2015; Jones *et al.* 2012), to those in formal roles with authority and oversight around institutional outcomes (Cipriano 2011; Gmelch and Miskin 1995; Knight and Trowler 2000). Each individual will experience a progressive journey of leadership identity formation, testing and refinement, with each new experience guiding them toward increased knowledge of themselves, their leadership context and the organisational setting in which they lead. Situational leadership of this nature is strengthened by an engaged and informed leadership community, including the opportunity to learn from and with others, in both formal and informal contexts. Thus, leadership capacity building is strengthened by leaders who:

- monitor and evaluate their performance and leadership impact;
- seek ways to enhance their leadership effectiveness and practices;
- actively share their knowledge and expertise with other colleagues through networks and forums;
- mentor and sponsor other leaders;
- prioritise attendance at key development activities.

Leadership capacity building is situated within a larger, institutionalised/collective context, which experiences shifting cultures, contexts and contemporaneous challenges (Edwards and Turnbull 2013). While there are many techniques and tools that support leadership practice (skillsets), the enactment of effective leadership requires an ongoing process of review, reframing and renewal of approaches to being a leader (mindset) (Kennedy *et al.* 2013). Thus, the goal of building a robust and engaged leadership community is to move it toward these transformational processes of situated, reflexive and responsive leadership. Given the span of leaders in an institution and the limited formalised support that can be offered, the development of an active and supportive leadership community is very necessary.

The higher education development service

As the facilitative service that can assist in promoting good leadership practices, the HE service provides an important bridge across the university community and tiers of leadership. It benefits from an executive sponsor who is also a strong advocate for good leadership (often the provost or senior deputy vice-chancellor).

Effective facilitation of leadership capacity building might be evidenced by an HED service that:

- meets regularly with key executive members to explore emerging leadership, cultural or organisational issues;

- provides a range of support strategies to enable effective leadership across the university community;
- engages leaders in their guidance of institutional reforms;
- develops appropriate strategies to address leadership challenges;
- assists institutional leaders in managing complex leadership problems or contexts;
- designs and delivers programs and other forms of learning support that are well attended, recognised as adding value to the institution, and promoted by leaders to other leaders.

In order to achieve these outcomes, sufficient budget needs to be allocated to support the leadership activities, as programs, multi-source feedback and coaching are a major component of these activities and require dedicated funding. In turn, evidence of impact provides a stronger case for funding of these initiatives (see Chapter 21).

HE developers can have a large impact on the university leadership community. Their capacity to deliver high-quality support is dependent on the following:

- their relationship capabilities;
- their professional standing and credibility as leadership and management experts;
- the suite of professional capabilities on which they can draw;
- the modes and scope of delivery approaches;
- their responsiveness to emerging issues.

The ability to build strong and sustained relationships with talented, innovative leaders is an essential foundation for this work (Ligon *et al.* 2011). A diverse professional toolkit can be a considerable advantage. The capacity to administer and debrief 360-degree reviews, coach, conduct reviews and evaluations, facilitate strategic planning, guide group learning, design and deliver complex leadership programs, as well as support complex change processes, enables a complete service to be offered. This will be particularly important as more complex needs are identified. Much of this work is contingent on the initial relationship that has been established with leaders or client groups.

Universities may employ external facilitators for this high-end leadership development. The HE developer is then likely to act as a broker, selecting the facilitator, briefing them, coordinating the program delivery and monitoring the quality of provision. These external agents will need to be well informed about institutional context and complexities.

Developing reflexive leaders

The goal of leadership capacity building is to encourage reflexive leadership, that is, leaders who are capable of reflecting on their context, actions and experiences, and to frame their insights within a broader consideration of good leadership principles and practices. This process draws on self-discovery, a review of critical learning moments and mentorship (Muir 2014). The development of an informed and nuanced leadership identity encourages ongoing reflection as a regular process.

To enable this transformative process, leadership capacity building strategies are context-sensitive and feedback-intensive (King and Santana 2010). As Figure 20.1 illustrates, they provide an important opportunity to explore actions and experiences through an evaluative lens that is supported by leadership communities, mentorship and/or more formalised support. Individual leaders are

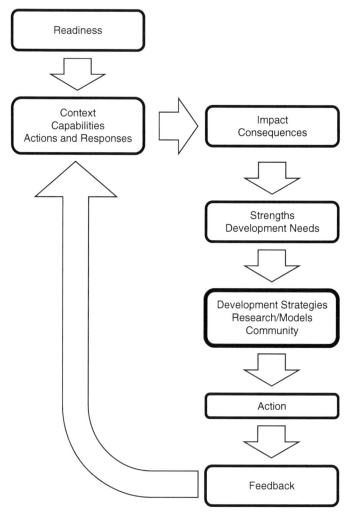

Figure 20.1 Developing leadership capacity.

encouraged to evaluate their leadership behaviours in terms of the context, actions and capabilities that were employed, and the resultant impact and consequences. These self-insights inform an assessment of strengths and development needs, which assists their efforts to evolve as leaders. Access to a range of development strategies, consideration of the research and models relating to leadership, as well as drawing on community support, all give the leaders new insights about themselves and their roles. Programs facilitate guided testing of ideas and principles, drawing on feedback from a range of sources. However, this process can also be undertaken via mentorship or in collaboration with other leaders. Readiness is configured at the top of this diagram. Leaders need to be open to these reflective processes. They will need to own, rather than deflect, their leadership impact and consequences. HED developers can stimulate readiness by offering prompts and reflective questions.

In planning development strategies, particular motifs or themes that are likely to shape the development experiences might include:

- leadership identity (knowledge of self and strengths, philosophy, goals and intentions);
- leadership roles and context (e.g. distributed vs formal) (Jones *et al.* 2012);
- the reflective leader (critical incidents, learning points, application and action) (Jarvis *et al.* 2013);
- the constructive leader (focusing on people, processes, culture) (Middlehurst 1993);
- the adaptive leader (contextual leadership, leading change and leading in uncertainty);
- the strategic leader (within a university context; achieving progress and outcomes);
- the academic leader (exploring the nature of academic work and its implications);
- the connected leader (examining context, culture, partnerships, relationships and interdependencies) (Edwards and Turnbull 2013).

As advanced learners (Grunefeld *et al.* 2015), leaders anticipate the capacity to negotiate and manage the development context to ensure they will have highly relevant outcomes. Their learning focus will draw on reflection and exploration of their leadership context, reflecting their different perspectives of being acted on, being actors and being agents of change.

Building leadership capacity

Leadership capacity building requires dedicated and persistent effort. The leadership community is highly dynamic, with its membership including formal and distributed leaders. There will be restructures and organisational renewal. New campuses may be added and others closed. Executive leaders and institutional agendas may change seemingly overnight in some instances. Within faculties, there will be a constant churn of academics and researchers moving into more senior roles, building a new team or group, or being promoted into the professoriate. Through all of this tumult, the HED service offers a source of guidance, expertise and reassurance. It needs to be a visible, professional presence that connects with new leaders, is supportive of established leaders and able to maintain strong engagement with the existing leadership community.

There are many forms of support that can be offered to leaders. Some common approaches are described in the following sections.

Leadership attributes/framework

Given the diversity, different experiences and interpretations of leadership, there is considerable advantage in articulating institutional leadership principles and concepts. The development of a leadership framework that articulates the desired attributes that leaders might evidence, for example, offers a rich opportunity to explore and build some communal understanding about leadership and its enactment. The framework supports executive sponsorship of these ideals and facilitates common usage by leaders and developers across all programs and activities. A consistent, research-informed framework or model enables its use for cultural audits (e.g. staff motivation, morale, turnover), multi-source reviews, development programs, workshops and other specific diagnostic tools. It encourages a common language and meaning to support each leader's interpretation of their own particular leadership narrative. Frameworks can also assist in clarifying accepted and unacceptable behaviour as part of a larger institutional transformation (Gedro and Wang 2013).

Leadership orientations

Attempts to provide a standardised, hosted orientation are not likely to draw large numbers. A more effective alternative would be the development of a leadership website with some focused self-help guides that can be accessed at point of need. Ideally, these would integrate institutional information that leaders need to know. These might be developed in partnership with experienced heads, managers and other specialist agencies in the university, or could be sourced from external avenues.[1]

New deans and heads, who have the largest span of responsibilities and influence, will benefit from individualised support, exploring the university systems and agencies and the role that the HED service might play. This can be the start of an ongoing relationship.

Workshops and forums

Leaders need to be agile and responsive to new challenges, emerging opportunities or shifts in university strategy. Workshops offer an efficient learning avenue to guide people toward improved leadership and management strategies. Their purpose is to explore specific capabilities, challenges or approaches that support better leadership. Thus, they are often focused on enhancing leaders' skillsets. Despite the relevance of many of these workshops, it is possible that more senior leaders may not manage to attend. The timing may be wrong, or they may not wish to attend sessions that are open to all and sundry, where they cannot discuss the real issues that must be addressed.

Forums offer a more targeted focus, and can be directed to certain roles, levels or needs. These can explore strategic issues or more generic leadership challenges, and may incorporate some integration of capability enhancement. The development of authentic case studies, exemplars, checklists or other useful guidance can be provided. Some pre-reading might be integrated to increase the richness and depth of discussions. The participants will value the opportunity to interact and map good strategies across their leadership community.

A particular advantage of these types of activities is the building of a collective purpose around the issue or initiative. The sessions may encourage collaboration or the formation of project groups to take the issue further. The HED developer might also prepare and disseminate a summary of key insights from the session, which will be reviewed with interest by the participants and the executive. These summaries should be carefully designed to be informative and readily digestible. Value adding is important for this group. The executive sponsor will anticipate a leadership role in these forums and may influence planning if collective pooling of ideas is likely to be an outcome.

Programs

Universities generally offer a range of leadership programs in recognition that there are a number of key skills and capabilities that need to be developed (Bolman and Gallos 2011; Debowski and Blake 2007; Ladyshewsky and Flavell 2012; Vilkinas *et al.* 2009). The advantage of these programs is their focused attention on the key roles being played by participants. They encourage reflection, action learning, feedback seeking, modelling from other leaders, testing of different practices and the ability to learn from others. Programs of this nature can be costly, as they may integrate residential components to encourage reflection and peer learning, the use of external expert consultants, a diagnostic feedback instrument and, potentially, coaching sessions. The choice of cohort is often strategically determined and may be influenced by the capacity to secure a sponsor.

Multi-source feedback

Given the role of leadership is to influence others and effect enhancements that improve the institutional culture and outcomes, the actions of each leader can impact on many people. It can be difficult to perceive those effects. Multi-source feedback offers nuanced feedback from multiple sources to help the leader see the effect of their behaviours on others. 360-degree reviews are normally drawn from supervisors, peers, subordinates and self, while 270- or 180-degree feedback will reflect fewer segments of impact. These different perspectives guide the learner toward a more accurate understanding of their leadership style, impact and influence (Tornow and London 1998). This guidance provides a rich basis for planning development and measuring shifts in behaviour over time. While these tools are often integrated into leadership programs, they are also useful diagnostic supports for formal leaders at the commencement of and during their role enactment. These diagnostic tools can reveal particular challenges that may be impeding the leader's efforts.

Universities that offer this support might reserve it for those engaged in leadership development programs or situated in complex and highly responsible formal leadership roles. The initial diagnostic review needs to be supported with a careful debrief, mapping of developmental needs and ongoing coaching to support desired shifts in leadership practice. Ideally, the same diagnostic tool would be used biennially to identify the impact of these changes and to establish new development goals.

A potential source of contention can occur if more senior leaders wish to view the results of multi-source feedback. These tools are best employed as developmental sources of information, to be used by the individual and shared if they so choose. If the results were to be public, the nature of the responses and the willingness to engage in seeking feedback will be compromised. Further, many of these tools are provided on the understanding that they will be confidential. A policy on their use is advisable. If there is a desire to use a multi-feedback process for performance review or summative purposes, a different instrument or process should be considered. There should be clear differentiation and clear guidance on how each will be employed.

Coaching

Coaching offers in-situ support, enabling the individual to identify and test enhanced approaches to their leadership (Beattie *et al.* 2014; Frankovelgia and Riddle 2010; Jones *et al.* 2015; Nieminen *et al.* 2013; Rogers 2012). The HED staff might take on this role as part of their service delivery, or it might be undertaken by an external coach. Leaders can also be trained as coaches, providing support to their colleagues (Nieminen *et al.* 2013). The HED might source a pool of coaches to enable support at point of need. External coaches will need to be knowledgeable about the institutional values and priorities to guide situated, reflexive leadership.

Leadership network

The role of leader can be an isolating experience. Tough decisions often need to be made. Heads of school, deans and senior research leaders may be particularly challenged as they grapple with staffing, funding, strategic choices and the necessary balancing of the needs of their different constituents. The capacity to manage a balanced budget is a pressing concern for all three groups, and often, may be further confounded by broader shifts in policy or government funding.

Academic leaders will value opportunities to talk about leadership with like colleagues and to hear of the common dilemmas they also experience. Deans may have this opportunity through regular meetings with their executive leader. Heads and research leaders, on the other hand, often lack a university-based forum of this nature, although they may be able to attend faculty-based meetings. Many note that these meetings can be very operationally focused rather than future-focused. Brokered network meetings provide an ideal forum for more wide-ranging discussions and can generate considerable solution generation (Debowski and Blake 2007; McCauley-Smith *et al*. 2015). The support of a network broker can ensure they remain active. Although academics are well intentioned, the scheduling of meetings can fall away unless it is managed by a good planner. There are different networking formats that might be considered. For example, the group might like formal sessions with an invited speaker where one theme is explored. Alternatively, they might prefer a self-organised approach, where key issues are uncovered and discussed. A third option is to occasionally invite the president or vice-chancellor to the meeting to explore strategic matters and share insights. The group can become a powerful lobbying network when this occurs.

Program scheduling

Programs are complex and require substantially more funding than other forms of HED activity. It is likely that the university will underwrite the cost of a select few each year. The challenge, then, is to consider which audiences are in most need of customised support. There will be many leadership groups who seek access to program support. These might include: deans, heads, professors and faculty leaders (e.g. associate deans, coordinators, deputy heads); research or teaching leaders, women or under-represented; or under-represented minority groups. Unfortunately, the capacity to support all of these communities is likely to be limited. However, it may be possible to offer programs on a rotating basis.

Some rules of thumb that can guide judgements as to frequency and depth of support include:

- Has this group been identified (by the executive or other senior leaders) as being at high risk of poor performance?
- Is this group key to new institutional initiatives or priorities?
- What is the likely impact of this leadership group in terms of strategy, culture and outcomes (e.g. financial outcomes, student impact, reputation, research productivity)?

- What is the size of this cohort? Are there economies of scale to be had by offering a program rather than individualised support?
- What roles do members of the group fill? Is there sufficient uniformity to support specialised workshops or programs?
- What are the primary leadership/management skills that underpin the role these individuals play? Is there sufficient support from related, generic services that are offered?
- Is there evidence of institutional desire to have this group supported?

Chapter 8 offered some principles and guidelines relating to program design and delivery. The targeted cohort and their identified learning needs should guide the structure and design of the program. To illustrate, two common program types are outlined below. They illustrate the different foci and approaches that might be used.

Supporting heads and deans

Heads normally attend within their first 2 years of appointment. Their program will be time limited, often comprising a 2-day residential followed by ½-day sessions. The foci might relate to leadership identity, constructive and ethical leadership and reflective, evaluative practices. Multi-source feedback, coaching, models and problem-based learning support effective decision-making, consultation and negotiation in their roles. The program is likely to promote improved linkages with executive leaders and a strong articulation with university mission, goals and priorities. A key outcome is the building of strong networks and connections with leadership colleagues. Ongoing support through a head's network will be valued (Debowski and Blake 2007).

Women and under-represented minorities

The goal of these programs is to increase representation of these members in more senior leadership roles (O'Connor *et al.* 2014; White 2012). Programs are likely to emphasise individual leadership and positioning within a politicised and system-level leadership context (Bonebright *et al.* 2012). An exploration of organisational climate and the capacity to explore ways of enacting leadership provides assurance as to effective approaches and encourages stronger leadership identity formation (Hornsby *et al.* 2012; Madsen 2012; Madsen *et al.* 2012; Tessens *et al.* 2011). The provision of mentorship (Debowski 2013), action-learning projects and narratives are important components of these programs.

It can be seen that these cohorts will seek a very different experience from their programs, although both focus on identity and role development within highly authentic and contextualised sessions. The goal of any program is to enable informed, insightful leaders to progress and move confidently through the typical experiences they will encounter.

Leadership in context

Things go wrong in academic communities. Sometimes, this is due to poor leadership. Other times, it may be a progressive decline that reaches a crisis point, or the causes may be diverse and unpredicted. Whatever the reason, there may come a point where changes must be made. Often, this will need to be guided by the leader and may require considerable courage and determination on that leader's part.

The HE developer fills a range of roles to support leaders in these circumstances: as guide, diagnostician, interventionist and consultant (Wakefield and Bunker 2010). Beginning with preliminary consultations to clarify the nature of the challenge/s, there are then likely to be progressive phases of interventions, monitoring the outcome, consulting with the leader and supporting their progressive re-engineering of the community systems, expectations, processes or strategies. At the same time, guidance as to better leadership and management practices may be necessary. Thus, coaching may also come into play. A mentor who has experienced similar challenges and successfully turned their community around may be particularly helpful. This can be arranged by the HED service in consultation with the leader.

The role of the HED developer is to advise and support, not to effect any necessary changes. There will be times when, despite the best efforts of the HED service, there is limited evidence of making a difference. Leaders who deflect blame on to others, who are unwilling to take responsibility for their actions or lack the courage to change will benefit little from supportive efforts. It is important to recognise these contexts and to withdraw after making sure this is the case. Referral to an external support coach or agency might be an alternative option.

Conclusion

Academic leaders live in a complex, messy and unpredictable world that requires adaptive, conscious, reflective approaches to ensure optimal solutions and responses are accomplished. The HED service has a particular brief in guiding the development of leaders to facilitate their preparedness and responsiveness. The provision of different opportunities and avenues for learning enables expanded leadership capability across the university. These services can offer an invaluable channel for peer learning, sharing of good practice and group learning, along with the development of a common language and rhetoric about leadership and its impacts. Specialised diagnostic services may also be provided. The internal capacity of the HED service will determine the extent of this service and its prioritisation. Ideally, synergy with highly functional executive leaders will create the right environment for this element of HED work to be a significant influence on university outcomes.

Note

1 See, for example, the University Leadership and Management program developed by Epigeum in consultation with university stakeholders: www.epigeum.com/courses/leadership-management/university-leadership-management.

References

Beattie, R.S., Kim, S., Hagen, M.S., Egan, T.M., Elinger, A.D. and Hamlin, R.G., 2014. Managerial coaching: a review of the empirical literature and development of a model to guide future practice. *Advances in Developing Human Resources*, 16(2), pp. 184–201.

Bolden, R., Petrov, G. and Gosling, J., 2009. Distributed leadership in higher education: rhetoric and reality. *Educational Management Administration & Leadership*, 37(2), pp. 257–277.

Bolman, L.G. and Gallos, J.V., 2011. *Reframing academic leadership*, 1st edition, San Francisco, CA: Jossey-Bass.

Bonebright, D.A., Cottledge, A.D. and Lonnquist, P., 2012. Developing women leaders on campus: a human resources-women's center partnership at the University of Minnesota. *Advances in Developing Human Resources*, 14(1), pp. 79–95.

Cipriano, R.E., 2011. *Facilitating a collegial department in higher education: strategies for success*, 1st edition, San Francisco, CA: Jossey-Bass.

Debowski, S., 2013. Creating fertile learning spaces: mentorship strategies to support academic success. In S. Frielick, N. Buissink-Smith, P. Wyse, J. Billot, J. Hallas and E. Whitehead, eds, *Research and Development in Higher Education: The Place of Learning and Teaching*, Auckland, New Zealand, 1–4 July 2013, Milperra, NSW: HERSDA, pp. 113–123.

Debowski, S. and Blake, V., 2007. Collective capacity building of academic leaders: a university model of leadership and learning in context. *International Journal of Learning and Change*, 2(3), p. 307.

Edwards, G. and Turnbull, S., 2013. A cultural approach to evaluating leadership development. *Advances in Developing Human Resources*, 15(1), pp. 46–60.

Floyd, A. and Fung, D., 2015. Focusing the kaleidoscope: exploring distributed leadership in an English university. *Studies in Higher Education*, pp. 1–16.

Frankovelgia, C.C. and Riddle, D.D., 2010. Leadership coaching. In E. Van Velsor, C.D. McCauley, and M.N. Ruderman, eds, *The Center for Creative Leadership handbook of leadership development*. San Francisco, CA: Wiley, pp. 125–146.

Gedro, J. and Wang, J., 2013. Creating civil and respectful organizations through the scholar-practitioner bridge. *Advances in Developing Human Resources*, 15(3), pp. 284–295.

Gmelch, W.H. and Miskin, V.D., 1995. *Chairing an academic department*, Thousand Oaks: SAGE Publications.

Grove, J., 2012. Choose a civil servant. Choose a business guru. Choose an international globetrotter. *Times Higher Education*, 15 November, pp. 37–41.

Grunefeld, H., Van Tartwijk, J., Jongen, H. and Wubbels, T., 2015. Design and effects of an academic development programme on leadership for educational change. *International Journal for Academic Development*, 20(4), pp. 306–318.

Hornsby, E.E., Morrow-Jones, H.A. and Ballam, D.A., 2012. Leadership development for faculty women at the Ohio State University: the president and provost's leadership institute. *Advances in Developing Human Resources*, 14(1), pp. 96–112.

Jarvis, C., Gulati, A., McCririck, V. and Simpson, P., 2013. Leadership matters: tensions in evaluating leadership development. *Advances in Developing Human Resources*, 15(1), pp. 27–45.

Jones, S., Lefoe, G., Harvey, M. and Ryland, K., 2012. Distributed leadership: a collaborative framework for academics, executives and professionals in higher education. *Journal of Higher Education Policy and Management*, 34(1), pp. 67–78.

Jones, R.J., Woods, S.A. and Guillaume, Y.R.F., 2015. The effectiveness of workplace coaching: a meta-analysis of learning and performance outcomes from coaching. *Journal of Occupational and Organizational Psychology*, 89(2), pp. 249–277.

Kennedy, F., Carroll, B. and Francoeur, J., 2013. Mindset not skill set: evaluating in new paradigms of leadership development. *Advances in Developing Human Resources*, 15(1), pp. 10–26.

King, S.N. and Santana, L.C., 2010. Feedback-intensive programs. In E. Van Velsor, C.D. McCauley, and M.N. Ruderman, eds, *The Center for Creative Leadership handbook of leadership development*, San Francisco, CA: Wiley, pp. 97–124.

Knight, P. and Trowler, P., 2000. *Departmental leadership in higher education*, Philadelphia, PA: Society for Research into Higher Education and Open University.

Ladyshewsky, R.K. and Flavell, H., 2012. Transfer of training in an academic leadership development program for program coordinators. *Educational Management Administration & Leadership*, 40(1), pp. 127–147.

Ligon, G.S., Wallace, J.H. and Osburn, H.K., 2011. Experiential development and mentoring processes for leaders for innovation. *Advances in Developing Human Resources*, 13(3), pp. 297–317.

McCauley-Smith, C., Williams, S.J., Gillon, A.C. and Braganza, A., 2015. Making sense of leadership development: developing a community of education leaders. *Studies in Higher Education*, 40(2), pp. 311–328.

Madsen, S.R., 2012. Women and leadership in higher education: current realities, challenges, and future directions. *Advances in Developing Human Resources*, 14(2), pp. 131–139.

Madsen, S.R., Longman, K.A. and Daniels, J.R., 2012. Women's leadership development in higher education: conclusion and implications for HRD. *Advances in Developing Human Resources*, 14(1), pp. 113–128.

Middlehurst, R., 1993. *Leading academics*, Buckingham, England: Society for Research into Higher Education.

Muir, D., 2014. Mentoring and leader identity development: a case study. *Human Resource Development Quarterly*, 25(3), pp. 349–379.

Nieminen, L.R.G., Smerek, R., Kotrba, L. and Denison, D., 2013. What does an executive coaching intervention add beyond facilitated multisource feedback? Effects on leader self-ratings and perceived effectiveness. *Human Resource Development Quarterly*, 24(2), pp. 145–176.

O'Connor, P., Carvalho, T. and White, K., 2014. The experiences of senior positional leaders in Australian, Irish and Portuguese universities: universal or contingent? *Higher Education Research & Development*, 33(1), pp. 5–18.

Rogers, J., 2012. *Coaching skills: a handbook*, Maidenhead, Berkshire: Open University Press.

Tessens, L., White, K. and Web, C., 2011. Senior women in higher education institutions: perceived development needs and support. *Journal of Higher Education Policy and Management*, 33(6), pp. 653–665.

Tornow, W.W. and London, M. (eds), 1998. *Maximizing the value of 360-degree feedback: a process for successful individual and organizational development*, 1st edition, San Francisco, CA: Jossey-Bass.

Vilkinas, T., Leask, B. and Ladyshewsky, R., 2009. *Academic leadership: fundamental building blocks*, Strawberry Hills, NSW: Australian Learning and Teaching Council.

Wakefield, M. and Bunker, K.A., 2010. *Leader development in times of change*. In E. Van Velsor, C.D. McCauley and M.N. Ruderman (eds), *The Center for Creative Leadership handbook of leadership development*, San Francisco, CA: Wiley, pp. 197–220.

Watkins, K.E., Lyso, I.H. and de Marrais, K., 2011. Evaluating executive leadership programs: a theory of change approach. *Advances in Developing Human Resources*, 13(2), pp. 208–239.

White, J.S., 2012. HERS Institutes: curriculum for advancing women leaders in higher education. *Advances in Developing Human Resources*, 14(1), pp. 11–27.

Part IV

Evaluating and researching HED practice and impact

A key question that faces the modern HED service is: does it make a difference? Is it encouraging changes to the learner in terms of their practice, insights, attitudes or impact on others? Are communities performing more effectively as a result of the support being offered to them? Can improved institutional performance be attributed to the interventions that have been undertaken?

Evidence of impact serves four important functions. First, it provides professional validation that the methodologies and practices employed by the HED team are appropriate and have an impact on the learner. Second, it offers sound evidence to the executive and other stakeholders as to the degree to which the service is adding value to the institutional outcomes. Third, it provides leaders with important evidence as to the way their communities are functioning and performing and, in some cases, the impact of their leadership on those communities. Fourth, it supports ongoing research and investigation into the academic learning context.

Chapter 21 opens up this focus by outlining the types of evaluative processes that might be undertaken, highlighting the critical importance of building evaluation into the design of learning activities. Chapter 22 explores the nature of HED scholarship and research, offering guidance on how deeper investigations into the impact of HED can be framed and undertaken.

Chapter 21

Evaluating the impact and effectiveness of HED strategies

Higher education development (HED) requires ongoing validation and testing of its methodologies to ensure the implemented processes are fit for purpose and can achieve the desired outcomes. There is increasing concern in the field as to the direct impact of HED on learners, and more broadly, the institution (Bamber and Stefani 2015; Chalmers and Gardiner 2015; Hoessler *et al.* 2015; Saroyan and Trigwell 2015). These commentaries recognise the inadequacy of past approaches, which tended to solicit immediate feedback from participants, rather than building in more rigorous evaluations of the longer-term impact of the learning experience. Given the increasing complexity of demonstrating value, it is time to reposition the evaluation cycle to ensure it provides the necessary evidence base to show that HED matters. This is important for the service as a whole, and for each developer, who relies on feedback to evaluate their own professional practice. It is also an important verification for leaders to ensure any interventions are generating the desired capacity building across their communities. This chapter therefore outlines the key principles of HED evaluation and review, affirming the importance of monitoring outcomes and shifts in organisational practice as a consequence of learning and development activities, particularly those that require intensive investment of funding, time and commitment.

Why evaluate HED?

Kennedy *et al.* (2013) suggests there are three purposes of evaluation: accountability, development and knowledge. At the *accountability* level, a strong evidence base demonstrates that participants who engage in development activities have adapted their practices, attitudes, knowledge or self-awareness to reach a higher level of functionality. However, the absence of persuasive evidence makes it hard to claim these benefits and also increases the vulnerability of the HED group when institutional assessments of value and contribution are undertaken (Hum *et al.* 2015; Taylor and Znajda 2015). A further challenge at this level is the differing perspectives on what counts: executive concern for return on investment seeks a direct causal linkage between the HED activities and the generative output of academics who participate (Jarvis *et al.* 2013). However, this does not recognise that the greater impact from HED activities will be evidenced by both process and outcome measures. Thus, there is a need to build greater clarity around the type of impact that this work generates.

From a *development* perspective, the design and delivery of learning interventions are predicated on an assumption that they will make a difference to the learner, and potentially, to their wider community. There are many different sources of evidence that could inform this review. For the most part, HED initiatives are evaluated either informally or via immediate user satisfaction. Assessment and evaluation is not integrated into many HED activities, resulting in limited or no evidence as to whether the particular approaches were effective, or that learning transfer was achieved.

At the *knowledge* level, the field is, again, vulnerable. There has been little effort to verify and test the efficacy of different methods and approaches. The evaluation methodologies that are used often lack power and rigour, thereby reducing the capacity to build a valid evidence base that demonstrates that the field makes a difference. Further, the field lacks a clear methodology or set of indicators that are consistently applied across institutions, thereby making benchmarking more difficult (Chalmers and Gardiner 2015).

Yeo and Gold (2011) suggest that HED evaluation is a broad-based, holistic approach that assesses the behavioural changes evident in each learner and the broader impact on organisational learning and practices. The initial guidance of the Kirkpatrick Model (Kirkpatrick 1975), while still widely evident in many HED groups, is now recognised as being insufficiently focused on the real learning outcomes and other factors that influence learning transfer (Holton 1996). Evaluation is about assessing the utility of HED interventions (Swanson and Holton 1999). It verifies that HED activities do impact on the learner and their subsequent professional practice. It also has the potential to monitor other causal factors that may influence the learner's ability to transfer their acquired skills, knowledge or insights into their ongoing professional practice.

To illustrate, Table 21.1 provides a short summation of some of the ways in which evaluative information might be used to inform leaders, the developer and the individual learner. It can be seen that well-designed evaluation can offer considerable richness in better understanding the learning context and outcomes.

To summarise, the development of a well-articulated and integrated evaluation process enables a number of benefits including:

- clarifying the ways in which different forms of development activity impact on learner outcomes;
- informing the HED practitioner's own self-review and reflection on their professional practice;
- supporting the development of a more informed pedagogy to ensure design and delivery mechanisms are fit for purpose;
- enabling the assessment of longitudinal growth of capabilities;

Table 21.1 Assessing HED impact on learner processes and outcomes

Focus	Leaders	Developer	Individual
Impact	Assessing return on investment. Identification of emerging issues. Mapping enhancements to organisational processes (e.g. student engagement; staff commitment). Evaluating changes to organisational productivity or outputs. Determining HED service value and impact.	Assessing changes in learner behaviours and enhanced capabilities. Identifying shifts in attitudes, confidence, self-efficacy. Determining evidence of broader impact on organisational functioning/outcomes.	Improved capacity to reflect, act and draw upon informed foundations. Increased confidence to enact role/apply learning. Changes to enacted behaviour. Participation in relevant academic communities of practice.
Learning design/process	Cost/benefit ratio: was the expenditure justified in terms of learning impact?	Did the design deliver the intended outcomes and experiences for the learners? Were there ways to improve the design? Were all participants engaged? If not, why not? What could be done differently?	Did the design generate optimised value for the time and effort invested? Were the learning activities meaningful? Did the experience increase knowledge/skills/strategy/confidence? Was the experience transformative?

- mapping the learning culture and related environment in which the participants are operating, thus supporting more integrated interventions if required;
- building a stronger understanding of the learning needs and expectations of the participants;
- identifying particular concepts or skills that may necessitate a broader range of support to accomplish the necessary threshold learning;
- providing a strong evidence base to justify requests for funding, sponsorship and ongoing continuation of the HED service.

However, at present, this is an area that still needs considerable consolidation. Developers often test multi-dimensional clusters of processes and outcomes (Saroyan and Trigwell 2015; Taylor and Znajda 2015), and the constructs being measured remain largely ill-defined, generating considerable variation in their interpretation and application (Chalmers and Gardiner 2015).

The evaluation context

The evaluation of higher education development is complex, as the actual impact may be influenced by many external factors. Figure 21.1 illustrates the complex setting in which HED operates. While the HED activities and support can be very influential in encouraging improved learning processes and outcomes, they also rely on other enabling influences within the faculty, work group or university.

There will be a number of factors that may affect the learner's capacity to act on the new knowledge and insights that they may have gained. The university focus, messages, systems and practices will drive the individual academic to prioritise certain behaviours and activities (Schein 2010). Similarly, the faculty or work group, as the most proximal influence, will guide an individual's capacity to engage in learning activities, prioritise the transfer of new skills to their work roles and support the learning process (Swanson and Holton 1999). The academic determines the degree of engagement with learning activities based on contextual factors (e.g. workload or role requirements), their capability assessment, their own personal agency with respect to learning and their prioritisation of the learning goals. The final factor is the effectiveness of the developer and the experience that was offered. In addition to the actual learning design, the developer can magnify the learning impact by integrating feedback support and assistance to encourage transfer of the learning back into the workplace.

These four levels of influence affect the learner's capacity to build new mental schema or professional capabilities. Learning takes time to test, explore and consolidate. Attendance at programs will offer more consolidated support to effect these shifts, while workshops may be less influential, given their temporal nature. Outcomes can be personal or professional, and will have wider impact if the learner's span of influence is large (e.g. a head of school). It is also important to consider what is being measured in terms of performance: "excellence" for example, may be an institutional metric that does not resonate with the participant (O'Connor and O'Hagan 2015).

Determining the evaluation purpose

Evaluation should be considered at the very start of the learning design planning process (Hum *et al.* 2015). An evaluation plan assists with identifying the desired purpose of the learning activity, the learning outcomes to be evaluated and any indicators of impact that might be subsequently measured. The integration of evaluation activities requires forward planning, as it may be necessary to set up surveys, negotiate approvals, recruit and encourage participant responses, and analyse preliminary results (if relevant) to inform the learning design.

The choice of evaluation strategy will depend, to some extent, on the nature of the learning design and delivery process. Questions to be asked include:

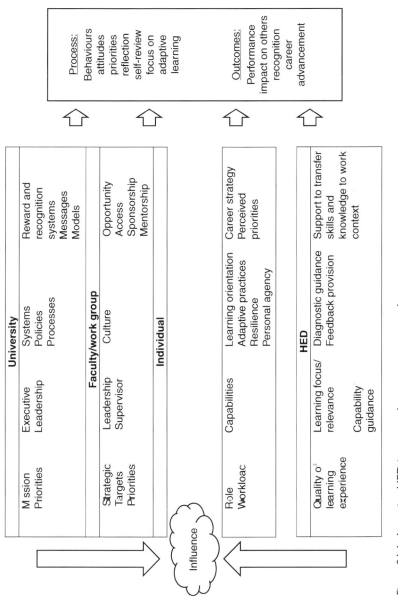

Figure 21.1 Assessing HED impact on learner processes and outcomes.

- What is the time frame for the learning activity? What level of evaluation is reasonable? For example, workshop evaluations are likely to be rapid, single-capture assessments that integrate a small range of responses, while programs warrant a more integrated sequence of evaluations that may capture many of the contextual elements depicted in Figure 21.1.
- What should be investigated? The way the learner has engaged and interacted with the learning experience, ideas and other stimuli (*Processes*) or the impact on learner behaviours and performance (*Outcomes*)? Or both? Perhaps the learning ecology or a desire to benchmark with other colleagues is a focus? The evaluative focus needs to be clearly defined and appropriate (Hoessler *et al.* 2015).
- What are the primary outcomes the development activity aims to encourage? How can those outcomes best be mapped and assessed? Will this require a longitudinal assessment to capture changes in behaviour or practice over time?
- Which sources of evidence will best demonstrate learning impact? What measures have other HE developers employed?
- When should evaluations be scheduled? It will be important to map the key dates for evaluation phases so that the necessary set up, communication and follow-up activities can be efficiently managed.
- How will participants respond to the evaluation process? Will they be willing to contribute the time and requested information?
- What is the best mechanism for data collection? Paper? Online?
- How will the results be analysed and reported?
- Are there core assessment measures that should be integrated as general practice across all development activities? How would this data be used and reviewed?

These are all important questions to consider when developing an evaluation plan. They will help to identify the purpose and scope of the evaluation focus and the methodologies to be employed.

When data is collected from or about participants, there is an understanding that it will be analysed, treated appropriately and used to enhance the professional delivery of the HED service. There are a number of principles that underpin evaluation:

- The analyses should be undertaken in a thorough and timely manner.
- The evaluation strategy must meet the institutional guidelines and expectations with respect to ethics and confidentiality.
- No individual respondent should be identified or singled out.
- The findings should be interpreted objectively and openly.

In planning an evaluation strategy, consider how this data might be used for additional evaluative purposes. For example, there are four ways in which the evaluations might be employed to provide richer and more impactful evidence.

- *Cumulative reviews* support the evaluation and benchmarking of a range of comparable activities, using a common set of evaluative measures (Sword 2014). Workshop delivery, for example, might integrate standard questions concerning the design and facilitation of each event. The feedback from participants can be compared with HED norms and might be segmented to test for differences across different delivery formats or cohorts. Many HED services undertake these regular evaluations as part of their standard cycle, with the collection of data managed by the HED administrative staff. The reporting of quantitative survey outcomes and qualitative commentary offers one source of feedback to the individual developer and informs HED performance reviews.
- *Program reviews* are designed to validate the content, delivery and impact of a substantial program of learning and development. In many cases, the funds to run such programs are substantial, and have required sponsorship from executive leaders. The decision to fund further programs of this nature will be predicated on a desire to know that the program did make a difference to the participants and met its promised deliverables. These programs are normally designed around a specific, high-priority target cohort. An advantage of this format is the increased commitment of participants to contribute to the evaluation process. This can be further enhanced by offering an executive summary of the outcomes back to those participants. The evaluative review will likely encompass a range of complex measures, including longitudinal analyses of capabilities and attitudinal responses, climate measures and other identified factors. These analyses may be contrasted with other comparable programs, or may integrate some generic program measures that ensure participants are content with the management, promotion and support offered throughout the duration. The development of generic program measures provides an important form of validation across different programs and enables benchmarking with other institutions.
- From another angle, the HED service may seek to build some institutional measures that provide *baseline and longitudinal data*. These evaluation processes may be less concerned with workshop or program outcomes, and more fully focused on organisational enhancement, institutional trends, cultural challenges, practices or impediments to excellence. Many universities, for example, undertake a cultural audit every 2 years to identify trends in staff morale, productivity and culture. The data offer an important cue for new programs and interventions, and can also assist in identifying communities at risk. There is potential to implement a capability audit for a specific target group (e.g. new teachers, early career researchers, heads). These holistic reviews map the context in which academics work and provide a rigorous mechanism to explore the differences across the institution and enhanced practices over time.
- The capacity to *benchmark* across institutions, using a common framework ultimately offers considerable promise. This is still at a very formative stage, with Chalmers and Znajda (2015) illustrating the challenges associated with employing a common framework across multiple institutions.

Thus, the context and purpose will influence the evaluation strategy and how the results are mapped, aggregated and reported. Cumulative reviews, for example, might be summarised each year to monitor the quality of the delivery and the ongoing participation by certain groups. Program reviews might be undertaken as single program evaluations, followed by an external evaluation after a designated period (e.g. De Vries 2005). These intensive evaluation projects offer rich pools of data that can contribute to scholarly papers or research into HED practices. The final choice of evaluation, focus and measures may be partly determined by:

- accessible models or instruments already available;
- the way the information will be used once collected;
- the degree to which the data will assist in guiding future practices or initiatives;
- the capacity of the HED team to analyse and review the results and their implications;
- the fit of the evaluation to the type of activity being reviewed.

Evaluating the HED activity

HED evaluations will primarily draw on three key sources of evidence:

- surveys that solicit quantitative and/or qualitative responses from the participants;
- reflective or authentic evidence sources that illustrate the application of learning outcomes to the individual's own context and setting (e.g. observation of behaviours; portfolios; performance metrics);
- feedback from other sources, such as supervisors, peers, students, staff or other stakeholders on changes in behaviour or outcomes.

This is an area of vulnerability at present, with most of the evaluative evidence drawing on personal reports, qualitative responses and small scale case studies (Saroyan and Trigwell 2015). Recent evidence still shows a strong reliance on descriptive statistics (e.g. percentages, tallies), which can limit the value of the data being presented (see, for example, Sword 2014; Taylor and Znajda 2015).

The following examples are designed to illustrate the various ways evaluations might be undertaken. They offer guidance on increasing the power, replicability and reliability of the investigations. Mixed method processes enable better use of quantitative strategies, integrating inter-rater reliability measures and the capacity to correlate constructs (Saroyan and Trigwell 2015).

Was the design and delivery of the learning activity engaging and effective?

The skill and calibre of the facilitator/s greatly influences how participants engage with their learning opportunity. If the design and the delivery of the session/s is poorly planned or executed, academics will quickly lose interest and either disengage or leave. The reputation of the presenter is a factor that they will take into account when deciding to participate in the first place, and may also generate more take-up by other colleagues through recommendations or may deter others from enrolling. Thus, the presenter needs to regularly seek and review feedback from their participants to check that the design, delivery and level of the development activity were well targeted for the audience. This feedback also assists the developer in articulating their own professional pedagogy and principles, with a strong evidence base to identify the best practices and learning design for particular groups. Questions that might be asked, for example, include:

- The workshop/program was well planned and managed.
- There were good opportunities to engage with and learn from my colleagues.
- I was kept engaged and interested during the session.
- I would recommend this workshop to other colleagues.

These are the questions that are generally tested at the conclusion of any event, providing quick feedback on the learner's reactions to the experience (Kirkpatrick 1975). Many HED groups have a standardised evaluation instrument that is used for this purpose, with the results then collated and summarised. They offer useful evidence as to each developer's immediate impact on learners, and also help to monitor the overall effectiveness of certain offerings or forms of delivery. These items, for example, work equally well for online, blended and face-to-face contexts, offering guidance on the different learning contexts and their effectiveness.

What did the learners gain from participating?

There is little value in offering a development opportunity if the participants leave without any new insights, stimuli for reflection or intention to review, adapt or critique their professional practice as a result of their participation. Some of the immediate benefits of a learning engagement may include:

- an opportunity to review and reflect on one's own attitudes, beliefs or positioning;
- an enhanced sense of motivation to effect some form of professional change;
- affirmation and social support from interacting with other colleagues and seeing others modelling good practice;
- the development of new learning insights or knowledge scaffolds;
- an opportunity to test and apply different skills;
- time to view the broader framing of their professional practice and their career directions.

While assessment immediately after a learning experience is too soon to measure capability changes, the *intention to change* can be a valuable test to see if the learner has shifted the goalposts in terms of the desired skills and capabilities. Some questions that might assist in determining these intentions include:

- I gained a deeper understanding as to how I can describe the key focus area.
- The session challenged me to review my current practices.
- I plan to change or improve at least one practice as a result of attending this workshop.

Kaye Hart *et al.* (2008) offer a different approach, in which participants register their commitment to taking their learning forward.

Did the experience influence their attitudes, beliefs or values?

Attitudes and beliefs are hard to change. They are influenced by many different stimuli, models and experiences over time. However, different learning activities can be influential, particularly if they integrate socialised learning, modelling and time for self-review and reflection. The transition from stimulus/challenge to embedded learning will take time and may be influenced by the environment in which each individual works and their own pre-disposition to reflect and learn. Despite this complexity, many of the learning experiences offered through HED will encourage a questioning of existing attitudes and self-belief, and may serve as a strong stimulus for reviewing and, possibly, remapping existing personal structures. However, it would be naïve to think that a 1-day session might strongly influence professional attitudes or beliefs, although it may be a key stimulus in some circumstances. The following questions might provide some indication as to whether this influence was generated:

- The workshop/program provided me with useful insights and opportunities to reflect.
- The activities and discussion challenged me.
- I gained new insights and perspectives through attending the workshop/ program.

It is possible to go more deeply and to explore how the participant sees their learning context. The following questions, for example, seek feedback from participants who do not have a mentor. They help to clarify the contextual or personal influences on mentorship take-up:

- I don't feel confident in asking anyone to help me.
- I don't think I need a mentor.
- I haven't found mentors to be very helpful.
- I am too senior to seek a mentor.
- I am too busy to take time out to engage in mentorship.
- I want a mentor, but am not sure how to go about getting one.

- I am keen to learn how to find a mentor.
- Setting up a mentoring relationship is very important to me.

Have learners changed their behaviours or practices?

To answer this question, it is first necessary to identify the core capabilities that are being targeted. The mapping of the capabilities may be drawn from existing capability frameworks, research or other sources, including the developer's own knowledge. Figure 21.2 illustrates a simple capability assessment relating to research strategy and performance. When used as a pre-test, the results provide the facilitator with a useful insight into the learning cohort's readiness and capabilities. These same measures can be re-administered as a post-test at the conclusion of the session to identify perceived changes in capabilities. This evidence can be very useful in identifying areas that require further consolidation or support. Capability assessments are useful additions to workshop evaluations, as they incorporate specific monitoring of learning outcomes.

The embedding of changed practices is a longer process that requires time to test, review, practice, seek feedback and consolidate the skills that have been targeted (Van Waes *et al.* 2015). In the case of the research capabilities outlined above, this same assessment can be conducted several times to assess changes in perceptions of capability. If these capabilities were part of a program, for example, a capability assessment might occur at the start of the program, at the conclusion of the core program, following the full program completion and once again, some months later. These four assessments will offer a resilient measure of capability gains. They are an essential feature of program evaluation.

Another method to verify learning impact is to seek feedback from multiple sources. The HED discipline is vulnerable with its considerable reliance on self-reported feedback from participants. Multi-source feedback can assist by triangulating capability or attitudinal assessments, particularly for a program operating over a substantial period of time. In these instances, the capacity to seek input from knowledgeable peers, supervisors and the individual, provides an important mechanism for verifying evidence of changes in behaviour and outcomes. This might be undertaken as part of a multi-source review process, via a customised tool that seeks feedback on designated capabilities or through the administration of a specific survey or phone interviews.

Portfolios of reflection and evidence developed by the individual as part of their learning journey also verify the learning and skill enhancement that has occurred (Boerboom *et al.* 2015). Often employed by learning and teaching developers, they have potential for research and leadership development. The encouragement of an evidence-based focus supports deeper reflection and the testing of different methodologies by the individual. The process of collecting evidence to verify claims also encourages a more reflective, evaluative approach to the learner's professional practice. This would necessitate review and evaluation by the developer to test for evidence of learning and application.

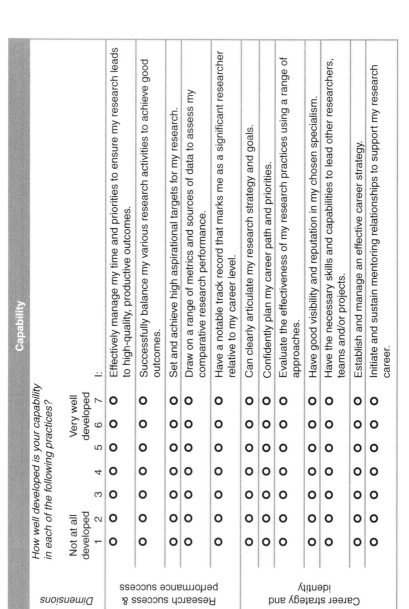

Figure 21.2 Sample capability assessment relating to research strategy.

A further mechanism for measuring enhanced professional capabilities is to evaluate the targeted behaviours in situ. A variety of options might be available, including mapping institutional metrics related to individual performance (e.g. improved publications, grant success, teaching awards), improved student outcomes, observation of teaching performance, peer review of targeted outcomes, evidence of improved cultural audits or increased team productivity. In each of these examples, longitudinal measures demonstrate that there have been shifts in practice.

Did learners have the right disposition when they participated in the learning opportunity?

In general, academics choose to participate. Their motivation to gain maximum value from these volitional activities is likely to be high. However, they may be required to attend some activities to comply with university governance or other commitments. (For example, training to support ethical conduct, records management or health and safety practices is typically expected of all staff.) In these instances, the compliance-driven approach may reduce their willingness to fully participate. This may affect their learning outcomes and quality of participation. Thus, it can be useful to see if learners are pre-disposed to gain the maximum value from their learning experience (Kruglanski *et al.* 2002; Locke and Latham 2006; Touré-Tillery and Fishbach 2011). The following questions, for example, review different views as to learning and its value:

- I like to develop new skills and insights.
- I want to build excellence in my skills relating to this field of expertise.
- When I am learning I like to be challenged and extended.
- I like to learn how to do things properly.
- I want to be seen as an expert in this field.
- I am required to complete this course.
- I will be recognised for promotion if I finish the course.
- I plan to do the minimum required to finish this course.

Are learners able to transfer their learning back to their own organisational context?

The capacity to transfer one's learning back to the real world of academe is affected by many factors, including the type of culture in which the individual works; the leadership that is dominant in that community; the communal encouragement to take risks and test new ideas, and the presence and evidence of interest from colleagues (Edwards and Turnbull 2013; Van Schalkwyk *et al.* 2015). Difficult transfer climates may greatly impede a willingness to participate in learning opportunities (Bates *et al.* 2012; Holton *et al.* 1997). Some would-be learners may even be penalised or prevented from "taking time" from their work context to learn new skills. They may find it harder to apply those insights once they return to work and could benefit from some additional support if they have attended, despite the negative context.

Many developers will have a clear sense of which communities are learning oriented. They will see more participants coming forward, the leaders will often sponsor their staff to attend and there will be evidence of innovation and responsiveness in the workplace. In these settings, if issues are identified during development activities, leaders will be keen to hear of emergent concerns and to discuss how they might be addressed.

The integration of climate measures can be particularly valuable for programs where the acquisition of new capabilities and learning will be predicated on good support within the local academic community. Early investigation of learning climate can offer a valuable cue as to issues that may emerge over time. The following list illustrates the types of questions that might be employed:

- My supervisor encouraged me to participate in this workshop/program.
- It will be easy for me to apply any new insights or skills into my particular work roles or setting.
- My peers generally offer supportive feedback when I try something new.
- When I learn something new, my supervisor is keen to explore what I have learnt.
- I am encouraged to seek support from mentors and sponsors.

Thus, the measures can explore a range of constructs and facets of learning. They may comprise standardised items that are consistently applied across different contexts (e.g. facilitator feedback) and customised measures to suit the particular learning context (e.g. capability statements). The use of Likert scales, where the participants can choose a response that best reflects their opinion, is a common methodology employed for self-reviews of perceptions and capability enhancements. This allows the reporting of means and standard deviations for the aggregated responses, and facilitates more complex analyses should they be required.

Managing the evaluative process

From this overview, it can be seen that the framing of evaluation requires careful planning to ensure it captures the right data. The purpose of the evaluation and the ways in which it will be analysed and reported will need to be considered as part of the initial scoping process. Careful management ensures the process is completed professionally and in a timely manner.

There is merit in building some standardised tools and templates that ensure the instruments are well-designed and readily adapted. The choice of review mechanism will reflect the goals and purpose of the evaluation and the capacity of the HED service to develop the instrumentation, collect and analyse the data. Assistance from in-house or commercial services can provide professional support in setting up standard evaluation templates and collection processes if internal capability is low. There is also potential to develop collaborative or common tools across the various HED groups, enabling benchmarking and the sharing of strategies. Cross-institutional comparisons can support increased scholarship and testing of the methodologies and approaches that are being applied.

It may be necessary to seek ethics approval to undertake evaluations. Many institutions now require ethics approval if data on staff or students is being collected. A blanket approval might be negotiated for standardised instruments. If it is hoped that the evaluations will feed into scholarly works or public sharing of the outcomes, participants will need to be asked for informed consent before sharing their insights, and the evaluation plan should be vetted by an experienced researcher.

Some key points have emerged from this section:

- Evaluation should be considered when planning any learning activity.
- HED staff need access to evaluative feedback to enhance their professional practice. This should target learner impact and outcomes, not simply reactions to the learning event.
- The development of a pool of verified results for comparable activities supports HED performance standards and validated benchmarking.
- The data that is collected should be appropriate and at the right level for the particular development experience that was offered.
- The development of core measures that reflect the pedagogical framing of the HED strategy provide an important foundation by which to undertake longitudinal sampling across programs.
- Triangulation of the results across multi-sources, polls and outcome-based evidence increases the power of the evaluative outcomes.
- Benchmarking (e.g. between programs within the same institution or across institutions) supports the identification of points of excellence or improvement.

Conclusion

This chapter has outlined a very important element of HED service delivery that is still in an early phase of its development. It has demonstrated the importance of building HED capabilities with respect to:

- integrating a reflective, evaluative focus as to the developer's role and influence;
- developing appropriate evaluation frames to suit each design context;
- designing and collecting data suited to the evaluation need;
- analysing and reviewing the findings from the data.

Evaluation plays a key part in affirming the value and impact of the HED service, capacity building activities and leadership effectiveness. Without evidence, it is

References

Bamber, V. and Stefani, L., 2015. Taking up the challenge of evidencing value in educational development: from theory to practice. *International Journal for Academic Development*, pp. 1–13. Available online at DOI 10.1080/1360144X.2015.1100112

Bates, R., Holton, E.F. and Hatala, J.P., 2012. A revised learning transfer system inventory: factorial replication and validation. *Human Resource Development International*, 15(5), pp. 549–569.

Boerboom, T.B.B., Stalmeijer, R.E., Dolmans, D.H.J.M. and Jaarsma, D.A.D.C., 2015. How feedback can foster professional growth of teachers in the clinical workplace: a review of the literature. *Studies in Educational Evaluation*, 46, pp. 47–52.

Chalmers, D. and Gardiner, D., 2015. An evaluation framework for identifying the effectiveness and impact of academic teacher development programmes. *Studies in Educational Evaluation*, 46, pp. 81–91.

De Vries, J., 2005. *More than the sum of its parts: 10 years of the Leadership Development for Women Programme at the University of Western Australia*, Crawley, W.A.: Organisational and Staff Development Services, University of Western Australia.

Edwards, G. and Turnbull, S., 2013. A cultural approach to evaluating leadership development. *Advances in Developing Human Resources*, 15(1), pp. 46–60.

Hoessler, C., Godden, L. and Hoessler, B., 2015. Widening our evaluative lenses of formal, facilitated, and spontaneous academic development. *International Journal for Academic Development*, 20(3), pp. 224–237.

Holton, E.F., 1996. The flawed four-level evaluation model. *Human Resource Development Quarterly*, 7(1), pp. 5–21.

Holton, E.F., Sayler, D.L. and Carvalho, M.B., 1997. Toward construct validation of a transfer climate instrument. *Human Resource Development Quarterly*, 8(2), pp. 95–113.

Hum, G., Amundsen, C. and Emmioglu, E., 2015. Evaluating a teaching development grants program: our framework, process, initial findings, and reflections. *Studies in Educational Evaluation*, 46, pp. 29–38.

Jarvis, C., Gulati, A., McCririck, V. and Simpson, P., 2013. Leadership matters: tensions in evaluating leadership development. *Advances in Developing Human Resources*, 15(1), pp. 27–45.

Kaye Hart, R., Conklin, T.A. and Allen, S.J., 2008. Individual leader development: an appreciative inquiry approach. *Advances in Developing Human Resources*, 10(5), pp. 632–650.

Kennedy, F., Carroll, B. and Francoeur, J., 2013. Mindset not skill set: evaluating in new paradigms of leadership development. *Advances in Developing Human Resources*, 15(1), pp. 10–26.

Kirkpatrick, D.L., 1975. *Evaluating training programs*, New York: McGraw-Hill.

Kruglanski, A.W., Shah, J. Y., Fishbach, A., Friedman, R., Woo, Y.C. and Sleeth-Keppler, D., 2002. A theory of goal systems. In *Advances in experimental social psychology*, Amsterdam: Elsevier, pp. 331–378.

Locke, E.A. and Latham, G.P., 2006. New directions in goal-setting theory. *Current Directions in Psychological Science*, 15(5), pp. 265–268.

O'Connor, P. and O'Hagan, C., 2015. Excellence in university academic staff evaluation: a problematic reality? *Studies in Higher Education*, pp. 1–15. DOI 10.1080/03075079.2014.1000292

Saroyan, A. and Trigwell, K., 2015. Higher education teachers' professional learning: process and outcome. *Studies in Educational Evaluation*, 46, pp. 92–101.

Schein, E.H., 2010. *Organizational culture and leadership*, 4th edition, San Francisco, CA: Jossey-Bass.

Swanson, R.A. and Holton, E.F., 1999. *Results: how to assess performance, learning, and perceptions in organizations*, San Francisco, CA: Berrett-Koehler.

Sword, H., 2014. Dancing on the bottom line: an unruly cost-benefit analysis of three academic development initiatives. *Higher Education Research & Development*, 33(4), pp. 783–793.

Taylor, K.L. and Znajda, S.K., 2015. Demonstrating the impact of educational development: the case of a course design collaborative. *Studies in Educational Evaluation*, 46, pp. 39–46.

Touré-Tillery, M. and Fishbach, A., 2011. The course of motivation. *Journal of Consumer Psychology*, 21(4), pp. 414–423.

Van Schalkwyk, S., Leibowitz, B., Herman, N. and Farmer, J., 2015. Reflections on professional learning: choices, context and culture. *Studies in Educational Evaluation*, 46, pp. 4–10.

Van Waes, S., Van den Bossche, P., Moolenaar, N.M., Stes, A. and Van Petegem, P., 2015. Uncovering changes in university teachers' professional networks during an instructional development program. *Studies in Educational Evaluation*, 46, pp. 11–28.

Yeo, R.K. and Gold, J., 2011. The inseparability of action and learning: unravelling Revans' action learning theory for Human Resource Development (HRD). *Human Resource Development International*, 14(5), pp. 511–526.

Chapter 22

Undertaking HED scholarship and research

When planned and managed effectively, the evaluation of development activities can offer guidance on how interventions have been perceived by the participants, the ways in which individuals are changing their capabilities and the degree to which the learners have transferred their insights into their work practices. This is important validation of the influence of HE developments within the university context, providing evidence of effect and potentially increasing sponsorship and recognition of the value-added function of these activities. However, if this evidence remains localised and internalised, it will be very quickly forgotten and subsumed into the archives as yet another piece of ephemera. Further, intensive investigations that may have been undertaken will largely lie fallow, failing to contribute to the broader field and its scholarly enhancement.

There is evidence of a growing concern for building a robust foundation of scholarship and research relating to higher education development (Boyer 1990; Clegg 2012a; Clegg 2012b; Middlehurst 2014; Saroyan and Trigwell 2015; Trigwell *et al.* 2000). While the field is enriched by the presence of different voices, perspectives, origins and methodologies, this has also created considerable challenges in building a coherent research identity that encourages others to join in scholarly debate. Middlehurst (2014) notes the risks attached to being too beholden to policy makers (for funding and sponsorship) when designing research. The desire to show impact from funding or policy-driven activities can reduce the focus on real questions that need to be addressed. In the allied field of human resource development, Chermack and Swanson (2015) offer a salutary warning over the risks of treating methodologies as "theology," allowing them to be the focus of research, rather than focusing on more fundamental testing of assumptions and theories. This concern over lack of theory is also evidenced by other key voices in the field (Ashwin 2012; Clegg 2012b; Krause 2012; Trowler 2014).

Certainly, the higher education field is challenged by its eclectic base: it is multi-disciplinary (Tight 2013), open-access (Harland 2012) and its members bring their own prior disciplinary grounding to their practice. The inclusion of both professional and academic staff adds both richness and complexity. The national context in which the developer operates also influences the methodologies (Tight 2013), viewpoints and theoretical orientation (Blair 2014; Boughey and Niven 2012; Chen and Hu 2012; Jones 2012). Thus, higher education development research and scholarship offers vast potential but considerable complexity in building some common threads and theories that might be communally adopted.

Many HE developers have contributed to the development of a strong scholarly base, with respect to learning and teaching, offering core foundational principles and practices (Amundsen and Wilson 2012; Kandlbinder and Peseta 2009; Peseta and Kandlbinder 2011). More recently, a study of learning and teaching scholarship from 2007–2012, mapped a range of topics that had been investigated (Velliaris *et al.* 2012). Many of these related to the enactment of educational practice in university settings: assessment and feedback; critical thinking; student disadvantage; educational technology; graduate attributes; health and wellbeing; higher degrees by research; internationalisation; student experience; work-integrated learning; transition; and student retention were popular topics (ibid.). Less represented were specific HED practice-related themes, with only three identified: leadership and professional development; learning and teaching; and research into higher education.

Amundsen and Wilson (2012) offer a useful path in exploring the previous scholarly output relating to the support of learning and development in higher education. Their study identified 137 papers published between 1995 and 2008. Six reporting foci were mapped: skills (e.g. how did the participants enhance their skills and techniques?); method (e.g. the process of building mastery of a particular methodology); reflection (e.g. assessing the changes to the participant's conceptions or perspectives); disciplinary (e.g. exploring the impact of disciplinary knowledge on the learners' practice); institutional (e.g. reflecting policy or institutional foci and outcomes); and action research or enquiry (where learners have explored their own authentic experiences and actions). While the pool of publications is quite confined, they offer a useful lens to consider how HED scholarship is evolving. They note, for example, that scholars generally focused on either outcomes or process and that there was considerable evidence that the presuppositions of scholars informed the focus of these papers and the questions they chose to investigate. A key concern that is noted is the limited recognition of the broader context in which the investigations were situated: there was little acknowledgement of the social and academic contexts in which learners operated. As Boud and Brew (2013) note, it is important to recognise that scholarship and, indeed, higher education development, is located within the academic workplace.

Saroyan and Trigwell (2015) note further concerns in their more recent review of published works. In particular, they recognised the considerable variation in the key terms being used to describe issues under investigation; that the phenomena under investigation are complex and multi-dimensional, requiring depth and breadth of investigation; that the research generally avoided the use of quantitative methodologies, making it difficult to build evidence that is generalisable; and that the papers ranged across theory building and theoretical frameworks, but showed limited theoretical exploration in general. Their investigation highlighted other trends: many projects were linked to institutional sponsorship with the research generally small in scale (10–35 participants), and with volunteer participants. They incorporated common mechanisms relating to reflection, engagement in scholarship of teaching and learning, communities of practice and situated learning to encourage learning transfer. The authors also noted evidence of a concern for academic or professional identity and consideration of conditions that enabled or impeded learning and its transfer. In this analysis, they noted the emerging effort to measure impact and change. Thus, there is evidence of an increasing maturation in the ways investigations are being designed and analysed.

Potential research foci

There is considerable scope to build a more rigorous and theory-driven body of knowledge as we explore the full span of academic activity and the impact of higher education development. A particular need relates to building more evidence and theory relating to HED methodologies and assumptions. Substantive evidence of the HED influence on university functioning, change or outcomes is particularly helpful in demonstrating value to university leaders. The testing of HED impact with respect to the individual, work group and organisational learning is a critical question (Saroyan and Trigwell 2015). A focus on the direct impact of HED services on university practices and outcomes offers many enticing areas of possible research, such as:

- How does HED influence academic practices, outcomes and organisational cultures?
- What is the impact of sponsor relationships on HED functioning?
- What do university executives want from their HED services? What do they understand with respect to HED and its potential purpose?
- What are the challenges that academic-related HE developers face in melding their academic and service roles?
- What are the primary methodologies being employed by HE developers? Do these differ according to the type of academics/researchers being supported?
- What do developers understand about their role and methodologies? How are they inducted and developed?
- What are the key measures that should be used to evaluate HED impact?

More broadly, there has been little investigation of the university environment and how it functions as a learning context for its employees. At the organisational and cultural levels, improved understanding of the different ways that academic and research communities operate and flourish, and the impact of leaders and HED services in supporting their advancement, would be a watershed in the theoretical underpinning of HED. Increased insight into academic leadership and culture; university management of organisational change; the challenges facing mid-career and senior academics as they transition to more senior roles; and the impact of university leadership on productivity, morale and commitment would all contribute to a deeper understanding of the academic condition and factors that impact academic capacity building.

Research strategies

Chermack and Swanson (2015) offer some useful guidance on framing research questions. They suggest that the research should be problem-driven, rather than directed toward proving a certain philosophical approach. When seeking evidence to justify a particular methodology, for example, there is considerable risk that the real questions about learning are ignored. They therefore suggest that research on development should emphasise a focus on the purpose or theorising intent. Further, they emphasise the importance of identifying the boundaries for the research. Typical boundaries might relate to the institution, context, target learning group or timeframes. Considering how, where and when to bound the research influences its scope and generalisability. Finally, they recommend that the research design be carefully aligned, so that the research purpose, content, measurement, strategies and analytical techniques are mutually compatible.

It is obvious, then, that there is still much to be considered in framing a stronger theoretical grounding to this applied field.

Research approaches and methods

As noted in the earlier reviews, the methodologies that are employed for many of the published papers evidence a high degree of variability. Papers seeking to demonstrate HED impact, for example, are often case study based, reporting on an internal intervention and its outcomes. There is little evidence of benchmarking, cross-institutional studies, systematic review methodology (Bearman *et al.* 2012), exploration of longitudinal impact or questioning of established models and methods. This potentially places the field at risk, given its emergent status and reliance on sponsorship. University leaders raised in a scientific paradigm (Goodall 2015) may find it difficult to relate to papers that are largely descriptive in nature and with little causal evidence of long-term impact. Thus, this is a good time to encourage more rigorous scholarship and research that addresses pivotal questions vexing the field.

Complex questions can be explored in a range of different ways. To date, the evidence suggests that the major methodology employed to describe programs or interventions and their outcomes is that of case studies with a strong reliance on qualitative reviews (Saroyan and Trigwell 2015). Case studies are a valuable form of grounded research, offering an important method of delving into a particular environment and analysing outcomes from a range of perspectives (Yin 2014).

These are a logical first step in building a scholarly investigative focus, as they can be readily developed, conducted within the existing organisation and melded with existing HED activities. However, there is considerable potential to deepen and increase the insights from these studies (Hammersley 2012). Many studies emphasise participant self-reports as the primary evidence base (Amundsen and Wilson 2012; Saroyan and Trigwell 2015). This leaves the field continuing to beg for evidence of making a difference. Case study research needs to be planned prior to the commencement of the targeted activity, as various sources of evidence, including pre- and post-intervention data, can be integrated. The incorporation of quantitative and qualitative data assists with triangulating the findings from a number of sources.

The following strategies support good case study research:

- review the extant literature to identify current approaches and research on the desired intervention and its impact;
- identify the key questions to be addressed through the study;
- develop the research plan, including any survey or interview questions, data sources and likely timings of data capture phases;
- consider sources of evidence that might be accessed as additional evidence/verification. How might access be gained to those sources?
- identify the key respondents/targets to be canvassed and consider how this process will benefit their evaluation purposes;
- develop a summary of the planned research and discuss it with the key targets to determine their willingness to participate or sponsor the project and any concerns that will need to be addressed;
- ensure any necessary permissions (e.g. the sponsor) are obtained before commencing;
- develop the full instruments and associated information sheets;
- seek ethics approval for the study;
- integrate the timing for the data gathering components into the planning schedule;
- implement the research plan and collect data through the project;
- analyse the results and draft a preliminary review of the findings;
- is additional triangulation/exploration needed? Are there results that could be drilled down further? Could follow-up interviews with key stakeholders be beneficial? How might these be conducted?
- draft the paper and seek input from the stakeholders and other mentors.

Many HED studies rely heavily on qualitative interviews from participants to verify the impact of an intervention. When preparing a paper for publication, there should be good clarity as to how the data was collected, the response rate, the way the data was analysed and how it was validated by another analyst. The capacity to provide some quantitative data in addition to anecdotal evidence to support these findings can greatly strengthen the research and its argument (Nimon and Astakhova 2015).

The development of some core measures that are consistently used across different activities provides an important form of validation and testing of impact. As outlined in Chapter 21, it is desirable to move beyond satisfaction measures and toward more progressive measures that will map the adaptive practices that participants evidence, as well as to identify relevant contextual factors that may impact on learning. The integration of a common item bank can facilitate the development of longitudinal and cross-program comparisons, support internal reporting and enable collaboration with other institutions. The capacity to map one's own professional impact is also beneficial to the individual developer when strongly supported by rigorous data.

The translation of evaluation findings into a scholarly paper may require further research, and possibly, replication with another similar intervention to increase the strength of the findings.

Draft papers may be subject to various internal controls and reviews before they can be submitted. Checking the protocols for publishing beforehand is a wise precaution. Developers with academic positions may have more latitude than those in professional roles with respect to publishing about their activities. However, universities are generally keen to see people promote the university's work more broadly.

Collaboration

The choice of research method will be partly driven by the research questions, the context, the form of intervention being measured and the capabilities of the researcher/s. This is an area where there can be particular merit in building a collaborative partnership with others to enrich the research capabilities and insights of the group. Developers from different elements of the HED service can offer very different perspectives (Patel 2014). Key stakeholders may wish to be involved in the review, particularly if the intervention is a negotiated activity where they have invested considerable leadership and intellectual capital. Academics from business or education faculties may provide complementary theoretical and quantitative research capabilities. While these additional contributors offer rich specialist insights, the developer will need to ensure the primary concern of delivering a quality intervention or service is not compromised. Access to academic communities is precious and difficult to gain. The protection of participant's rights and sensitivities will need to be monitored carefully to ensure they do not feel violated at a time of vulnerability. To avoid having the academic community react negatively to perceptions of being "guinea pigs" to serve another person's academic goals, ensure they understand the purpose of the investigation and how the results will be used. The research should not undermine the development priority.

A challenge for HED research projects is that they are often applied, thereby engaging many stakeholders in their design and management. There are risks attached to this form of collaboration, as this personal story will demonstrate. In 2007, I led a collaborative project called the *Future Research Leaders Program* (FRLP). The project was conceived and scoped out by HE developers, and gained significant funding from the Australian Government. The objective was to develop a blended learning program that supported researchers in building better research management practices. 1,000 academics and researchers participated in the project, contributing to capability assessments (pre- and post-test), evaluating the online modules and related workshops, and mapping their enhanced outcomes following participation. Given the programs were comparable across all eight institutions, the evaluation enabled the identification of causal relationships between learning experiences and outcomes, and provided benchmarking to compare the effectiveness of different workshop approaches for the same modules. This was a very early benchmarking program that could have generated considerable insight into blended learning and research capacity building. However, an error for this project was the failure to integrate a publication strategy into the initial project plan and ensure it was signed off early in the process. By the time the evidence could be shared, there were many new stakeholders who had sponsored the project, with a number then wishing to embargo the results while the project offered strong competitive advantage. As a result, the findings of this project have only ever been shared via conference presentations. This lesson will hopefully be noted by other HED collaborators: integrate a publishing strategy as part of the project or program plan, including formal approval to publish planned papers.[1]

Collaboration across different institutions that structure and deliver quite different experiences to achieve similar goals will be more complex in terms of scoping legitimate measures and comparable indicators. The collaboration might require a series of tests to first identify the differences and commonalities in the outcomes, and then further explore these in more depth. It will be important to recognise that the measures may not make sense unless a range of mixed-methods are used to ensure strong validation and testing is achieved. Early permission and clarification as to how the research may be published and disseminated is essential.

Ethics and development

The collection and reporting of data about university members requires approval to ensure the rights and privacy of individuals are fully protected. There is a slightly grey area when the results are intended for internal evaluation only. Even in these cases, it is wise to seek approval, as the later analysis of a series of assessments can reveal important insights that are worth publishing. It may be possible to seek a blanket clearance for generic evaluative measures; that is, if there are broad practices that are being applied across workshops and programs, an outline of the measures, their purpose and the collection processes can support permission for their general use. However, once larger questions that inform research are posed, and where deep investigations are being undertaken, a new ethics approval will be required.

Ethics applications will need to be lodged as early as possible. It is likely that these applications will spark considerable interest from the Ethics Committee, given the target audience and the focus (Parsell *et al.* 2014). Evidence of support from the target community will assist in the application. The Committee will expect to see the instruments or questions to be asked and will wish to know about the sampling and other methodological matters. Although the process of documenting these matters is arduous, it creates an excellent framing for the subsequent research once it is approved. If students are a target group, the vigilance will be even stronger, as there is strong reluctance to load them down with numerous research requests. Research of this nature may require quite senior sponsorship.

Disseminating the research

A paper focusing on higher education development has the potential to reach many audiences. Within the university, it can help to inform the sponsor and senior leaders about key interventions or areas of concern. It can provide guidance on the types of activities that are making a difference. It may also serve to highlight emergent issues that may require more attention. Importantly, it also encourages the HE developer to view their practice with more rigour and professionalism, and to contribute to the emerging body of knowledge.

Publications that have been particularly influential in guiding the development of HED theory and practice include the *International Journal of Academic Development* (IJAD), *Higher Education Research and Development* (HERD), *To Improve the Academy*, *The International Journal for Researcher Development* and *Studies in Higher Education*. These scholarly publications have formed the main vehicles for those seeking to publish on their professional HED activities. The sponsorship of governments and public agencies to encourage research on higher education development matters has acted as a major stimulus for many, and certainly ensured there are many substantial pieces of work that have been undertaken. A challenge is to integrate more summative reviews of core areas (Bearman *et al.* 2012) to facilitate the guidance of new practitioners entering the field. Some executive summaries of evidence and impact would also provide a valuable source of credible information, particularly if published in key journals or via academic societies.

Conclusion

This chapter has explored the nature of HED research and scholarship. It has possibly raised more questions than it has resolved, given the emergent nature of this discipline. However, the importance of building collective knowledge and insights about the work that is undertaken, the way in which it is positioned in universities and the impact it achieves in enhancing academic practice and well-being needs to be recognised. In universities, evidence counts. We need, though, to ensure the right type of evidence is proffered. Academic audiences will judge the quality of the research as well as its focus.

Note

1   An overview of the program can be found at: https://go8.edu.au/programs-and-fellowships/go8-future-research-leaders-program. This program is now publicly available for any university, but the rich evaluative data remains hidden and forgotten.

References

Amundsen, C. and Wilson, M., 2012. Are we asking the right questions? A conceptual review of the educational development literature in higher education. *Review of Educational Research*, 82(1), pp. 90–126.

Ashwin, P., 2012. How often are theories developed through empirical research into higher education? *Studies in Higher Education*, 37(8), pp. 941–955.

Bearman, M., Smith, C.D., Carbone, A., Slade, S., Baik, C., Hughes-Waring, M. and Neumann, D.L., 2012. Systematic review methodology in higher education. *Higher Education Research & Development*, 31(5), pp. 625–640.

Blair, E., 2014. Academic development through the contextualization of the Scholarship of Teaching and Learning: reflections drawn from the recent history of Trinidad and Tobago. *International Journal for Academic Development*, 19(4), pp. 330–340.

Boud, D. and Brew, A., 2013. Reconceptualising academic work as professional practice: implications for academic development. *International Journal for Academic Development*, 18(3), pp. 208–221.

Boughey, C. and Niven, P., 2012. The emergence of research in the South African Academic Development movement. *Higher Education Research & Development*, 31(5), pp. 641–653.

Boyer, E.L., 1990. *Scholarship reconsidered: priorities of the professoriate*, New York: Carnegie Foundation for the Advancement of Teaching.

Chen, S.-Y. and Hu, L.-F., 2012. Higher education research as a field in China: its formation and current landscape. *Higher Education Research & Development*, 31(5), pp. 655–666.

Chermack, T.J. and Swanson, R.A., 2015. When methodologies become theologies, applied disciplines falter. *Human Resource Development Review*, 14(4), pp. 509–513.

Clegg, S., 2012a. Conceptualising higher education research and/or academic development as 'fields': a critical analysis. *Higher Education Research & Development*, 31(5), pp. 667–678.

Clegg, S., 2012b. On the problem of theorising: an insider account of research practice. *Higher Education Research & Development*, 31(3), pp. 407–418.

Goodall, A., 2015. The leaders of the world's top 100 universities. *International Higher Education*, 42. Available online at https://ejournals.bc.edu/ojs/index.php/ihe/article/download/7877/7028

Hammersley, M., 2012. Troubling theory in case study research. *Higher Education Research & Development*, 31(3), pp. 393–405.

Harland, T., 2012. Higher education as an open-access discipline. *Higher Education Research & Development*, 31(5), pp. 703–710.

Jones, G.A., 2012. Reflections on the evolution of higher education as a field of study in Canada. *Higher Education Research & Development*, 31(5), pp. 711–722.

Kandlbinder, P. and Peseta, T., 2009. Key concepts in postgraduate certificates in higher education teaching and learning in Australasia and the United Kingdom. *International Journal for Academic Development*, 14(1), pp. 19–31.

Krause, K.L., 2012. Addressing the wicked problem of quality in higher education: theoretical approaches and implications. *Higher Education Research & Development*, 31(3), pp. 285–297.

Middlehurst, R., 2014. Higher education research agendas for the coming decade: a UK perspective on the policy-research nexus. *Studies in Higher Education*, 39(8), pp. 1475–1487.

Nimon, K.F. and Astakhova, M., 2015. Improving the rigor of quantitative HRD research: four recommendations in support of the general hierarchy of evidence. *Human Resource Development Quarterly*, 26(3), pp. 231–247.

Parsell, M., Ambler, T. and Jacenyik-Trawoger, C., 2014. Ethics in higher education research. *Studies in Higher Education*, 39(1), pp. 166–179.

Patel, F., 2014. Promoting a culture of scholarship among educational developers: exploring institutional opportunities. *International Journal for Academic Development*, 19(3), pp. 242–254.

Peseta, T. and Kandlbinder, P. (eds), 2011. *Higher education research & development anthology*, Milperra, NSW: HERDSA.

Saroyan, A. and Trigwell, K., 2015. Higher education teachers' professional learning: process and outcome. *Studies in Educational Evaluation*, 46, pp. 92–101.

Tight, M., 2013. Discipline and methodology in higher education research. *Higher Education Research & Development*, 32(1), pp. 136–151.

Trigwell, K., Martin, E., Benjamin, J. and Prosser, M., 2000. Scholarship of teaching: a model. *Higher Education Research and Development*, 19(2), pp. 155–168.

Trowler, P., 2014. Depicting and researching disciplines: strong and moderate essentialist approaches. *Studies in Higher Education*, 39(10), pp. 1720–1731.

Velliaris, D., Palmer, E., Picard, M., Guerin, C., Smith, S., Green, I. and Miller, J., 2012. *Australian tertiary learning and teaching scholarship and research 2007–2012*, Milperra, NSW: HERDSA.

Yin, R.K., 2014. *Case study research: design and methods*, 5th edition, Los Angeles, CA: SAGE Publications.

Part V

Positioning the HED service for success

This final section explores the HED leadership context, highlighting the importance of shaping a high-quality professional service that best meet the needs of its university constituents. To flourish, the HED service needs to have good sponsorship, strong usage by university members, and be recognised as a core component of university activity. This is not achieved overnight. This part of the book examines some factors that will contribute to the effective placement of the HED service/s and the establishment of robust partnerships with key leaders.

Chapter 23, explores the role of the HED head and the team in build-ing a responsive, agile and effective service will be explored. Chapter 24 then looks more deeply at the nature of the political context in which HED centres operate, outlining the political competencies which will assist in positioning the group for success. Chapter 25 maps a potential path that HED might forge as it builds more influence and takes stronger shape as a credible discipline that offers research-informed, evidence-based, fit-for-purpose support to encourage academic capacity building. The integral role of the executive and leaders in both sponsoring and encouraging the right development context is affirmed.

Chapter 23

Leading high-performing HED services

The variable nature of HED groups can make it difficult to benchmark against other comparable centres as the range of functions may be very diverse, and the methods of evaluation may differ markedly. In a single university, there may be three central service groups that support HE development (e.g. research, teaching, leadership/organisational development), with three different sponsors, budgeting arrangements and forms of delivery. Additional faculty-based services may also exist to serve the specific requirements of those local communities. In other universities, the central services may be amalgamated, with strong linkages to any decentralised support hosted in the faculties. How then, might one evaluate the performance and functional fit of the HED centre?

There are universities that include services of this nature in their regular quality audits. This is a sensible way of monitoring accountability and performance, ensuring that the activities and quality of delivery are of a suitable standard and meet the needs of the university community. Even without these forms of validation, the HED service can identify some key indicators that will guide assessment of their activities and service delivery (Bamber and Stefani 2015; Stefani 2013; Sword 2014).

A high-functioning HED group might demonstrate the following:

- growth in, and enhancements to, the provision of a range of agreed services and support activities to facilitate capacity building of the targeted university community;
- growth in demand for services and support;
- high service productivity (e.g. number of hours of participant engagement per year) relative to staffing;
- successful delivery of support for institutional enhancements and priorities, including strong take-up by university groups;
- evidence of successful innovations, service or systems enhancements or scholarship, including their impact on usage, adoption or integration into policy and practice;
- contribution to the enhancement or development of institutional services, systems or strategies relating to higher education development;

- evidence of high impact of the service on such aspects as learner capability enhancement, improved cultures, leadership confidence, leadership performance, promotion success and other institutional metrics;
- positive participant perceptions of learning experience quality, relationship quality and production, design and delivery quality (Gronroos 2012).

This chapter explores two critical factors in delivering these outcomes. First, it outlines potential strategies to build HED leadership that effectively frames and guides an adaptive service attuned to the needs of the academic community and the university priorities (Gibbs 2013). Second, the HE developers and other team members need to be similarly aligned, supportive and reflective of these goals and readily able to build the necessary relationships across the university. These are the key challenges of any HED service, no matter how it is configured. This chapter focuses on the specific contextual challenges that occur in HED services, building on the guidance offered some years ago (Blackmore and Blackwell 2006; Blackwell et al. 2003). More guidance on leadership and leading change can be found in Chapters 9 and 19.

Envisioning the HED service

HED services can be shaped in many ways. While there is some discretion to focus the service toward particular ends, there is also an expectation that it will provide institutionally relevant and valued services (Baker et al. 2015; Moses 2012). Each HED leader needs to carefully position their group and its activities to ensure optimal quality delivery relative to the size of the team and its scope of work. As the head of this group, the HED leader has a major influence over the "branding" and envisioning processes. The purpose, functions and core activities are often shaped by the leader's view of the context and needs. However, this needs to be carefully considered, as it can set up the service for either success or minimal impact. The sponsor, executive, leaders and university client expectations should inform these judgements and, at times, may have quite a large influence if high-priority initiatives are to be supported. Some questions that can be asked when reviewing or revisioning the service and its activities include:

- Who are the stakeholders supported by this service?
- What are the core functions to be fulfilled?
- Are these the core functions that the clients wish to see provided?
- What outcomes should be emphasised?
- Are there added-value services that might be offered on request to high-priority clients? How would these be prioritised?
- What do other allied development services do? Are there gaps that need to be supported (e.g. career management, research development, leadership)? Are these appropriate areas to integrate?
- What indicators will be used to evaluate success?

A new head is likely to undertake this review as part of the establishment process. Ideally, the positioning would draw on input from key stakeholders and a knowledge of the broader sector. This may result in extension or reduction of the scope of services. It is wise to review the range of services and balance of core and customised activities every few years; universities are volatile places and the needs may have shifted. This may be even more critical if there is turnover at the executive or sponsor level. Individuals at those levels will have particular priorities and assumptions that will need to be clarified and supported.

Thus, the establishment of a clear identity and purpose for the service needs to be undertaken and reviewed on a regular basis. In this envisioning process, there are likely to be different paths that might be taken, depending on the sponsor, learners, team capabilities and positioning of the service. However, the development of a strong professional collective identity is a foundation for all of these services (Boud and Brew 2013).

Leading HED teams

Another factor that may influence the envisioning process is the calibre and capacity of the team. While the HED leader sets the tone and the focus for the team, this is contingent on the group having the skills, openness and willingness to embrace new ideas, different approaches and innovation. The HED leader will need to offer clear guidance on what should be achieved by the service and the core priorities that will need to be reflected. This sense of purpose or mission helps to guide each team member's focus, development and performance.

The nature of the HED team

The leadership and management of HED teams can be complex. The team may include the following types of personnel:

- academics
- professional developers
- administrative staff
- technical staff.

Each of these groups will seek different forms of support and guidance from their leader. Academics, for example, will need to explore their evolving academic identities, progress their career strategy and build a suitable scholarship and research portfolio as part of their professional strategy (Kensington-Miller et al. 2015; Kinash and Wood 2013; Sutherland 2015; van Schalkwyk et al. 2013). This can be a delicate balancing act between dedicating time to do research and undertaking the educational/outreach functions that are part of the development role. Research is more readily managed if the foci are related to development, but this is not always the case. Many developers retain a strong allegiance to their initial discipline through their ongoing research activities. This is particularly necessary if they are seconded into the development group for a specified period. Developers with academic appointments will therefore anticipate time allocations to publish and undertake investigative work. They will seek funding and support to attend conferences and present their outcomes, and may build collaborations with other colleagues outside the development group. A key responsibility of the HED leader is to guide their career planning, helping them to articulate a clear academic identity around the educational role they fill. This will need to be further articulated when these staff seek promotion or recognition, as these roles are somewhat different to the norm.

The employment context for professional developers operates slightly differently: they will not be required to research or publish about their work. However, close proximity to the academic context and the nature of the development sphere may encourage them to broaden their ambitions, including undertaking a doctorate. Some will already hold doctoral qualifications, and may wish to continue to undertake research-informed practice. The head will need to explore how this might be undertaken as part of, or in addition to, the substantive role. A complexity in this field is the occasional re-assignment of academic developers to professional staff appointments (Fraser and Ling 2014). Thus, professional developers may be seeking opportunities to remain scholars as part of their professional practice. A scholarly, critical stance is desirable, given the audience being supported (Bovill and Mårtensson 2014).

These services rely on administrative staff to provide a range of services that may include financial management, marketing, event management, reception services and administrative/secretarial activities. The establishment of a stable, customer-focused group that is professional, reliable, responsive and able to work relatively autonomously is a significant asset. It is likely that this group will also have responsibility for preparing a range of marketing resources, such as programs, flyers and website information. Thus, they will need to be skilled in using many different software packages as well as providing an exceptional customer interface.

Technical staff may be responsible for designing and managing technological services and their delivery. Typically, these may relate to student evaluations of teaching, the online teaching interface for the university, learning databases, blended learning program delivery, design and delivery of new programs or courseware development. While the technical skills of each member need to be at a high level, the capacity to relate and communicate with staff will be most important. It is likely that their role will include the development of manuals, guides and help sheets to assist staff learning about these systems. Some of these members may progress to substantive roles as trainers, particularly if the university emphasises a strong technological interface for students.

Recruiting developers

HE development is a highly specialised role. As outlined in earlier chapters, it is likely to attract people who wish to support their colleagues, and who may have been actively engaged in the academic or research community prior to transitioning to the group. It is possible that some degree of compromise may be required when seeking to recruit new people. The role benefits from dual capabilities in development as well as a deep professional grounding in learning and teaching, research or leadership. It is rare to find people expert in both when they move into the HED space. Instead, they will need to acquire intensive grounding quite quickly.

Given these limitations, the HED leader is well advised to consider the key criteria that need to be clearly evidenced before employing a new staff member. These might include:

- evidence of successfully working in a team;
- the capacity to design and deliver engaging learning activities;
- a strong professional grounding in academic/research/leadership/technological methodologies and practices;
- the capacity to communicate effectively across a range of media;
- evidence of the ability to negotiate and work collaboratively.

These are pre-conditions for these roles, but in many cases, the new staff member will require considerable guidance on the real context of development and how it operates. Ongoing training, mentoring and coaching may be required. Given the diversity of backgrounds and experience that members bring to their roles (Green and Little 2016), the provision of a focused induction to the role and its implications is most critical (Kensington-Miller *et al*. 2012). An understanding of the threshold concepts that can impact on a developer's capacity to deliver good quality service (Timmermans 2014) and a broader framing of the role in terms of its functions offer an initial grounding. The provision of regular in-services to encourage collegial exploration of role and service will further assist in building an understanding of this process (van Schalkwyk *et al*. 2013). Dipietro (2014) offers some useful reflections on what might be covered.

Building a high-performing HED team

It is likely that each member will have a specific role and responsibilities to be fulfilled. Good articulation of the overarching purpose of the service will guide collective understanding as to what each person contributes, how they link to other colleagues' roles and the ways in which each may need support. Teams of this nature work very intensively together: there may be opportunities to co-facilitate or to shadow more experienced members. Peer review of facilitation offers a particularly rich context to explore development philosophies and variations in approaches. The establishment of a strong collective identity and lexicon relating to service goals encourages this collective understanding. Clarification of cultural expectations and codes of conduct as to confidentiality, knowledge sharing and respectful interactions with each other assists in establishing a basic set of protocols.

Establishing role and performance expectations

Effective establishment of role expectations, how the service measures its impact and effectiveness (Gray and Radloff 2006; Stefani 2013) and guidance on performance expectations will ensure a fair and equitable approach to workloads and outcomes. Development work varies greatly in terms of complexity. There needs to be some equity in assessing workload and providing space for innovation and creative enhancement. This can be quite a vexatious issue, and is not dissimilar to the challenges faced by academic staff members who are allocated a certain number of teaching or student hours to ensure equitable workloads, despite differences in complexity, size of student cohort and coordination responsibilities.

Determining workloads for developers is particularly complex in that different activities demand variable levels of effort and oversight. Consider, for example, the differences between designing and delivering a workshop and a program; between long-standing, somewhat formulaic sessions vs new and innovative offerings; between events to be attended by hundreds of participants and a small activity; or negotiated support that requires considerable shaping and negotiating compared with those where the process is well-tested. Each of these circumstances will affect the consideration of workload. There may also be different expectations based on the calibre of each staff member and the degree to which they are capable of delivering some of the more sophisticated services. Thus, the head will need to be quite considered when determining the load to be carried by each individual, particularly as more expert developers may be asked to add negotiated activities in addition to planned commitments. If some of the added-value services outlined in this book are employed, they will put further demands on the developer. This will need to be recognised. Clarification of service priorities and the groups with highest needs can assist in this regard. It may also be necessary to think carefully about whether individualised support can be sustained (Sword 2014).

Integrating a strong service ethic

The entire team needs a strong service ethic (Gronroos 2012) with a clear understanding of user expectations. The team members need to be highly professional, possessing the critical skills and knowledge required to perform their roles. Their attitudes and behaviours need to emphasise a concern for clients and an interest in supporting their needs in a positive and responsive way. The service should be accessible and flexible in meeting the needs of its users. The service, systems and team will need to reflect high levels of reliability, trustworthiness and consistency.

If something goes wrong, every effort should be made to address the issue or offer an alternative solution. The environment in which the service is delivered should be attractive, encouraging interactions with the learner population. Finally, the service needs to be credible and reputable (Gronroos 2012). Explicit exploration of these principles offers an important scaffold to the whole team. It provides an important basis for induction, performance reviews and debriefs if something goes wrong.

An important goal of the service is to provide the best quality experience within the allocated resources. A team that is willing to share, listen, learn and create together offers a rich and fertile environment for creativity. The development of a shared repository, templates and models further encourages productive collaboration and is particularly helpful for new staff who have come into the group. Of course, it will also be important to recognise that certain activities, methodologies or models might be better used for specific learning contexts. The group needs to trust each other in terms of how knowledge and ideas will be adopted and respected. This needs to be clearly established and reiterated.

Chapter 21 outlined the critical need for evaluation and evidence gathering (McAlpine and Amundsen 2012; Stefani 2011; Chalmers and Gardiner 2015). The development of an evaluation strategy and clarity as to what is measured, when and by whom will assist team members in engaging with this professional activity. Allied to this group capability is the encouragement of scholarship across the team. At the least, each developer should ensure that they are familiar with their specialist development literature. However, this might be extended further to encourage new skills, methodologies and practices.

Ensuring quality outcomes

As this work has outlined, poor performance is a major risk to a service group of this nature. There are few second chances if an experience has been unfortunate or ill-received. Establishing and maintaining high standards of service and delivery is therefore an essential element of the leadership role. The HED leader must be particularly vigilant in quality assurance, ensuring that each offering and staff member is delivering optimal outcomes. As a first precaution, new staff will need to be carefully guided through core methodologies and a deep understanding of the academic context. They might shadow more experienced colleagues and consider how their particular role will articulate the broader framing. Their first "solo" activities could be beneficially mentored and observed by a supportive peer.

Where issues arise, the individual concerned might be assisted with a thorough debrief, coaching, further development, mentorship or shadowing of more experienced colleagues. There may be some instances where the individual is clearly not suited to this type of work. The capacity to be empathetic, creative, flexible and adaptive is essential for these roles. If someone is ill-suited, early discussions to explore where they might better fit are advisable.

Performance reviews and targets

In this context, performance reviews play an essential part in setting clear expectations and monitoring outcomes. Developers benefit from preparing a portfolio relating to their work as part of their annual review, perhaps encompassing:

- articulation of their *career goals and plans*;
- an outline of their *development and service philosophy*, explaining the groups they support and their developmental needs, how this support is designed and structured and the particular approaches that have proven beneficial;
- an overview of the *key activities and support* that have been delivered in the last year;
- *evidence* of learner satisfaction, outcomes and impact;
- a review of *research or scholarship activities and outcomes* (if appropriate);
- a review of *leadership, management and collaborative* contributions and outcomes;
- identification of *new goals and development strategies* to assist ongoing development.

It can be seen that this portfolio would have three key foci:

- building a conscious and professional approach to the development role;
- enabling career management and long-term planning;
- integrating a strong focus on evidence-based professional practice.

Performance discussions can then be richly contextualised, drawing on these reflections, and including career and development discussions. Ideally, new challenges and innovations can be mapped as part of the goals for the incoming year. Developers, like academics, need to transition toward coordination and leadership responsibilities as they consolidate their skills and seek career progression. They will also need to balance their developmental role with research, scholarship and potentially, collaboration as part of their broader outreach role (Willis and Strivens 2015).

Designing HED policies and systems

Part of the HED infrastructure relates to the establishment of underlying policies and systems that will support the service activities and the staff. Policies offer important guidance on the standard behaviours and expectations that should be reflected by all individuals in the group. They support consistent application of principles across the team, and provide certainty with respect to decision making. While it is unlikely that a HED service will have a large number of policies, there are some that will assist in clarifying service delivery principles or internal management practices. For example, service-related policies might explore who should be prioritised for negotiated support and to what degree; co-contribution payments and how they will be applied; evaluation and its application across the HED service; and the use and confidentiality of multi-source reviews. HED staff-related policies might include conference and professional development support, workload policies, time in lieu for residential development activities or external consultancies. It can be seen that these policies are often related to issues that may be difficult to resolve when rapid decisions are required.

The service will need to build and maintain a range of systems to support its work. Again, some of these systems will be institutionally focused, designed to provide access to key services by any staff member, while others will be more internally focused. Institutional systems might include the learning management system, student evaluations, research management platform, capability or performance frameworks, performance management systems and/or booking systems for learning activities. These systems are often relatively stable, requiring limited adjustment and refinements until they are deemed too outdated and replaced. Staff involved in managing these large, complex systems need to monitor system functionality and usage, ensuring any issues are addressed quickly. They may operate a help-desk or some other form of customer support.

More internally based systems might include: a records system to capture the resources, communications and records related to HED activities, acting as both an archive and shared repository; an evaluation database that is regularly analysed and summarised; budgetary and registrant systems to monitor demand and costs; a customer relationship management database; administrative records; guidance on setting up and managing networks, events or programs; marketing information; and other forms of public communication/reporting. Each of these systems may be configured in different ways, with some designed to encourage individual input and responsibility, while others will be managed by an authorised delegate. The design of many of these internal systems is likely to be a work in progress. Technology is advancing and systems that were once costly to introduce are now more accessible. In many cases, the initial systems will have been designed in-house, while newer options are more likely to be off the shelf. An implication of these different systems is that all HED staff should be trained in their use and should have a clear understanding as to their responsibilities for data entry and upkeep.

A key part of the delivery process is the building of consistent systems, principles and methodologies. Templates for marketing, workshop and program design can ensure there is a high-quality presentation and approach being used. The integration of a standardised evaluation system that ensures core questions are being canvassed from all participants, as well as providing some flexible options for more customised interrogation, can greatly assist analysis and benchmarking. The development of standardised annual programs, reports and executive summaries offers helpful models, ensuring consistently high-quality planning and delivery.

Developing the HED capability

The development of HED capability will be an ongoing challenge. First, the repertoire and methodologies are evolving and expanding each year. Second, the service may identify additional capabilities that it feels need to be added (e.g. multi-source reviews or facilitation skills). Third, the university may determine the need for additional streams of support (e.g. moving to an online institutional strategy). Finally, the team is likely to grow or evolve over time. Staff will need regular development opportunities to build new skills, including in-service sessions, external courses, conference attendance, visits to other institutions or mentorship. Deepening professional skills so that at least two members are able to perform any role is an important risk management strategy and supports succession planning.

The university is likely to have a number of people undertaking development roles. Often, they will be seen as "dissimilar" because their functions or target groups may be different (Green and Little 2013; Patel 2014). However, many of the concerns, methodologies and strategies will be comparable. Developers will benefit from learning about the diversity of support offered across the institution. An internal network and shared repository where people can exchange knowledge and insights, regular meetings and development sessions will increase the institutional capability and open opportunities to explore mutual interests, research questions and potential partnerships (Quinn and Vorster 2014). Benchmarking may also be enabled through this collegial exchange.

This collaboration may be taken further, providing a forum for those in the region to collaborate and share their practice, ideas and questions. Network meetings can generate powerful alliances, including the development of shared programs, identification of best practice and lobbying for funding.

Resetting the goal posts

The HED service needs to be adaptive and responsive to institutional and sectoral shifts in expectation, practice and emphasis. The quest to build significant impact, a more strategic focus and robust partnerships with faculty and leaders, for example, requires regular retuning of the service and its delivery mechanisms. The HED leader will be a key sensor for this recalibration, drawing on both formal discussions and interpretations of the climate and strategy. The capacity to be proactive and to anticipate likely changes is a particular benefit. This will allow time to canvass opinions, explore other practices, identify possible strategies to recommend and build evidence to support those recommendations. The capacity to bring the team along will also require careful management. They will need time to work through the evidence, consider consequences and relinquish attachment to the current practices.

The integrated HED service

A trend in many universities is to divide, merge, shift or amalgamate HED centres. The motivations for these restructures may be attributable to a leader's vision, cost savings or other political or ideological reasons. Although many universities operate segmented services (e.g. teaching, research, leadership), there will be times when these centres are merged.

An integrated service offers many benefits. It encourages collaboration and exchange across the different HED groups, avoiding duplication. It is easier to design conjoint programs and services. Costs can be contained through the use of joint facilities, systems, policies and resources. Users are able to source all support from one area and website. They are also able to learn about other services through interaction with any of the developers.

Disadvantages also exist, of course. The head of an integrated HED service may report to two or three sponsors and will need to be even more fully politically attuned. It is possible that all three sponsors will anticipate another colleague is acting as the primary sponsor, so clarification as to who will speak on behalf of the group is advisable. The HED leader will need to build strong relationships with each sponsor, and there will be increased participation in forums or committees. This will place more onus on other senior developers to fill leadership and management functions.

The adaptive HED service

If the service has experienced a restructure or change in functions and team members, regular reviews and mapping of key areas of activity will ensure the essential emphases have been incorporated. Sponsors will anticipate seeing a revitalised and energised service configuration and design. Consultation with key stakeholders can offer rich insights into the past elements that were valued and those that weren't. Be prepared to abandon the elements that were less valued. It is time to build a different identity and image. The team will require considerable support and guidance. The development of a new vision, common protocols, culture and expectations will need to be prioritised. Many past systems and practices are likely to require reconfiguration, unlearning or review. This can be disconcerting to staff, particularly if they helped shape old practices. The building of a unified focus and approach may require focused attention.

It is likely that some of the HED members will find it hard to adapt. They may find the new mode of working to be difficult, or feel the loss of roles or activities that were close to their heart. While they will need time to adapt and come to terms with their loss, they will need to come on board as quickly as possible. The university will anticipate many wins from this new initiative and will wish to see high energy, focus and options coming forward.

Conclusion

Good leadership of an HED service is predicated on:

- a clear and well-articulated vision;
- the right team to deliver this vision;
- a strong understanding of service and its enactment;
- well-developed systems and policies to support delivery;
- a well-attuned sense of any changes that may affect the service and its positioning.

Adaptive and capable teams are essential to high-quality HED service delivery. The leader plays a key role in selecting the right people, building capability and ensuring all are able to consistently apply the established policies, systems and principles. The team needs to demonstrate a broad range of skills and capabilities and to be learning and development orientated. Good performance management and clear performance expectations will support these outcomes.

References

Baker, V.L., Lunsford, L.G. and Pifer, M.J., 2015. Systems alignment for comprehensive faculty development in liberal arts colleges. *To Improve the Academy*, 34(1–2), pp. 91–116.

Bamber, V. and Stefani, L., 2015. Taking up the challenge of evidencing value in educational development: from theory to practice. *International Journal for Academic Development*, pp.1–13, Available online at DOI 10.1080/1360144X.2015.1100112

Blackmore, P. and Blackwell, R., 2006. Strategic leadership in academic development. *Studies in Higher Education*, 31(3), pp. 373–387.

Blackwell, R., Blackmore, P. and Society for Research into Higher Education, 2003. *Towards strategic staff development in higher education*, Maidenhead, Berkshire: Society for Research into Higher Education and Open University Press.

Boud, D. and Brew, A., 2013. Reconceptualising academic work as professional practice: implications for academic development. *International Journal for Academic Development*, 18(3), pp. 208–221.

Bovill, C. and Mårtensson, K., 2014. The challenge of sustaining academic development work. *International Journal for Academic Development*, 19(4), pp. 263–267.

Chalmers, D. and Gardiner, D., 2015. An evaluation framework for identifying the effectiveness and impact of academic teacher development programmes. *Studies in Educational Evaluation*, 46, pp. 81–91.

DiPietro, M., 2014. Tracing the evolution of educational development through the POD Network's Institute for New Faculty Developers. *To Improve the Academy*, 33(2), pp. 113–130.

Fraser, K. and Ling, P., 2014. How academic is academic development? *International Journal for Academic Development*, 19(3), pp. 226–241.

Gibbs, G., 2013. Reflections on the changing nature of educational development. *International Journal for Academic Development*, 18(1), pp. 4–14.

Gray, K. and Radloff, A., 2006. Quality management of academic development work: implementation issues and challenges. *International Journal for Academic Development*, 11(2), pp. 79–90.

Green, D.A. and Little, D., 2013. Academic development on the margins. *Studies in Higher Education*, 38(4), pp. 523–537.

Green, D.A. and Little, D., 2016. Family portrait: a profile of educational developers around the world. *International Journal for Academic Development*, 21(2), pp. 135–150.

Gronroos, C., 2012. *Service management and marketing: customer management in service competition*, New Delhi: Wiley.

Kensington-Miller, B., Brailsford, I. and Gossman, P., 2012. Developing new academic developers: doing before being? *International Journal for Academic Development*, 17(2), pp. 121–133.

Kensington-Miller, B., Renc-Roe, J. and Morón-García, S., 2015. The chameleon on a tartan rug: adaptations of three academic developers' professional identities. *International Journal for Academic Development*, 20(3), pp. 279–290.

Kinash, S. and Wood, K., 2013. Academic developer identity: how we know who we are. *International Journal for Academic Development*, 18(2), pp. 178–189.

McAlpine, L. and Amundsen, C., 2012. Challenging the taken-for-granted: how research analysis might inform pedagogical practices and institutional policies related to doctoral education. *Studies in Higher Education*, 37(6), pp. 683–694.

Moses, I., 2012. Views from a former vice-chancellor. *International Journal for Academic Development*, 17(3), pp. 275–277.

Patel, F., 2014. Promoting a culture of scholarship among educational developers: exploring institutional opportunities. *International Journal for Academic Development*, 19(3), pp. 242–254.

Quinn, L. and Vorster, J.A., 2014. Isn't it time to start thinking about 'developing' academic developers in a more systematic way? *International Journal for Academic Development*, 19(3), pp. 255–258.

van Schalkwyk, S., Cilliers, F., Adendorff, H., Cattell, K. and Herman, N., 2013. Journeys of growth towards the professional learning of academics: understanding the role of educational development. *International Journal for Academic Development*, 18(2), pp. 139–151.

Stefani, L. (ed.), 2011. *Evaluating the effectiveness of academic development: principles and practice*, New York: Routledge.

Stefani, L., 2013. Performance measurement for academic development: risk or opportunity? *International Journal for Academic Development*, 18(3), pp. 294–296.

Sutherland, K.A., 2015. Precarious but connected: the roles and identities of academic developers. *International Journal for Academic Development*, 20(3), pp. 209–211.

Sword, H., 2014. Dancing on the bottom line: an unruly cost–benefit analysis of three academic development initiatives. *Higher Education Research & Development*, 33(4), pp. 783–793.

Timmermans, J.A., 2014. Identifying threshold concepts in the careers of educational developers. *International Journal for Academic Development*, 19(4), pp. 305–317.

Willis, I. and Strivens, J., 2015. Academic developers and international collaborations: the importance of personal abilities and aptitudes. *International Journal for Academic Development*, 20(4), pp. 333–344.

Chapter 24

Positioning the HED service in a political world

Universities have faced increasing pressure to be more agile and adaptive (Middlehurst 2013). This has created a ripple effect through the various institutional levels, as new initiatives are implemented, leaders are recruited to lead reforms and the systems and processes underpinning university practices are reviewed and scrutinised with increased vigour. The quest to find better and different ways to deliver outcomes has driven many changes that have profoundly impacted how universities function and the ways in which different academic and service groups operate.

These changes have generated considerable upheaval in HED services (Debowski et al. 2012; Fraser and Ryan 2012; Holt et al. 2011). Many have experienced some or all of the following shifts over the last few years:

- changes to the executive reporting line as new roles are added;
- diminished direct access to senior leaders in the executive;
- greater accountability for how funds are spent;
- increased emphasis on demonstrating evidence of impact;
- requirements to increase productivity with less resources;
- an expectation that the HED services will be active in promoting institutional change strategies;
- changes to budgetary principles and/or funding arrangements;
- increased casualisation of appointments;
- increased competition for available funding sources;
- demotion of directors of HED centres to associate director or coordinator roles;
- integration of additional functions and roles into the HED;
- re-employment of academic developers as professional staff.

While some of these changes might be highly confronting and distressing, they are symptomatic of a changing university ecology. All areas of the university are facing a tougher regimen of being more accountable for the provided funds and needing to demonstrate adaptive and strategic approaches to their functions and outcomes. Service groups are also expected to demonstrate how they add value to the university's core goals of attracting and retaining students or enhancing research, in order to justify their continued existence. This can be challenging where the service is less directly linked to operational mechanisms that support the delivery of teaching or research outcomes. The HED service role acts as a mediating influence on academic and leadership productivity, practices and outcomes, making it more difficult to demonstrate this added value, particularly with respect to short-term gains. In many cases, despite enormous investment in a key initiative, the HED contribution will be largely unacknowledged. The HED leader and team need to seek alternative ways of positioning and promoting the value and benefits of the services that are delivered.

Pfeffer (2010) notes that political contexts like universities are not necessarily fair or just, with many stakeholders and voices to be accommodated when decisions are made. In this context, the HED service needs to be attuned to the dynamic university context, working in tandem with other institutional forces. It needs to be seen as part of the solution, not one of the problems. This alignment affords protection as uncertainty, risk, change and dynamic decision contexts are encountered.

Effective HED services and leaders need to be well connected, wired into the DNA of their university community, with strong linkages and relationships that encourage partnerships, alliances and collaborations. The service needs to be seen as a key agency that can help the stakeholders achieve their aspirations and targets. Their mediating impact should be evident through the growth of capable academics and leaders. A service that operates in isolation, without allies or strong support from stakeholders, is very vulnerable. Its invisibility is a major risk to long-term sustainability.

There are various ways in which the political landscape of higher education might be viewed. Kauko (2013), for example, aptly identifies *reform, gridlock, consensual change* and *friction* as change contexts. Saarinen and Ursin (2012), in their analysis of HE policy, suggest that there are various ways in which policy is enacted. *Structural reform* is framed by a bounded reality which defines the broad focus and intent; the *actor approach* supports both individuals and collective actors in effecting change; while the *agency approach* is interactive and action-focused. These concepts have been the subject of much debate in this discipline's literature as the role of HED in terms of being an actor, agency or bound by structures is debated (Cordiner 2014; Debowski 2014; Di Napoli 2014; Szkudlarek and Stankiewicz 2014). The fluidity of placement, influence and sponsorship is a particular challenge for HED groups with most possessing limited authority (Johnson 2008a). The achievement of effective integration and positioning therefore requires considerable political competence to successfully navigate strong political currents.

Being politically competent

Political competence has been described as having three key features: the capacity to accurately map the terrain in which one operates; the ability to build allies and coalitions to support initiatives; and the skills to execute and take action to achieve desired results (Johnson 2008b). This is an important capability for HE developers. A further element of political competence is the ability to share and promote successful outcomes to stakeholders and allies. This assists in increasing awareness and knowledge of the group's impact. These elements can provide considerable protection and support for the HED leader and team. Each of these will be discussed in turn.

Map the terrain

Universities comprise numerous communities, powerbrokers, factions, tribes and territories (Becher and Trowler 2001), with each seeking access to resources and opportunity. Each will be motivated by their own contexts, goals, priorities, values, experiences and anxieties. These influences will strongly determine the ways in which they view the HED service and its activities. Some will be highly defensive in orientation, protecting their space with strong barriers and aggressive stances against any perceived encroachment on their territory. Others will be open to new ideas, innovations, support and partnerships or may be quite neutral, but ready to consider how mutual benefit might be possible. In all cases, these groups will anticipate benefiting from any alliance with the HED service.

The ability to read the landscape is an important HED capability (Johnson 2008b). The following questions assist in this environmental scan:

- Who is influential and powerful? (Normally this relates to the capacity to make decisions and direct resources.)
- How do they distribute resources and sponsorship? (For example, do they chair budgetary committees or have discretionary funding to allocate? Do they determine what budget should be apportioned for these types of activities?)
- What do they understand with respect to the HED service and its activities?
- Is there any history or experience with the HED service? Was it a good or poor experience? If they are new to the university, what experience have they had in the past? (Consider, for example, how their old services functioned. Are there some likely assumptions that may need to be influenced?)
- How aligned is the HED service with their goals, priorities and targets?
- What do they want to achieve? Is this aligned with the potential services and support that the HED service can offer?
- If they need something more adaptive or innovative, is there capacity to provide that?
- Are there other groups competing for attention and sponsorship?
- Are there groups or individuals who are adversarial or resistant to the value of the HED service? Why? Do they have good reason to be so, or is this motivated by a quest for power, resources or influence?

These questions can open up considerable insight into the landscape and the key players. Some of the dominant forces, for example, will include particular members of the executive, deans or heads of research institutes, those with strong connections to external groups, or others who have the ear of senior people. Some of the influential people may be support staff who provide guidance, or who oversee important functions in the university. There will be people who *should* be influential, but are largely negligible: they may hold positions of authority but be poor in managing their time, relationships or outcomes. Knowledge of those who are ineffectual is as important as an awareness of those who are generally shaping the directions and priorities. It is also critical to ascertain the disposition of those who need to be influenced or are desirable sponsors.

These mapping processes will require a range of approaches. Observation and listening are essential. While it is not advisable to be seen as a gossip, the capacity to garner information from a range of sources can be invaluable. Anecdotes, evidence of new, successful initiatives, official communications and input from other service leaders all facilitate a deeper perspective on key people. An awareness of the political structures of the university, the role of different decision-making groups and the line of command for certain outcomes all assist with mapping the landscape. Involvement in university committees and boards will provide further insight into how particular people act and hold influence. Thus, there are many different ways to develop a deep insight into how politics operates in the university, and the variable influence of different groups or individuals.

This knowledge enables the next step: building alliances and partnerships with key people or groups.

Build allies and coalitions

The HED service is likely to sustain many different alliances and partnerships. Some of these will be directed toward supporting the overall purpose and delivery of the service, while others may be more functionally targeted toward achievement of specific outcomes. There are a number of factors that will assist in building these connections.

First, it is important that the HED leader and team are recognised for their expertise, personal integrity, reliability and credibility. Any group or leader who sponsors or partners with this group needs to be assured that agreed outcomes will be delivered to a high quality. They will choose to engage based on this initial assessment. As noted earlier in this book, the reputation and standing of the service and its members will be critical to the sustainability of the group.

University members are responsible for generating the necessary outcomes and growth that supports the university's long-term directions. The HED service's capacity to ensure strong wins for these stakeholders will encourage loyalty and long-term relationships. HED members need to be politically attuned to the shifts and dynamics of the university terrain; their ability to talk coherently and intelligently about these matters, and to recognise the needs of their stakeholders will be integral to success. Most critically, developers need to be actively focused on establishing and maintaining these connections, rather than waiting on invitations (Pfeffer 2010).

The provision of ongoing core services that build academic or university capacity and support for key initiatives or new innovations rely on a suitable budget, facilities, encouragement of staff to attend and many other forms of support. Senior stakeholders will seek evidence of strong benefits and value from the activities, looking for approaches that are consonant with their own priorities, and verifying that the HED group is the best avenue to achieve the outcomes. The process of building support can therefore be complex, requiring lobbying, advocacy and (re)education. A frustration for many HED leaders is that well-established and highly valued core services, such as foundational programs and orientations, may lose sponsorship over time. A compelling and persuasive vision for the service can help frame the message (Kotter 2012; Pfeffer 2010). Evidence is an essential part of illustrating value (Bamber and Stefani 2015; McAlpine and Amundsen 2012; Stefani 2011). Evaluations and reviews, affirmations from key stakeholders, advisory panels and benchmarking all reinforce the continuing importance and impact of these ongoing activities. It is strategic to source sponsors and advocates who will attest to their value and contribution as part of the evaluative process.

Seeking sponsors for new proposals or ideas is even more complex. It will be necessary to gain commitment to the ideas, initiatives or service elements that are being promoted. Innovations and new ideas or services will require substantiation in terms of the prospective benefits. The proposals will require careful documentation, outlining how they might benefit the community and support the agenda of that stakeholder. Tailor the messages to reflect the priorities and agendas of each sponsor. Research and evidence from other universities provide a clear rationale for the initiative. While it may be clear that a critical gap or deficit requires addressing, care should be taken in exploring this deficiency, particularly if stakeholders have contributed to that particular context. A deficit-based model can generate frustration, anger, offence or irritation. Instead, focus on an asset-based approach, which explores how new enhancements will benefit the community and build further capacity.

It can take considerable time to achieve sponsorship and/or consensus. It may be necessary to adapt ideas and concepts to reach an agreed approach. New sponsors or partners are likely to have ideas that they would like to see incorporated. They may wish to discuss the costs and scope of the initiatives, or shift the focus toward some different goals and outcomes. The HED team will need to be responsive and creative over this negotiation, recognising that the goal is to achieve commitment and engagement to effect broad strategy. Pfeffer (2010) also suggests that it is wise to consider what constitutes "victory." There is little sense in fighting hard for a particular element if it serves only to hamper the overall goal. On the other hand, the need to employ practice wisdom to ensure initiatives will work in real contexts is essential (Bamber and Stefani 2015).

There will be other times where ideas are taken up with alacrity along with an expectation of rapid implementation. An executive member, for example, may wish to see their vision put in place as an urgent priority. However, innovations do need to be carefully scoped, and, if they are to be whole of institutional reforms, careful piloting should be undertaken. The approval of a well-designed plan for implementation will provide important assurance to the sponsor and increase their knowledge and understanding as to what will be required. However, there may be times when they require or suggest changes that have the potential to greatly undermine critical components of the initiative. The capacity to offer expert guidance, including a rationale based on research and evidence, with alternative recommendations for consideration, will assist.

Unfortunately, in some cases, rational argument may not win out! There will be some occasions where resigned acquiescence and making the best of something is a wiser political course. Political competence also relates to the identification of things that one can and can't control and determining when to take action or stay inactive. The delicate balance between building alliances and partnerships and acting as an expert is likely to be an ongoing challenge in our politicised universities.

Achieve the desired results

With approval or alliances gained, the delivery of high-quality, successful outcomes must then be achieved. These should be managed in a timely and highly professional manner. Strategic initiatives that are high priority need to be escalated, ensuring rapid progression of the plans. However, development services can sometimes take considerable time to plan and implement approved innovations. While delays may be necessary because of the need to build in some pre-steps (e.g. system design or further consultation and research), impatient stakeholders may see the time lags as symptomatic of larger inadequacies in the service. In some cases, they might be correct, reflecting a service that is potentially moving to a different pace than the rest of the university. In other cases, the lengthy process could be necessary to ensure good success. As noted in Chapter 10, it is important to provide a thorough briefing to the sponsor on the planned process and scheduling. Regular communication and updates on progress should be prioritised to maintain good will across all parties.

From the stakeholder perspective, these initiatives will need to have strong visibility and generate good will and engagement across the community. The sponsor/s will hope for some referred benefit from successful activities, such as publicity or recognition. They will relish opportunities to be profiled and to show that they have guided this successful innovation. Planning in advance and issuing invitations to related events and media engagements that feature such innovations will allow stakeholders to attend and see for themselves.

Promote the outcomes and impact

As noted in Chapters 21 and 22, the integration of evaluation and ongoing research into the HED service and its impact can build influence. University sponsors and stakeholders are research focused: they look for evidence and like to be assured that their support is leading to better outcomes. The collection, analysis and presentation of evaluative data will be highly valued, providing reassurance that the HED service is professional, effective and on top of its game.

The HED service is also well advised to widely promote outcomes. Internal university media releases ensure the university community is kept informed of the HED service and its impact. Quotes from more senior leaders or sponsors in these communiqués add further authenticity to such releases. There may be potential to extend the publicity around an initiative to external media sources. Consider, for example, the tenth anniversary of a core program. This is an event to be celebrated, and may be of interest to internal and external audiences. The development of connections with the media department will facilitate promotion around such an event.

The integration of research and evaluation as part of new initiatives to show impact and contribution to the university's goals will offer considerable benefit. The sharing of papers and reports of translation to other universities or contexts validates the HED service. The annual report provides an important vehicle for a summary of the key activities being delivered, and may assist in guiding more awareness of the totality of the service and its influence. Reviews on a periodic basis of particular initiatives (e.g. programs) by an independent third party increase the credibility of the offerings. Similarly, external accreditation, such as that offered by the Higher Education Academy, benchmarks and validates the offerings, making a program harder to discredit. This form of recognition also encourages ongoing quality assurance and critique, and may promote wider input from various stakeholders in the university.

There is merit in seeking external recognition for innovations developed or overseen by the HED service, including national, professional, or disciplinary awards. A strong evaluative evidence base is necessary for these forms of quality assurance and recognition. The development of a portfolio and submission, along with commendations and letters of support from key university leaders, focuses attention on the achievements and merits of the intervention/s. This, in itself, is a strong outcome. The gaining of awards or recognition as a finalist (or winner!) provides further affirmation about the value of the strategy.

HED leaders can build more visibility through attendance at university and faculty committees, boards and working parties. These are ideal forums to influence, present cases, and listen to the emerging debates that are occurring. They also provide an invaluable platform to view senior leaders in action, and to revise initial assessments of the landscape and influential players. Additional profile and credibility can be gained from participating or leading national and professional groups (Debowski *et al.* 2012).

Engaging the university community as partners

A risk for centralised development services is their remoteness from faculty locations and activities. The capacity to maintain a presence and to be an active stimulus, encouraging reflection and engagement with the HED priorities, can contribute to the service's likely success. HED services benefit from building regular connections with their communities and providing a more targeted form of interaction to suit particular segments of the population. Useful strategies include:

- Ensure that the institutional directions, policies and priorities are aligned with the service's priorities, while designing clear reports on the strategic outcomes that are being delivered.
- Develop a shared HED interactive database of key institutional contacts to be maintained by all developers. The database provides a centralised record of who is using the service and the types of services that are being sourced. It can also be used to note the key challenges that are being evidenced in each community, and what has been done to support them.
- Encourage interchange across program cohort members. The development of networks and shared communications of useful resources, tips or innovations increases the relevance of the service to those members.
- Share the results of evaluations and reviews back to senior leaders, particularly if they have been instrumental in guiding the progress of cohort members. The identification of emerging issues or risks might also be discussed, encouraging further dialogue and additional support. Ensure influential contributors are acknowledged in reports.
- Prepare and share tailored updates to support key groups.
- Build effective mechanisms to provide just-in-time support to address key challenges, such as FAQs, quick tip guides, case studies, online programs for skill enhancement and links to useful websites.
- When offering guidance on generic issues or challenges, aim for well-framed, pithy summaries that can be readily digested and applied. This "grey literature" is highly valued by practitioners (Gibbs 2013). Any recommended resources need to be carefully selected, easily navigable and suitably targeted to the real challenges people wish to address. Many academics have little spare time, so they value summaries of any key research that is pertinent to their needs. They will perhaps not be able to look at the substantive literature. The HED service can add considerable value by undertaking the investigative work on their behalf, providing a summary of the key points or strategies to apply.
- Develop a strong service ethic across the HED team. All members of the team play a key role in ensuring there is strong responsiveness. Ensure everyone understands the types of services that are delivered and who to contact for different forms of support;

- Integrate new technologies to increase the HED connections with members, including social media and blogs (Guerin *et al.* 2015).
- Ensure that the website is highly interactive, user-focused and supports targeted searching.
- For key institutional projects, develop a shared repository of useful ideas and resources that can be accessed by university members. Consider, for example, the benefit of sharing ideas and approaches when mass-curriculum reform or restructure is underway. When combined with forums where good practices or challenges are shared, the service is adding considerable value.

When things go wrong

Unfortunately, despite the best of efforts, things can go wrong. There are many examples of massive, sometimes cataclysmic, changes to HED groups, including the redesign of the identity and composition of the HED service or disestablishment of all or part it (Debowski *et al.* 2012; Holt *et al.* 2011). There are many likely reasons for this outcome: perhaps the group had not been sufficiently proactive in building its allies and sponsors; perhaps the designated sponsor lacked the power or will to be a strong advocate; there might have been other groups lobbying for the HED service budget or functions; the sponsor might have perceived little value in the services offered; there might have been conflicting demands for the funds to be allocated; the group may have chosen to remain remote from institutional initiatives; the service may have been too focused on being a research rather than service centre; and many other variables.

Whatever the cause, there is often little chance to present a different viewpoint or to be heard when decisions are made. The HED leader is likely to feel disempowered, devalued and guilty about the actions being taken. The team will be uncertain, angry, anxious and demotivated as it explores what the future is likely to bring. If the group is being relocated under different leadership, or split and shifted to different functional areas, it is likely to feel very adrift. The following tips may assist in this situation:

- Recognise that the decision has been made. Aim to think about the future and how the best can be made of the possible options available.
- Document and celebrate the past achievements of the service and make sure these are acknowledged to the team. Ideally, this should be conveyed by a more senior leader.
- Identify a memento that can go with each member and have an intimate ceremony to bid farewell to those who are departing (McGugan and Petichakis 2009).
- Give the team time to grieve, but then focus on the next steps and keep them busy. They are better being kept active than brooding. Part of the legacy will be documenting the key initiatives, and, if necessary, handing over

to the next incumbent. Set up clear transition plans and build momentum around these.
- Conduct an exit interview with each member, exploring their plans and their career strategies. Ensure they have the necessary documentation and portfolio to present their best case to their next supervisor or employer.
- Invite stakeholders to a farewell meeting or event. Be gracious and celebrate the wins that have occurred. Acknowledge the partnerships and alliances that have been a strength for the group.
- Work with new leaders who are taking parts of the group into their fold. Discuss how you might support any transitions and what resources or data they might like access to.
- Prepare a gracious message to key stakeholders about the imminent changes, focusing particularly on where they might now seek assistance. In this message, outline how the changes will affect the broad areas of both core and strategic support that have been offered in the past. This is an important signal which clarifies what has been lost or changed.

As a leader, ensure there is no evidence of bitterness or devastation. Your persona needs to be confident, assured and in charge. People will be watching for signs of frailty or vulnerability. Stay strong; it will be noted.

If the service was well attuned to its community and their needs, there is high likelihood that new opportunities will emerge as gaps in support and provision are recognised. These may seem very different to the old approaches, but the same principles of mapping needs, designing suitable strategies and delivering high-quality support will remain fundamental to future success.

Conclusion

Universities are volatile environments. The HED service is likely to be targeted at some time or other for reform or enhancement. The political capabilities of the HED leader and senior staff can help to minimise associated impacts. The ability to map the terrain, build strong alliances and partnerships and ensure the results are well suited to the needs of the organisation will strengthen the support base of the service. Even so, there may be times when changes are enacted, regardless of how politically savvy the leader is. The capacity to adapt and take good advantage from this time of renewal is an important watershed for many leaders, and can be used as an ideal time for review, innovation and cleansing. The capacity to return with a renewed and invigorated focus can create many unexpected opportunities.

References

Bamber, V. and Stefani, L., 2015. Taking up the challenge of evidencing value in educational development: from theory to practice. *International Journal for Academic Development*, pp. 1–13. Available online at DOI 10.1080/1360144X.2015.1100112

Becher, T. and Trowler, P.R., 2001. *Academic tribes and territories: intellectual enquiry and the culture of disciplines*, Buckingham, England: Society for Research in Higher Education and Open University Press.

Cordiner, M., 2014. Academic developers as change agents improving quality in a large interprofessional undergraduate subject. *International Journal for Academic Development*, 19(3), pp. 199–211.

Debowski, S., 2014. From agents of change to partners in arms: the emerging academic developer role. *International Journal for Academic Development*, 19(1), pp. 50–56.

Debowski, S., Stefani, L., Cohen, P. and Ho, A., 2012. Sustaining and championing teaching and learning: in good times or bad. In J.E. Groccia, M.A. Al-Sudairy and W. Buskist, eds, *Handbook of college and university teaching: a global perspective*, Thousand Oaks, CA: SAGE Publications, pp. 125–142.

Di Napoli, R., 2014. Value gaming and political ontology: between resistance and compliance in academic development. *International Journal for Academic Development*, 19(1), pp. 4–11.

Fraser, K. and Ryan, Y., 2012. Director turnover: an Australian academic development study. *International Journal for Academic Development*, 17(2), pp. 135–147.

Gibbs, G., 2013. Reflections on the changing nature of educational development. *International Journal for Academic Development*, 18(1), pp. 4–14.

Guerin, C., Carter, S. and Aitchison, C., 2015. Blogging as community of practice: lessons for academic development? *International Journal for Academic Development*, 20(3), pp. 212–223.

Holt, D., Palmer, S. and Challis, D., 2011. Changing perspectives: teaching and learning centres' strategic contributions to academic development in Australian higher education. *International Journal for Academic Development*, 16(1), pp. 5–17.

Johnson, L.K., 2008a. Exerting influence without authority. *Harvard Business Review*, February 28, 2008.

Johnson, L.K., 2008b. Sharpen your political competence. *Harvard Business Review*, February 27, 2008. Available online at https://hbr.org/2008/02/sharpen-your-political-compete-1

Kauko, J., 2013. Dynamics in higher education politics: a theoretical model. *Higher Education*, 65(2), pp. 193–206.

Kotter, J.P., 2012. Accelerate! *Harvard Business Review*, November. Available online at https://hbr.org/2012/11/accelerate

McAlpine, L. and Amundsen, C., 2012. Challenging the taken-for-granted: how research analysis might inform pedagogical practices and institutional policies related to doctoral education. *Studies in Higher Education*, 37(6), pp. 683–694.

McGugan, S. and Petichakis, C., 2009. Messengers of the extraordinary: the role of souvenirs in academic development. *International Journal for Academic Development*, 14(3), pp. 233–235.

Middlehurst, R., 2013. Changing internal governance: are leadership roles and management structures in United Kingdom universities fit for the future? *Higher Education Quarterly*, 67(3), pp. 275–294.

Pfeffer, J., 2010. Power play. *Harvard Business Review*, July–August, pp. 85–92.

Saarinen, T. and Ursin, J., 2012. Dominant and emerging approaches in the study of higher education policy change. *Studies in Higher Education*, 37(2), pp. 143–156.

Stefani, L. (ed.), 2011. *Evaluating the effectiveness of academic development: principles and practice*, New York: Routledge.

Szkudlarek, T. and Stankiewicz, Ł., 2014. Future perfect? Conflict and agency in higher education reform in Poland. *International Journal for Academic Development*, 19(1), pp. 37–49.

Chapter 25

The Age of Influence

This book has explored many different aspects of the higher education development environment. It has mapped the converging fields of teaching, research and leadership development, illustrating that many of the methodologies, concerns and focus areas of these fields are strongly allied. At the same time, the significant influence of the executive sponsor, organisational structures and historical precedent have served to locate each of these fields in distinctively different domains of university activity. This segregation has encouraged a silo mentality that has served as a divisive barrier between these groups, reducing the potential to share good practices, expertise and common concerns. It has also limited the collective capacity of these groups to build more influence and reach across their universities and the sector. A notable consequence of these practices has been the tendency to compartmentalise development to reflect the particular focus of the designated HED service. However, this is a frustration for many academics and leaders who must seek support from different agencies that employ different approaches and with differing degrees of effectiveness.

The new age HED developer

In this book, a range of new approaches have been recommended, drawing on the best of all three fields. It has been argued that the effective developer must recognise that they are a dual professional, bringing their substantive disciplinary knowledge to their role, along with the cultivation of advanced development repertoires. Developers benefit from integrating holistic insights into the academic/researcher experience and context to increase the likely relevance of their interventions and support. There needs to be particular consideration of the nature of identity and its (re)formation as a key part of this academic life cycle, and the criticality of career strategy and mentorship. The complex roles of leaders across all three fields is a similar motif that requires additional support and guidance. Integration of versatile methodologies and approaches enriches the professional HED repertoire, encouraging multi-layered support, including the provision of core and more customised, negotiated guidance that may be prolonged, embedded and strongly focused on collaborative partnerships. This expanded brief opens up many new and exciting possibilities for a number of development groups. Importantly, the move toward this more adaptive service may necessitate collaboration across the various HED services if they are separate. There is much to learn from each other.

The successful developer needs to build many different capabilities in addition to an enhanced professional theory base and toolkit. Effective negotiation of this liminal space requires strong alignment with the institutional goals and priorities and the capacity to intuit, interpret and negotiate the political landscape (Schroeder 2011). The ability to be a translator, disseminator and effective communicator will be fundamental to success in this dynamic university ecology. Additional capabilities that support the HED role include highly honed relationship management, marketing and self-reflective skills. This work has also encouraged a deeper consideration of research and evaluation as core components of the HE development activities. I have argued that the absence of clear evidence of impact and outcomes has been a significant impediment and, possibly, a cause of vulnerability when financial cuts are being considered. The capacity to build strong connections with sponsors and stakeholders is greatly enhanced when credible and persuasive evidence is made available (Di Napoli 2014; Johnson 2008).

Some commentators might see the changeable university context as a concern and risk for HED centres and services (Golding 2014). Certainly, if they remain attached to traditional approaches, core service delivery and passive engagement with university leaders, they will be vulnerable (Gibbs 2013). Universities want more from their HED services: they anticipate seeing agile, adaptive and responsive groups that are willing to move toward new models of delivery, increase their volume of support using online and blended options, provide customised, negotiated support to critical priority areas and embrace new roles and responsibilities (Van Note Chism 2011). This is a big expectation, but certainly, it is more than possible if the groups have a stronger sense of their purpose and role within the institution. The repositioning of these services as key agencies for capacity building and collaborative partnerships creates a very different dynamic for the role to be played.

Transitioning to the Age of Influence

Reflecting on Sorcinelli et al.'s suggestions as to the different stages of development of teaching and learning centres (Sorcinelli *et al.* 2006; Austin and Sorcinelli 2013), it is clear that higher education development is moving to a new age: The Age of Influence. The previous stage, the Age of the Networker, reflected the need to clarify and enhance the purposes of faculty development, and to network with faculty and institutional leaders to create the right context for dealing with complex challenges. In this work, I have suggested that these foundations need to be taken further: to increase the messages that are shared across the university and, particularly with senior leaders, to build stronger consideration of the need for development within each university and faculty group. Most particularly, the capacity to work in partnership with academic leaders to build capacity encourages enhanced university functioning.

Influencing therefore needs to operate at a number of levels. At the senior executive level, the HED developer needs to be articulate in framing the importance of development and demonstrating how it supports the promotion and enhancement of university performance and expectations. The capacity to influence will be dependent on clear articulation of the university's and sponsor's priorities and targets. The construction of tailored arguments and cases to encourage stronger executive engagement with development strategies is now an integral part of the role. The ability to show evidence and long-term impact, and to draw on research to support claims, will greatly strengthen this lobbying and influencing role. On the other hand, the capacity to be authentic, authoritative and credible also helps to build influence (Loads and Campbell 2015; Gibbs 2013; Peseta 2014).

Access to executive sponsors is essential, but potentially difficult. There may be high volatility at this level, with considerable turnover of key contacts. This can make the process of building long-term connections challenging. Nevertheless, a HED service that is distant from such contacts, poorly represented to executive members and only marginally linked to new strategies or priorities will be at great risk of being regarded as superfluous to need.

The shift from networking and connecting with other university leaders to building intensive and enduring development partnerships substantively changes the nature of the HED role. As outlined in this work, the recognition that leaders and the academy also contribute extensive knowledge and expertise to the development process, creates a more equitable partnership. In fact, development needs alliances to be effective in encouraging learning transfer and transformed communities. The HED developer will be likely to transition across a range of roles and identities through these dynamic relationships (Neame 2013). Fundamental to this partnership, however, will be the confident assurance in drawing on a knowledge of development methodologies and options and a situated awareness as to how academe and each local area operate. Recognition that there is much to be learnt across this two-way process will ensure strong reciprocity in building optimal solutions. The establishment of strong trust between developers and the academy also provides essential channels to explore complex issues relating to culture, leadership impact and innovative approaches to harness the potential of faculty members. This deep influence is a long-term outcome from working closely with key stakeholders and their constituents.

Part of this transition toward influencing is the debate around the role that development plays. In this book, some contentious terms have been used quite freely: *service, client, sponsors* and *stakeholder* are concepts that may be strongly resisted by some. However, these have been consciously and purposely used to reposition the function and priorities of the HED centres and teams. The recognition that they are dependent on perceived value-adding and directing benefit back to their learners encourages new ways of conceptualising and articulating the collective and individual professional identities of developers (Debowski 2014). Those who move into the development space from faculty roles may find the notion of service to be somewhat confronting. However, there are many parallels in the academic world itself, as the concept of impact and engagement gains increasing currency. There is growing recognition that the academy needs to be located in, and contributing to, a better world. The focus of HE development may be more internally directed, but it is similarly charged with enhancing, enriching and influencing the broader environment in which it is located (Di Napoli 2014).

Positive interaction with leaders is a particularly important message in this work. I have strongly argued for more engagement and stronger relationship management of these connections. A willingness to design customised solutions and support that best suits the particular context will greatly increase the valuing of the developer (Sherlock 2012). Adaptive work of this nature is the most influential in terms of its likely impact, as it has the capacity to embed enhanced practices within whole communities. Thus, influence can be achieved through working within a community as well as across it. The brokering of networks and collaborative alliances across different schools, departments, faculties and/or centres also encourages collective investigation of more complex issues and the identification of peer mentors and models. A further form of influence is through the provision of accessible guides, tools and tips to support key roles at point of need. Thus, the influencing of leaders may be through direct action, brokerage of networks and indirect self-help support.

Positioning the new HED service

While each HED service may support a specific element of academic work, their overarching goal is to enhance academic outcomes and increase academic capacity (Moses 2012; Gibbs 2013). Recognising that they are all part of the quest to facilitate academic enhancement offers considerable potential for articulating common principles, a professional lexicon and consistent methodology. The development of conjoint systems, templates, marketing and user interfaces across each institution makes considerable sense. While the overall branding for each group may remain distinct, the creation of a single user interface for all relevant guidance and information creates a powerful source of institutional influence. The key focus here is thinking about how the academic and related populations can best be served. The transition from seeking distinctiveness to building consistency is a strong marker of moving from what is convenient for the development group to increased focus on user support and ease of access. The melding of these different sources also offers considerable opportunity for benchmarking and collective refinement. Increased joint offerings, co-facilitation, network meetings, shared practice and mentorship would further assist in building disciplinary strength across the HED community. Those who are located in faculty development roles would greatly benefit from this increased connectedness and professional exchange.

Taking this further, the hosting of meetings with colleagues from other colleges and universities in the local region opens up additional opportunities to explore the academic context, methodological innovations and sharing of research and evaluative findings. Collaboration, benchmarking and peer mentoring could be facilitated through these initiatives.

The discipline of higher education development

In Chapter 2, I suggested that HE development was ready to move toward a new phase in its development, arguing that it was poised to be an identifiable discipline with responsibility to influence and shape the future of higher education learning and development. A number of features of disciplines were mapped (Messer-Davidow *et al.* 1993), illustrating their emergent nature at this stage. This work has explored a number of strategies to support HED capacity building, illustrating some possible approaches to strengthening a disciplinary identity that can straddle the respective specialist areas. These are reviewed below:

1 *The consolidation of a professional identity.* This work has provided a foundational handbook to encourage enhanced understanding of the roles, functions and professional methodologies that underpin higher education development (Boud and Brew 2013).
2 *The identification of scope and focus of the discipline.* The breadth and focus of HED functions and roles have been mapped, illustrating the potential scope and focus of higher education development. Increased clarity as to the boundaries of HED activities facilitates enhanced research, professional interaction and identity formation.
3 *The identification of problems and tools to address those challenges.* The absence of a clear HED methodology, scholarship or toolkit has limited the HED community's capacity to identify or address evident challenges facing the profession. Academic capacity building has been introduced as a HED framework, encouraging more reflexive practice concerning methodologies, strategies, risks and opportunities facing the field. The importance of building a strong collective voice through research, scholarship, advocacy and partnerships has been explored.
4 *The recognition and rewarding of intellectual and professional achievements.* Many HE developers feel invisible and marginalised (Gravett and Bernhagen 2015; Green and Little 2016; Little and Green 2012). This work has mapped the standards and capabilities that support excellent performance as a HE developer. This will assist HED leaders in setting up their team for success and in advocating their recognition through traditional academic channels. Guidance on performance standards also supports effective performance and career management.

5 *The capacity to distribute status and recognition.* An increased understanding of the HED role within universities and across the sector will encourage more discussion as to how status and recognition might be accorded. Central to this, however, is the development of a stronger research and scholarship base to demonstrate the capacity to impact and transform learning.
6 *The enhancement of relevant expertise and capabilities.* This book has emphasised the critical importance of building professional methodologies that can assist those entering the field as well as more experienced developers (DiPietro 2014; Timmermans 2014). It has noted the importance of building some sophisticated approaches, including facilitation and consultancy capabilities.
7 *Demarcate novices and experts.* The differentiation of HED roles, including the mapping of entry-level, specialist and HED leadership capabilities provides a useful framework to articulate the different roles that developers will fill. A benefit of building a more inclusive framing for this field is the potential to move toward formal professional qualifications, accreditation and recognition of professional practice. This has remained a largely underdeveloped element of HED (DiPietro 2014), and one that would build further credence for the field.
8 *Encourage intellectual engagement, knowledge production and communication.* The development of a collective HED scholarly space remains a significant gap. While HED members are publishing in various sources, the sharing across the sub-disciplines and an opportunity to collectively explore common challenges would increase the capacity to advance the field. Encouragement of more stringent research and evaluative practices, including benchmarking and cross-institutional collaboration, would also assist the development of core methodologies.
9 *Attract passionate advocates who seek to make a better context for their colleagues and stakeholders.* The HED discipline is filled with passionate people who act in isolation. This work has encouraged more professional interchange across the development fraternity, particularly through the establishment of intra- and inter-institutional networking and collaboration. Mentorship to assist those venturing into the HED field would be particularly valuable.
10 *Advocate and influence.* An increased assurance as to identity, purpose and impact encourages a more powerful capacity to both advocate and influence. This is an important step forward for a discipline. The provision of standards and recommendations would greatly assist HED groups and university leaders in framing their expectations from an informed, well-articulated stance. HED societies' statements relating to the support that academics, researchers, leaders and the institution might reasonably anticipate from effective development services, for example, offer informed external advocacy. With new nations seeking to establish good-quality development in their universities, this would be timely and greatly appreciated. The International Consortium for Educational Development (ICED), perhaps, plays a key role in starting these explorations.

Implications for university leaders

In writing this work, I have been cognisant of the role that university leaders, faculty members and HED developers all play in supporting academic capacity building. This book offers considerable guidance on the nature of academic development and the challenges that people are likely to encounter in progressing their capabilities and performance.

There has been a clear thread through the chapters relating to the role that executives play in facilitating and steering support for academic enhancement. It is clear that the power and influence of university leaders is increasing as they become more instrumental in directing academic priorities, rewards, recognition and sanctions. Unfortunately, there can be limited recognition of the complex demands generated by multiple executives on the reform trail. Executive bullying, rapid shifts in policy and little understanding of the way changes can be accomplished with good will, commitment and strong results have significant potential to damage the well-being of university communities.

Changes in executives have also seen many development groups marginalised rather than well deployed. This reduces the use of the HED service as an important enabler. The ideal is to ensure that the executive is well informed about the support they might expect from their development agencies. This could be part of the induction of each new executive member, as access to a highly professional, proactive service is a highly desirable asset for leaders with a mission. There are also strong implications for the designated sponsor of HED services: they need to be informed, articulate and strong advocates in executive discussions. Their role is to educate their colleagues as to the potential benefits of drawing on an effective and creative HED service. Additionally, an executive that is willing to embark on its own leadership evaluation and development journey offers powerful affirmation about the importance of learning and self-reflection.

As learning collaborators and partners, faculty leaders play a key role in engaging with HE developer/s, enabling their integration and connections with other faculty members, and ensuring that they have the necessary sponsorship, time, access and contacts to achieve the agreed outcomes. In-depth understanding of HE development supports these dialogues and negotiations.

However, this book has also suggested that faculty leaders are both recipients of, and active contributors to, the provision of HED support (Lieberman 2011). The capacity to transfer learning back into the academic workplace is strongly contingent on supportive supervisors and leaders, cultures and colleagues. Thus, the encouragement of a supportive learning community that publicly advocates learning and professional enhancement is an important role for faculty leaders (Middlehurst 1993). They need to take active responsibility for building effective infrastructure that enables the ongoing acculturation and development of their staff. Effective inductions, retreats, commissioned programs or workshops, mentorship and the enactment of quality performance management practices (particularly feedback-giving) enable a high-functioning academic community.

The leaders' willingness to participate in their own ongoing development is a further contributory factor. The capacity to reflect, learn and adapt one's leadership to increase constructive and productive work settings has true potential to make a profound difference. Thus, faculty leaders fill a number of roles in sponsoring development: as learning partners, sponsors, models, developers and learners.

Conclusion

Academic work is exciting, changeable, daunting and challenging. It continues to escalate in pace and demands, requiring considerable skill to identify what matters and how each work component can best be managed. Higher education development fills an important function in helping individuals navigate their professional capabilities, academic identity and career strategy. However, this influence is variable at present, and may be affected by many factors, including the basic capabilities of the developers and the context in which the academic is situated. This work has offered new guidance on the HE development context, role and strategies. It has outlined how these roles can be further enhanced by articulating and mapping HED methodologies; building a consistent and inclusive identity around the field; encouraging further scholarship and research about the discipline; and increasing the focus on building robust partnerships with university leaders to ensure good alignment of support. It is time to move into the Age of Influence with confidence, a full toolkit and the capacity to show that well-designed and executed development truly does make a difference to individuals and institutional outcomes.

References

Austin, A.E. and Sorcinelli, M.D., 2013. The future of faculty development: where are we going? *New Directions for Teaching and Learning*, 2013(133), pp. 85–97.

Boud, D. and Brew, A., 2013. Reconceptualising academic work as professional practice: implications for academic development. *International Journal for Academic Development*, 18(3), pp. 208–221.

Debowski, S., 2014. From agents of change to partners in arms: the emerging academic developer role. *International Journal for Academic Development*, 19(1), pp. 50–56.

Di Napoli, R., 2014. Value gaming and political ontology: between resistance and compliance in academic development. *International Journal for Academic Development*, 19(1), pp. 4–11.

DiPietro, M., 2014. Tracing the evolution of educational development through the POD Network's Institute for New Faculty Developers. *To Improve the Academy*, 33(2), pp. 113–130.

Gibbs, G., 2013. Reflections on the changing nature of educational development. *International Journal for Academic Development*, 18(1), pp. 4–14.

Golding, C., 2014. Blinkered conceptions of academic development. *International Journal for Academic Development*, 19(2), pp. 150–152.

Gravett, E.O. and Bernhagen, L., 2015. A view from the margins: situating CTL staff in organizational development. *To Improve the Academy*, 34(1–2), pp. 63–90.

Green, D.A. and Little, D., 2016. Family portrait: a profile of educational developers around the world. *International Journal for Academic Development*, 21(2), pp. 135–150.

Johnson, L.K., 2008. Sharpen your political competence. *Harvard Business Review*, February 27, 2008. Available online at https://hbr.org/2008/02/sharpen-your-political-compete-1.html.

Lieberman, D., 2011. Nurturing institutional change: collaboration and leadership between upper-level administrators and faculty developers. In C.M. Schroeder, ed., *Coming in from the margins: faculty development's emerging organizational development role in institutional change*, 1st edition, Sterling, VA: Stylus Publishing, pp. 60–76.

Little, D. and Green, D.A., 2012. Betwixt and between: academic developers in the margins. *International Journal for Academic Development*, 17(3), pp. 203–215.

Loads, D. and Campbell, F., 2015. Fresh thinking about academic development: authentic, transformative, disruptive? *International Journal for Academic Development*, 20(4), pp. 355–369.

Messer-Davidow, E., Shumway, D.R. and Sylvan, D. (eds), 1993. *Knowledges: historical and critical studies in disciplinarity*, Charlottesville, VA: University Press of Virginia.

Middlehurst, R., 1993. *Leading academics*, Buckingham, England: Society for Research into Higher Education.

Moses, I., 2012. Views from a former vice-chancellor. *International Journal for Academic Development*, 17(3), pp. 275–277.

Neame, C., 2013. Democracy or intervention? Adapting orientations to development. *International Journal for Academic Development*, 18(4), pp. 331–343.

Peseta, T.L., 2014. Agency and stewardship in academic development: the problem of speaking truth to power. *International Journal for Academic Development*, 19(1), pp. 65–69.

Schroeder, C.M., 2011. Recentering within the web of institutional leadership. In Schroeder, ed., *Coming in from the margins: faculty development's emerging organizational development role in institutional change*, 1st edition. Sterling, VA: Stylus Publishing, pp. 273–292.

Sherlock, J., 2012. The HR transition to strategic partner: the rarely discussed identity challenges. In W.J. Rothwell and G.M.B. Benscoter, eds, *The encyclopedia of human resource management*, San Francisco, CA: Pfeiffer, pp. 161–172.

Sorcinelli, M.D., Austin, A.E., Eddy, P.L. and Beach, A.L. (eds), 2006. *Creating the future of faculty development: learning from the past, understanding the present*, Bolton, MA: Anker Publishing.

Timmermans, J.A., 2014. Identifying threshold concepts in the careers of educational developers. *International Journal for Academic Development*, 19(4), pp. 305–317.

Van Note Chism, N., 2011. Getting to the table: planning and developing institutional initiatives. In C.M. Schroeder, ed., *Coming in from the margins: faculty development's emerging organizational development role in institutional change*, 1st edition, Sterling, VA: Stylus Publishing, pp. 47–59.

Index

academic capabilities: engagement 176–8; research 183–90; teaching 211–13
academic careers: enablers 8–9; management 6, 70, 136–42, 150; paths 136, 138, 141, 148–57; success indicators 134–5
academic collegiality: bullying 159; collegial practices 160–1; definition 158; evidence of 160–1; non-collegial practices 161–2; non-contributing academics 164–5; political competence 163; service as an expression of collegiality 162–4; strategies to encourage collegiality 165–9; threats 159
academic culture: bullying 159; enabling environments 134–5; learning support 7–8, 67–9; promoting mediocrity 159; supporting new staff 154–5; *see also* academic collegiality; learning transfer
academic developer *see* developer, higher education
academic development *see* higher education development
academic employment: acculturating new staff 154–5; early career entry 136–7; expectations 4; research focused-roles 152–3; precariousness 5; professional entry 154; teaching-focused roles 153–4
academic engagement: benefits of 173; capabilities 176–8; definition 172; determining an engagement strategy 173–6; impact 172; role 4; support strategies 179; types of engagement activities 172
academic freedom 162; *see also* academic collegiality
academic identity: academic goals 133–4; as developer 62–3, 319; as teacher 210–11; authentic identities 141–2; building identity 6, 133–47; career narratives 143–4; challenges 141–4; early career phase 136–8; identity influences 142; mid-career phase 138–40; professionals 154; researcher 182–3; senior academics 140–1; teacher 210–11
academic impact: on colleagues 162; definition 172; strategies to build impact 172–4; university expectations 4; *see also* academic engagement
academic leadership: adaptive leadership 237–9; capability frameworks 250; development approaches 246–54; dysfunctional leaders 235; evaluation and review 239–40; formal leaders 237–9; good leadership 235–7; institutional capacity building 240–1; leadership strategy 237–8; roles 235; success indicators 190; teaching 229–30
academic learning: context 66–9; designing meaningful learning experiences 69–71
academic performance: impact 172; measures 5, 135
academic probation 138
academic self-management 61–2
academic writing strategies: circles 228; retreats 203
academics: definition 3; diversity 3; engagement roles 4, 172–8; leadership roles 4; potential services 56; research roles 4, 182–93; teaching roles 3–4, 210–11
action learning projects 105
Age of the Networker 317
Amundsen, C. 279

Ashwin, P. 279
associate deans: support from the development services 45
AUSSE 224

baseline data 267; *see also* evaluation
Baume, D. 39
benchmarking 267
Blackham, A. 140
blended learning 73–4, 202, 226
Boud, D. 279
Bovill, C. 228
Brew, A. 279
Bridges, W. 110–11
Buller, J. L. 158–9
bullying 159; *see also* Academic Collegiality

capability assessment instruments 271–2
capability frameworks: academic careers 135–41; purpose 92–3; research 199–200; Vitae Research Capability Framework 30
capacity building: definition 10–11; encouraging leadership capacity building 244; factors affecting teaching capacity building 220–1; historical approaches 17–22; research 194–8
case study research 281–3
Chermack, T. J. 279, 281
Cipriano, R. E. 158–9
Clegg, S. 278
clients, university staff 42
climate measures 274
codes of conduct 160, 165
collaboration: capabilities 4; with other developers 283–4; skill building 150, 177, 187–8; success indicators 188;
collegiality *see* academic collegiality
communication: academic capabilities 176–7; during organizational change 112, 116
communities of practice 76, 229
constructive leadership 245
consultancy role: communication with clients 123–4; process 122–4; strategies 54, 118–20
consultation: during organizational change 118–19
core services 43–7, 52
course coordinators 227–8
culture *see* academic culture
cumulative reviews 267–8; *see also* evaluation

curriculum design 212
customised services 47, 52, 205–6, 319

De Vries, J. 268
deans/executive directors: development and support 254; HED services to 44, 125–6; promoting collegiality 167–8; promoting good leadership 246; role 140–1; supporting learning and teaching 229–30
demand for development offerings 90–1
developer, higher education *see* higher education developer
development portfolios: higher education development 296; reflective 105, 271; research 197–8; teaching 213–14
discipline(s): higher education development as 17, 21–4, 320–1; purpose 17
dissemination of higher education development research 285
distributed leadership 236–7
doctoral training: career support 7; as entry path to academe 7, 149–51; program design 7, 151, 200–1; research supervision success indicators 189; supervision 188–9, transferable skills 149–50

early career academics 136–8, 151–5, 200–3, 210–11, 225–7
employee disengagement 164–5
employee engagement 162
environmental scanning 306–7
evaluation, higher education development: assessing impact 227; benefits 262–3; context 264; leadership capabilities 239–40; learning design 263; planning 264–8; principles 266; purpose 261–3, 264–8; survey design 268–75; *see also* research, higher education development
Evans, L. 182, 194
event coordination 57
evidence building 210, 213–14; teaching 222–4; *see also* development portfolios
executive leaders: accessibility 126; change initiatives 109, 245, 305–11; as clients 124, 128–9; functions 32, 245; impact 245; interactions with HED groups 31–3, 39, 43–4, 122–30, 322–3; leadership 245–6, 322; services to 44; sponsorship of university leaders 245; turnover 245, 293

facilitation 55, 74–5, 80–1, 205–6
faculty-based development 31, 227, 231, 311
follow-up support 91
foundational programs 97, 226–7
funding development activities: funding model 41, 83; program costing 100–2
funding, higher education development: funding model 41
funding, research *see* research funding

Gedro, J. 162
Gibbs, G. 18
Gordon, G. 182
graduate certificates 226
grant seeking *see* research funding
group management 60–1, 74–5

heads of school/department, services to 45, 125–6
HED *see* higher education development
HERD *see* Higher Education Research and Development
HERDSA *see* Higher Education Research and Development Society of Australasia
Higher Education Academy 19, 226
higher education developer roles: coach 55; communicator 60; consultant 54, 122–5; core capabilities 53, 58–62, 68, 295; diagnostician 55, 59; educator 54; evaluator/analyst 54; event coordinator 56; expert adviser 54, 126–8; facilitator 55, 60; influencer 317–19; learning partner 56; network broker 56; observer 55; overview 9–10, 35, 52–3; policy/system developer 56; project manager 56; promoting collegiality 168–9; relationship manager 59; researcher 128; role definition 9–10, 21–2; scholar and researcher 56
higher education development: capabilities 35, 53–63, 71; challenges 34–6, 304–5, 312–13; core services 39–40, 43–7, 52; customised services 43, 47–8, 52, 205–6, 319; definition 10, 21–2; as a discipline 17, 23–4, 320–3; marginalization 36, 126–7; principles 50; promotion of outcomes 310; reputation building 68; research challenges 279; restructures 41, 312–13; services 32–3, 38–9, 42–3; service success indicators 10, 41, 69, 291–2; sponsors 33–4, 39, 126–8, 304, 318–19; strategy 292; systems 298–9; trends 22–3, 31
higher education development leadership: adaptive leadership 301; assessing the university landscape 306–7; developing systems and quality assurance 297–9; establishing a service vision 292–3; establishing alliances within the university 307–9; key principles 301–2; political context 304–6, 316–17; promotional strategies 310; role 34; team building 293–7; stakeholder management 309
higher education development research *see* research, higher education development
higher education development services: facilitating organizational reform 109–20; guiding strategic initiatives 309; leadership capacity building 246–55; research capacity building 194–206; service success indicators 10, 41, 69, 291–2; supporting university communities 311–12; teaching capacity building 220–31; types of services 32–3; 42–3, 38–9
higher education development teams: composition 293–4; recruitment 19, 29, 295; team building 295–6
higher education development units: challenges 304–5; collaboration across units 319–20; composition 293–4; disestablishment 312–13; integrated development services 31, 300–1; location 30–1, 39; mission and focus 40; multiple providers 31, 35, 319–20; restructures 312–13
Higher Education Research and Development (HERD) 285
Higher Education Research and Development Society of Australasia (HERDSA) 19
higher education: trends 3, 18–21, 109–21
Holland, B. 173
Holten, E. F. 67
human resource management services 21, 30
Human Synergistics 240, 242

ICED *see* International Consortium for Educational Development
IJAD *see* International Journal of Academic Development

imposter syndrome: academics 136; developers 62–3
individual learning factors 7, 66–9, 133–5, 273
individualized support to academics 48
influencing strategies, higher education development 316–19
information sessions 72
institutional strategies: to encourage collegiality 165–6; teaching and learning 209, 220–2, 224, 230–1; to support leadership capacity building 240–1
instructional design *see* learning design
intention to change-measures 269–70
International Consortium for Educational Development 19
International Journal for Researcher Development 285
International Journal of Academic Development 285
intrinsic motivation 66, 133–5

Kandlbinder, P. 226, 279
Kauko, J. 305
Kaye Hart, R. 270
Kirkpatrick, D. L. 269
Kligyte, G. 70
Krause, K. L. 279
Kreber, C. 214

leadership developer *see* developer, higher education
leadership development: coaching 252; frameworks 250; human resource development services 20–1, 30; leaders in crisis 255; multi-source feedback 251–2; network support 252–3; orientation programs 250; programs 95–108, 251, 253; reflexive leadership 247–9; target groups 254; types of support offered 246–7; workshops 250–1
Leadership Foundation for Higher Education 21
Leadership Impact (Human Synergistics) 240, 242
leadership *see* academic leadership; higher education development leadership
learning and development principles: for higher education development 69–71; 81–8; for leadership 246–9
learning and teaching *see* teaching and learning

learning communities: enabling leadership identity formation 246; to support learning 7–8, 67–9, 273–4; *see also* networks
learning culture 273–4
learning design: development experiences 61, 67–76, 81–7; development planning template 84–8; evaluating outcomes 269–75; learner-centred design 92; student learning 212–14
learning gaps 67
learning outcomes: academics 82–3; assessing development outcomes 269–70; quality teaching metrics 222–4
learning partnerships 56, 231, 307–8, 311–12, 318–19
learning portfolios *see* development portfolios
learning spaces, development 88–9
learning transfer 67, 91, 227, 273

Macfarlane, B. 141
Mamiseishvili, K. 163
measurement challenges 264
mentorship 91, 105, 137, 143, 161, 202–4, 239–40
Messer-Davidow, E. 17, 23
micromanagement 5
mid-career academics 138–9, 163, 203–4
Middlehurst, R. 236, 279
middlescence 139
modes of delivery 49, 71–6; *see also* blended learning; online learning; programs; workshops
multi-source feedback 104–5, 240, 251–2, 271

narrative building: principles 141, 143–4, 173; research narrative 196–7; as sense-making 70
Neame, C. 110
network brokering 57, 76, 104, 229, 252–3
networking skills: academic 150, 177; developer 57, 307–9; 311–12, 317–19
NSSE 224

online learning 73, 89–90, 213
organizational change: academic responses to change 109, 110–12; communication strategies 112, 116; consultation strategies 118–19; cultural influences 111–12; higher education development

service leadership of change 116–18; higher education development service role 110, 113–15; impact of 109–10; leadership role in change 112–16; reasons for change 109; transitions 110–11
orientations: to introduce development programs 103; leadership orientations 250; research orientations 201–2; teaching orientations 224–5

participant: attitudinal measures 270–1; attrition 91; engagement measures 268–9; feedback 268–9; interviews 104; recruitment 102
peer review of teaching 213, 223
performance expectations: developers 296, 298; research 183–90; teaching 222–4
performance metrics 5, 20, 135
Perkmann, M. 173
personal agency 142, 264
Peseta, T. 226, 279
Pfeffer, J. 305
planning development experiences 81–4
POD *see* Professional and Organizational Development
political competence: academics 163; developers 305–10
portfolios: developers 298; teaching 213–14
practice wisdom xxii, 41, 308–9
precarious employment 5, 137
problem-driven research 281
Professional and Organizational Development 19
professional developers 294
professional entry into academe 154
professional staff, potential support 56
professoriate 141
programs: comparison with workshops 96; costing 100–2; design 75, 95–108; evaluation 105–6; features 98, 104–5; planning 98–102; post-program support 104; preparing participants 104; purpose 75; types 97
promotion: development opportunities 90–1; outcomes 310
publishing: as a foundational capability 183; institutional expectations 183; indicators of success 184; strategies to develop capabilities 184

quality assurance 297–8

reflection: leadership 23, 236–7; learning 70; programs 105, 213–14; reflexive leadership 247–9
reflective portfolios *see* development portfolios
relationship management: academic role 4, 160–1; developer role 177–8
research capabilities: collaboration 187–8; funding research 185–6; publishing 183–5; research capabilities 183; research leadership and management 189–90; research project management 186–7; research strategy 182; research supervision 188–9
research capacity building: approaches 198; development options 195–7; doctoral candidates 200–1; early career researchers 202–3; high impact capacity building 195–7; mid-career researchers 203–4; programs 202–6; research capability frameworks 199–200; research leaders 204–6; research narrative building 197–8; research orientation 201–2; success indicators 196; whole of institutional reforms 198–9
research developer *see* developer, higher education
research development: history 19–20; national initiatives 20; purpose 29, 194–206; *see also* research capacity building
research focused roles 152–3
research funding: as an indicator of research success 185; capabilities 185; funding context 150; indicators of a successful funding track record 186; proposal development 185; success indicators 186
research leadership 189–90
research project management: as part of doctoral training 150; benefits 186; indicators of success 187; Research Project Management Checklist 186, 191
research publishing *see* publishing
research, higher education development: case studies 281–3; collaboration 283–4; dissemination 285; ethics 284–5; foci 280–1; strategies 281–3; supporting research teams 205
residential programs 101, 103
return on investment 261–3
Rowland, S. 158

Saarinen, T. 305
Saroyan, A. 279–81
Schein, E. 112
scholarship: on higher education development 278–80; of teaching and learning 214–15, 228–9; *see also* research, higher education development
SEDA 226
self-management: academic self-evaluation 178; academic self-knowledge 160, 168; collegial behavior 168; developer self-management 61–2
Seligman, M. 134–5
seminars 72; *see also* workshops
senior academics 140–1, 204–6
service, higher education development: assumptions 42–3; definition 41–2; delivery mechanisms 39–50; ethic 296–7; management of strategic initiatives 309; prioritization 48
socialization of learning 68–9
Sorcinelli, M. D. 18, 29, 35, 317
SOTL *see* scholarship of teaching and learning
sponsorship: of higher education development units 33–4; 39, 126–8; of programs 100
stakeholder management 39, 43, 128–9, 307–8
students: diversity 212; feedback on teaching 223; as learners 211–13
Studies in Higher Education 285
Stupnisky, R. H. 135
success indicators: collaboration 188; funding 186; higher education development 291–2, 317; publishing 184; research capacity building 194–6; research leadership 190; research project management 187; research supervision 189; teaching capacity building 221
supervisors: promoting collegiality 167–8
Sutherland, K. 134–5

Swanson, R. A. 279, 281
system design, higher education development 56, 298–9

talent programs 203
targeted support 47–8
teaching and learning development: history 18–19; scope of functions 29, 221, 229
teaching portfolio *see* development portfolios
teaching, university: course coordinators 227–8; feedback sources 213–14; leaders 215, 229–30; metrics 215; quality 19, 222–4; roles 3–4, 153–4, 209–10; success indicators 221; teaching leaders 229–30; tutor preparation 227
Teelken, C. 110
tenure track 152
timing of development opportunities 68, 83, 92
To Improve the Academy 285
transitions 109–11
Trigwell, K. 279–81
Trowler, P. 279

University and College Teaching (Epigeum) 226
Ursin, J. 305

Velliaris, D. 279
Vitae: Career Framework for Researcher Developers 25, 30; description 30, 200

Wang, J. 162
Wilson, M. 279
women's programs 97, 254
work-integrated learning 213
workloads: academics 163–4; developers 296
workshops: design 82–9; purpose 47, 72; 202, 204, 205, 250–1